# BLEEDING SHADOWS

# BLEEDING SHADOWS

Stories by

## JOE R. LANSDALE

Subterranean Press 2013

**First Edition**

**ISBN**

978-1-59606-599-4

Subterranean Press
PO Box 190106
Burton, MI 48519

**subterraneanpress.com**

# TABLE OF CONTENTS

*This book is dedicated to the memory of my good friend, Ardath Mayhar.*

# A LITTLE BIT OF MY BLOOD

## BY JOE R. LANSDALE

This collection is the largest I've ever offered to readers. There are short stories and long stories and those that are in-between. There are also poems.

It's a varied box of words. Some of the words are obviously just for fun, and some have more weight, some are a combination of those things, but I hope all of them are interesting to read and that they stick with you for awhile.

There are horror stories and crime stories and a mystery story with an unusual, elderly investigator. There are realistic stories and historical tales and... Well, enough of that. That's your discovery to have, and it's not for me to spoil it.

If you want to know more about the individual stories, then you can go to the end of the book and see my comments on them. I don't recommend this until you've finished the book, or the individual story you want to know about. My comments on the stories might spoil things for you.

I hate it when that happens.

I appreciate all the readers over the years who have read my books and made my life comfortable, not only in a material way, but have allowed me the satisfaction to keep writing and making a living at it, to keep thinking of stories and writing them down.

Again, I offer to you sincere thanks. I hope after putting the book down you will feel your money is well spent.

Joe R. Lansdale
Nacogdoches, Texas

# TORN AWAY

**H**e was a young man in an old black car, parked out by the railroad tracks near an oil well that still pumped, pulling up that East Texas crude. I got word of the car from Mrs. Roark who lived on the far side of the tracks. She called my office and told me car and man had been sitting there since late afternoon, and from her kitchen window she had seen the driver get out of the car once, while it was still light, walk to the other side, probably to relieve himself. She said he was dressed in black and wore a black hat and just the outfit spooked her.

Now, at midnight, the car was still there, though she hadn't seen him in a quite a while, and she was worried about going to sleep, him being just across the tracks, and she wondered if I'd take a look and make sure he wasn't a robber or killer or worse.

Being Chief of Police of a small town in East Texas can be more interesting than you might think. But not my town. It had a population of about three hundred and was a lazy sort of place where the big news was someone putting a dead armadillo in the high school principal's mailbox.

I had one deputy, and his was the night shift, but he had called in sick for a couple of days, and I knew good and well he was just spending a little extra time at home with his new bride. I didn't tell him I knew, because I didn't care. I had been married once, and happily, until my wife died suddenly in childbirth, losing the baby in the process.

Frankly, I've never gotten over it. The house seemed too large and the rooms too empty. Sometimes, late at night, I looked at her photograph and cried. Fact was I preferred the night shift. I didn't sleep much.

So, when Mrs. Roark called and told me about the car, I drove out there, and sure enough, the car was still there, and when I hit my lights on high, I saw that it looked like it had seen a lot of road. It was caked in dust and the tires looked thin. I bumped the siren once, and saw someone sit up in the seat and position his hands on the steering wheel.

I left the light on to keep him a little blinded, got out and went over tapped on the glass. The driver rolled it down.

"Hello, sir," I said. "May I see your license?"

He turned his face into my flashlight and blinked, and took out his wallet and pushed his license out to me. It said his name was Judah Wilson. The license was invalid by a couple of months, and the photo on it looked somewhat like him but it was faded and not reliable. I told him so.

"Oh," he said. "I should have noticed it was out of date."

"This is your picture, here?" I asked.

He nodded.

I thought about giving him a ticket for the problem with the license, sending him on his way, but there was something about him that made me suspicious; the photo not being quite right. I said, "I tell you what, Mr. Wilson. You follow me to the station and we can talk there."

"Is that necessary?" he said.

"I'm afraid so," I said.

〉〈

At the station I found myself a little nervous, because the man was over six feet tall and well built and looked as if he could be trouble. His hat and suit were a bit worn, and out of style, but had at one time been of good quality. His shoes needed a shine. But so did mine. I had him seat himself in front of my desk and I went around to my chair and without thinking about it, unfastened my holster flap where he couldn't see me do it. I studied the photo. I said, "This looks like you, but...not quite."

"It's me," he said. "I'm older by a few years. A few years can make a difference."

"I just need to make a call," I said. I wasn't able to go somewhere private and call, since I was the only one there, and yet I was not in a position where I felt comfortable locking him up. I made the call and he listened, and when I finished, I said, "I guess you heard that?"

"The owner of the license is dead?"

"That's right. That means you have another man's out of date license."

He sighed. "Well, it wasn't out of date when I first got it and it's not another man. Exactly. It's just that I can't duplicate another person completely, and some less than others, and this man was one of the hard ones. I don't know what the difference is with one and then another, but there's sometimes a difference. Like you buy a knock-off product that has the same general appearance, but on closer inspection, you can tell it's not the real deal."

"I'm not sure I understand," I said, "but, I'm going to ask you to stand up and walk over to the wall there, and put your hands on it, spread your legs for a pat down. I got reason to hold you."

He did what I asked, sighing as he did. I gave him his Miranda rights. He listened and said he understood. I marched him back to one of the two cages we had in the back. I put him in one and locked the door.

"You really ought not do this," he said.

"Is that a threat?"

"No, it's a warning."

"You're behind bars, sir, not me."

"I know," he said, and went and sat on the bunk and looked at a space between his shoes.

I was about to walk away, when he said, "Watch this."

I turned, and his body shifted, as if there were something inside of him trying to get out, and then his face popped and crawled, and I let out a gasp. He lifted his chin and looked up. Inside his black suit, under his black hat, he looked almost exactly like me.

>><<

I felt weak in the knees and grabbed the bars for support. He said, "Don't worry, I can shift the way I look because I do not have a core, but I can't turn to smoke and flow through the bars. You've got me. And that ought to worry you."

There was a bench on the outside of the bars for visitors to sit and talk to their friends or loved ones on the other side, and I sat down there and tried to get my breath. I kept staring at him, seeing my face under that black hat. It wasn't quite right. There was something missing in the face, same as the one he had before, but it was close enough.

A long moment passed before he spoke. "Now watch."

He closed his eyes and tightened his mouth, shifted back and looked the way he had before, like Wilson. Or almost like Wilson.

"It's best you let me out," he said.

I shook my head.

He sighed. "I'm not like anyone you've dealt with before."

"I don't doubt that," I said, and took my pistol out of its holster and laid it on my knee. He was behind bars, but the whole thing with his face, the way his body shifted under his suit, I couldn't help but think I might have to shoot him. I thought I ought to call my deputy and have him come in, but I wasn't sure what he could do. I wanted to call someone, but I couldn't think of anyone to call. I felt as if every thought I had ever possessed was jumbled up inside my head, knotted up and as confused as Alexander's Gordian knot.

I made myself breathe slowly and deeply.

He took off his hat and placed it on the bunk beside him and stared at me.

I said, "Tell me who you really are. What you are? Why you're here?"

"You wouldn't understand."

"Try me."

"It wouldn't make any difference," he said, and smiled at me. The smile had about as much warmth as a hotel ice machine.

"Are you... Are you from somewhere else?"

"You mean am I from Mars? From somewhere out there?" He pointed up to give his words emphasis.

"Yes."

"No. I'm not. I'm from right here on Earth, and I am a human being. Or, at least I once was."

I bent forward, overwhelmed, feeling light-headed and strange.

"What I can tell you is there is something coming, and when it gets here, you won't like it. Let me out."

"I can't do that."

"Because I'm not who I say I am?"

I nodded. "And because the man you look like is dead."

"Don't worry. I didn't kill him. He died and I took his identity. It was simple really. I was in the hospital, for a badly sprained wrist; had to have a kind of support cast. Accident. Silly, really. I fell off a ladder working in a bookstore. But I was there and Wilson died because of a car accident. It was time for me to move on anyway. I can't stay anywhere very long, because it'll find me."

"It?"

"Just listen. His family was in his room, and when they left out to do what was needed to be done about having the body dismissed, I went in and found his pants and looked through his pockets and took his wallet. I pulled back the sheet and studied his face. I became him. It was okay until tonight, long as I kept on the move and didn't have trouble with the law. But tonight, me being tired and you checking me out... It's come to an end."

"You could be me if you wanted to?"

"I could. If I killed you and hid the body, I could go right on being you. But not here. I wouldn't know your ways, your mannerisms, your experiences, but I could use the face and body and move on; become you somewhere else. Or use the face and not the name. There's all kinds of ways to play it. But I'm behind bars and you're out there, so you've got no worries. Besides, I don't kill. I'm not a murderer. Thing is, none of it matters now, I've lost time and I've lost ground. It's coming and I need to put enough miles between me and it to give myself time to truly rest."

"You're crazy?"

"You saw me change."

"I saw something."

"You know what you saw."

I nodded. "Yeah. Yeah, I do." I got up and slipped the gun in its holster and took hold of the bars and said, "Tell me about yourself. Tell me now."

"If I do, will you let me out?"

For a moment I didn't know what to say to that. Finally I said, "Maybe."

"Ha. You're pulling my leg. You're the law. You're dedicated."

"I don't know the law covers this," I said. "I don't know what I might do. I know this, what you got is a story, and I got a gun and you behind bars, and you say something's coming, so it seems the problem is yours."

"Something is coming all right, and if you're in the way, it could bother you. It could do more than just bother. Look here. Listen up." He stood up and spread his arms and stood under the light on the ceiling. "What do you see?"

"A man."

"Yes. But what is missing? What do you not see?"

I shook my head.

"Look at the floor where you stand. What do you see?"

I looked. I saw nothing, and said as much.

"No. You see something all right. Think about it... Here. Listen. Move to your right."

I stepped to my right.

"What moved with you?" he asked.

"Nothing moved with me."

"Look at me."

I looked. He stepped right. "Look on the ground. What do you see?"

"Nothing."

"Correct, now follow me when I step left."

He stepped left. "What do you see now?"

"Still nothing."

He nodded. "Look at your feet again. Step left."

I did.

"Step right."

I did...and then I got it. I had a shadow and it moved with me. I jerked my head toward him and saw that where he stood there was nothing. No shadow.

He stepped right, then left. He spun about like a top.

"My husk is empty," he said. "I am without shadow."

I took hold of the bars again, stood there trembling. I said, "Tell me."

"Will it matter? Will you help me out?"

"Perhaps. Tell me."

He sat down on the bunk again. "All right," he said. "I will."

〉〈

"My troubles began during the War Between the States. For me that was a year or two after the war started. 1862."

"The Civil War?"

"That's what I said."

"You're a time traveler?"

"In a way we all are time travelers. We travel from our date of birth until our date of death. We travel through time as it happens. Not around it, but through it. I am like that, same as you. But I have traveled farther and longer. I was born in 1840. I fought in the Civil War. I was killed in 1864."

"Killed?" I said.

"I was struck with a musket ball, during... Never mind. The where and how of it is unimportant. But I was struck dead and laid down in a shallow grave, and I was uncovered by wild dogs who meant to tear at my flesh. I know this because she told me."

I took my seat on the bench again. I didn't know what to think. What to feel.

"An old woman chased the dogs away and finished digging me up and took me home and I came alive again on her kitchen table, stretched out there naked as the day I was born, my chest and legs covered in designs made in chicken blood. Standing by the table with a big fruit jar full of something dark was the old woman. And she told me then I was hers. She was a witch. A real witch. She had rescued me from death and brought me to life with a spell, but she had kept my shadow; had torn it away from me with her enchantments. If I had it back, she said, after being brought back from the dead, I would die as others die, and I would not have the powers that I have now."

"The shape changing?" I said.

Wilson, for I knew no other name to call him, nodded. "That, and my ability to live on and on and on."

"And the jar of shadow?"

"She kept it on a shelf. My shadow was small at first, miniscule, like a piece of folded cloth. As time went on, it swelled and filled the jar. The jar could only hold my shadow for so long, and when it swelled enough, the jar would break, unless moved to some larger container, but once it was free, it could never be contained again. Even then, as long as I stayed away from it, I would remain ageless, be able to change my shape. But, if it found me it would take me and I would age the way I should have aged;

all the years that had passed would collect inside me, turn me inside out."

"Why didn't the witch use the spell on herself, to keep from aging?"

"Because you had to be young for it to work, or so she told me. But perhaps it was because she knew that eventually, no matter what it was contained within, it would get out. You had to worry about it forever pursing you, forever fleeing.

"As time went on, my shadow grew, and the old woman placed the jar in a crock, and one day we heard the jar crack inside the crock, and we knew the shadow was growing. During the day I did her bidding. I chopped and gathered wood. I worked her garden. I cooked her meals and washed her clothes. At night I lay on the floor in the thin clothes she had given me, shivering or sweating, according to the weather, unable to move because of the magic marks the old witch had made on my body. And my shadow, I could hear it moving around inside the crock, like insects in a hive.

"Then, one morning I awoke and nothing held me. The spell was broken. In the night the old woman had died. I buried the crock deep in the ground inside the floorless cabin and I set the place on fire and burned it and the old woman's body up. I went away then, walking as fast and as far as I could go.

"All I could think about was my shadow. When I laid down at night I felt as if I could hear it swell inside that crock, under the ground, and that it was breaking free, and coming up through the earth, taking to the wind, moving deliberately after me. I knew this as surely as if I could see it. I knew this because it was part of me and it was missing. I knew it traveled only at night, and found dark places during the day, for it had lost its host, and without me, it couldn't stand the light of day. I knew all of this instinctively, the way a chicken knows to set a nest, the way a fish knows to swim or a dog knows to bark.

"I moved across the land, year after year, ahead of my shadow, moving when it moved, at night, sleeping during the days, sometimes, but often driving day and night until exhaustion took me. The decades ticked by. I grew weary. That's why I was in the car during the night when I should have been moving. I slept the day and planned to move on when night came. Kept telling myself, you're too tired to drive. Just a few more minutes. A half hour. And then you can go. It's only just dark. Thoughts like that; the kind of thoughts an exhausted man thinks. I had been that way before, all tuckered out, and it had almost caught me. I was down with some disease or another. Down for three days, and I awoke, some kind of internal clock ticking louder and louder, and I knew it was near. This was over a hundred years ago, that near catch, and I still remember it sharp as a moment ago. The air turned cold in the dead of summer, and the world felt strange and out of whack, as if something had tilted. I took to a horse and rode out. As I rode, I looked back, and there it was, a dark swirl of gloom tumbling toward me, dead as a distant star.

"I whipped that horse and rode it until it keeled over. I whipped it to its feet, rode it until it fell over dead. I ran on foot and found a barn and stole another horse, rode it for miles. I caught a train and just kept going. But it had been close. I had felt it coming, and that had saved me. I feel that way now. In this damn cell I'll meet my Waterloo, and there you'll stand, watching it happen."

I stood there for a long moment, and then I got the cell key and opened the door. I said, "Not if you run."

Wilson stood up and adjusted his hat and came out of the cell, showed me a thin smile. "Bless you... By the way. The real name, it's Elton Bloodline. Thank you, thank you."

"Go!"

I followed as Bloodline moved swiftly toward the door, opened it and stepped out. The wind was chill and Bloodline stopped as if something wet had crawled up his spine, he went white under the overhanging light. He turned his head and looked, and I looked too.

Way down the street the darkness pulsed and moved toward us on the breeze; it twisted and balled and sometimes resembled a giant dark and faceless man, running.

"It's found me." Bloodline seemed frozen to the spot. "Torn away, and now it's coming back."

I grabbed his arm. "Come. Come with me. Now!"

He came alert then. We darted toward the police car. He got in and I got behind the wheel and started up the engine and drove away in a roar and a squeal of tires. I glanced in the rearview. And there it was, a shadow man, maybe ten feet high, passing under streetlights, pulling their glow into its ebony self. It ran swiftly on what looked like long wide, black, paper-wobble legs, and then its legs fluttered out from under it and it was a writhing wraith, a tumbleweed of darkness.

I put my foot to the floor and the car jumped and we put space between us and it, and then I hit something in the road, a pot hole maybe, but whatever it was it was a big bad bump and the right front tire blew. The car swerved and the back end spun to where the front should be. As it did, through the windshield I saw that the shadow looked like an inkblot, then I saw lights from the streetlamps and then the car flipped and bounced and I didn't see much of anything for a while.

## 》《

I couldn't have been out longer than a few seconds. When I awoke, I discovered I was hanging upside down. Through habit, I had fastened my seat belt. Bloodline, in his haste and fear, had not; he was wadded up on the ceiling of the car and he was starting to move. I unfastened my belt and managed not drop too hard or too fast by bracing my hands on the ceiling of the car and twisting my feet around to catch myself. I glanced about. The front and back glass were still intact. The glass on the driver's side was knocked out and the passenger's side was cracked in such a way you couldn't see out of it.

Bloodline sat up, shook his head, and looked at me. I saw the hope drain out of him and he began to shake. "You tried," he said, and then the car was flung upright and we crashed together, and then I heard glass break, and a big dark hand jutted through the shattered windshield. It grabbed at Bloodline. He tried to slide backwards, but it stretched and followed and got him around the waist. I grabbed his legs and tugged, but the thing was strong. It pulled him through the glass, cutting him with jagged shards stuck together by the windshield's safety goo, and then it pulled so hard he was snatched from my grasp.

I wiggled through the busted-out driver's window, and on my hands and knees I crawled along the street, glass sticking in my hands, the reek of spilled fuel in the air. I got to one knee and looked; saw that Bloodline's shadow was completely in the shape of a large man. It had grown from only moments ago, standing now twenty feet high and four feet wide. It lifted Bloodline high into the air, tilted its head back and carefully swallowed him.

The shadow swelled and vibrated. There was a pause, and then it throbbed even more. With a sound like metal being torn it grew smaller, rapidly. Smaller and smaller, and then, there it stood, a shadow the shape and size of a man. It looked at me, or would have had it had it eyes. The darkness it was made of began to whirl in upon itself. The shape grew pale, and finally it was Bloodline standing there, the way I had seen him before, but nude, his suit and hat and shoes all gone; his nude body shivering in the wind. He looked at me and a strange expression ran across his face, the kind you might have when someone points a loaded gun at you and you know they are going to pull the trigger. He turned his head and looked to his left, and there, poking out from him, framed by the streetlights behind him, was his shadow.

Then he withered. He bent and he bowed and his skin creaked and his bones cracked, and his flesh began to fall in strips off of his broken skeleton. The strips fell into the street and the bones came down like dominoes dropped, rattled on the concrete; the skull rolled between my feet. When I looked down at it, it was grinning, and shadows moved behind the sockets, and then even they were gone and the darkness that replaced them was thin. The skull collapsed. I stepped back, let out an involuntary cry.

Then all of it, the skull, the bones and the strips of flesh, they were caught up on the chill wind, and then they were dust, and then they were gone, and then the air warmed up and the night brightened, and the lights all along the street seemed clearer, and I was left standing there, all alone.

# THE BLEEDING SHADOW

I was down at the Blue Light Joint that night, finishing off some ribs and listening to some blues, when in walked Alma May. She was looking good, too. Had a dress on and it fit her the way a dress ought to fit every woman in the world. She was wearing a little flat hat that leaned to one side, like an unbalanced plate on a waiter's palm. The high heels she had on made her legs look tight and way all right.

The light wasn't all that good in the joint, which is one of its appeals. It sometimes helps a man or woman get along in a way the daylight wouldn't stand, but I knew Alma May enough to know light didn't matter. She'd look good wearing a sack and a paper hat.

There was something about her face that showed me right off she was worried, that things weren't right. She was glancing left and right, like she was in some big city trying to cross a busy street and not get hit by a car.

I got my bottle of beer, left out from my table, and went over to her.

Then I knew why she'd been looking around like that. She said, "I was looking for you, Richard."

"Say you were," I said. "Well, you done found me."

The way she stared at me wiped the grin off my face.

"Something wrong, Alma May?"

"Maybe. I don't know. I got to talk, though. Thought you'd be here, and I was wondering you might want to come by my place."

"When?"

"Now."

"All right."

"But don't get no business in mind," she said. "This isn't like the old days. I need your help, and I need to know I can count on you."

"Well, I kind of like the kind of business we used to do, but all right, we're friends. It's cool."

"I hoped you'd say that."

"You got a car?" I said.

She shook her head. "No. I had a friend drop me off."

I thought, friend? Sure.

"All right then," I said, "let's strut on out."

## 〉《

I guess you could say it's a shame Alma May makes her money turning tricks, but when you're the one paying for the tricks, and you are one of her satisfied customers, you feel different. Right then, anyway. Later, you feel guilty. Like maybe you done peed on the Mona Lisa. Cause that gal, she was one fine dark-skin woman who should have got better than a thousand rides and enough money to buy some eats and make some coffee in the morning. She deserved something good. Should have found and married a man with a steady job that could have done all right by her.

But that hadn't happened. Me and her had a bit of something once, and it wasn't just business, money changing hands after she got me feeling good. No, it was more than that, but we couldn't work it out. She was in the life and didn't know how to get out. And as for deserving something better, that wasn't me.

What I had were a couple of nice suits, some two-tone shoes, a hat and a gun—.45 caliber automatic, like they'd used in the war a few years back.

Alma May got a little on the dope, too, and though she shook it, it had dropped her down deep. Way I figured, she wasn't never climbing out of that hole, and it didn't have nothing to do with dope now. What it had to do with was time. You get a window open now and again, and if you don't crawl through it, it closes. I know. My window had closed some time back. It made me mad all the time.

We were in my Chevy, a six-year-old car, a forty-eight model. I'd had it reworked a bit at a time: new tires, fresh windshield, nice seat covers and so on. It was shiny and special.

We were driving along, making good time on the highway, the lights racing over the cement, making the recent rain in the ruts shine like the knees of old dress pants.

"What you need me for?" I asked.

"It's a little complicated," she said.

"Why me?"

"I don't know... You've always been good to me, and once we had a thing goin'."

"We did," I said.

"What happened to it?"

I shrugged. "It quit goin'."

"It did, didn't it? Sometimes I wish it hadn't."

"Sometimes I wish a lot of things," I said.

She leaned back in the seat and opened her purse and got out a cigarette and lit it, then rolled down the window. She remembered I didn't like cigarette smoke. I never had got on the tobacco. It took your wind and it stunk and it made your breath bad too. I hated when it got in my clothes.

"You're the only one I could tell this to," she said. "The only one that would listen to me and not think I been with the needle in my arm. You know what I'm sayin'?"

"Sure, baby, I know."

"I sound to you like I been bad?"

"Naw. You sound all right. I mean, you're talkin' a little odd, but not like you're out of your head."

"Drunk?"

"Nope. Just like you had a bad dream and want to tell someone."

"That's closer," she said. "That ain't it, but that's much closer than any needle or whisky or wine."

Alma May's place is on the outskirts of town. It's the one thing she got out of life that ain't bad. It's not a mansion. It's small, but its tight and bright in the daylight, all painted up canary yellow color with deep blue trim. It didn't look bad in the moonlight.

Alma May didn't work with a pimp. She didn't need one. She was well known around town. She had her clientele. They were all safe, she told me once. About a third of them were white folks from on the other side of the tracks, up there in the proper part of Tyler Town. What she had besides them was a dead mother and a runaway father, and a brother, Tootie, who liked to travel around, play blues and suck that bottle. He was always needing something, and Alma May, in spite of her own demons, had always managed to make sure he got it.

That was another reason me and her had to split the sheets. That brother of hers was a grown-ass man, and he lived with his mother and let her tote his water. When the mama died, he sort of went to pieces. Alma May took mama's part over, keeping Tootie in whisky and biscuits, even bought him a guitar. He lived off her whoring money, and it didn't bother him none. I didn't like him. But I will say this. That boy could play the blues.

When we were inside her house, she unpinned her hat from her hair and sailed it across the room and into a chair.

She said, "You want a drink?"

"I ain't gonna say no, long as it ain't too weak, and be sure to put it in a dirty glass."

She smiled. I watched from the living room doorway as she went and got a bottle out from under the kitchen sink, showing me how tight that dress fit across her bottom when she bent over.

She pulled some glasses off a shelf, come back with a stiff one. We drank a little of it, still standing, leaning against the door frame between living room and kitchen. We finally sat on the couch. She sat on the far end, just to make sure I remembered why we were there. She said, "It's Tootie."

I swigged down the drink real quick, said, "I'm gone."

As I went by the couch, she grabbed my hand. "Don't be that way, baby."

"Now I'm baby," I said.

"Hear me out, honey. Please. You don't owe me, but can you pretend you do?"

"Hell," I said and went and sat down on the couch.

She moved, said, "I want you to listen."

"All right," I said.

"First off, I can't pay you. Except maybe in trade."

"Not that way," I said. "You and me, we do this, it ain't trade. Call it a favor."

I do a little detective stuff now and then for folks I knew, folks that recommended me to others. I don't have a license. Black people couldn't get a license to shit broken glass in this town. But I was pretty good at what I did. I learned it the hard way. And not all of it was legal. I guess I'm a kind of private eye. Only I'm really private. I'm so private I might be more of a secret eye.

"Best thing to do is listen to this," she said. "It cuts back on some explanation."

There was a little record player on a table by the window, a stack of records. She went over and opened the player box and turned it on. The record she wanted was already on it. She lifted up the needle and set it right, stepped back and looked it me.

She was oh so fine. I looked at her and thought maybe I should have stuck with her, brother or no brother. She could melt butter from ten feet away, way she looked.

And then the music started to play.

》《

It was Tootie's voice. I recognized that right away. I had heard him plenty. Like I said, he wasn't much as a person, willing to do anything so he could lay back and play that guitar, slide a pocket knife along the strings to squeal out just the right sound, but he was good at the blues, of that, there ain't no denying.

His voice was high and lonesome, and the way he played that guitar, it was hard to imagine how he could get the sounds out of it he got.

"You brought me over here to listen to records?" I said.

She shook her head. She lifted up the needle, stopped the record, and took it off. She had another in a little paper cover, and she took it out and put it on, dropped the needle down.

"Now listen to this."

First lick or two, I could tell right off it was Tootie, but then there came a kind of turn in the music, where it got so strange the hair on the back of my neck stood up. And then Tootie started to sing, and the hair on the back of my hands and arms stood up. The air in the room got thick and the lights got dim, and shadows come out of the corners and sat on the couch with me. I ain't kidding about that part. The room was suddenly full of them, and I could hear what sounded like a bird, trapped at the ceiling, fluttering fast and hard, looking for a way out.

Then the music changed again, and it was like I had been dropped down a well, and it was a long drop, and then it was like those shadows were folding around me in a wash of dirty water. The room stunk of something foul. The guitar no longer sounded like a guitar, and Tootie's voice was no longer like a voice. It was like someone dragging a razor over concrete while trying to yodel with a throat full of glass. There was something inside the music; something that squished and scuttled and honked and raved, something unsettling, like a snake in a satin glove.

"Cut it off," I said.

But Alma May had already done it.

She said, "That's as far as I've ever let it go. It's all I can do to move to cut it off. It feels like it's getting more powerful the more it plays. I don't want to hear the rest of it. I don't know I can take it. How can that be, Richard? How can that be with just sounds?"

I was actually feeling weak, like I'd just come back from a bout with the flu and someone had beat my ass. I said, "More powerful? How do you mean?"

"Ain't that what you think? Ain't that how it sounds? Like it's getting stronger?"

I nodded. "Yeah."

"And the room—"

"The shadows?" I said. "I didn't just imagine it?"

"No," she said, "Only every time I've heard it, it's been a little different. The notes get darker, the guitar licks, they cut something inside me, and each time it's something different and something deeper. I don't know if it makes me feel good or it makes me feel bad, but it sure makes me feel."

"Yeah," I said, because I couldn't find anything else to say.

"Tootie sent me that record. He sent a note that said: Play it when you have to. That's what it said. That's all it said. What's that mean?"

"I don't know, but I got to wonder why Tootie would send it to you in the first place. Why would he want you to hear something makes you almost sick... And how in hell could he do that, make that kind of sound, I mean?"

She shook her head. "I don't know. Someday, I'm gonna play it all the way through."

"I wouldn't," I said.

"Why?"

"You heard it. I figure it only gets worse. I don't understand it, but I know I don't like it."

"Yeah," she said, putting the record back in the paper sleeve. "I know. But it's so strange. I've never heard anything like it."

"And I don't want to hear anything like it again."

"Still, you have to wonder."

"What I wonder is what I was wondering before. Why would he send this shit to you?"

"I think he's proud of it. There's nothing like it. It's...original."

"I'll give it that," I said. "So, what do you want with me?"

"I want you to find Tootie."

"Why?"

"Because I don't think he's right. I think he needs help. I mean, this... It makes me think he's somewhere he shouldn't be."

"But yet, you want to play it all the way through," I said.

"What I know is I don't like that. I don't like Tootie being associated with it, and I don't know why. Richard, I want you to find him."

"Where did the record come from?"

She got the sheath and brought it to me. I could see through the little doughnut in the sheath where the label on the record ought to be. Nothing but disk. The package itself was like wrapping paper you put meat in. It was stained.

"I think he paid some place to let him record," I said. "Question is, what place? You have an address where this came from?"

"I do." She went and got a large manila envelope and brought it to me. "It came in this."

I looked at the writing on the front. It had as a return address, the Hotel Champion. She showed me the note. It was on a piece of really cheap stationery that said the Hotel Champion and had a phone number and an address in Dallas. The stationery looked old and it was sun-faded.

"I called them," she said, "but they didn't know anything about him. They had never heard of him. I could go look myself, but...I'm a little afraid. Besides, you know, I got clients, and I got to make the house payment."

I didn't like hearing about that, knowing what kind of clients she meant, and how she was going to make that money. I said, "All right. What you want me to do?"

"Find him."

"And then what?"

"Bring him home."

"And if he don't want to come back?"

"I've seen you work, bring him home to me. Just don't lose that temper of yours."

I turned the record around and around in my hands. I said, "I'll go take a look. I won't promise anything more than that. He wants to come, I'll bring him back. He doesn't, I might be inclined to break his leg and bring him back. You know I don't like him."

"I know. But don't hurt him."

"If he comes easy, I'll do that. If he doesn't, I'll let him stay, come back and tell you where he is and how he is. How about that?'

"That's good enough," she said. "Find out what this is all about. It's got me scared, Richard."

"It's just bad sounds," I said. "Tootie was probably high on something when he recorded it, thought it was good at the time, sent it to you because he thought he was the coolest thing since Robert Johnson."

"Who?"

"Never mind. But I figure when he got over his hop, he probably didn't even remember he mailed it."

"Don't try and tell me you've heard anything like this. That listening to it didn't make you feel like your skin was gonna pull off your bones, that some part of it made you want to dip in the dark and learn to like it. Tell me it wasn't like that. Tell me it wasn't like walking out in front of a car and the headlights in your face, and you just wanting to step out there even though it scared hell out of you and you knew it was the devil or something even worse at the wheel. Tell me you didn't feel something like that."

I couldn't. So I didn't say anything. I just sat there and sweated, the sound of that music still shaking down deep in my bones, boiling my blood.

"Here's the thing," I said. "I'll do it, but you got to give me a photograph of Tootie, if you got one, and the record so you don't play it no more."

She studied me a moment. "I hate that thing," she said, nodding at the record in my hands, "but somehow I feel attached to it. Like getting rid of it is getting rid of a piece of me."

"That's the deal."

"All right," she said, "take it, but take it now."

》《

**Motoring along by** myself in the Chevy, the moon high and bright, all I could think of was that music, or whatever that sound was. It was stuck in my head like an axe. I had the record on the seat beside me, had Tootie's note and envelope, the photograph Alma May had given me.

Part of me wanted to drive back to Alma May and tell her no, and never mind. Here's the record back. But another part of me, the dumb part, wanted to know where and how and why that record had been made. Curiosity, it just about gets us all.

Where I live is a rickety third-floor walk-up. It's got the stairs on the outside, and they stop at each landing. I was at the very top.

I tried not to rest my hand too heavy on the rail as I climbed, because it was about to come off. I unlocked my door and turned on the light and watched the roaches run for cover.

I put the record down, got a cold one out of the ice box. Well, actually it was a plug-in. A refrigerator. But I'd grown up with ice boxes, so calling it that was hard to break. I picked up the record again and took a seat.

Sitting in my old armchair with the stuffings leaking out like a busted cotton sack, holding the record again, looking at the dirty brown sleeve, I noticed the grooves were dark and scabby looking, like something had gotten poured in there and had dried tight. I tried to determine if that had something to do with that crazy sound. Could something in the grooves make that kind of noise? Didn't seem likely.

I thought about putting the record on, listening to it again, but I couldn't stomach the thought. The fact that I held it in my hand made me uncomfortable. It was like holding a bomb about to go off.

I had thought of it like a snake once. Alma May had thought of it like a hit and run car driven by the devil. And now I had thought of it like a bomb. That was some kind of feeling coming from a grooved up circle of wax.

### »«

Early next morning, with the .45 in the glove box, a razor in my coat pocket, and the record up front on the seat beside me, I tooled out toward Dallas, and the Hotel Champion.

I got into Big D around noon, stopped at a café on the out-skirts where there was colored, and went in where a big fat mama with a pretty face and a body that smelled real good made me a hamburger and sat and flirted with me all the while I ate it. That's all right. I like women, and I like them to flirt. They quit doing that, I might as well lay down and die.

While we was flirting, I asked her about the Hotel Champion, if she knew where it was. I had the street number of course, but I needed tighter directions.

"Oh, yeah, honey, I know where it is, and you don't want to stay there. It's deep in the colored section, and not the good part, that's what I'm trying to tell you, and it don't matter you brown as a walnut yourself. There's folks down there will cut you and put your blood in a paper cup and mix it with whisky and drink it. You too good-looking to get all cut up and such. There's better places to stay on the far other side."

I let her give me a few hotel names, like I might actually stay at one or the other, but I got the address for the Champion, paid up, giving her a good tip, and left out of there.

The part of town where the Hotel Champion was, was just as nasty as the lady had said. There were people hanging around on the streets, and leaning into corners, and there was trash everywhere. It wasn't exactly a place that fostered a lot of pride.

I found the Hotel Champion and parked out front. There was a couple fellas on the street eyeing my car. One was skinny. One was big. They were dressed up with nice hats and shoes, just like they had jobs. But if they did, they wouldn't have been standing around in the middle of the day eyeing my Chevy.

I pulled the .45 out of the glove box and stuck it in my pants, at the small of my back. My coat would cover it just right.

I got out and gave the hotel the gander. It was nice looking if you were blind in one eye and couldn't see out the other.

There wasn't any doorman, and the door was hanging on a hinge. Inside I saw a dusty stairway to my left, a scarred door to my right.

There was a desk in front of me. It had a glass hooked to it that went to the ceiling. There was a little hole in it low down on the counter that had a wooden stop behind it. There were fly specks on the glass, and there was a man behind the glass, perched on a stool, like a frog on a lily pad. He was fat and colored and his hair had blue blanket wool in it. I didn't take it for decoration. He was just a nasty sonofabitch.

I could smell him when he moved the wooden stop. A stink like armpits and nasty underwear and rotting teeth. Floating in from somewhere in back, I could smell old cooking smells, boiled pig's feet and pig's tails that might have been good about the time the pig lost them, but now all that was left was a rancid stink. There was also a reek like cat piss.

I said, "Hey, man, I'm looking for somebody."

"You want a woman, you got to bring your own," the man said. "But I can give you a number or two. Course, I ain't guaranteeing anything about them being clean."

"Naw. I'm looking for somebody was staying here. His name is Tootie Johnson."

"I don't know no Tootie Johnson."

That was the same story Alma May had got.

"Well, all right, you know this fella?" I pulled out the photograph and pressed it against the glass.

"Well, he might look like someone got a room here. We don't sign in and we don't exchange names much."

"No? A class place like this."

"I said he might look like someone I seen," he said. "I didn't say he definitely did."

"You fishing for money?"

"Fishing ain't very certain," he said.

I sighed and put the photograph back inside my coat and got out my wallet and took out a five-dollar bill.

Frog Man saw himself as some kind of greasy high roller. "That's it? Five dollars for prime information?"

I made a slow and careful show of putting my five back in my wallet. "Then you don't get nothing," I said.

He leaned back on his stool and put his stubby fingers together and let them lay on his round belly. "And you don't get nothing neither, jackass."

I went to the door on my right and turned the knob. Locked. I stepped back and kicked it so hard I felt the jar all the way to the top of my head. The door flew back on its hinges, slammed into the wall. It sounded like someone firing a shot.

I went on through and behind the desk, grabbed Frog Man by the shirt and slapped him hard enough he fell off the stool. I kicked him in the leg and he yelled. I picked up the stool and hit him with it across the chest, then threw the stool through a doorway that led into a kitchen. I heard something break in there and a cat made a screeching sound.

"I get mad easy," I said.

"Hell, I see that," he said, and held up a hand for protection. "Take it easy, man. You done hurt me."

"That was the plan."

The look in his eyes made me feel sorry for him. I also felt like an asshole. But that wouldn't keep me from hitting him again if he didn't answer my question. When I get perturbed, I'm not reasonable.

"Where is he?"

"Do I still get the five dollars?"

"No," I said, "now you get my best wishes. You want to lose that?"

"No. No, I don't."

"Then don't play me. Where is he, you toad?"

"He's up in room 52, on the fifth floor."

"Spare key?"

He nodded at a rack of them. The keys were on nails and they all had little wooden pegs on the rings with the keys. Numbers were painted on the pegs. I found one that said 52, took it off the rack.

I said, "You better not be messing with me."

"I ain't. He's up there. He don't never come down. He's been up there a week. He makes noise up there. I don't like it. I run a respectable place."

"Yeah, it's really nice here. And you better not be jerking me."

"I ain't. I promise."

"Good. And, let me give you a tip. Take a bath. And get that shit out of your hair. And those teeth you got ain't looking too good. Pull them. And shoot that fucking cat, or at least get him some place better than the kitchen to piss. It stinks like a toilet in there."

I walked out from behind the desk, out in the hall, and up the flight of stairs in a hurry.

》《

I rushed along the hallway on the fifth floor. It was covered in white linoleum with a gold pattern in it; it creaked and cracked as I walked along. The end of the hall had a window, and there was a stairwell on that end too. Room 52 was right across from it.

I heard movement on the far end of the stairs. I had an idea what that was all about. About that time, two of the boys I'd seen on the street showed themselves at the top of the stairs, all decked out in their nice hats and such, grinning.

One of them was about the size of a Cadillac, with a gold tooth that shone bright when he smiled. The guy behind him was skinny with his hand in his pocket.

I said, "Well, if it isn't the pimp squad."

"You funny, nigger," said the big man.

"Yeah, well, catch the act now. I'm going to be moving to a new locale."

"You bet you are," said the big man.

"Fat ass behind the glass down there, he ain't paying you enough to mess with me," I said.

"Sometimes, cause we're bored, we just like messin'."

"Say you do?"

"Uh-huh," said the skinny one.

It was then I seen the skinny guy pull a razor out of his pocket. I had one too, but razor work, it's nasty. He kept it closed.

Big guy with the gold tooth flexed his fingers, and made a fist. That made me figure he didn't have a gun or a razor; or maybe he just liked hitting people. I know I did.

They come along toward me then, and the skinny one with the razor flicked it open. I pulled the .45 out from under my coat, said, "You ought to put that back in your pocket," I said, "save it for shaving."

"Oh, I'm fixing to do some shaving right now," he said.

I pointed the .45 at him.

The big man said, "That's one gun for two men."

"It is," I said, "but I'm real quick with it. And frankly, I know one of you is gonna end up dead. I just ain't sure which one right yet."

"All right then," said the big man, smiling. "That'll be enough." He looked back at the skinny man with the razor. The skinny man put the razor back in his coat pocket and they turned and started down the stairs.

I went over and stood by the stairway and listened. I could hear them walking down, but then all of a sudden, they stopped on the stairs. That's the way I had it figured.

Then I could hear the morons rushing back up. They weren't near as sneaky as they thought they was. The big one was first out of the chute, so to speak; come rushing out of the stairwell and onto the landing. I brought the butt of the .45 down on the back of his head, right where the skull slopes down. He did a kind of frog hop and bounced across the hall and hit his head on the wall, and went down and laid there like his intent all along had been a quick leap and a nap.

Then the other one was there, and he had the razor. He flicked it, and then he saw the .45 in my hand.

"Where did you think this gun was gonna go?" I said. "On vacation?"

I kicked him in the groin hard enough he dropped the razor, and went to his knees. I put the .45 back where I got it. I said, "You want some, man?"

He got up, and come at me. I hit him with a right and knocked him clean through the window behind him. Glass sprinkled all over the hallway.

I went over and looked out. He was lying on the fire escape, his head against the railing. He looked right at me.

"You crazy cocksucker. What if there hadn't been no fire escape?"

"You'd have your ass punched into the bricks. Still might."

He got up quick and clambered down the fire escape like a squirrel. I watched him till he got to the ground and went limping away down the alley between some overturned trash cans and a slinking dog.

I picked up his razor and put it in my pocket with the one I already had, walked over and kicked the big man in the head just because I could.

》《

I knocked on the door. No one answered. I could hear sounds from inside. It was similar to what I had heard on that record, but not quite, and it was faint, as if coming from a distance.

No one answered my knock, so I stuck the key in the door and opened it and went straight away inside.

I almost lost my breath when I did.

The air in the room was thick and it stunk of mildew and rot and things long dead. It made those boiled pig feet and that shitting cat and that rotten-tooth bastard downstairs smell like perfume.

Tootie was lying on the bed, on his back. His eyes were closed. He was a guy usually dressed to the top, baby, but his shirt was wrinkled and dirty and sweaty at the neck and arm-pits. His pants were nasty too. He had on his shoes, but no socks. He looked like someone had set him on fire and then beat out the flames with a two-by-four. His face was like a skull, he had lost so much flesh, and he was as bony under his clothes as a skeleton.

Where his hands lay on the sheet, there were blood stains. His guitar was next to the bed, and there were stacks and stacks of composition notebooks lying on the floor. A couple of them were open and filled with writing. Hell, I didn't even know Tootie could write.

The wall on the far side was marked up in black and red paint; there were all manner of musical notes drawn on it, along with symbols I had never seen before; swiggles and circles and stick figure drawings. Blood was on the wall too, most likely from Tootie's bleeding fingers. Two open paint cans, the red and the black, were on the floor with brushes stuck up in them. Paint was splattered on the floor and had dried in humped-up blisters. The guitar had blood stains all over it.

A record player, plugged in, sitting on a nightstand by the bed, was playing that strange music. I went to it right away and picked up the needle and set it aside. And let me tell you, just making my way across the room to get hold of the player was like wading through mud with my ankles tied together. It seemed to me as I got closer to the record, the louder it got, and the more ill I felt. My head throbbed. My heart pounded.

When I had the needle up and the music off, I went over and touched Tootie. He didn't move, but I could see his chest rising and falling. Except for his hands, he didn't seem hurt. He was in a deep sleep. I picked up his right hand and turned it over and looked at it. The fingers were cut deep, like someone had taken a razor to the tips. Right off, I figured that was from playing his guitar. Struck me, that to get the sounds he got out of it, he really had to dig in with those fingers. And from the looks of this room, he had been at it non-stop, until recent.

I shook him. His eyes fluttered and finally opened. They were bloodshot and had dark circles around them.

When he saw me, he startled, and his eyes rolled around in his head like those little games kids get where you try to shake the marbles into holes. After a moment, they got straight, and he said, "Ricky?"

That was another reason I hated him. I didn't like being called Ricky.

I said, "Hello, shithead. Your sister's worried sick."

"The music," he said. "Put back on the music."

"You call that music?" I said.

He took a deep breath, rolled out of the bed, nearly knocking me aside. Then I saw him jerk, like he'd seen a truck coming right at him. I turned. I wished it had been a truck.

》《

Let me try and tell you what I saw. I not only saw it, I felt it. It was in the very air we were breathing, getting inside my chest like mice wearing barbed-wire coats. The wall Tootie had painted and drawn all that crap on shook.

And then the wall wasn't a wall at all. It was a long hallway, dark as original sin. There was something moving in there, something that slithered and slid and made smacking sounds like an anxious old drunk about to take his next drink. Stars popped up; greasy stars that didn't remind me of anything I had ever seen in the night sky; a moon the color of a bleeding fish eye was in the background, and it cast a light on something moving toward us.

"Jesus Christ," I said.

"No," Tootie said. "It's not him."

Tootie jumped to the record player, picked up the needle, and put it on. There came that rotten sound I had heard with Alma May, and I knew what I had heard when I first came into the room was the tail end of that same record playing, the part I hadn't heard before.

The music screeched and howled. I bent over and threw up. I fell back against the bed, tried to get up, but my legs were like old pipe cleaners. That record had taken the juice out of me. And then I saw it.

There's no description that really fits. It was...a thing. All blanket wrapped in shadow with sucker mouths and thrashing tentacles and centipede legs mounted on clicking hooves. A bulb-like head plastered all over with red and yellow eyes that seemed to creep. All around it, shadows swirled like water. It had a beak. Well, beaks.

The thing was coming right out of the wall. Tentacles thrashed toward me. One touched me across the cheek. It was like being scalded with hot grease. A shadow come loose of the thing, fell onto the floorboards of the room, turned red and raced across the floor like a gush of blood. Insects and maggots squirmed in the bleeding shadow, and the record hit a high spot so loud and so goddamn strange, I ground my teeth, felt as if my insides were being twisted up like wet wash. And then I passed out.

## 》《

When I came to, the music was still playing. Tootie was bent over me.

"That sound," I said.

"You get used to it," Tootie said, "but the thing can't. Or maybe it can, but just not yet."

I looked at the wall. There was no alleyway. It was just a wall plastered in paint designs and spots of blood.

"And if the music stops?" I said.

"I fell asleep," Tootie said. "Record quits playing, it starts coming."

For a moment I didn't know anything to say. I finally got off the floor and sat on the bed. I felt my cheek where the tentacle hit me. It throbbed and I could feel blisters. I also had a knot on my head where I had fallen.

"Almost got you," Tootie said. "I think you can leave and it won't come after you. Me, I can't. I leave, it follows. It'll finally find me. I guess here is as good as any place."

I was looking at him, listening, but not understanding a damn thing.

The record quit. Tootie started it again. I looked at the wall. Even that blank moment without sound scared me. I didn't want to see that thing again. I didn't even want to think about it.

"I haven't slept in days, until now," Tootie said, coming to sit on the bed. "You hadn't come in, it would have got me, carried me off, taken my soul. But, you can leave. It's my lookout, not yours... I'm always in some kind of shit, ain't I, Ricky?"

"That's the truth."

"This though, it's the corker. I got to stand up and be a man for once. I got to fight this thing back, and all I got is the music. Like I told you, you can go."

I shook my head. "Alma May sent me. I said I'd bring you back."

It was Tootie's turn to shake his head. "Nope. I ain't goin'. I ain't done nothin' but mess up Sis's life. I ain't gonna do it."

"First responsible thing I ever heard you say," I said.

"Go on," Tootie said. "Leave me to it. I can take care of myself."

"If you don't die of starvation, or pass out from lack of sleep, or need of water, you'll be just fine."

Tootie smiled at me. "Yeah. That's all I got to worry about. I hope it is one of them other things kills me. Cause if it comes for me... Well, I don't want to think about it."

"Keep the record going, I'll get something to eat and drink, some coffee. You think you can stay awake a half hour or so?"

"I can, but you're coming back?"

"I'm coming back," I said.

Out in the hallway I saw the big guy was gone. I took the stairs.

>> <<

When I got back, Tootie had cleaned up the vomit, and was looking through the notebooks. He was sitting on the floor and had them stacked all around him. He was maybe six inches away from the record player. Now and again he'd reach up and start it all over.

Soon as I was in the room, and that sound from the record was snugged up around me, I felt sick. I had gone to a greasy spoon down the street, after I changed a flat tire. One of the boys I'd given a hard time had most likely knifed it. My bet was the lucky son-of-a-bitch who had fallen on the fire escape.

Besides the tire, a half dozen long scratches had been cut into the paint on the passenger's side, and my windshield was knocked in. I got back from the café, I parked what was left of my car behind the hotel, down the street a bit, and walked a block. Car looked so bad now, maybe nobody would want to steal it.

I sat one of the open sacks on the floor by Tootie.

"Both hamburgers are yours," I said. "I got coffee for the both of us here."

I took out a tall, cardboard container of coffee and gave it to him, took the other one for myself. I sat on the bed and sipped. Nothing tasted good in that room with that smell and that sound. But, Tootie, he ate like a wolf. He gulped those burgers and coffee like it was air.

When he finished with the second burger, he started up the record again, leaned his back against the bed.

"Coffee or not," he said, "I don't know how long I can stay awake."

"So what you got to do is keep the record playing?" I said.

"Yeah."

"Lay up in bed, sleep for a few hours. I'll keep the record going. You're rested, you got to explain this thing to me, and then we'll figure something out."

"There's nothing to figure," he said. "But, god, I'll take you up on that sleep."

He crawled up in the bed and was immediately out.

I started the record over.

I got up then, untied Tootie's shoes and pulled them off. Hell, like him or not, he was Alma May's brother. And another thing, I wouldn't wish that thing behind the wall on my worst enemy.

》《

I sat on the floor where Tootie had sat and kept restarting the record as I tried to figure things out, which wasn't easy with that music going. I got up from time to time and walked around the room, and then I'd end up back on the floor by the record player, where I could reach it easy.

Between changes, I looked through the composition notebooks. They were full of musical notes mixed with scribbles like the ones on the wall. It was hard to focus with that horrid sound. It was like the air was full of snakes and razors. Got the feeling the music was pushing at something behind that wall. Got the feeling too, there was something on the other side, pushing back.

》《

It was dark when Tootie woke up. He had slept a good ten hours, and I was exhausted with all that record changing, that horrible sound. I had a headache from looking over those notebooks, and I didn't know any more about them than when I first started.

I went and bought more coffee, brought it back, and we sat on the bed, him changing the record from time to time, us sipping.

I said, "You sure you can't just walk away?"

I was avoiding the real question for some reason. Like, what in hell is that thing, and what is going on? Maybe I was afraid of the answer.

"You saw that thing. I can walk away, all right. And I can run. But wherever I go, it'll find me. So, at some point, I got to face it. Sometimes I make that same record sound with my guitar, give the record a rest. Thing I fear most is the record wearing out."

I gestured at the notebooks on the floor. "What is all that?"

"My notes. My writings. I come here to write some lyrics, some new blues songs."

"Those aren't lyrics, those are notes."

"I know," he said.

"You don't have a music education. You just play."

"Because of the record, I can read music, and I can write things that don't make any sense to me unless it's when I'm writing them, when I'm listening to that music. All those marks, they are musical notes, and the other marks are other kinds of notes, notes for sounds that I couldn't make until a few days back. I didn't even know those sounds were possible. But now, my head is full of the sounds and those marks and all manner of things, and the only way I can rest is to write them down. I wrote on the wall cause I thought the marks, the notes themselves, might hold that thing back and I could run. Didn't work."

"None of this makes any sense to me," I said.

"All right," Tootie said, "this is the best I can explain something that's got no explanation. I had some blues boys tell me they once come to this place on the south side called Cross Road Records. It's a little record shop where the streets cross. It's got all manner of things in it, and it's got this big colored guy with a big white smile and bloodshot eyes that works the joint. They said they'd seen the place, poked their heads in, and even heard Robert Johnson's sounds coming from a player on the counter. There was a big man sitting behind the counter, and he waved them in, but the place didn't seem right, they said, so they didn't go in.

"But, you know me. That sounded like just the place I wanted to go. So, I went. It's where South Street crosses a street called Way South.

"I go in there, and I'm the only one in the store. There's records everywhere, in boxes, lying on tables. Some got labels, some don't. I'm looking, trying to figure out how you told about anything, and this big fella with the smile comes over to me and starts to talk. He had breath like an un-wiped butt, and his face didn't seem so much like black skin as it did black rock.

"He said, 'I know what you're looking for.' He reached in a box, and pulled out a record didn't have no label on it. Thing was, that whole box didn't have labels. I think he's just messing with me, trying to make a sale. I'm ready to go, cause he's starting to make my skin crawl. Way he moves ain't natural, you know. It's like he's got something wrong with his feet, but he's still able to move, and quick like. Like he does it between the times you blink your eyes.

"He goes over and puts that record on a player, and it starts up, and it was Robert Johnson. I swear, it was him. Wasn't no one could play like him. It was him. And here's the thing. It wasn't a song I'd ever heard by him. And I thought I'd heard all the music he'd put on wax."

Tootie sipped at his coffee. He looked at the wall a moment, and then changed the player again.

I said, "Swap out spots, and I'll change it. You sip and talk. Tell me all of it."

We did that, and Tootie continued.

"Well, one thing comes to another, and he starts talking me up good, and I finally I ask him how much for the record. He looks at me, and he says, 'For you, all you got to give me is a little blue soul. And when you come back, you got to buy something with a bit more of it till it's all gone and I got it. Cause you will be back.'

"I figured he was talking about me playing my guitar for him, cause I'd told him I was a player, you know, while we was talking. I told him I had my guitar in a room I was renting, and I was on foot, and it would take me all day to get my guitar and get back, so I'd have to pass on that deal. Besides, I was about tapped out of money. I had a place I was supposed to play that evening, but until then, I had maybe three dollars and some change in my pocket. I had the rent on this room paid up all week, and I hadn't been there but two days. I tell him all that, and he says, 'Oh, that's all right. I know you can play. I can tell about things like that. What I mean is, you give me a drop of blood and a promise, and you can have that record.' Right then, I started to walk out, cause I'm thinking, this guy is nutty as fruit cake with an extra dose of nuts, but I want that record. So, I tell him, sure, I'll give him a drop of blood. I won't lie none to you, Ricky, I was thinking about nabbing that record and making a run with it. I wanted it that bad. So a drop of blood, that didn't mean nothin'.

"He pulls a record needle out from behind the counter, and he comes over and pokes my finger with it, sudden like, while I'm still trying to figure how he got over to me that fast, and he holds my hand and lets blood drip on—get this—the record. It flows into the grooves.

"He says, 'Now, you promise me your blues playing soul is mine when you die.'

"I thought it was just talk, you know, so I told him he could have it. He says, 'When you hear it, you'll be able to play it. And when you play it, sometime when you're real good on it, it'll start to come, like a rat easing its nose into hot dead meat. It'll start to come.'

"'What will?' I said. 'What are you talking about?'

"He says, 'You'll know.'

"Next thing I know, he's over by the door, got it open and he's smiling at me, and I swear, I thought for a moment I could see right through him. Could see his skull and bones. I've got the record in my hand, and I'm walking out, and as soon as I do, he shuts the door and I hear the lock turn.

"My first thought was, I got to get this blood out of the record grooves, cause that crazy bastard has just given me a lost Robert

Johnson song for nothing. I took out a kerchief, pulled the record out of the sleeve, and went to wiping. The blood wouldn't come out. It was in the notches, you know.

"I went back to my room here, and I tried a bit of warm water on the blood in the grooves, but it still wouldn't come out. I was mad as hell, figured the record wouldn't play, way that blood had hardened in the grooves. I put it on and thought maybe the needle would wear the stuff out, but as soon as it was on the player and the needle hit it, it started sounding just the way it had in the store. I sat on the bed and listened to it, three or four times, and then I got my guitar and tried to play what was being played, knowing I couldn't do it, cause though I knew that sound wasn't electrified, it sounded like it was. But, here's the thing. I could do it. I could play it. And I could see the notes in my head, and my head got filled up with them. I went out and bought those notebooks, and I wrote it all down just so my head wouldn't explode, cause every time I heard that record, and tried to play it, them notes would cricket-hop in my skull."

All the while we had been talking, I had been replaying the record.

"I forgot all about the gig that night," Tootie said. "I sat here until morning playing. By noon the next day, I sounded just like that record. By late afternoon, I started to get kind of sick. I can't explain it, but I was feeling that there was something trying to tear through somewhere, and it scared me and my insides knotted up.

"I don't know any better way of saying it than that. It was such a strong feeling. Then, while I was playing, the wall there, it come apart the way you seen it, and I seen that thing. It was just a wink of a look. But there it was. In all its terrible glory.

"I quit playing, and the wall wobbled back in place and closed up. I thought, Damn, I need to eat or nap, or something. And I did. Then I was back on that guitar. I could play like crazy, and I started going off on that song, adding here and there. It wasn't like it was coming from me, though. It was like I was getting help from somewhere.

"Finally, with my fingers bleeding and cramped and aching, and my voice gone raspy from singing, I quit. Still, I wanted to hear it, so I put on the record. And it wasn't the same no more. It was Johnson, but the words was strange, not English. Sounded like some kind of chant, and I knew then that Johnson was in that record, as sure as I was in this room, and that that chanting and that playing was opening up a hole for that thing in the wall. It was the way that fella had said. It was like a rat working its nose through red hot meat, and now it felt like I was the meat. Next time I played the record, the voice on it wasn't Johnson's. It was mine.

"I had had enough, so I got the record and took it back to that shop. The place was the same as before, and like before, I was the only one in there. He looked at me, and comes over, and says, 'You already want to undo the deal. I can tell. They all do. But that ain't gonna happen.'

"I gave him a look like I was gonna jump on him and beat his ass, but he gave me a look back, and I went weak as kitten.

"He smiled at me, and pulls out another record from that same box, and he takes the one I gave him and puts it back, and says, 'You done made a deal, but for a lick of your soul, I'll let you have this. See, you done opened the path, now that rat's got to work on that meat. It don't take no more record or you playing for that to happen. Rat's gotta to eat now, no matter what you do.'

"When he said that, he picks up my hand and looks at my cut up fingers from playing, and he laughs so loud everything in the store shakes, and he squeezes my fingers until they start to bleed.

"'A lick of my soul?' I asked.

"And then he pushed the record in my hand, and if I'm lying, I'm dying, he sticks out his tongue, and it's long as an old rat snake and black as a hole in the ground, and he licks me right around the neck. When he's had a taste, he smiles and shivers, like he's just had something cool to drink."

Tootie paused to unfasten his shirt and peel it down a little. There was a spot halfway around his neck like someone had worked him over with sandpaper.

"'A taste,' he says, and then he shoves this record in my hand, which is bleeding from where he squeezed my fingers. Next thing I know, I'm looking at the record, and it's thick, and I touch it, and it's two records, back to back. He says, 'I give you that extra one cause you tasted mighty good, and maybe it'll let you get a little more rest that way, if you got a turntable drop. Call me generous and kind in my old age.'

"Wasn't nothing for it but to take the records and come back here. I didn't have no intention of playing it. I almost threw it away. But by then, that thing in the wall, wherever it is, was starting to stick through. Each time the hole was bigger and I could see more of it, and that red shadow was falling out on the floor. I thought about running, but I didn't want to just let it loose, and I knew, deep down, no matter where I went, it would come too.

"I started playing that record in self-defense. Pretty soon, I'm playing it on the guitar. When I got scared enough, got certain enough that thing was coming through, I played hard, and that hole would close, and that thing would go back where it come from. For awhile.

"I figured though, I ought to have some insurance. You see, I played both them records, and they was the same thing, and it was my voice, and I hadn't never recorded or even heard them songs before. I knew then, what was on those notes I had written, what had come to me was the counter song to the one I had been playing first. I don't know if that was just some kind of joke that record store fella had played on me, but I knew it was magic of a sort. He had give me a song to let it in and he had give me another song to hold it back. It was amusing to him, I'm sure.

"I thought I had the thing at bay, so I took that other copy, went to the Post Office, mailed it to Alma, case something happened to me. I guess I thought it was self-defense for her, but there was another part was proud of what I had done. What I was able to do. I could play anything now, and I didn't even need to think about it. Regular blues, it was a snap. Anything on that guitar was easy, even things you ought not to be able to play on one. Now, I realize it ain't me. It's something else out there.

"But when I come back from mailing, I brought me some paint and brushes, thought I'd write the notes and such on the wall. I did that, and I was ready to pack and go roaming some more, showing off my new skills, and all of a sudden, the thing, it's pushing through. It had gotten stronger cause I hadn't been playing the sounds, man. I put on the record, and I pretty much been at it ever since.

"It was all that record fella's game, you see. I got to figuring he was the devil, or something like him. He had me playing a game to keep that thing out, and to keep my soul. But it was a three-minute game, six if I'd have kept that second record and put it on the drop. If I was playing on the guitar, I could just work from the end of that record back to the front of it, playing it over and over. But it wore me down. Finally, I started playing the record nonstop. And I have for days.

"The fat man downstairs, he'd come up for the rent, but as soon as he'd use his key and crack that door, hear that music, he'd get gone. So here I am, still playing, with nothing left but to keep on playing, or get my soul sucked up by that thing and delivered to the record store man."

## »«

Tootie minded the record, and I went over to where he told me the record store was with idea to put a boot up the guy's ass, or a .45 slug in his noggin. I found South Street, but not Way South. The other street that should have been Way South was called Back Water. There wasn't a store either, just an empty, unlocked building. I opened the door and went inside. There was dust everywhere, and I could see where some tables had been, cause their leg marks was in the dust. But anyone or anything that had been there, was long gone.

I went back to the hotel, and when I got there, Tootie was just about asleep. The record was turning on the turntable without any sound. I looked at the wall, and I could see the beak of that thing, chewing at it. I put the record on, and this time, when it come to the end, the thing was still chewing. I played it another time, and another, and the thing finally went away. It was getting stronger.

I woke Tootie up, said, "You know, we're gonna find out if this thing can outrun my souped-up Chevy."

"Ain't no use," Tootie said.

"Then we ain't got nothing to lose," I said.

We grabbed up the record and his guitar, and we was downstairs and out on the street faster than you can snap your fingers. As we passed where the toad was, he saw me and got up quick and went into the kitchen and closed the door. If I'd had time, I'd have beat his ass on general principles.

When we walked to where I had parked my car, it was sitting on four flats and the side windows was knocked out and the aerial was snapped off. The record Alma May had given me was still there, lying on the seat. I got it and put it against the other one in my hand. It was all I could do.

As for the car, I was gonna drive that Chevy back to East Texas like I was gonna fly back on a sheet of wet newspaper.

Now, I got to smellin' that smell. One that was in the room. I looked at the sky. The sun was kind of hazy. Green even. The air around us trembled, like it was scared of something. It was heavy, like a blanket. I grabbed Tootie by the arm, pulled him down the street. I spied a car at a curb that I thought could run, a V-8 Ford. I kicked the back side window out, reached through and got the latch.

I slid across the seat and got behind the wheel. Tootie climbed in on the passenger side. I bent down and worked some wires under the dash loose with my fingers and my razor, hot-wired the car. The motor throbbed and we was out of there.

>><<

It didn't make any kind of sense, but as we was cruising along, behind us it was getting dark. It was like chocolate pudding in a big wad rolling after us. Stars was popping up in it. They seemed more like eyes than stars. There was a bit of a moon, slightly covered over in what looked like a red fungus.

I drove that Ford fast as I could. I was hitting the needle at a hundred and ten. Didn't see a car on the highway. Not a highway cop, not an old lady on the way to the store. Where the hell was everybody? The highway looped up and down like the bottom was trying to fall out from under us.

To make it all short, I drove hard and fast, and stopped once for gas, having the man fill it quick. I gave him a bill that was more than the gas was worth, and he grinned at me as we burned rubber getting away. I don't think he could see what we could see—that dark sky with that thing in it. It was like you had to hear the music to see the thing existed, or for it to have any effect in your life. For him, it was daylight and fine and life was good.

By the time I hit East Texas, there was smoke coming from under that stolen Ford's hood. We came down a hill, and it was daylight in front of us, and behind us the dark was rolling in; it was splittin', making a kind of corridor, and there was that beaked thing, that...whatever it was. It was bigger than before and it was squirming its way out of the night sky like a weasel working its way under a fence. I tried to convince myself it was all in my head, but I wasn't convinced enough to stop and find out.

I made the bottom of the hill, in sight of the road that turned off to Alma May's. I don't know why I felt going there mattered, but it was something I had in my mind. Make it to Alma

May's, and deliver on my agreement, bring her brother into the house. Course, I hadn't really thought that thing would or could follow us.

It was right then the car engine blew in an explosion that made the hood bunch up from the impact of thrown pistons.

The car died and coasted onto the road that led to Alma May's house. We could see the house, standing in daylight. But even that light was fading as the night behind us eased on in.

I jerked open the car door, snatched the records off the back-seat, and yelled to Tootie to start running. He nabbed his guitar, and a moment later, we were both making tracks for Alma May's.

Looking back, I saw there was a moon back there, and stars too, but mostly there was that thing, full of eyes and covered in sores and tentacles and legs and things I can't even describe. It was like someone had thrown critters and fish and bugs and beaks and all manner of disease into a bowl and whipped it together with a whipping spoon.

When we got to Alma May's, I beat on the door. She opened it, showing a face that told me she thought I was knocking too hard, but then she looked over my shoulder, and went pale, almost as if her skin was white. She had heard the music, so she could see it too.

Slamming the door behind us, I went straight to the record player. Alma May was asking all kinds of questions, screaming them out, really. First to me, then to Tootie. I told her to shut up. I jerked one of the records out of its sheath, put it on the turntable, lifted the needle, and—

—the electricity crackled and it went dark. There was no playing anything on that player. Outside the world was lit by that blood-red moon.

The door blew open. Tentacles flicked in, knocked over an end table. Some knickknacks fell and busted on the floor. Big as the monster was, it was squeezing through, causing the door frame to crack; the wood breaking sounded like someone crack-ing whips with both hands.

Me and Alma May, without even thinking about it, backed up. The red shadow, bright as a camp fire, fled away from the monster and started flowing across the floor, bugs and worms squirming in it.

But not toward us.

It was running smooth as an oil spill toward the opposite side of the room. I got it then. It didn't just want through to this side. It wanted to finish off that deal Tootie had made with the record store owner. Tootie had said it all along, but it really hit me then. It didn't want me and Alma at all.

It had come for Tootie's soul.

There was a sound so sharp I threw my hands over my ears, and Alma May went to the floor. It was Tootie's guitar. He had hit it so hard, it sounded electrified. The pulse of that one hard chord made me weak in the knees. It was a hundred times louder than the record. It was beyond belief, and beyond human ability. But, it was Tootie.

The red shadow stopped, rolled back like a tongue.

The guitar was going through its paces now. The thing at the doorway recoiled slightly, and then Tootie yelled, "Come get me. Come have me. Leave them alone."

I looked, and there in the faint glow of the red moonlight through the window, I saw Tootie's shadow lift that guitar high above his head by the neck, and down it came, smashing hard into the floor with an explosion of wood and a springing of strings.

The bleeding shadow came quickly then. Across the floor and onto Tootie. He screamed. He screamed like someone having the flesh slowly burned off. Then the beast came through the door as if shot out of a cannon.

Tentacles slashed, a million feet scuttled, and those beaks came down, ripping at Tootie like a savage dog tearing apart a rag doll. Blood flew all over the room. It was like a huge strawberry exploded.

Then another thing happened. A blue mist floated up from the floor, from what was left of Tootie, and for just the briefest of moments, I saw Tootie's face in that blue mist; the face smiled a toothless kind of smile, showing nothing but a dark hole where his mouth was. Then, like someone sniffing steam off soup, the blue mist was sucked into the beaks of that thing, and Tootie and his soul were done with.

The thing turned its head and looked at us. I started to pull my .45, but I knew there wasn't any point to it. It made a noise like a thousand rocks and broken automobiles tumbling down a cliff made of gravel and glass, and it began to suck back toward the door. It went out with a snapping sound, like a wet towel being popped. The bleeding shadow ran across the floor after it, eager to catch up; a lap dog hoping for a treat.

The door slammed as the thing and its shadow went out, and then the air got clean and the room got bright.

I looked where Tootie had been.

Nothing.

Not a bone.

Not a drop of blood.

I raised the window and looked out.

It was morning.

No clouds in the sky.

The sun looked like the sun.

Birds were singing.

The air smelled clean as a newborn's breath.

I turned back to Alma May. She was slowly getting up from where she had dropped to the floor.

"It just wanted him," I said, having a whole different kind of feeling about Tootie than I had before. "He gave himself to it. To save you, I think."

She ran into my arms and I hugged her tight. After a moment, I let go of her. I got the records and put them together. I was going to snap them across my knee. But I never got the chance. They went wet in my hands, came apart and hit the floor and ran through the floorboards like black water, and that was all she wrote.

# A VISIT
# WITH FRIENDS

**M**ary said, "You don't visit Mason and Jane much anymore."

"No," I said. "I don't."

"It's been maybe a month. You don't even mention them anymore. Maybe you should see them."

"You don't like them," I said.

"I don't. I can't tell you why, but you like them, so I don't want you to keep from seeing them. You knew them before things changed."

"So did you."

"Yes," Mary said. "I did, and I didn't like them, and I feel bad about it, but I didn't and I still don't. I can't explain it."

"You have good radar."

"Say what?"

"You were correct about them," I said. "You sensed a potential for something wrong, and it was there, and it had to have been there all along. Me, I didn't notice it, didn't realize it. You were right, and I was wrong."

Mary came away from the barred and wire-netted window where she was looking out and sat down at the table.

"What are you saying?" she asked.

"I'm saying you're right, and I'm wrong."

"Why do you say that?"

I sipped my coffee and looked at my watch. I didn't have to go to work for another hour. "All right," I said. "But it's not a pretty story."

"Nothing these days is pretty."

"You are," I said.

Mary blushed. I loved that about her. She always seemed amazed that anyone would notice how lovely she was. Perhaps because she didn't realize how fine she looked.

I said, "I think before the dead came back, and everyone had to change things, Jane and Mason may have been all right. But they were what they are now back then, but they didn't have the opportunity."

Mary furrowed her brows. "I don't follow."

"They can do what they're doing now and get away with it, but back then there wasn't that opportunity. I guess in one way it doesn't matter as much if they were doing what they are doing now, because, well, there is a difference. But the difference doesn't settle well with me, because it makes me realize how they are. If they're that way now, they were that way then."

"Now I really don't follow."

"I drove over to their place the other day. After work. I had to drive the long way around because the dead were all over the main streets, and the government sweeper had yet to come through, or maybe it had gone through and the dead people had come back thick again. It usually doesn't happen that way that quick, but I guess it could be like that.

"But the thing is, I thought since the streets to our house were full of the rascals, I might drive over and see Jane and Mason and have a drink. Nothing much, of course, since I was driving, but something. A soda, maybe. Kill a little time and visit. I always liked our visits. They are always so funny."

"They give good parties," Mary said. "I know that."

"You only went to one," I said.

"Yes, but it was a good one. If I had liked them better, I would have gone to another. But tell me the rest of it."

"There's not much to it, really. I told you I have a key to their garage?"

"No. I didn't know that."

"I do," I said. "I have a key because of the dead, and because they like me to come visit them. I use the key to get in through the barrier they've built, and then I use it again to get in through the garage. They trust me to watch out for the dead and not let them in. It's a peculiar setup they have. You pull under a carport, and then there's a barrier wall that runs up to the top of the extended garage, and you have to unlock a door there, and then it's kind of like a narrow maze. You got to deal with any dead if they're there before you get to the door, but that's only a few feet, and you can see easily from the car if any are around. That way you know if you should get out of the car or not. It's a good setup. They said they designed it that way so that if the dead got inside the door, they couldn't come easily in a group. That there was only room for one to go through the maze at a time. It was easier to fight them back if they were jammed in like that, and it gave time to get through the main door and into the house."

"Smart idea."

"Yeah," I said. "They're smart. Anyway, there wasn't any threat in the garage, even if the front yard was filled with the things, wandering about, stinking up the air.

"I unlocked the door and went into the maze and went along the path, and then I came to the garage door and unlocked it. After you do the unlocking, the doors lock themselves when you close them, and then you have to go through another narrow tunnel that comes to a wire door, and you use the key to unlock it, and then you have to unlock another metal door to get in the house. Same key on all the doors."

"That's serious," Mary said. "But if one of them got in there with you, you'd do better to fight it instead of trying to unlock all those doors. While you're unlocking, they'd be on you."

"That's the benefit of the narrow path. And for themselves they have automatic locks. They work on some kind of battery device they have. They've got the better deal, of course, but the key, you're paying attention to what's around you, and you don't let them through that first door to the carport, then you got it made.

"I went through the doors and went into the house, and for a moment, I thought no one was there, and then I heard that moan. You know the one. The one the dead make."

"Oh, god, yes. It's awful. Were Jane and Mason okay?"

"Yes, they were okay."

"Good. Good. I don't like them, but I don't want that for anyone. I feel so sorry for the ones who are like that. I hear them I almost cry. I think it could be me. It might some day be me."

I reached across the table and took Mary's hand. "No. It won't be you. And it won't be me. We're too careful. We'll die of old age. We won't get bitten by them, and the disease is long gone. If we were going to get it, going to die and come back, it would have happened long ago. We're among the immune."

"But we still don't know why," Mary said.

"No, we don't. Some of the scientists say it's because we took a flu shot that year. There were so many that didn't, and they got the disease, the new flu, but we didn't."

"We almost didn't get the shots, remember?"

"I do. But we did. We did and we're fine."

"If we hadn't, in just a matter of days, we'd have gotten the flu, and died, and then—"

"It's best not to worry about something that didn't happen," I said.

"I can't believe I stopped your story. I get so scared just thinking about them, you know."

"I know," I said.

"So you heard a sound you thought was the dead, but wasn't."

"I didn't say that."

"You said they were okay."

"Yes."

"Go on," she said.

"I heard the sound, I looked around, and saw across the way a fire poker by the fireplace. I went over and got it and listened again, and now I heard the moaning; the way they moan, you know, kind of continuous, and I thought, heavens, those things have gotten in the house and they've cornered or killed Jane and Mason upstairs. I decided I had to see if they were okay, if they needed help. I thought about running, too, but I didn't. I carried the poker upstairs, going softly. Those things have that great hearing, you know. For whatever reason they have that. Even the deaf, they die and come back, they got that ability to hear, and when they hear a noise—"

"They come," Mary said.

"Yes, they come. So I went up the stairs carefully, and when I got to the top of the stairs I could see their bedroom door was open, and I crept along the hall, all the while hearing that noise, and when I got to the doorway and looked in... It wasn't good."

"Zombies?"

"Yes. But not the way you think. On the bed was one of the dead. A fresh one, a bite mark on her arm, but other than that, she looked normal. Except for the eyes, you know how the eyes are. I could see them from where I was and they looked horrible and she was trying to bite Mason. You see, she was tied spread-eagle on the bed. Naked. She was tied that way and Mason was trying to tie a rag over her mouth, something to keep her from biting, maybe something to control her head."

"But why on the bed?"

I looked at her.

"Oh."

"They were naked too. And Jane, she had a broom handle, and she... Well, she was using it on the dead woman. Using it in a way it shouldn't be used."

"My god," Mary said.

"Yes. Mason, he was... Well, sexual ready. Like he was waiting his turn, second to the broom."

"What did you do?"

"There wasn't anything I could do. Technically, the dead are dead, so they weren't really abusing a living being. But it let me know who they were. It let me know how they thought, and made me think they might have wanted to do those kinds of things to the living before the flu event, but hadn't for fear of being caught. Or maybe they had done those kinds of things and hadn't been caught."

"They were always inviting us over," Mary said. "Do you think...?"

"I don't know they're killers, but maybe they wanted to enlist us in some fun and games and we just never got the hint, and then you quit coming, and they kept inviting me over... I mean, it doesn't matter. That's okay. We weren't interested, but if we had been, that's okay. That's just a choice, an adult choice. But maybe they would have carried it farther."

"No."

"Maybe. And maybe they never did anything to anybody, but then the opportunity with this dead woman, maybe others, was there, and they saw their chance and took it. But to me, dead or alive, on one level, it's still the same thing. Just because they aren't alive doesn't change much. Maybe it changes something, but for me it didn't change that much. It told me something about them. It told me everything about them."

"Did they see you?"

"Yes," I said. "They did. They turned and saw me there."

"What did you do?"

I hesitated before I answered. "I left. I just left."

"Good grief. Is there someone to tell? The law?"

"It's not a crime. With all that's going on, no one, law or otherwise, cares about the dead. They don't care as long as the dead get completely dead. They have enough to worry about without worrying about if that kind of thing is immoral or if it isn't."

"But it's not right."

"No. And I'm done with them. I left the key there when I went out. I went out through the front door. I took the chance. I went out that way and to the carport and the yard was full of them, but it was like they didn't see me. And by the time they did see me, I was in the car. I got in and drove home, and I thought I wouldn't mention it, but now that time has passed and you asked, I've told you."

"It's horrible."

"We're done with them," I said.

"But if I see them in the store, or something, I know what they did. I don't know if I can make chit chat."

"Maybe you won't see them."

"I hope not. Jesus, how horrible are they?"

"Pretty horrible."

》《

Two days later I went to the supermarket, and as I was driving up to the plastic tunnel that led into it, the guards let me pass when I waved at them because the dead don't drive and the dead don't wave. I drove inside and wheeled my car up to the upper parking berth and used the stairs to go down to the market. Once I got groceries, I'd use the elevator back up to the car.

I went in and shopped. Through the reinforced plastic that served as windows for the store, I could see men in the lot shooting the dead, shooting them in the head. It was messy, as always, and it made me feel odd to see them do it and not think too much about it. Them shooting the dead and blowing their skulls and dry brains all over the lot didn't bother me, but yet I couldn't get that young dead girl out of my mind.

I bought the groceries and started home. The dead were thick that day, and I kept wondering: how many of them are there? How do they just keep coming, keep showing up. With all of them that were being killed you'd think there'd be a lot fewer. But, hell,

Houston is a big city and therefore it has a big population, so statistically there should be a lot of the dead. Still, it seemed like way too many of them.

I had to drive by Jane and Mason's house, and when I did I saw the front door was still open, the way I had left it. I didn't tell Mary that I didn't close it and I lied about going out of it. There were dead in the yard, wandering about. One came out of the front door as I drove past.

That day I had slipped away quietly unseen and had gone downstairs and opened their front door because I knew their yard was filled with the dead. When I opened the door, I knew those things would hear that moaning upstairs, because not all of it was the dead girl moaning. Some of it was from Jane and Mason, moans of enjoyment at what they were doing. The dead know the difference in their own moans and the moans of the living, and it's the sounds the living make that excites them.

So I opened that door and went back through the house and through the tunnels. I kept the poker with me until I came into the carport. There was one of the dead nearby, but not so close I wasn't able to get in the car and back out. I hit one doing that, running over it, and I remember thinking I had no trouble doing that but I was bothered by what Jane and Mason were doing upstairs.

As I was driving away the dead were already going through the front door. The house would soon be thick with them. Up the stairs they would go, and there they would find Jane and Mason, naked, preoccupied. The rest of it I didn't like to think about, and the thing that bothered me most was how I made a judgment to let happen to them what I know must have happened.

I felt bad for a dead woman, but I didn't feel bad for them. I thought for awhile I might not be any better than them. Or that I might be worse. For in a way, I had committed murder, and they had not murdered that girl. I told myself that they might have done other things before to the living, and I told myself if they hadn't, they might yet when the dead were no longer fun. Then I decided I didn't know that either of these things was true, and I was just trying to make myself feel better.

I did feel better, and that didn't seem right, considering what I had done.

As the days passed, and I thought about that dead girl and how Jane and Mason looked, the sweat on their faces and the eager way they moved and the excitement they had about it all, the fun they were having at that dead girl's expense, I began to get over it.

# CHRISTMAS MONKEYS

The Christmas monkeys came again this year. The little bastards.

They brought monkey poo to throw. They always do.

They came down the chimney, amid scratches and chatters and all manner of hulabaloo.

They had good aim with that poo. My little sister lost an eye. She wears a patch now.

They tore down the Christmas tree and kicked the dog.

The cat was sodomized. He won't turn his back on you anymore.

They ate the parakeet and left its bones on a window sill.

It wasn't as bad as last year, though.

Last year the Christmas monkeys ate mom and dad, left their skeletons in the closet, on hangers. Hung them there with a tie fastened tight and correct around Dad's bony neck, Mama wearing a feathered Easter hat on her shiny skull, the hat turned backwards. On the floor, beneath her swinging skeleton feet, was her bathrobe, wadded.

But this Christmas was different.

The monkeys came and none of us died. We don't count the para-keet. We all hated that goddamn bird.

The monkeys set fire to a bed and left the bathtub full of poo, rearranged our shoes, mismatched our socks.

They left little red fez hats and matching vests in the kitchen, enough to dress a ten man crew.

But me and Sis, we survived.

We put out their treats like we're supposed to do. Do that, it means they usually let somebody live.

But this year, me and Sis left out poison bananas with the hot cocoa.

We wondered why we hadn't thought of it before.

When the monkeys finished beating me up, setting fire to the overturned Christmas tree, peeing in a flower pot, making my one-eyed sister wear her pants backwards, they ate their treats, took the presents, and went up the chimney.

But not quite so brisk as they came down.

And there wasn't as much chattering.

They won't be back next year.

Or the year after that.

We found them dead. On the roof. Near the reindeer and the dropped presents and banana peels. And the sleigh, which was packed tight with monkey poo, an address book and a well marked map.

# CHRISTMAS
# WITH THE DEAD

I t was a foolish thing to do, and Calvin had not bothered
with it the last two years, not since the death of his wife and
daughter, but this year, this late morning, the loneliness and
the monotony led him to it. He decided quite suddenly, having kept fairly good record on the calendar, that tomorrow was
Christmas Eve, and zombies be damned. The Christmas lights
and decorations were going up.

He went into the garage to look for the lights. He could hear
the zombies sniffing around outside the garage door. The door was
down and locked tight, and on top of that, though the zombies
could grab and bite you, they weren't terribly strong most of the
time, so the door was secure. The windows inside were boarded
over, the doors were locked, and double locked, and boarded.
The backyard the dead owned, but the windows and doors were
boarded really well there, so he was shut in tight and safe.

Prowling through the holiday ornaments, he found immediately the large plastic Santa, and three long strings of lights.
They were the ones he had ripped down in anger about two
years back.

He managed all of the strings of lights into his living room. He plugged the wires into the extension cord that was hooked up to the generator he had put in the kitchen, and discovered most of the lights were as dead as the proverbial dodo bird. Many were broken from him having ripped the whole thing off the house in anger two years back.

He sat for a moment, then went to the little refrigerator he had replaced the big one with—used less energy—and pulled a bottled coffee out, twisted off the cap, and walked over to the living room window.

Unlike the garage on the side of the house, or the backyard, he had fenced the front yard off with deeply buried iron bars to which he had attached chicken wire, overlapped with barbed wire. The fence rose to a height of eight feet. The gate, also eight feet tall, was made of the same. He seldom used it. He mostly went out and back in through the garage. There was no fence there. When he went out, they were waiting.

More often than not, he was able to run over and crush a few before hitting the door device, closing the garage behind him. On the way back, he rammed a few more, and with the touch of a button, sealed himself inside. When they were thin in the yard, he used that time to stack the bodies in his pickup truck, haul them somewhere to dump. It kept the stink down that way. Also, the rotting flesh tended to attract the hungry dead. The less he made them feel at home, the better.

Today, looking through the gaps between the boards nailed over the window, he could see the zombies beyond the fence. They were pulling at the wire, but it was firm and they were weak. He had discovered, strangely, that as it grew darker, they grew stronger. Nothing spectacular, but enough he could notice it. They were definitely faster then. It was as if the day made them sluggish, and the night rejuvenated them; gave them a shot of energy, like maybe the moon was their mistress.

He noticed too, that though there were plenty of them, there were fewer every day. He knew why. He had seen the results, not only around town, but right outside his fence. From time to time they just fell apart.

It was plain old natural disintegration. As time rolled on, their dead and rotten bodies came apart. For some reason, not as fast as was normal, but still, they did indeed break down. Of course, if they bit someone, they would become zombies, fresher ones, but, after the last six months there were few if any people left in town, besides himself. He didn't know how it was outside of town, but he assumed the results were similar. The zombies now, from time to time, turned on one another, eating what flesh they could manage to bite off each other's rotten bones. Dogs, cats, snakes, anything they could get their hands on, had been devastated. It was new world, and it sucked. And sometimes it chewed.

Back in the garage, Calvin gathered up the six large plastic snowmen and the Santa, and pulled them into the house. He plugged them in and happily discovered they lit right up. But the strings of lights were still a problem. He searched the garage, and only found three spare bulbs—green ones—and when he screwed them in, only one worked. If he put up those strings they would be patchy. It wasn't as if anyone but himself would care, but a job worth doing was a job worth doing right, as his dad always said.

He smiled.

Ella, his wife, would have said it wasn't about doing a job right, it was more about fulfilling his compulsions. She would laugh at him now. Back then a crooked picture on the wall would make him crazy. Now there was nothing neat about the house. It was a fortress. It was a mess. It was a place to stay, but it wasn't a home.

Two years ago it ended being a home when he shot his wife and daughter in the head with the twelve gauge, put their bodies in the Dumpster down the street, poured gas on them, and set them on fire.

All atmosphere of home was gone. Now, with him being the most desirable snack in town, just going outside the fence was a dangerous endeavor. And being inside he was as lonely as the guest of honor at a firing squad.

》《

Calvin picked the strapped shotgun off the couch and flung it over his shoulder, adjusted the .38 revolver in his belt, grabbed the old-fashioned tire tool from where it leaned in the corner, and went back to the garage.

He cranked up the truck, which he always backed in, and using the automatic garage opener, pressed it.

He had worked hard on the mechanism so that it would rise quickly and smoothly, and today was no exception. It yawned wide like a mouth opening. Three zombies, one he recognized faintly as Marilyn Paulson, a girl he had dated in high school, were standing outside. She had been his first love, his first sexual partner, and now half of her face dangled like a wash cloth on a clothes line. Her hair was falling out, and her eyes were set far back in her head, like dark marbles in crawfish holes.

The two others were men. One was reasonably fresh, but Calvin didn't recoginize him. The other was his next-door neighbor, Phil Tooney. Phil looked close to just falling apart, and so was his nose.

As Calvin roared the big four-seater pickup out of the garage, he hit Marilyn with the bumper and she went under, the wing mirror clipped Phil and sent him winding. He glanced in the rearview as he hit the garage mechanism, was pleased to see the door go down before the standing zombie could get inside. From time to time they got in when he left or returned, and he had to seal them in, get out and fight or shoot them. It was a major annoyance, knowing you had that waiting for you when you got back from town.

The last thing he saw as he drove away was the remaining zombie eating a mashed Marilyn as she squirmed on the driveway; he had shattered her legs with the truck. She was unable to rise or fight back. The way their teeth bit into her, how skin stretched, it looked as if they were trying to pull old bubble gum loose from the sidewalk.

Another glance in the mirror showed him Phil was back on his feet. He and the other zombie got into it then, fighting over the writhing meal on the cement. And then Calvin turned the truck along Seal Street, out of their view, and rolled on toward town.

» «

**Driving, he glanced** at all the Christmas decorations. The lights strung on houses, no longer lit. The yard decorations, most of them knocked over: Baby Jesus flung south from an over-turned manger, a deflated blow-up Santa Claus in a sleigh with hooked up reindeer, now laying like a puddle of lumpy paint spills in the high grass of a yard fronting a house with an open door.

As he drove, Calvin glanced at the Dumpster by the side of the road. The one where he had put the bodies of his wife and daughter and burned them. It was, as far as he was concerned, their tomb.

One morning, driving into town for supplies, a morning like this, he had seen zombies in the Dumpster, chewing at bones, strings of flesh. It had driven him crazy. He had pulled over right then and there and shotgunned them, blowing off two heads, and crushing in two others with the butt of the twelve gauge. Then, he had pulled the tire tool from his belt and beat their corpses to pieces. It had been easy, as they were rotten and ragged and almost gone. It was the brain being destroyed that stopped them, either that or their own timely disintegration, which with the destruction of the brain caused the rot to accelerate. But even with them down for the count, he kept whacking at them, screaming and crying as he did.

He swallowed as he drove by. Had he not been napping after a hard day's work, waiting on dinner, then he too would have been like Ella and Tina. He wasn't sure which was worse, becoming one of them, not knowing anything or anyone anymore, being eternally hungry, or surviving, losing his wife and daughter and having to remember them every day.

>> <<

Mud Creek's Super Saver parking lot was full of cars and bones and wind-blown shopping carts. A few zombies were wandering about. Some were gnawing the bones of the dead. A little child was down on her knees in the center of the lot gnawing on the head of a kitten.

As he drove up close to the Super Saver's side door, he got out quickly, with his key ready, the truck locked, the shotgun on his shoulder, and the tire tool in his belt.

He had, days after it all came down, finished off the walking dead in the supermarket with his shotgun, and pulled their bodies out for the ones outside to feast on. While this went on, he found the electronic lock for the sliding plasti-glass doors, and he located the common doors at side and back, and found their keys. With the store sealed, he knew he could come in the smaller doors whenever he wanted, shop for canned and dried goods. The electricity was still working then, but in time, he feared it might go out. So he decided the best way to go was to start with the meats and fresh vegetables. They lasted for about six weeks. And then, for whatever reason, the electricity died.

It may have been attrition of power, or a terrific storm, though not nearly as terrific as the one Ella and Tina had described. The one that had changed things. But something killed the electricty. He managed to get a lot of meat out before then, and he tossed a lot away to keep it from rotting in the store, making the place stink.

By then, he had a freezer and the smaller refrigerator both hooked to gas generators he had taken from the store. And by siphoning gas from cars, he had been able to keep it running. He also worked out a way to maintain electricity by supplanting the gas-powered generators with car batteries that he wired up and used until they died. Then he got others, fresh ones from the car parts house. He didn't know how long that supply would last. Someday he feared he would be completely in the dark when night fell. So, he made a point of picking up candles each time he went to the store. He had hundreds of them now, big fat ones, and plenty of matches.

The weather was cool, so he decided on canned chili and crackers. There was plenty of food in the store, as most of the town had seen the storm and been affected by it, and had immediately gone into zombie mode. For them, it was no more cheese and crackers, salads with dressing on the side, now it was hot, fresh meat and cold dead meat, rotting on the bone.

As he cruised the aisle, he saw a rack with bags of jerky on it. He hadn't had jerky in ages. He grabbed bags of it and threw them in the cart. He found a twelve pack of bottled beer and put that in the cart.

He was there for about six hours. Just wandering. Thinking. He used the restrooms, which still flushed. He had the same luxury at his house, and he could have waited, but the whole trip, the food, walking the aisles, using the toilet, it was akin to a vacation.

After awhile he went to the section of the store that contained the decorations. He filled another basket with strings of lights, and even located a medium-sized plastic Christmas tree. Three baskets were eventually filled, one with the plastic tree precariously balanced on top. He found a Santa hat, said, "What the hell," and put it on.

He pushed all three baskets near the door he had come in. He slung the shotgun off his shoulder, and took a deep breath. He hated this part. You never knew what was behind the door. The automatic doors would have been better in this regard, as they were hard plastic and you could see through them, but the problem was if you went out that way, you left the automatic door working, and they could come and go inside as they pleased. He liked the store to be his sanctuary, just like the pawn shop down town, the huge car parts store, and a number of other places he had rigged with locks and hidden weapons.

He stuck the key in the door and heard it snick. He opened it quickly. They weren't right at the door, but they were all around his truck. He got behind one of the baskets and pushed it out, leaving the door behind him open. It was chancy, as one of them might slip inside unseen, even ·be waiting a week or two later when he came back, but it was a chance he had to take.

Pushing the basket hard, he rushed out into the lot and to the back of the truck. He had to pause to open up with the shotgun. He dropped four of them, then realized he was out of fire power. For the first time in ages, he had forgot to check the loads in the gun; his last trek out, a trip to the pawn shop, had used most of them, and he hadn't reloaded.

He couldn't believe it. He was slipping. And you couldn't slip. Not in this world.

He pulled the .38 revolver and popped off a shot, missed. Two were closing. He stuck the revolver back in his belt, grabbed a handful of goodies from the basket and tossed them in the back of the pickup. When he looked up, four were closing, and down the way, stumbling over the parking lot, were more of them. A lot of them. In that moment, all he could think was: at least they're slow.

He pulled the .38 again, but one of them came out of nowhere, grabbed him by the throat. He whacked at the arm with revolver, snapped it off at the shoulder, leaving the hand still gripping him. The zombie, minus an arm, lunged toward him, snapping its teeth, filling the air with its foul stench.

At close range he didn't miss with the revolver, got Armless right between the eyes. He jerked the arm free of his neck, moved forward quickly, and using the pistol as a club, which for him was more precise, he knocked two down, crushing one's skull, and finishing off the other with a close skull shot. A careful shot dropped another.

He looked to see how fast the other zombies were coming.

Not that fast. They were just halfway across the lot.

There was one more dead near the front of his truck. It had circled the vehicle while he was fighting the others. He hadn't even seen where it came from. He watched it as he finished unloading the cart. When it was close, he shot it at near point-blank range, causing its rotten skull to explode like a pumpkin, spewing what appeared to be boiled, dirty oatmeal all over the side of his truck and the parking lot.

Darting back inside, he managed to push one cart out, and then shove the other after it. He grabbed the handles of the carts, one in each hand, and guided them to the back of the truck. The zombies were near now. One of them, for some reason, was holding his hand high above his head, as if in greeting. Calvin was tempted to wave.

Calvin tossed everything in the back of the truck, was dismayed to hear a bulb or two from his string of bulbs pop. The last thing he tossed in back was the Christmas tree.

He was behind the wheel and backing around even before the zombies arrived. He drove toward them, hit two and crunched them down.

As if it mattered, as he wheeled out of the lot, he tossed up his hand in a one-finger salute.

》《

"They were so pretty," Ella had said about the lightning flashes.

She had awakened him as he lay snoozing on the couch.

"They were red and yellow and green and blue and all kinds of colors," Tina said. "Come on, Daddy, come see."

By the time he was there, the strange lightning storm was gone. There was only the rain. It had come out of nowhere, caused by who knew what. Even the rain came and went quickly; a storm that covered the earth briefly, flashed lights, spit rain, and departed.

When the rain stopped, the people who had observed the colored lightning died, just keeled over. Ella and Tina among them, dropped over right in the living room on Christmas Eve, just before presents were to be opened.

It made no sense. But that's what happened.

Then, even as he tried to revive them, they rose.

Immediately, he knew they weren't right. It didn't take a wizard to realize that. They came at him, snarling, long strings of mucus flipping from their mouths like rabid dog saliva. They tried to bite him. He pushed them back, he called their names, he yelled, he pleaded, but still they came, biting and snapping. He stuck a couch cushion in Ella's mouth. She grabbed it and ripped it. Stuffing flew like a snow storm. And he ran.

He hid in the bedroom, locked the door, not wanting to hurt them. He heard the others, his neighbors, outside, roaming around the house. He looked out the window. There were people all over the backyard, fighting with one another, some of them living, trying to survive, going down beneath teeth and nails. People like him, who for some reason had not seen the weird storm. But the rest were dead. Like his wife and daughter. The lights of the storm had stuck something behind their eyes that killed them and brought them back—dead, but walking, and hungry.

Ella and Tina pounded on his bedroom door with the intensity of a drum solo. Bam, bam, bam, bam, bam, bam. He sat on the bed for an hour, his hands over his ears, tears streaming down his face, listening to his family banging at the door, hearing the world outside coming apart.

He took a deep breath, got the shotgun out of the closet, made sure it was loaded, opened the bedroom door.

It was funny, but he could still remember thinking as they went through the doorway, here's my gift to you. Merry Christmas, family. I love you.

And then two shots.

Later, when things had settled, he had managed, even in the midst of a zombie takeover, to take their bodies to the Dumpster, pour gas on them, and dispose of them as best he could. Months later, from time to time, he would awaken, the smell of their burning flesh and the odor of gasoline in his nostrils.

Later, one post at a time, fighting off zombies as he worked, he built his compound to keep them out, to give him a yard, a bit of normalcy.

>> <<

Calvin looked in the rearview mirror. His forehead was beaded with sweat. He was still wearing the Santa hat. The snowball on its tip had fallen onto the side of his face. He flipped it back, kept driving.

He was almost home when he saw the dog and saw them chasing it. The dog was skinny, near starved, black and white spotted, probably some kind of hound mix. It was running all out, and as it was nearing dark, the pace of the zombies had picked up. By deep nightfall, they would be able to move much faster. That dog was dead meat.

The dog cut out into the road in front of him, and he braked. Of the four zombies chasing the dog, only one of them stopped to look at him. The other three ran on.

Calvin said, "Eat bumper," gassed the truck into the zombie who had stopped to stare, knocking it under the pickup. He could hear it dragging underneath as he drove. The other zombies were chasing the dog down the street, gaining on it; it ran with its tongue hanging long.

The dog swerved off the road and jetted between houses. The zombies ran after it. Calvin started to let it go. It wasn't his problem. But, as if without thought, he wheeled the truck off the road and across a yard. He caught one of the zombies, a fat slow one that had most likely been fat and slow in life. He bounced the truck over it and bore down on the other two.

One heard the motor, turned to look, and was scooped under the bumper so fast it looked like a magic act disappearance. The other didn't seem to notice him at all, it was so intent on its canine lunch. Calvin hit it with the truck, knocked it against the side of a house, pinned it there, gassed the truck until it snapped in two and the house warped under the pressure.

Calvin backed off, fearing he might have damaged the engine. But the truck still ran.

He looked. The dog was standing between two houses, panting, its pink tongue hanging out of its mouth like a bright power tie.

Opening the door, Calvin called to the dog. The dog didn't move, but its ears sprang up.

"Come on, boy...girl. Come on, doggie."

The dog didn't move.

Calvin looked over his shoulders. Zombies were starting to appear everywhere. They were far enough away he could make an escape, but close enough to be concerned. And then he saw the plastic Christmas tree had been knocked out of the back of the pickup. He ran over and picked it up and tossed it in the bed. He looked at the dog.

"It's now or never, pup," Calvin said. "Come on. I'm not one of them."

It appeared the dog understood completely. It came toward him, tail wagging. Calvin bent down, carefully extended his hand toward it. He patted it on the head. Its tail went crazy. The dog had a collar on. There was a little aluminum tag in the shape of a bone around its neck. He took it between thumb and forefinger. The dog's name was stenciled on it: BUFFY.

Looking back at the zombies coming across the yard in near formation, Calvin spoke to the dog, "Come on, Buffy. Go with me."

He stepped back, one hand on the open door. The dog sprang past him, into the seat. Calvin climbed in, backed around, and they were out of there, slamming zombies right and left as the truck broke their lines.

》《

As he neared his house, the sun was starting to dip. The sky was as purple as a hammered plum. Behind him, in the mirror, he could see zombies coming from all over, between houses, out of houses, down the road, moving swiftly.

He gave the truck gas, and then a tire blew.

The truck's rear end skidded hard left, almost spun, but Calvin fought the wheel and righted it. It bumped along, and he was forced to slow it down to what seemed like a near crawl. In the rearview, he could see the dead gaining; a sea of teeth and putrid faces. He glanced at the dog. It was staring out the back window as well, a look of concern on its face.

"I shouldn't have stopped for you," Calvin said, and in an instant he thought: If I opened the door and kicked you out, that might slow them down. They might stop and fight over a hot lunch.

It was a fleeting thought.

"You go, I go," Calvin said, as if he had owned the dog for years, as if it were a part of his family.

He kept driving, bumping the pickup along.

>> <<

When he arrived at his house, he didn't have time to back in as usual. He hit the garage remote and drove the truck inside. When he got out, Buffy clambering out behind him, the zombies were in the garage, maybe ten of them, others in the near distance were moving faster and faster toward him.

Calvin touched the remote, closed the garage door, trapping himself and the dog inside with those ten, but keeping the others out. He tossed the remote on the hood of the pickup, pulled the pistol and used what ammunition was left. A few of them were hit in the head and dropped. He jammed the empty pistol in his belt, pulled the tire iron free, began to swing it, cracking heads with the blows.

He heard growling and ripping, turned to see Buffy had taken one down and was tearing its throat out, pulling its near rotten head off its shoulders.

"Good dog, Buffy," Calvin yelled, and swung the iron. "Sic 'em."

They came over the roof of the truck, one of them, a woman, leaped on him and knocked him face down, sent his tire iron flying. She went rolling into the wall, but was up quickly and moving toward him.

He knew this was it. He sensed another close on him, and then another, and then he heard the dog bark, growl. Calvin managed to turn his head slightly as Buffy leaped and hit the one above him, knocking her down. It wasn't much, but it allowed Calvin to scramble to his feet, start swinging the tire iron. Left and right he swung it, with all his might.

They came for him, closer. He backed up, Buffy beside him, their asses against the wall, the zombies in front of them. There were three of the dead left. They came like bullets. Calvin breathed hard. He grabbed the tire iron off the garage floor, swung it as quickly and as firmly as he could manage, dodging in between them, not making a kill shot, just knocking them aside, finally dashing for the truck with Buffy at his heels. Calvin and Buffy jumped inside, and Calvin slammed the door and locked it. The zombies slammed against the door and the window, but it held.

Calvin got a box of .38 shells out of the glove box, pulled the revolver from his belt and loaded it. He took a deep breath. He looked out the driver's side window where one of the zombies, maybe male, maybe female, too far gone to tell, tried to chew the glass.

When he had driven inside, he had inadvertently killed the engine. He reached and twisted the key, started it up. Then he pushed back against Buffy, until they were as close to the other door as possible. Then he used his toe to roll down the glass where the zombie gnashed. As the window dropped, its head dipped inward and its teeth snapped at the air. The revolver barked, knocking a hole in the zombie's head, spurting a gusher of goo, causing it to spin and drop as if practicing a ballet move.

Another showed its face at the open window, and got the same reception. A .38 slug.

Calvin twisted in his seat and looked at the other window. Nothing. Where was the last one? He eased to the middle, pulling the dog beside him. As he held the dog, he could feel it shivering. Damn, what a dog. Terrified, and still a fighter. No quitter was she.

A hand darted through the open window, tried to grab him, snatched off his Santa hat. He spun around to shoot. The zombie arm struck the pistol, sent it flying. It grabbed him. It had him now, and this one, fresher than the others, was strong. It pulled him toward the window, toward snapping, jagged teeth.

Buffy leaped. It was a tight fit between Calvin and the window, but the starved dog made it, hit the zombie full in the face and slammed it backwards. Buffy fell out the window after it.

Calvin found the pistol, jumped out of the car. The creature had grabbed Buffy by the throat, had spun her around on her back, and was hastily dropping its head for the bite.

Calvin fired. The gun took off the top of the thing's head. It let go of Buffy. It stood up, stared at him, made two quick steps toward him, and dropped. The dog charged to Calvin's side, growling.

"It's all right, girl. It's all right. You done good. Damn, you done good."

Calvin got the tire iron and went around and carefully bashed in all the heads of the zombies, just for insurance. Tomorrow, he'd change the tire on the truck, probably blown out from running over zombies. He'd put his spare on it, the doughnut tire, drive to the tire store and find four brand new ones and put them on. Tomorrow he'd get rid of the zombies' bodies. Tomorrow he'd do a lot of things.

But not tonight.

He found the Santa hat and put it back on.

Tonight, he had other plans.

》《

First he gave Buffy a package of jerky. She ate like the starving animal she was. He got a bowl out of the shelf and filled it with water.

"From now on, that's your bowl, girl. Tomorrow... Maybe the next day, I'll find you some canned dog food at the store."

He got another bowl and opened a can of chili and poured it into it. He was most likely overfeeding her. She'd probably throw it up. But that was all right. He would clean it up, and tomorrow they'd start over, more carefully. But tonight, Buffy had earned a special treat.

He went out and got the tree out of the truck and put it up and put ornaments on it from two years back. Ornaments he had left on the floor after throwing the old dead and dried tree over the fence. This plastic one was smaller, but it would last, year after year.

He sat down under the tree and found the presents he had for his wife and child. He pushed them aside, leaving them wrapped. He opened those they had given him two Christmases ago. He liked all of them. The socks. The underwear. The ties he would never wear. DVDs of movies he loved, and would watch, sitting on the couch with Buffy, who he would soon make fat.

He sat for a long time and looked at his presents and cried.

**》《**

Using the porch light for illumination, inside the fenced-in yard, he set about putting up the decorations. Outside the fence the zombies grabbed at it, and rattled it, and tugged, but it held. It was a good fence. A damn good fence. He believed in that tediously built fence. And the zombies weren't good climbers. They got off the ground, it was like some of whatever made them animated slid out of them in invisible floods. It was as if they gained their living dead status from the earth itself.

It was a long job, and when he finished climbing the ladder, stapling up the lights, making sure the Santa and snowmen were in their places, he went inside and plugged it all in.

When he came outside, the yard was lit in colors of red and blue and green. The Santa and the snowmen glowed as if they had swallowed lightning.

Buffy stood beside him, wagging her tail as they examined the handiwork.

Then Calvin realized something. It had grown very quiet. The fence was no longer being shaken or pulled. He turned quickly toward where the zombies stood outside the fence. They weren't holding onto the wire anymore. They weren't moaning. They weren't doing anything except looking, heads lifted toward the lights.

Out there in the shadows, the lights barely touching them with a fringe of color, they looked like happy and surprised children.

"They like it," Calvin said, and looked down at Buffy.

She looked up at him, wagging her tail.

"Merry Christmas, dog."

When he glanced up, he saw a strange thing. One of the zombies, a woman, a barefoot woman wearing shorts and a tee-shirt, a young woman, maybe even a nice-looking woman not so long ago, lifted her arm and pointed at the lights and smiled with dark, rotting teeth. Then there came a sound from all of them, like a contented sigh.

"I'll be damned," Calvin said. "They like it."

He thought: I will win. I will wait them out. They will all fall apart someday soon. But tonight, they are here with us, to share the lights. They are our company. He got a beer from inside, came back out and pulled up a lawn chair and sat down. Buffy lay down beside him. He was tempted to give those poor sonofabitches outside the wire a few strips of jerky. Instead, he sipped his beer.

A tear ran down his face as he yelled toward the dead.

"Merry Christmas, you monsters. Merry Christmas to all of you, and to all a good night."

# QUARRY

(An associational sequel to Richard Matheson's "Prey")

T here had been better days in his life, and as Jeff drove home from the courthouse, the convertible top down, the wind blowing through his hair, he tried to put all that had gone before out of his mind and think about the book he was writing. He was at least two months behind on the deadline, and it seemed to him that if he doubled up, by working weekends, which he did not normally do, he might be able to make it.

Now that Brenda had left he should have plenty of time, fewer interruptions.

Brenda. It always came back to Brenda. It had been hard to concentrate on much else the last few months, and though he thought he should be angry and glad to be rid of her, all he felt was empty and sad and lonely. She always said, in spite of his financial success, that he was a loser who didn't know a thing about being a man. He could write books, but he wasn't like the men she knew, like her father and brother. Football players, hunters.

He sat in the dark in front of a word processor and made up stories.

"Not a manly profession, Jeff," she told him.

Considering she was always glad to spend his money and was now expecting more from the divorce, he was a little uncertain about her belief system, but still, it hurt to be considered a wimp.

Try as he might to put Brenda out of his mind, thoughts about the book wouldn't come. He needed to finish it, turn it in, get his other half of the advance and keep his publishing schedule, but it was more than a little hard to concentrate.

On the way home he stopped by the antique and curiosity shop. He had ordered a few things for the house from antique buyers who promised him some nice surprises. It had been exciting to him at the time, the idea of hiring someone to find him some new and interesting pieces for their new home, but now it was his new home, and if Brenda's lawyers handled things correctly, it might be her new home.

The shop was on the outskirts of the little community of Falling Rock, not real far from his home. The building was nestled in the mountains as securely as a tick in a fat man's armpit. It was backed up against a rock face and the front of it stuck out close to the highway. There were all manner of odds and ends out front, and these items were more junk than antiques, but inside the shop, which was as huge as a warehouse, there was old furniture, paintings, weird art objects. The place was called OLD STUFF AND ODD STUFF, and it was operated by a gay couple.

They were anything but stereotypical. Jason was about forty and was a body builder and had a macho swagger. His mate, Kevin, taught Mixed Martial Arts Combat Fighting, and had won a number of championships. They had bought the place from a cranky old man and his crankier old wife about a year ago. Jeff had always liked antiques and odd art objects, and had frequented the shop for years. The success of his books worldwide had given him the money to buy all manner of things. Colorful rugs from Morocco, tables and chairs hand made in the Appalachians, primitive art paintings from the Southern States and the Midwest.

As he pulled into the gravel drive out front of OLD STUFF AND ODD STUFF, he thought maybe he ought to cancel his order. He could use the money. Six months ago, he was a millionaire, and though he might still be considered one as of this moment, a lot of his money had already gone to lawyers, and soon more would be heading there, like a cue ball for a pool table pocket, ready to drop out of sight.

But the problem was he had asked Jason and Kevin to hand pick him a few items, and he had already paid half down. He knew Jason and Kevin well enough to know that they had gone to considerable trouble to find the items for him, had spent the last month looking high and low for just the right objects.

He decided the thing to do was to bite the bullet.

》《

Inside Jason greeted him with a handshake and a pat on the shoulder, and for a moment Jeff felt better. He always enjoyed Jason and Kevin's company. Jason, as usual, looked as if he had just stepped off the cover of a magazine, and Kevin, as usual, was in sweats with tennis shoes.

They talked briefly, and he sat and had a cup of coffee with them. After they had gone through the coffee, the pair walked him around the place, showed him a few primitive art pieces, three of them paintings, one a "sculpture" they referred to as "found" art. It was made with odds and ends, an old transistor radio, a little statuette of Elvis, a cell phone, and some light bulbs, all of this encased inside a wooden box. It was unique and interesting. The phone's insides had been replaced with a battery, and when you punched the call button, it played Elvis singing "Don't Be Cruel" and the lights lit up and the statuette of Elvis bobbed from one side to the other.

"That I like," Jeff said. "Best thing yet."

"No," Kevin said, and his eyes seemed to light up, "I don't think so. We have a very fine and different piece for you."

Kevin took Jeff by the elbow and guided him to a shelf at the back of the place, and on the shelf, in a black box, about twelve inches high and six inches wide, perched on a little platform inside the box, was a very strange thing indeed.

It was a kind of doll, dark as a rainy night with a shock of black hair that looked like dyed straw; it stood up from the doll's head as if it had been charged with electricity. Its body was skeletal and its mouth was open, revealing some jagged, but sharp-looking teeth. It had a little spear in its hand. Its hands were large for the rest of its body, the knuckles each the size of a shelled pecan. Its long fingers were tipped with sharp fingernails. There was a small coil of black rope hanging from a hook on one side of its leather belt, and on the other side was a miniature dagger the length of a sewing machine needle and the width of a fingernail file. The doll was sexless, smooth all over. It stood on a little platform about two inches high. As he got closer, Jeff saw that there was a chain around the doll's neck, and on the little chain a placard that read: HE WHO KILLS.

"My god," Jeff said, "it's wonderfully ugly."

"Isn't it?" Kevin said. "There's a little scroll inside the stand."

Kevin slid a sliding door aside on the platform beneath He Who Kills' feet, and took out the scroll. It was bound with a black ribbon. He gently removed the ribbon and opened the scroll. He read what was written on it: "This is a Zuni fetish doll, He Who Kills. He is deadly and ever persistent. The chain holds his warrior spirit at bay. Remove at your own peril, for he is a strong and mighty hunter."

"Isn't that just the thing?" Jason said. "This is very rare. There are only a few, and this is the only one we've ever seen. We've heard of them, and they have a story around them, about a curse and all, but considering the kind of fiction you write, we thought that wouldn't be a worry for you."

Kevin rolled up the scroll and bound it with the ribbon and replaced it in the compartment inside the platform. Jeff grinned. This was just the sort of thing he would love to have on the mantel. A nice conversation piece. He'd have to do some research on it.

"Guys, I like it all," Jeff said.

"Good," Jason said, "we can deliver it day after tomorrow."

"Let me pay up, and take the doll with me," Jeff said. "You can deliver the rest."

"I told you he'd like it," Jason said. Then to Jeff: "Isn't that doll just the bomb?"

"The Atomic bomb," Jeff said.

》《

At home Jeff got the good scissors out of the kitchen drawer and sat at the kitchen table and cut loose the wrapping Jason and Kevin had put around the box. He dropped the scissors on the table and took the doll out of the box and turned it over and looked at its back. It was polished there as smoothly as it was polished all over. It seemed to be made of some kind of light wood, or perhaps bone. He wasn't sure exactly. He tapped it with his knuckles. It sounded hollow... No. There might be something inside. He got the feeling that when he tapped, something shifted in there. He had heard a sound, like the beating of a moth's wings.

He laughed. The soul. The mighty hunter's soul shifted. That was the sound.

His dog, Fluffy, the poodle—his wife's name for their pet—trotted over, reared up on Jeff's knee, looked at the doll and growled at it.

"Don't worry, Fluffy. I won't let him get you. Besides, he's got his chain on."

Jeff touched the tip of the little spear, jerked his finger back. It was razor sharp. His finger was bleeding. He stuck it in his mouth and sucked. Damn, he thought. That thing is dangerous.

Jeff set the doll on the table, pushed back his chair and studied it carefully. Its features were very fine, and the eyes, he couldn't figure what they were made from. They didn't look like beads, or jewels, clam shell maybe. White clam shell with small black dots painted in the center.

"I should turn you loose on my wife," he said.

He stood the doll upright on the table, went into his study, turned on his computer, typed in ZUNI FETISH DOLL, HE WHO KILLS. As he typed, Sofia, his tabby, climbed up in his lap. He stroked the cat's head with one hand while she watched him work the mouse with the other. Maybe she thought it was a real mouse, and Dad had trapped it, holding it down for her to eat.

He smiled and looked at what he had brought up on the screen.

It was a photograph of a doll like the one he had. He skimmed the reading material. Apparently, only three of the dolls were known to exist. They had a kind of cult story about them, sort of like the Hope Diamond. Whoever owned the dolls met with a bad end. This was the reason they were popular, the story that went with them. Owning a doll that supposedly had a curse attached to it was the cool thing to have, or so it seemed.

He studied the photograph of the doll on the screen. It was very much like his doll. No. It was exactly like his doll. The photograph had been taken in the nineteen-thirties by an anthropologist. The doll was called a Zuni doll, but there seemed to be some question as to if it meant the Zuni Indians. There was also some question as to where the chains and the little placards around their necks, written in English, had come from.

No one seemed to have any answers.

Jeff was about to switch to another site, try and find more information. He figured that the dolls had been made in modern times as curios, and a legend had built up around them for sales purposes. He doubted they were Zuni or that they were ever found in a cave. But, it would make a great story. Maybe a novel. Sounded more interesting than the one he was working on at the moment, and—

There was a crashing noise, and then Fluffy yelped in the kitchen.

》《

When Jeff entered the kitchen he discovered the doll was missing from the table. He was immediately mad. Fluffy. That damn dog had grabbed the doll. She was bad about that sort of thing, climbing up in the chair to eat out of plates, get hold of anything she could grab, just to make sure she got attention, good or bad. The crash he had heard had most likely been his expensive doll, and worse, it was probable Fluffy had already begun to chew on his rare property.

Jeff noted that the sliding glass door to the garden was cracked open. He had opened it when he first came in with the doll, then left it open for the cat to come inside. He pushed the glass door wider and looked out at the garden inside the high walls that surrounded it.

There wasn't much moonlight tonight, and what light there was appeared gauzy, as if cheese cloth had been thrown over the quarter moon. Jeff went out into the garden and looked at the tall plants that made the place look like a little patch of tropical forest. Shadows draped between the plants like plaited ropes of black satin.

He and his wife had planted these, and it occurred to him that what she had said about never loving him was probably not true. She had loved him. She had loved him when they had made the garden. Now she didn't and she was saying she never had. The plants gave him comfort that once they truly had loved one another, made him feel less like an idiot.

The doll. Fluffy. His mind came back to the problem at hand. He was about to venture out into the garden, to see if Fluffy had gone out there, when he heard a noise in the house, a dragging noise.

Jeff stepped back inside and shut the door.

"Fluffy," he called.

He went around the table, and as he did, something shiny caught his eye. He looked down. It was the necklace with the placard for He Who Kills. Jeff bent down and picked it up and examined it. He was certain now that what had happened was the doll, perhaps when Fluffy bumped the table, had tipped over and fallen to the floor, losing its necklace. It had fallen on Fluffy, hence, the yelp. And then Fluffy, vengeful and dog-like, had grabbed it and carried it off and was probably in the living room, behind the couch, chewing its head off.

Jeff called the dog again, but nothing.

He went into the living room, pulled up sharp. There was a dark red swipe of blood beginning just as he stepped into the living room. Jeff studied the swipe, saw that it wiped across the wooden floor and disappeared behind the couch.

He took a deep breath, and careful not to step in the blood, went behind the couch and let out an involuntary cry.

Fluffy was there.

He was lying in a puddle of blood...and there was the doll's little spear sticking out of the side of his neck. It had penetrated an artery and Fluffy had bled out in seconds. Jeff bent over the dog, took hold of the little spear and pulled it free.

And then there was a crackle and the lights went out.

》《

Moving through the dark, accustomed enough to his home to make his way about, but not so accustomed to avoid bumping his knee on the edge of the couch, Jeff managed to cross the living room, stumble down the hall, to the closet. There was a fuse box in the closet, and he had some spare fuses inside, and he needed light. His stomach felt queasy. His heart was beating fast. He still had the little spear in his hand.

There was a bit of moonlight coming in through the back sliding door, across the kitchen and down the connecting hall. It fell into the hall where he stood, near the closet, making a little pool of glow. It wasn't much, but it made him feel better, being able to see something.

The closet door was open. His cat, Sofia, was standing outside of the closet, making a strange sound. The hair on her back stood up like quills.

He stepped into the closet and felt around for the flashlight he kept on a shelf, found it, and turned it on. The fuse box was open, and there were old shoe boxes stacked all the way up to it.

What the hell?

He thought again of the little spear. He looked at it with his flashlight. The blood on its tip was already drying, growing dark. He put the spear on top of the fuse box and took a deep breath. He looked at the shoe boxes again.

Someone, or something small had stacked them to get at the fuse box, which, now, as he flashed the light on the box, he saw had been wrecked. Someone...or something...had savagely ripped at the guts of the box and torn them out. But what had been used, and who...or what had done such a thing?

He had an idea, but it wasn't an idea he could completely wrap his mind around. It just did not make sense.

And if it was the doll—there, he had said it—how would it know to do such a thing?

Instinct?

Experience?

Oh, hell, he thought. Don't be silly. There's a perfectly reasonable explanation for all this, it's—

Jeff heard something, like a roach caught up in a match box. He turned the light around and around on the floor of the closet. Nothing. And then he saw the little black rope. It was dangling from the closet shelf, being slowly drawn up.

Swallowing, Jeff turned the light onto the shelf.

And there was the doll, just pulling up the last of its rope. The rope was clutched in one oversized hand, and the scissors that had been on the table were clutched in the other.

The doll leaped at him.

Swatting at the doll with the flashlight, he knocked it to the side, against the closet wall. It was such a hard strike, that after he hit the doll, his flashlight traveled into the edge of the closet doorway and came apart in an explosion of glass and batteries.

Jeff leaped backwards out of the closet and slammed the door.

Suddenly there was a savage yell inside the closet, and then the tip of the scissors poked through the wooden door and missed his knee by less than an inch. Jeff staggered back. In the faint moonlight he could see the tip of the scissors being driven through the door again and again, in a paced rhythm of strikes.

My God, the little beast was a psycho.

And then the stabbing stopped. Jeff stepped back, thinking. Okay. Okay. He's in the closet. It will take him awhile to work his way through the door, even as relentless as he seems to be.

The doorknob began to shake.

My God, he thought. It has leaped up and grabbed the knob, and he's hanging there, trying to open the door.

Don't just stand here, meathead, he told himself. Do something.

Jeff grabbed a chair from the kitchen and stuck the back of it against the knob. There, that would hold him.

He rushed into his study, opened up his desk drawer and got the .38 revolver out of it. He wasn't a great shot, but he had been known to hit targets with some regularity at the range. He also had another flashlight in the drawer, a smaller heavier one. He clicked it on.

The door knob continued to shake furiously, and then he heard the chair jar loose and fall to the floor. He rushed out of the study, into the hallway. The closet door was cracked open. Plenty wide for it to get out.

Was it out?

Or was it still waiting inside?

He felt something brush between his legs and Jeff jumped. He twisted, the flashlight in one hand, the gun in the other, saw something darting across the floor. He fired off a shot. There was a screech that he knew was his cat. He had missed her, but the bullet had slammed into the wall next to her. She had darted into the living room; he could see her shape just as she turned the corner.

Idiot, he told himself. Calm down. You're going to shoot the cat, or yourself.

Save the five left in the gun for the doll.

The doll!

Was he dreaming? This was crazy. A doll come to life, chasing him through his own house, killing his dog?

Ridiculous.

He was about to pinch himself when there came a ferocious yell, and then a screech from the cat, the sound of something tumbling, something falling, breaking, the terrible yells of the doll, a kind of high-pitched, "Eeeyah! Eeeyah! Eeeyah!"

Jeff made himself move toward the living room. Each step was an ordeal, but he made it. The screeching and the high-pitched Eeeyah continued the entire time. When he looked into the darkness of the room, he saw what at first appeared to be two tumbling shadows, but the shadows stopped rolling, and what he saw was Sofia, lying on the carpet, not moving. The doll was standing over the cat with the scissors upraised. It bent forward and examined its quarry, made a satisfied sound.

The doll turned its head and looked at Jeff.

Jeff raised the revolver. The doll came skittering across the carpet at a wild run, the scissors raised high in its hand.

"Eeyah! Eeeyah! Eeeyah!"

Jeff fired the gun and the sound of it in the living room was foreign and wrong to his ears, but he couldn't stop shooting. Each shot missed. He heard glass break. A thud as a bullet embedded in the couch, and then the doll was right on him. He fired, and this time he hit it. The bullet knocked the thing winding and he saw something dark fly up from it. It lay face down on the floor next to his dead cat.

He took a deep breath and dropped his hand to his side, clutching the empty revolver as if trying to strangle it. He pooled the flashlight beam around the shape on the floor. The thing raised its hand, the one with the scissors in it, and jammed them into the wood flooring, pulled itself forward a pace. It lifted its head, and looked at him. The eyes glowed in the flashlight beam like flaming match heads.

It put one knee under itself and started to stand.

Jeff could see that one of its large hands was missing a finger. That's what his bullet had hit.

And that wasn't good enough.

Jeff threw the empty revolver and then the flashlight. Neither hit its mark. He made a run for it, back down the hall, through the linking hall, across the kitchen and out the sliding back door and into the garden. He could hear the thing running behind him, still in the house, but coming fast. The sound of its feet running was like a soft drum roll. It came on yelling that horrible war cry: "Eeeyah! Eeeyah! Eeeyah!"

The garden was thick with plants and they rose up high, staked out professionally on posts. They gave the garden a jungle atmosphere, gathering in shadows, laying them deep within the greenery.

He darted into their midst, peeked around a twisty bit of plant growth, saw the thing coming through the open doorway, into the moonlight. It paused, lifted its head and sniffed the air. It turned to the side, made a few steps. As it crossed in front of the glass doorway, he could see its reflection in the glass. The reflection was huge, and wavery. It whipped and twisted like something being cooked alive on a griddle.

My god, Jeff thought. The glass is reflecting its soul. The soul of the hunter, He Who Kills.

Easing behind the foliage, resting on his knees, Jeff tried to get his breathing under control. Certainly He Who Kills would have heightened senses. He kept breathing like he was, the thing would hear him.

When he had taken a couple of deep breaths, he started to move again.

All of the long wide rows were crisscrossed with little narrow rows so he could move the wheelbarrow and gardening equipment about. He used one of the small crisscrossing rows to enter one of the wider rows, moved down it until he reached the wall that surrounded the garden. It was about twelve feet high, and it occurred to him if he could get over the wall, maybe the doll could not. But there was no time to consider that seriously. He would have to bide his time and think that one over, find a way to manage his way over twelve feet of substantial rock wall. But right now, he had to hide. He skulked through the rows as silently as he could manage. He could hear the doll moving through the garden, carelessly pushing foliage aside, yelling its war cry, and then... Everything went silent.

Jeff squatted in the middle of a row, breathed through his nose, long, deep breaths, and listened. Nothing. Not even a cricket. Then, he thought he heard the snapping of a plant. No. Maybe not. There was a gentle wind blowing. It could move things around. It could fool him, way his nerves were on edge.

The snapping again.

He wasn't sure what he was hearing. He looked down the row, saw that it was the one that ended at the water faucet and hose. The thick, coiled yellow hose with its squeeze handle and nozzle shone dully in the moonlight. It looked like some kind of metal-headed yellow anaconda. It lay next to the compost pile. The compost pile was up against the wall, and it was made of neatly arranged railroad ties with a tarpaulin thrown over it, weighted at the edges with bricks. If he could run and put a foot on the ties, he might be able to make a jump, grab the top of the wall with his hands and pull himself over.

It was iffy. But he couldn't stay here. The thing would find him eventually. There were only so many places to hide.

He decided to make a break for it.

》《

Jeff was about to run for the compost pile, leap for the wall, when a shadow fell across the row. The shadow came from the connecting row, and it was undoubtedly the shadow of He Who Kills. It looked like the shadow of something gigantic, but it was definitely the little warrior. The shadow writhed and vibrated as if powered by electricity. The thing was standing in the connecting row, and all it had to do to find him was step forward slightly and turn its head his way.

Jeff held his breath. The shadow gradually moved away, growing smaller, going in the other direction

Stooping, easing down the row, Jeff came to the connecting row and paused. He got down on his hands and knees and slowly peeked around the edge of the thick vegetation.

Nothing there.

He crossed the openness where the rows connected, made it to the other side, and then there was a flash as a limb on one of the plants snapped toward him at about knee height. And then he felt terrible pain in his kneecap.

He Who Kills had rigged a snare. The miniature knife the doll carried had been attached to a limb with a cut of the rope, bent back and let go.

Involuntary cries leaped from Jeff's mouth as he grabbed at the limb, jerked the needle-like knife out of his knee. He Who Kills sprang from the enclosure of the greenery brandishing the scissors, yelling, "Eeeyah! Eeeyah!"

"You devil!" Jeff said, and kicked at the doll. It dodged. The scissors were plunged into Jeff's foot. Jeff screamed. The scissors came down again, and again, ripping into Jeff's legs as he tried to dart past the little monster.

He finally managed to dodge around him. Limping, he made for the compost pile. He Who Kills attacked the back of his legs, driving the scissors in deep. Jeff yelled and wobbled toward the compost pile, managed to reach the water hose. He snapped it up, swung it around and hit the doll with the nozzle. It knocked the doll back about ten feet. Jeff lifted the hose and squeezed the lever on the nozzle. Water blew out in a hard, fast stream. He used it on the doll in the manner a fireman might use a fire hose on rioters.

The water kept knocking the doll down, and the doll kept getting up.

Jeff turned, tossed the hose over the top of the wall, pulled back, and the hand lever attached to the nozzle hung at the summit.

He leaped onto the compost pile, jerked the hose taut, and began to climb, his feet against the wall, his hands moving up the hose like a pirate climbing the rigging of a sailing ship.

When he reached the top, he stretched out on the wall and looked down.

He Who Kills was clambering up the hose with the scissors in his teeth. Jeff grabbed the nozzle, pulled it loose, flipped it back into the garden, sending the little monster sprawling.

He dropped to the other side of the wall, and in considerable pain, limped toward the garage. He looked back. The hose nozzle was flying up in the moonlight, hanging on the top of the wall. He Who Kills was stealing his method, and he was coming after him.

He saw the shape of the doll on the top of the wall just as he reached the garage door.

Locked.

He didn't have the device to work it. It was inside the car which was inside the garage.

Jeff stumbled around the side to a low-hung window, used his elbow to drive into one of the panes and break it. He knocked loose glass aside, reached through the missing pane, got hold of the lock and flipped it. He pushed the window up and squeezed through.

He felt a sudden moment of panic. He had trapped himself in the garage, and he wasn't even sure he had his keys.

He felt for them as he moved toward the car. He had them. He managed them from his pocket and hit the device that unlocked the car doors. He got inside and looked through the windshield and saw the shape of He Who Kills climbing through the window. He hit the door lock switch. He looked around for the garage door opener.

And then it hit him, and he felt his stomach roll. He had taken it inside. He was going to refresh the batteries. It was lying on the kitchen counter. Getting out of the car, going back into the house didn't seem like such a good idea.

Not with that thing out there.

He took only a moment to consider, stuck the key in the ignition. He Who Kills' head appeared, rising up over the hood of the car. Then it was standing on the hood.

Jeff jammed the car in reverse, hit the gas and sent He Who Kills flying.

The car struck the door and knocked it off its hinges, sent it hurtling across the drive and out into the connecting street. He had always loved the fact that his house was isolated, on a street he had built, where there were no neighbors. But right then he wished he had someone, anyone he could turn to for help.

But there was only himself to depend on. He was on his own.

He backed the car over the door, on out into the street, jammed it into drive. Just before he punched the gas, he looked in his side mirror. He Who Kills was running rapidly toward the car.

He stomped the gas. The convertible leaped with a growl. He turned on the lights.

He checked the mirror again.

It was coming, bathed in the red glow from the car's rear lights. Running ridiculously fast behind him. Closing.

It seemed impossible that it could be running that fast.

He let out a laugh. Impossible. Of course, it was impossible. Everything that had happened from the time he bought the doll was impossible.

Except, it was happening.

He gunned the engine harder, checked the rearview mirror. No doll.

He let out a sigh of relief, took the road past the dark community of Falling Rock, down toward the city. The car wound around one curve after another, the mountainous terrain little more than bumps and valleys of darkness.

And what about the doll? It was out there, running around. What did he do about that? Who would believe him? People would think him crazy, and he could hardly blame them.

But I'm not crazy. I'm fine. I'm all right.

His legs began to ache where He Who Kills had attacked him. He was losing blood. He felt a little dizzy.

He rounded a curve. Now he could see more than dark bumps and valleys, he could see city lights, way off in the distance, down in the lowlands, like someone had turned on a wadded-up handful of Christmas lights.

There was a hard metallic sound.

Jeff checked his rearview mirror. He felt the blood drain out of his face and his stomach turn sick. He Who Kills was on the back of the car. He was stabbing the scissors into the convertible's trunk with one hand, burying its claws into the trunk with the other. It was using this hand-over-hand method to crawl toward the back window of the car.

The damn thing had stayed after him, maybe grabbed onto the back of the bumper, or had worked its way along beneath the car... He didn't know how, but it had stayed after him and caught up with him, and now it was coming for him, and all he could do was watch it move toward him in the rearview mirror.

Whipping the car left and right, Jeff tried to shake the doll, but no luck. It hung tight, like a leech. It jerked the scissors free, leaped and landed on the roof of the convertible. He could hear it up there, scuttling along.

The scissors poked through the ceiling. Were withdrawn, poked again. The roofing began to rip in a long strip, and then the face of He Who Kills jutted through the slit and let out with its wild cry of "Eeeyah! Eeeyah! Eeeyah!"

He Who Kills dropped through the slit, onto the front seat. It ran across the seat in a fast scuttle, striking out with the scissors, burying them in Jeff's shoulder. Jeff groaned, swatted at the doll, knocked it back against the front passenger door, sent it rolling onto the floorboard.

The demon still had the scissors; nothing seemed able to dislodge them from its grasp. It jetted across the floorboard and stabbed at Jeff's feet, causing him to at first lift them, then jam his right foot back down on the gas.

He whipped the car hard right when another blow from the scissors went deep into the side of his calf. It was too late to swerve back. He was heading right for a guard rail. He moved the wheel some, but not enough. The car hit the railing, tore it apart with a horrid screech of metal against metal, and then the machine was flying through the air. It went for some distance before hitting the side of the mountain, blowing out its tires. The drop was so terrific, so violent, that Jeff's door was thrown open, and he was thrown from the car, sent tumbling head over heels down the side of the mountain until he fetched up against a lump of rock that knocked the wind out of him. He felt something shift in his back, and then the pain started.

The car kept going. It sailed down the mountainside, bouncing, throwing up sparks. It appeared to head deliberately for one old, dead, lightning-struck tree that jutted out from the side of the mountain like a deformed arm. The convertible slammed into it and burst into flames.

Jeff, crawling painfully around the rock he had hit, saw the flames whip up and scorch the night air. Blood ran down his face, into his left eye. He wiped it away with his sleeve. He watched the car burn. Good, he thought. I got him. I got him.

Out of the flames he saw something moving. He Who Kills. The doll started running up the hill, directly toward him. It still held the scissors. It blazed like a torch.

"No," Jeff said aloud. "No."

The doll was halfway to him when Jeff dislodged a rock about the size of his fist and threw it. It was a lucky shot. It hit the flaming hunter and knocked him down.

But, it wasn't enough. Still decorated with flames, He Who Kills got up and came running up the hill again.

Jeff tried to dig another rock out of the ground, scratching and pulling so hard his fingers bled. He got it loose, looked up. The doll was almost on him... And then its legs burned out from beneath it. It fell, face down. Flames licked off its smoldering corpse.

The hand holding the scissors shot out and stuck them in the ground. It pulled itself forward. It lifted its head and opened its mouth and flames licked out of it. It raised the scissors again, struck out, driving them into the dirt. It was coming for him, using the scissors to lurch toward him, inch by inch.

Jeff lifted the rock, rose to a sitting position, felt blood running down his legs, face and shoulder. "Come on," he said. "Come on, He Who Kills. Come and get some. You and me. Come on!"

The doll struck out with the scissors again, pulled itself forward another inch as the flames that bathed it slowed and blackened and turned to smoke. It struck one more blow with the scissors, and—

—the doll ceased to move. The smoke from its scorched body twisted up and became thick and full. The smoke took on the form of a savage face; the mouth opened and the smoke face jumped toward Jeff, yelled, "Eeeyah!" Then the smoke swirled rapidly skyward.

Jeff could still see the shape of the face in the smoke, but it had begun to spread and flatten. The smoke thinned and rose high and clouded Jeff's vision of the already murky quarter moon.

He looked back down at the doll. It had come apart. The burnt arms and legs and head had separated from the torso. Tendrils of smoke trailed off of its pieces.

"I won!" Jeff said. "I beat you, you monstrosity. If that isn't manly, nothing is. Nothing."

Laughing, he lay back. The last of the smoke faded away. The cloud cover faded as well. There was just the scimitar moon left, floating up there, nestled amongst the stars, bright and shiny in a clear, clean sky.

# SIX-FINGER JACK

**J**ack had six fingers. That's how Big O, that big, fat, white, straw-hatted son-of-a-bitch, was supposed to know he was dead. Maybe, by some real weird luck a man could kill some other black man with six fingers, cut off his hand and bring it in and claim it belonged to Jack, but not likely. So he put the word out whoever killed Jack and cut off his paw and brought it back was gonna get one hundred thousand dollars and a lot of goodwill.

I went out there after Jack just like a lot of other fellas, and one woman I knew of, Lean Mama Tootin', who was known for shotgun shootin' and ice pick work. She went out there too.

But the thing I had on them was I was screwing Jack's old lady. Jack didn't know it of course. Jack was a bad dude, and it wouldn't have been smart to let him know my bucket was in his well. Nope. Wouldn't have been smart for me or for Jack's old lady. He'd known that before he had to make a run for it, might have been good to not sleep, cause he might show up and be most unpleasant. I can be unpleasant too, but I prefer when I'm on the stalk, not when I'm being stalked. It sets the dynamics all different.

You see, I'm a philosophical kind of guy.

Thing was, though, I'd been laying the pipeline to his lady for about six weeks, because Jack had been on the run ever since he'd tried to muscle in on Big O's whores and take over that business, found out he couldn't. That wasn't enough, he took up with Big O's old lady like it didn't matter none, but it did. Rumor was, Big O put the old lady under about three feet of concrete out by his lake boat stalls, put her in the hole while she was alive, hands tied behind her back, lookin' up at that concrete mixer truck dripping out the goo, right on top of her naked self.

Jack hears this little tidbit of information, he quit foolin' around and made with the jack rabbit, took off lickity-split, so fast he almost left a vapor trail. It's one thing to fight one man, or two, but to fight a whole organization, not so easy. Especially if that organization belonged to Big O.

Loodie, Jack's personal woman, was a hot-flash number who liked to have her ashes hauled, and me, I'm a tall, lean fellow with good smile and a willing attitude. Loodie was ready to lose Jack because he had a bad temper and a bit of a smell. He was short on baths and long on cologne. Smell-good juice on top of his stinky smell, she said, made a kind of funk that would make a skunk roll over dead and cause a wild hyena to leave the body where it lay.

She, on the other hand, was like sweet wet sin dipped in coffee and sugar with a dash of cinnamon; God's own mistress with a surly attitude, which goes to show even God likes a little bit of the devil now and then.

She'd been asked about Jack by them who wanted to know. Bad folks with guns, and a need for dough. But she lied, said she didn't know where he was. Everyone believed her because she talked so bad about Jack. Said stuff about his habits, about how he beat her, how bad he was in bed, and how he stunk. It was convincin' stuff to everyone.

But me.

I knew that woman was a liar, because I knew her whole family, and they was the sort like my daddy used to say would rather climb a tree and lie than stand on the ground and tell the truth and be given free flowers. Lies flowed through their veins as surely as blood.

She told me about Jack one night while we were in bed, right after we had toted the water to the mountain. We're laying there lookin' at the ceilin', like there's gonna be manna from heaven, watchin' the defective light from the church across the way flash in and out and bounce along the wall, and she says in that burnt toast voice of hers, "You split that money, I'll tell you where he is?"

"You wanna split it?"

"Naw, I'm thinkin' maybe you could keep half and I could give the other half to the cat."

"You don't got a cat."

"Well, I got another kind of cat, and that cat is one you like to pet."

"You're right there," I said. "Tellin' me where he is, that's okay, but I still got to do the ground work. Hasslin' with that dude ain't no easy matter, that's what I'm tryin' to tell you. So, me doin' what I'm gonna have to do, that's gonna be dangerous as trying to play with a daddy lion's balls. So, that makes me worth more than half, and you less than half."

"You're gonna shoot him when he ain't lookin', and you know it."

"I still got to take the chance."

She reached over to the nightstand, nabbed up a pack, shook out a cigarette, lit it with a cheap lighter, took a deep drag, coughed out a puff, said, "Split, or nothin'."

"Hell, honey, you know I'm funnin'," I said. "I'll split it right in half with you."

I was lyin' through my teeth. She may have figured such, but she figured with me she at least had a possibility, even if it was as thin as the edge of playin' card.

She said, "He's done gone deep East Texas. He's over in Marvel Creek. Drove over there in his big black Cadillac that he had a chop shop turn blue."

"So he drove over in a blue Caddy, not a black," I said. "I mean, if it was black, and he had it painted blue, it ain't black no more. It's blue."

"Aren't you one for the details, and at a time like this," she said, and used her foot to rub my leg. "But, technically, baby, you are so correct."

»«

That night Loodie laid me out a map written in pencil on a brown paper sack, made me swear I was gonna split the money with her again. I told her what she wanted to hear. Next mornin', I started over to Marvel Creek.

Now, technically, Jack was in a place outside of the town, along the Sabine River, back in the bottom land where the woods was still thick, down a little trail that wound around and around, to a cabin Loodie said was about the size of a postage stamp, provided the stamp had been scissor trimmed.

I oiled my automatic, put on gloves, went to the store and bought a hatchet, cruised out early, made Marvel Creek in about and hour and fifteen, went glidin' over the Sabine River bridge. I took a gander at the water, which was dirty brown and up high on account of rain. I had grown up along that river, over near a place called Big Sandy. It was a place of hot sand and tall pines and no opportunity.

It wasn't a world I missed none.

I stopped at a little diner in Marvel Creek and had me a hamburger. There was a little white girl behind the counter with hair blond as sunlight, and we made some goo-goo eyes at one another. Had I not been on a mission, I might have found out when she got off work, seen if me and her could get a drink and find a motel and try and make the beast with two backs.

Instead I finished up, got me a tall Styrofoam cup of coffee to go. I drove over to a food store and went in and bought a huge jar of pickles, a bag of cookies and a bottle of water. I put the pickles on the floor board between the backseat and the front. It was a huge jar and it fit snugly. I laid the bag with the cookies and the water on the backseat.

The bottoms weren't far, about twenty minutes, but the roads were kind of tricky, some of them were little more than mud and a suggestion. Others were slick and shiny like snot on a water glass.

I drove carefully and sucked on my coffee. I went down a pretty wide road that became narrow, then took another road that wound off into the deeper woods. Drove until I found what I thought was the side road that led to the cabin. It was really a glorified path. Sun hardened, not very wide, bordered on one side by trees, and on the other side by marshy land that would suck the shoes off your feet, or bog up a car tire until you had to pull a gun and shoot the engine like a dying horse.

I stopped in the road and held Loodie's hand-drawn map, checked it, looked up. There was a curve went around and between the trees and the marsh. There were tire tracks in it. Pretty fresh. At the bend in the curve was a little wooden bridge with no railings.

So far Loodie's map was on the money.

I finished off my coffee, got out and took a pee behind the car and watched some big white water birds flying over. When I was growing up over in Big Sandy I used to see that kind of thing all the time, not to mention all manner of wildlife, and for a moment I felt nostalgic. That lasted about as long as it took me to stick my dick back in my pants and zipper up.

I got my hatchet out of the trunk and laid it on the front passenger seat as I got back in the car. I pulled out my automatic and checked it over, popped out the clip and slid it back in. I always liked the sound it made when it snapped into place. I looked at myself in the mirror, like maybe I was goin' on a date. Thought maybe if things fucked up, it might be the last time I got a good look at myself. I put the car in gear, wheeled around the curve and over the bridge, going at a slow pace, the map on the seat beside me, held in place by the hatchet.

I came to a wide patch, like on the map, and pulled off the road. Someone had dumped their garbage at the end of the spot where it ended close to the trees. There were broken-up plastic bags spilling cans and paper, and there was an old bald tire leaning against a tree, as if taking a break before rolling on its way.

I got out and walked around the bend, looked down the road. There was a broad pond of water to the left, leaked there by the dirty Sabine. On the right, next to the woods, was a log cabin. Small, but well made and kind of cool lookin'. Loodie said it was on property Jack's parents had owned. Twenty acres or so. Cabin had a chimney chuggin' smoke. Out front was a big blue Cadillac El Dorado, the tires and sides splashed with mud. It was parked up close to the cabin. I could see through the Cadillac's windows, and they lined up with a window in the cabin. I moved to the side of the road, stepped in behind some trees, and studied the place carefully.

There weren't any wires runnin' to the cabin. There was a kind of lean-to shed off the back. Loodie told me that was where Jack kept the generator that gave the joint electricity. Mostly the cabin was heated by the firewood piled against the shed, and lots of blankets come late at night. Had a gas stove with a nice sized tank. I could just imagine Jack in there with Loodie, his six fingers on her sweet chocolate skin. It made me want to kill him all the more, even though I knew Loodie was the kind of girl made a minx look virginal. You gave your heart to that woman, she'd eat it.

## 》《

I went back to the car and got my gun-cleaning goods out of the glove box, and took out the clip, and cleaned my pistol and reloaded it. It was unnecessary, because the gun was a clean as a model's ass, but I liked to be sure.

I patted the hatchet on the seat like it was a dog.

I sat there and waited, thought about what I was gonna do with one hundred thousand dollars. You planned to kill someone and cut off their hand, you had to think about stuff like that, and a lot.

Considering on it, I decided I wasn't gonna get foolish and buy a car. One I had got me around and it looked all right enough. I wasn't gonna spend it on Loodie or some other split tail in a big time way. I was gonna use it carefully. I might get some new clothes and put some money down on a place instead of rentin'. Fact was, I might move to Houston.

If I lived closed to the bone and picked up the odd bounty job now and again, just stuff I wanted to do, like bits that didn't involve me having to deal with some goon big enough to pull off one of my legs and beat me with it, I could live safer, and better. Could have some stretches where I didn't have to do a damn thing but take it easy, all on account of that one hundred thousand dollar nest egg.

Course, Jack wasn't gonna bend over and grease up for me. He wasn't like that. He could be a problem.

I got a paperback out of the glove box and read for awhile. I couldn't get my mind to stick to it. The sky turned gray. My light was goin'. I put the paperback in the glove box with the gun-cleaning kit. It started to rain. I watched it splat on the windshield. Thunder knocked at the sky. Lighting licked a crooked path against the clouds and passed away.

I thought about all manner of different ways of pullin' this off, and finally came up with somethin', decided it was good enough, because all I needed was a little edge.

The rain was hard and wild. It made me think Jack wasn't gonna be comin' outside. I felt safe enough for the moment. I tilted the seat back and lay there with the gun in my hand, my arm folded across my chest, and dozed for awhile with the rain pounding the roof.

》《

It was fresh night when I awoke. I waited about an hour, picked up the hatchet, and got out of the car. It was still raining, and the rain was cold. I pulled my coat tight around me, stuck the hatchet through my belt and went to the back of the car and unlocked the trunk. I got the jack handle out of there, stuck it in my belt opposite the hatchet, started walking around the curve.

The cabin had a faint light shining through the window that in turn shone through the lined-up windows of the car. As I walked, I saw a shape, like a huge bullet with arms, move in front of the glass. That size made me lose a step briefly, but I gathered up my courage, kept going.

When I got to the back of the cabin, I carefully climbed on the pile of firewood, made my way to the top of the lean-to. It sloped down off the main roof of the cabin, so it didn't take too much work to get up there, except that hatchet and tire iron gave me a bit of trouble in my belt and my gloves made my grip a little slippery.

On top of the cabin, I didn't stand up and walk, but instead carefully made my way on hands and knees toward the front of the place.

When I got there, I leaned over the edge and took a look. The cabin door was about three feet below me. I made my way to the edge so I was overlooking the Cadillac. A knock on the door wouldn't bring Jack out. Even he was too smart for that, but that Cadillac, he loved it. Bought a new one every year. I pulled out the tire iron, laid down on the roof, looking over the edge, cocked my arm back and threw the iron at the windshield. It made a hell of a crash, cracking the glass so that it looked like a spider web, setting off the car alarm.

I pulled my gun and waited. I heard the cabin door open, heard the thumping of Jack's big feet. He came around there mad as a hornet. He was wearing a long sleeve white shirt with the sleeves rolled up. He hadn't had time to notice the cold. But the best thing was it didn't look like he had a gun on him.

I aimed and shot him. I think I hit him somewhere on top of the shoulder, but I wasn't sure. But I hit him. He did a kind of bend at the knees, twisted his body, then snapped back into shape and looked up.

"You," he said.

I shot him again, and it had about the same impact. Jack was on the hood of his car and then on the roof, and then he jumped. That big bastard could jump, could probably dunk a basketball and grab the rim. He hit with both hands on the edge of the roof, started pulling himself up. I was up now, and I stuck the gun in his face, and pulled the trigger.

And, let me tell you how the gas went out of me. I had cleaned that gun and cleaned that gun, and now... It jammed. First time ever. But it was a time that mattered.

Jack lifted himself onto the roof, and then he was on me, snatching the gun away and flinging it into the dark. I couldn't believe it. What the hell was he made of? Even in the wet night, I could see that much of his white shirt had turned dark with blood.

We circled each other for a moment. I tried to decide what to do next, and then he was on me. I remembered the hatchet, but it was too late. We were going back off the roof and onto the lean-to, rolling down that. We hit the stacked firewood and it went in all directions and we splattered to the ground.

I lost my breath. Jack kept his. He grabbed me by my coat collar and lifted me and flung me around and against the side of the lean-to. I hit on my back and came down on my butt.

Jack grabbed up a piece of firewood. It looked to me that that piece of wood had a lot of heft. He came at me. I made myself stand. I pulled the hatchet free. As he came and struck down with the wood, I sidestepped and swung the hatchet.

The sound the hatchet made as it caught the top of his head was a little like what you might expect if a strong man took hold of a piece of cardboard and ripped it.

I hit him so hard his knees bent and hot blood jumped out of his head and hit my face. The hatchet came loose of my hands, stayed in his skull. His knees straightened. I thought: What is this motherfucker, Rasputin?

He grabbed me and started to lift me again. His mouth was partially open and his teeth looked like machinery cogs to me.

The rain was washing the blood on his head down his face in murky rivers. He stunk like roadkill.

And then his expression changed. It seemed as if he had just realized he had a hatchet in his head. He let go, turned, started walking off, taking hold of the hatchet with both hands, trying to pull it loose. I picked up a piece of firewood and followed after him. I went up behind him and hit him in the back of the head as hard as I could. It was like hitting an elephant in the ass with a twig. He turned and looked at me. The look on his face was so strange, I almost felt sorry for him.

He went down on one knee, and I hauled back and hit him with the firewood, hitting the top of the hatchet. He vibrated, and his neck twisted to one side, and then his head snapped back in line.

He said, "Gonna need some new pigs," and then fell out.

Pigs?

He was lying face forward with the stock of the hatchet holding his head slightly off the ground. I dropped the firewood and rolled him over on his back, which only took about as much work as trying to roll his Cadillac. I pulled the hatchet out of his head. I had to put my foot on his neck to do it.

I picked up the firewood I had dropped, put it on the ground beside him, and stretched his arm out until I had the hand with the six fingers positioned across it. I got down on my knees and lifted the hatchet, hit as hard as I could. It took me three whacks, but I cut his hand loose.

>> <<

I put the bloody hand in my coat pocket and dug through his pants for his car keys, didn't come across them. I went inside the cabin and found them on the table. I drove the Cadillac to the back where Jack lay, pulled him into the backseat, almost having a hernia in the process. I put the hatchet in there with him.

I drove the El Dorado over close to the pond and rolled all the windows down and put it in neutral. I got out of the car, went to the back of it and started shoving. My feet slipped in the mud, but finally I gained traction. The car went forward and slipped into the water, but the back end of it hung on the bank.

Damn.

I pushed and I pushed, and finally I got it moving, and it went in, and with the windows down, it sunk pretty fast.

I went back to the cabin and looked around. I found some candles. I turned off the light, and I went and turned off the generator. I went back inside and lit about three of the big fat candles and stuck them in drinking glasses and watched them burn for a moment. I went over to the stove and turned on the gas. I let it run a few seconds, looked around the cabin. Nothing there I needed.

I left, closed the door behind me. When the gas filled the room enough, those candles would set the air on fire, the whole place would blow. I don't know exactly why I did it, except maybe I just didn't like Jack. Didn't like that he had a Cadillac and a cabin and some land, and for a while there, he had Loodie. Because of all that, I had done all I could do that could be done to him. I even had his six-fingered hand in my pocket.

By the time I got back to the car, I was feeling weak. Jack had worked me over pretty good, and now that the adrenaline had started to ease out of me, I was feeling it. I took off my jacket and opened the jar of pickles in the floor board, pulled out a few of them and threw them away. I ate one, and had my bottle of water with it and some cookies.

I took Jack's hand and put it in the big pickle jar. I sat in the front seat, and was overcome with a feeling of nausea. I didn't know if it was the pickle or what I had done, or both. I opened the car door and threw up. I felt cold and damp from the rain. I started the car and turned on the heater. I cranked back my seat and closed my eyes. I had to rest before I left, had to. All of me seemed to be running out through the soles of my feet.

I slept until the cabin blew. The sound of the gas generator and stove going up with a one-two boom snapped me awake.

>> <<

I got out of the car and walked around the curve. The cabin was nothing more than a square dark shape inside an envelope of fire. The fire wavered up high and grew narrow at the top like a cone. The fire crackled like someone wadding up cellophane.

I doubted, out here, anyone heard the explosion, and no one could see the flames. Wet as it was, I figured the fire wouldn't go any farther than the cabin. By morning, even with the rain still coming down, that place would be smoked down to the mineral rights.

I drove out of there, and pretty soon the heater was too hot, and I turned it off. It was as if my body was as on fire as the cabin. I rolled down the window and let in some cool air. I felt strange. Not good, not bad. I had bounty hunted for years, and I had done a bit of head-whopping before, but this was my first murder.

I had really hated Jack and I had hardly known him.

It was the woman that made me hate him. The woman I was gonna cheat out of some money. But a hundred thousand dollars is a whole lot of money, honey.

>> <<

When I got home, the automatic garage opener lifted the door and I wheeled in and closed the place up. I went inside and took off my clothes and showered carefully and looked in the mirror. There was knot on my head that looked as if you might need mountaineering equipment to scale it. I got some ice and put it in a sock and pressed it to my head while I sat on the toilet lid and thought about things. If any thoughts actually came to me, I don't remember them well.

I dressed, bunched up my murder clothes, and put them in a black plastic garbage bag.

In the garage, I removed the pickle jar and cleaned the car. I opened the jar and looked at the hand. It looked like a black crab in there amongst the pickles. I studied it for a long time until it started to look like one hundred thousand dollars.

I couldn't wait until morning, and after awhile I drove toward Big O's place. Now, you would think a man with the money he's got would live in a mansion, but he didn't. He lived in three double-wide mobile homes that had been lined together by screened-in porches. I had been inside once, when I had done Big O a very small favor, and had never been inside since. But one of those homes was nothing but one big space, no rooms, and it was Big O's lounge. He hung in there with some ladies and some bodyguards. He had two main guys. Be Bop Lewis, who was a skinny white guy who always acted as if someone was sneaking up on him, and a black guy named Lou Boo (keep in mind, I didn't name them) who thought he was way cool and smooth as velvet.

The rain had followed me from the bottom land, on into Tyler, to the outskirts, and on the far side. It was way early morning, and I figured on waking Big O up and dragging his ass out of bed and showing him them six fingers and getting me one hundred thousand dollars, a pat on the head, and hell, he might ask Be Bop to give me a hand job, on account of I had done so well.

More I thought about it, more I thought he might not be as happy to see me as I thought. A man like Big O liked his sleep, so I pulled into a motel not too far from where I had to go to see Big O, the big jar of pickles and one black six-fingered hand beside my bed, the automatic under my pillow.

I dreamed Jack was driving the Cadillac out of that pond. I saw the lights first and then the car. Jack was steering with his nub laid against the wheel, and his face behind the glass was a black mass without eyes or smile or features of any kind.

It was a bad dream and it woke me up. I washed my face, went back to bed, slept this time until late morning. I got up and put back on my same clothes, loaded up my pickle jar and left out of there. I thought about the axe in Jack's head, his hand chopped off and in the pickle jar, and regret moved through me like shit through a goose and was gone.

I drove out to Big O's place.

» «

By the time I arrived at the property, which was surrounded by a barbed-wire fence, and had driven over a cattle guard, I could see there were men in a white pickup coming my way. Two in the front and three in the bed in the back, and they had some heavy-duty fire power. Parked behind them, up by the double-wides, were the cement trucks and dump trucks and backhoes and graders that were part of the business Big O claimed to operate. Construction. But his real business was a bit of this, and a little of that, construction being little more than the surface paint.

I stopped and rolled down my window and waited. Outside the rain had burned off and it was an unseasonably hot day, sticky as honey on the fingers.

When they drove up beside my window, the three guys in the bed pointed their weapons at me. The driver was none other than one of the two men I recognized from before. Be Bop. His skin was so pale and thin, I could almost see the skull beneath it.

"Well, now," he said. "I know you."

I agreed he did. I smiled like me and him was best friends. I said, "I got some good news for Big O about Six Finger Jack."

"Six Finger Jack, huh," Be Bop said. "Get out of the car."

I got out. Be Bop got out and frisked me. I had nothing sharp or anything full of bullets. He asked if there was anything in the car. I told him no. He had one of the men in the back of the pickup search it anyway. The man came back, said, "Ain't got no gun, just a big jar of pickles."

"Pickles," Be Bop said. "You a man loves pickles?"

"Not exactly," I said.

"Follow us on up," Be Bop said.

We drove on up to the trio of double-wides. There had been some work done since I had last been here, and there was a frame of boards laid out for a foundation, and out to the side there was a big hole that looked as if it was going to be a swimming pool.

I got out of the car and leaned on it and looked things over. Be Bop and his men got out of the truck. Be Bop came over.

"He buildin' a house on that foundation?" I asked.

"Naw, he's gonna put an extension on one of the trailers. I think he's gonna put in a pool room and maybe some gamin' stuff. Swimmin' pool over there. Come on."

I got my jar of pickles out of the backseat, and Be Bop said, "Now wait a minute. Your pickles got to go with you?"

I set the jar down and screwed off the lid and stepped back. Be Bop looked inside. When he lifted his head, he said, "Well, now."

》《

Next thing I know I'm in the big trailer, the one that's got nothin' but the couch, some chairs and stands for drinks, a TV set about the size of a downtown theater. It's on, and there's sports goin'. I glance at it and see it's an old basketball game that was played a year back, but they're watchin' it, Big O and a few of his boys, includin' Lou Boo, the black guy I've seen before. This time, there aren't any women there.

Be Bop came inside with me, but the rest of the pickup posse didn't. They were still protecting the perimeter. It seemed silly, but truth was, there was lots of people wanted to kill Big O.

No one said a thing to me for a full five minutes. They were waitin' for a big score in the game, somethin' they had seen before. When the shot came they all cheered. I thought only Big O sounded sincere.

I didn't look at the game. I couldn't take my eyes off Big O. He wasn't wearin' his cowboy hat. His head had only a few hairs left on it, like worms working their way over the face of the moon. His skin was white and lumpy like cold oatmeal. He was wearin' a brown pair of stretch overalls. When the fat moved, the material moved with him, which was a good idea, cause it looked as if Big O had packed on about one hundred extra pounds since I saw him last.

He was sitting in a motorized scooter, had his tree trunk legs stretched out in front of him on a leg lift. His stomach flowed up and fell forward and over his sides, like four hundred pounds of bagged mercury. I could hear him wheezing across the room. His right foot was missing. There was a nub there and his stretch pants had been sewn up at the end. On the stand, near his right elbow was a tall bottle of malt liquor and a greasy box of fried chicken.

His men sat on the couch to his left. The couch was unusually long and there were six men on it, like pigeons in a row. They all had guns in shoulder holsters. The scene made Big O looked like a whale on vacation with a male harem of sucker fish to attend him.

Big O spoke to me, his voice sounded small coming from that big body. "Been a long time since I seen you last."

I nodded.

"I had a foot then."

I nodded again.

"The diabetes. Had to cut it off. Dr. Jacobs says I need more exercise, but, hey, glandular problems, so what you gonna do? Packs the weight on. But still, I got to go there every Thursday mornin'. Next time, he might tell me the other foot's got to go. But you know, that's not so bad. This chair, it can really get you around. Motorized you know."

Be Bop, who was still by me, said, "He's got somethin' for you, Big O."

"Chucky," Big O said, "cut off the game."

Chucky was one of the men on the couch, a white guy. He got up and found a remote control and cut off the game. He took it with him back to the couch, sat down.

"Come on up," Big O said.

I carried my jar of pickles up there, got a whiff of him that made my memory of Jack's stink seem mild. Big O smelled like dried urine, sweat, and death. I had to fight my gag reflex.

I set the jar down and twisted off the lid and reached inside the blood stained pickle juice, and brought out Jack's dripping hand. Big O said, "Give me that."

I gave it to him. He turned it around and around in front of him. Pickle juice dripped off of the hand and into his lap. He started to laugh. His fat vibrated, and then he coughed. "That there is somethin'."

He held the hand up above his head. Well, he lifted it to about shoulder height. Probably the most he had moved in a while. He said, "Boys, do you see this? Do you see the humanity in this?"

I thought: Humanity?

"This hand tried to take my money and stuck its finger up my old lady's ass... Maybe all six. Look at it now."

His boys all laughed. It was like the best goddamn joke ever told, way they yucked it up.

"Well now," Big O said, "that motherfucker won't be touchin' nothin', won't be handlin' nobody's money, not even his own, and we got this dude to thank."

Way Big O looked at me then made me a little choked up. I thought there might even be a tear in his eye. "Oh," he said. "I loved that woman. God, I did. But, I had to cut her loose. She hadn't fucked around, me and her might have gotten married, and all this—" he waved Jack's hand around, "would have been hers to share. But no. She couldn't keep her pants on. It's a sad situation. And though I can't bring her back, this here hand, it gives me some kind of happiness. I want you to know that."

"I'm glad I could have been of assistance," I said.

"That's good. That's good. Put this back in the pickle jar, will you?"

I took the hand and dropped it in the pickle jar.

Big O looked at me, and I looked at him. After a long moment, he said, "Well, thanks."

I said, "You're welcome."

We kept looking at one another. I cleared my throat. Big O shifted a little in his chair. Not much, but a little.

"Seems to me," I said, "there was a bounty on Jack. Some money."

"Oh," Big O said. "That's right, there was."

"He was quite a problem."

"Was he now... Yeah, well, I can see the knot on your head. You ought to buy that thing its own cap. Somethin' nice."

Everyone on the couch laughed. I laughed too. I said, "Yeah, it's big. And, I had some money, like say, one hundred thousand dollars, I'd maybe put out ten or twenty for a nice designer cap."

I was smilin', waiting for my laugh, but nothin' came. I glanced at Be Bop. He was lookin' off like maybe he heard his mother callin' somewhere in the distance.

Big O said, "Now that Jack's dead, I got to tell you, I've sort of lost the fever."

"Lost the fever?" I said.

"He was alive, I was all worked up. Now that he's dead, I got to consider, is he really worth one hundred thousand dollars?"

"Wait a minute, that was the deal. That's the deal you spread all over."

"I've heard those rumors," Big O said.

"Rumors?"

"Oh, you can't believe everything you hear. You just can't."

I stood there stunned.

Big O said, "But I want you to know, I'm grateful. You want a Coke, a beer before you go?"

"No. I want the goddamn money you promised."

That had come out of my mouth like vomit. It surprised even me.

Everyone in the room was silent.

Big O breathed heavy, said, "Here's the deal, friend. You take your jar of pickles, and Jack's six fingers, and you carry them away. Cause if you don't, if you want to keep askin' me for money

I don't want to pay, your head is gonna be in that jar, but not before I have it shoved up your ass. You savvy?"

It took me a moment, but I said, "Yeah. I savvy."

》《

Lying in bed with Loodie, not being able to do the deed, I said, "I'm gonna get that fat sonofabitch. He promised me money. I fought Jack with a piece of firewood and a hatchet. I fell off a roof. I slept in my car in the cold. I was nearly killed."

"That sucks," Loodie said.

"Sucks? You got snookered too. You was gonna get fifty thousand, now you're gonna get dick."

"Actually, tonight, I'm not even gettin' that."

"Sorry, baby. I'm just so mad... Ever Thursday mornin', Big O, he goes to a doctor's appointment at Dr. Jacobs. I can get him there."

"He has his men, you know."

"Yeah. But when he goes in the office, maybe he don't. And maybe I check it out this Thursday, find out when he goes in, and next Thursday, I maybe go inside and wait on him."

"How would you do that?"

"I'm thinkin' on it, baby."

"I don't think it's such a good idea."

"You lost fifty grand, and so did I, so blowin' a hole in his head is as close as we'll get to satisfaction."

》《

So Thursday mornin', I'm goin' in the garage, to go and check things out, and when I get in the car, before I can open up the garage and back out, a head raises up in the back seat, and a gun barrel, like a wet kiss, pushes against the side of my neck.

I can see him in the mirror. It's Lou Boo. He says: "You got to go where I tell you, else I shoot a hole in you."

I said, "Loodie."

"Yeah, she come to us right away."

"Come on, man. I was just mad. I wasn't gonna do nothin'."

"So here it is Thursday mornin', and now you're tellin' me you wasn't goin' nowhere."

"I was gonna go out and get some breakfast. Really."

"Don't believe you."

"Shit," I said.

"Yeah, shit," Lou Boo said.

"How'd you get in here without me knowin'?"

"I'm like a fuckin' ninja... And the door slides up you pull it from the bottom."

"Really?"

"Yeah, really."

"Come on, Lou Boo, give a brother a break. You know how it is?"

Lou Boo laughed a little. "Ah, man. Don't play the brother card. I'm what you might call one of them social progressives. I don't see color, even if it's the same as mine. Let's go, my man."

》《

It was high morning and cool when we arrived. I drove my car right up to where the pool was dug out, way Lou Boo told me. There was a cement mixer truck parked nearby for cementing the pool. We stopped and Lou Boo told me to leave it in neutral. I did. I got out and walked with him to where Big O was sitting in his motorized scooter with Loodie on his lap. His boys were all around him. Be Bop pointed his finger at me and dropped his thumb.

"My man," Be Bop said.

When I was standing in front of Big O, he said, "Now, I want you to understand, you wouldn't be here had you not decided to kill me. I can't have that, now can I?"

I didn't say anything.

I looked at Loodie, she shrugged.

"I figured you owed me money," I said.

"Yeah," Big O said. "I know. You see, Loodie, she comes and tells me she's gonna make a deal with you to kill Jack and make you think you made a deal with her. That way, the deal I made was with her, not you. You followin' me on this, swivel dick? Then, you come up with this idea to kill me at the doctor's office. Loodie, she came right to me."

"So," I said, "you're gettin' Loodie out of the deal, and she's gettin' one hundred thousand."

"That sounds about right, yeah," Big O said.

I thought about that. Her straddlin' that fat bastard in his scooter. I shook my head, glared at her, said, "Damn, girl."

She didn't look right at me.

Big O said, "Loodie, you go on in the house there, and amuse yourself. Get a beer, or somethin'. Watch a little TV. Do your nails. Whatever."

Loodie started walking toward the trailers. When she was inside, Big O said, "Hell, boy. I know how she is, and I know what she is. It's gonna be white gravy on sweet chocolate bread for me. And when I get tired of it, she gonna find a hole out here next to you. I got me all kind of room here. I ain't usin' the lake boat stalls no more. That's risky. Here is good. Though I'm gonna have to dig another spot for a pool, but that's how it is. Ain't no big thing, really."

"She used me," I said. "She's the one led me to this."

"No doubt, boy. But, you got to understand. She come to me and made the deal before you did anything. I got to honor that."

"I could just go on," I said. "I could forget all about it. I was just mad. I wouldn't never bother you. Hell, I can move. I can go out of state."

"I know that," he said, "but, I got this rule, and it's simple. You threaten to kill me, I got to have you taken care of. Ain't that my rule, boys?"

There was a lot of agreement.

Lou Boo was last. He said, "Yep, that's the way you do it, boss."

Big O said, "Lou Boo, put him in the car, will you?"

Lou Boo put the gun to back of my head, said, "Get on your knees."

"Fuck you," I said, but he hit me hard behind the head. Next thing I know I'm on my knees, and he's got my hands behind my back, and has fastened a plastic tie over my wrists.

"Get in the car," Lou Boo said.

I fought him all the way, but Be Bop came out and kicked me in the nuts a couple of times, hard enough I threw up, and then they dragged me to the car and shoved me inside behind the wheel and rolled down the windows and closed the door.

They went behind the car then and pushed. The car wobbled, then fell, straight down, hit so hard the air bag blew out and knocked the shit out of me. I couldn't move with it the way it was, my hands bound behind my back, the car on its nose, its back wheels against the side of the hole. It looked like I was tryin' to drive to hell. I was stunned and bleeding. The bag had knocked a tooth out. I heard the sound of a motor above me, a little motor. The scooter.

I could hear Big O up there. "If you hear me, want you to know I'm having one of the boys bring the cement truck around. We're gonna fill this hole with cement, and put, I don't know, a tennis court or somethin' on top of it. But the thing I want you to know is this is what happens when someone fucks with Big O."

"You stink," I said. "And you're fat. And you're ugly."

He couldn't hear me. I was mostly talking into the air bag.

I heard the scooter go away, followed by the sound of a truck and a beeping as it backed up. Next I heard the churning of the cement in the big mixer that was on the back of it. Then the cement slid down and pounded on the roof and started to slide over the windshield. I closed my eyes and held my breath, and then I felt the cold wet cement touch my elbow as it came through the open window. I thought about some way out, but there was nothing there, and I knew that within moments there wouldn't be anything left for me to think about at all.

# MR. BEAR

For Michelle Lansdale

Jim watched as the plane filled up. It was a pretty tightly stacked flight, but last time, coming into Houston, he had watched as every seat filled except for the one on his left and the one on his right. He had hit the jackpot that time, no row mates. That made it comfortable, having all that knee and elbow room.

He had the middle seat again, an empty seat to his left, and one to his right. He sat there hoping there would be the amazing repeat of the time before.

A couple of big guys, sweating and puffing, were moving down the aisle, and he thought, yep, they'll be the ones. Probably one of them on either side. Shit, he'd settle for just having one seat filled, the one by the window, so he could get out on the aisle side. Easy to go to the bathroom that way, stretch your legs.

The big guys passed him by. He saw a lovely young woman carrying a straw hat making her way down the center. He thought, someone has got to sit by me, maybe it'll be her. He could perhaps strike up a conversation. He might even find she's going where he's going, doesn't have a boyfriend. Wishful thinking, but it was a better thing to think about than big guys on either side of him, hemming him in like the center of a sandwich.

But no, she passed him by as well. He looked up at her, hoping she'd look his way. Maybe he could get a smile at least. That would be nice.

Course, he was a married man, so that was no way to think.

But he was thinking it.

She didn't look and she didn't smile.

Jim sighed, waited. The line was moving past him. There was only one customer left. A shirtless bear in dungarees and work boots, carrying a hat. The bear looked peeved, or tired, or both.

Oh, shit, thought Jim. Bears, they've got to stink. All that damn fur. He passes me by, I'm going to have a seat free to myself on either side. He doesn't, well, I've got to ride next to him for several hours.

But, the bear stopped in his row, pointed at the window seat. "That's my seat."

"Sure," Jim said, and moved out of the middle seat, and out into the aisle, let the bear in. The bear settled in by the window and fastened his seat belt and rested his hat on his knee. Jim slid back into the middle seat. He could feel the heat off the bear's big hairy arm. And there was a smell. Nothing nasty or ripe. Just a kind of musty odor, like an old fur coat hung too long in a closet, dried blood left in a carpet, a whiff of cigarette smoke and charred wood.

Jim watched the aisle again. No one else. He could hear them closing the door. He unfastened his seat belt and moved to the seat closest to the aisle. The bear turned and looked at him. "You care I put my hat in the middle seat?"

"Not at all," Jim said.

"I get tired of keeping up with it. Thinking of taking it out of the wardrobe equation."

Suddenly it snapped. Jim knew the bear. Had seen him on TV. He was a famous environmentalist. Well, that was something. Had to sit by a musty bear, helped if he was famous. Maybe there would be something to talk about.

"Hey," the bear said, "I ask you something, and I don't want it to sound rude, but...can I?"

"Sure."

"I got a feeling, just from a look you gave me, you recognized me."

"I did."

"Well, I don't want to be too rude, sort of leave a fart hanging in the air, though, I might... Deer carcass. Never agrees. But, I really don't want to talk about me or what I do or who I am... And let me just be completely honest. I was so good at what I do... Well, I am good. Let me rephrase that. I was really as successful as people think, you believe I'd be riding coach? After all my years of service to the forest, it's like asking your best girl to ride bitch like she was the local poke. So, I don't want to talk about it."

"I never intended to ask," Jim said. That was a lie, but it seemed like the right thing to say.

"Good. That's good," said the bear, and leaned back in his seat and put the hat on his head and pulled it down over his eyes.

For a moment Jim thought the bear had gone to sleep, but no, the bear spoke again. "Now that we've got that out of the way, you want to talk, we can talk. Don't want to, don't have to, but we can talk, just don't want to talk about the job and me and the television ads, all that shit. You know what I'd like to talk about?"

"What's that?"

"Poontang. All the guys talk about pussy, but me, I'm a bear, so it makes guys uncomfortable, don't want to bring it up. Let me tell you something man, I get plenty, and I don't just mean bear stuff. Guy like me, that celebrity thing going and all, I can line them up outside the old motel room, knock 'em off like shooting ducks from a blind. Blondes, redheads, brunettes, bald, you name it, I can bang it."

This made Jim uncomfortable. He couldn't remember the last time he'd had sex with his wife, and here was a smelly bear with a goofy hat knocking it off like there was no tomorrow. He said, "Aren't we talking about your celebrity after all? I mean, in a way?"

"Shit. You're right. Okay. Something else. Maybe nothing. Maybe we just sit. Tell you what, I'm going to read a magazine, but you think of something you want to talk about, you go ahead. I'm listening."

Jim got a magazine out of the pouch in front of him and read a little, even came across an ad with the bear's picture in it, but he didn't want to bring that up. He put the magazine back and thought about the book he had in the overhead, in his bag, but it was the usual thriller, so he didn't feel like bothering with it.

After a while the flight attendant came by. She was a nice-looking woman who looked even nicer because of her suit, way she carried herself, the air of authority. She asked if they'd like drinks.

Jim ordered a diet soda, which was free, but the bear pulled out a bill and bought a mixed drink, a Bloody Mary. They both got peanuts. When the flight attendant handed the bear his drink, the bear said, "Honey, we land, you're not doing anything, I could maybe show you my wild side, find yours."

The bear grinned showed some very ugly teeth.

The flight attendant leaned over Jim, close to the bear, said, "I'd rather rub dirt in my ass than do anything with you."

This statement hung in the air like backed-up methane for a moment, then the flight attendant smiled, moved back and stood in the aisle, looked right at Jim said, "If you need anything else, let me know," and she was gone.

The bear had let down his dining tray and he had the drink in its plastic cup in his hand. The Bloody Mary looked very bloody. The bear drank it one big gulp. He said, "Flight drinks. You could have taken a used Tampax and dipped it in rubbing alcohol and it would taste the same."

Jim didn't say anything. The bear said, "She must be a lesbian. Got to be. Don't you think?"

The way the bear turned and looked at him, Jim thought it was wise to agree. "Could be."

The bear crushed the plastic cup. "No could be. Is. Tell me you agree. Say, IS."

"Is," Jim said, and his legs trembled slightly.

"That's right, boy. Now whistle up that lesbian bitch, get her back over here. I want another drink."

»«

When they landed in Denver the bear was pretty liquored up. He walked down the ramp crooked and his hat was cocked at an odd angle that suggested it would fall at any moment. But it didn't.

The plane had arrived late, and this meant Jim had missed his connecting flight due to a raging snowstorm. The next flight was in the morning and it was packed. He'd have to wait until tomorrow, mid-afternoon, just to see if a flight was available. He called his wife on his cell phone, told her, and then rang off feeling depressed and tired and wishing he could stay home and never fly again.

Jim went to the bar, thinking he might have a nightcap, catch a taxi to the hotel, and there was the bear, sitting on a stool next to a blonde with breasts so big, they were resting on the bar in front of her. The bear, his hat still angled oddly on his head, was chatting her up.

Jim went behind them on his way to a table. He heard the bear say, "Shid, darlin', you dun't know whad yer missin'. 'ere's wimen all o'er 'is world would lige to do it wid a bear."

"I'm not that drunk, yet," the blonde said, "and I don't think they have enough liquor here to make me that drunk." She got up and walked off.

Jim sat down at a table with his back to the bar. He didn't want the bear to recognize him, but he wanted a drink. And then he could smell the bear. The big beast was right behind him. He turned slightly. The bear was standing there, dripping saliva onto his furry chest thick as sea foam.

"Eh, buddy, 'ow you doin'." The bear's words were so slurred, it took Jim a moment to understand.

"Oh," he said. "Not so good. Flight to Seattle is delayed until tomorrow."

"Me too," the bear said, and plopped down in a chair at the table so hard the chair wobbled and Jim heard a cracking sound that made him half-expect to see the chair explode and the bear go tumbling to the floor. "See me wid dat gal? Wus dryin' to roun me ub sum, ya know."

"No luck?"

"Les'bin. The're eberyware."

Jim decided he needed to get out of this pretty quick. "Well, you know, I don't think I'm going to wait on that drink. Got to get a hotel room, get ready for tomorrow."

"Naw, dunt do 'at. Er, led me buy ya a drank. Miz. You in dem tidht panss."

So the waitress came over and the bear ordered some drinks for them both. Jim kept trying to leave, but, no go. Before he knew it, he was almost as hammered as the bear.

Finally, the bear, just two breaths short of a complete slur, said, "Eber thang 'ere is den times duh prize. Leds go ta a real bar." He paused. "Daby Crogett killed a bar." And then the bear broke into insane laughter.

"Wen e wus ony tree...three. Always subone gad ta shood sub bar subware. Cum on, eds go. I know dis town ligh duh bag ob muh 'and."

》《

They closed down a midtown bar. Jim remembered that pretty well. And then Jim remembered something about the bear saying they ought to have some companionship, and then things got muddled. He awoke in a little motel room, discovered the air was full of the smell of moldy bear fur, alcohol farts, a coppery aroma, and sweaty perfume.

Sitting up in bed, Jim was astonished to find a very plump girl with short blond hair next to him in bed. She was lying face down, one long, bladder-like tit sticking out from under her chest, the nipple pierced with a ring that looked like a washer.

Jim rolled out of bed and stood up beside it. He was nude and sticky. "Shit," he said. He observed the hump under the sheet some more, the washer in the tit. And then, as his eyes adjusted, he looked across the room and saw another bed, and he could see on the bed post the bear's hat, and then the bear, lying on the bed without his pants. There was another lump under the blanket. One delicate foot stuck out from under the blanket near the end of the bed, a gold chain around the ankle. The bear was snoring softly. There were clothes all over the floor, a pair of panties large enough to be used as a sling for the wounded leg of a hippopotamus was dangling from the light fixture. That would belong to his date.

Except for his shoes and socks, Jim found his clothes and put them on and sat in a chair at a rickety table and put his head in his hands. He repeated softly over and over, "Shit, shit, shit."

With his hands on his face, he discovered they had a foul smell about them, somewhere between working-man sweat and a tuna net. He was hit with a sudden revelation that made him feel ill. He slipped into the bathroom and showered and re-dressed; this time he put on his socks and shoes. When he came out the light was on over the table and the bear was sitting there, wearing his clothes, even his hat.

"Damn, man," the bear said, his drunk gone, "that was some time we had. I think. But, I got to tell you, man, you got the ugly one."

Jim sat down at the table, feeling as if he had just been hit by a car. "I don't remember anything."

"Hope you remembered she stunk. That's how I tracked them down, on a corner. I could smell her a block away. I kind of like that, myself. You know, the smell. Bears, you know how it is. But, I seen her, and I thought, goddamn, she'd have to sneak up on a glass of water, so I took the other one. You said you didn't care."

"Oh, god," Jim said.

"The fun is in the doing, not the remembering. Trust me, some things aren't worth remembering."

"My wife will kill me."

"Not if you don't tell her."

"I've never done anything like this before."

"Now you've started. The fat one, I bet she drank twelve beers before she pissed herself."

"Oh, Jesus."

"Come on, let's get out of here. I gave the whores the last of my money. And I gave them yours."

"What?"

"I asked you. You said you didn't mind."

"I said I don't remember a thing. I need that money."

"I know that. So do I."

The bear got up and went over to his bed and picked up the whore's purse and rummaged through it, took out the money. He then found the other whore's purse on the floor, opened it up and took out money.

Jim staggered to his feet. He didn't like this, not even a little bit. But, he needed his money back. Was it theft if you paid for services you didn't remember?

Probably. But...

As Jim stood, in the table light, he saw that on the bear's bed was a lot of red paint, and then he saw it wasn't paint, saw too that the whore's head was missing. Jim let out a gasp and staggered a little.

The bear looked at him. The expression on his face was oddly sheepish.

"Thought we might get out of here without you seeing that. Sometimes, especially if I've been drinking, and I'm hungry, I revert to my basic nature. If it's any consolation, I don't remember doing that."

"No. No. It's no consolation at all."

At this moment, the fat whore rolled over in bed and sat up and the covers dropped down from her, and the bear, moving very quickly, got over there and with a big swipe of his paw sent a spray of blood and a rattle of teeth flying across the room, against the wall. The whore fell back, half her face clawed away.

"Oh, Jesus. Oh, my god."

"This killing I remember," the bear said. "Now come on, we got to wipe everything down before we leave, and we don't have all night."

>> <<

They walked the streets in blowing snow, and even though it was cold, Jim felt as if he were in some kind of fever dream. The bear trudged along beside him, said, "I had one of the whores pay for the room in cash. They never even saw us at the desk. Wiped down the prints in the room, anything we might have touched. I'm an expert at it. We're cool. Did that cause I know how these things can turn out. I've had it go bad before. Employers have got me out of a few scrapes, you know. I give them that. You okay, you look a little peaked."

"I...I..."

The bear ignored him, rattled on. "You now, I'm sure you can tell by now, I'm not really all that good with the ladies. On the plane, I was laying the bullshit on... Damn, I got all this fur, but that don't mean I'm not cold. I ought to have like a winter uniform, you know, a jacket, with a big collar that I can turn up. Oh, by the way. I borrowed your cell phone to call out for pizza last night, but before I could, dropped it and stepped on the motherfucker. Can you believe that? Squashed like a clam shell. I got it in my pocket. Have to throw it away. Okay. Let me be truthful. I had it in my back pocket and I sat my fat ass on it. That's the thing... You a little hungry? Shit. I'm hungry. I'm cold."

That was the only comment for a few blocks, then the bear said, "Fuck this," and veered toward a car parked with several others at the curb. The bear reached in his pocket and took out a little packet, opened it. The streetlights revealed a series of shiny lock-pick tools. He went to work on the car door with a tool that he unfolded and slid down the side of the car window until he could pull the lock. He opened the door, said, "Get inside." The bear flipped a switch that unlocked the doors, and Jim, as if he was obeying the commands of a hypnotist, walked around to the other side and got in.

The bear was bent under the dash with his tools, and in a moment, the car roared to life. The bear sat in the seat and closed the door, said, "Seat belts. Ain't nobody rides in my car, they don't wear seat belts."

Jim thought: It's not your car. But he didn't say anything. He couldn't. His heart was in his mouth. He put on his seat belt.

》《

They tooled along the snowy Denver streets and out of town and the bear said, "We're leaving this place, going to my stomping grounds. Yellowstone Park. Know some back trails. Got a pass. We'll be safe there. We can hang. I got a cabin. It'll be all right."

"I…I…" Jim said, but he couldn't find the rest of the sentence.

"Look in the glove box, see there's anything there. Maybe some prescription medicine of some kind. I could use a jolt."

"I…" Jim said, and then his voice died and he opened the glove box. There was a gun inside. Lazily, Jim reached for it.

The bear leaned over and took it from him. "You don't act like a guy been around guns much. Better let me have that." The bear, while driving, managed with one hand to pop out the clip and slide it back in. "A full load. Wonder he's got a gun permit. You know, I do. Course, not for this gun. But, beggars can't be choosers, now can they?"

"No. No. Guess not," Jim said, having thought for a moment that he would have the gun, that he could turn the tables, at least make the bear turn back toward Denver, let him out downtown.

"See any gum in there," the bear said. "Maybe he's got some gum. After that whore's head, I feel like my mouth has a pair of shitty shorts in it. Anything in there?"

Jim shook his head. "Nothing."

"Well, shit," the bear said.

The car roared on through the snowy night, the windshield wipers beating time, throwing snow wads left and right like drunk children tossing cotton balls.

The heater was on. It was warm. Jim felt a second wave of the alcohol blues; it wrapped around him like a warm blanket, and without really meaning to, he slept.

"I should be hibernating," the bear said, as if Jim were listening. "That's why I'm so goddamn grumpy. The work. No hibernation. Paid poon and cheap liquor. That's no way to live."

The bear was a good driver in treacherous weather. He drove on through the night and made good time.

>> <<

When Jim awoke it was just light and the light was red and it came through the window and filled the car like blood-stained streams of heavenly piss.

Jim turned his head. The bear had his hat cocked back on his head and he looked tired. He turned his head slightly toward Jim, showed some teeth at the corner of his mouth, then glared back at the snowy road.

"We got a ways to go yet, but we're almost to Yellowstone. You been asleep two days."

"Two days."

"Yeah. I stopped for gas once, and you woke up once and you took a piss."

"I did."

"Yeah. But you went right back to sleep."

"Good grief. I've never been that drunk in my life."

"Probably the pills you popped."

"What?"

"Pills. You took them with the alcohol, when we were with the whores."

"Oh, hell."

"It's all right. Ever now and again you got to cut the tiger loose, you know. Don't worry. I got a cabin. That's where we're going. Don't worry. I'll take care of you. I mean, hell, what are friends for?"

## 》《

The bear didn't actually have a cabin, he had a fire tower, and it rose up high into the sky overlooking very tall trees. They had to climb a ladder up there, and the bear, sticking the automatic in his belt, sent Jim up first, said, "Got to watch those rungs. They get wet, iced over, your hand can slip. Forest Ranger I knew slipped right near the top. We had to dig what was left of him out of the ground. One of his legs went missing. I found it about a month later. It was cold when he fell so it kept pretty good. Wasn't bad, had it with some beans. Waste not, want not. Go on, man. Climb."

Inside the fire tower it was very nice, though cold. The bear turned on the electric heater and it wasn't long before the place was toasty.

The bear said, "There's food in the fridge. Shitter is over there. I'll sleep in my bed, and you sleep on the couch. This'll be great. We can hang. I got all kinds of movies, and as you can see, that TV is big enough for a drive-in theater. We ain't got no bitches, but hell, they're just trouble anyway. We'll just pull each other's wieners."

Jim said, "What now?"

"I don't stutter, boy. It ain't so bad. You just grease a fellow up and go to work."

"I don't know."

"Nah, you'll like it."

»«

**As night neared,** the light that came through the tower's wrap-around windows darkened and died, and Jim could already imagine grease on his hands.

But by then, the bear had wetted his whistle pretty good, drinking straight from a big bottle of Jack Daniel's. He wasn't as wiped out as before, not stumbling drunk, and his tongue still worked, but fortunately the greased weenie pull had slipped from the bear's mind. He sat on the couch with his bottle and Jim sat on the other end, and the bear said: "Once upon a goddamn time the bears roamed these forests and we were the biggest, baddest, meanest motherfuckers in the woods. That's no shit. You know that?"

Jim nodded.

"But, along come civilization. We had fires before that, I'm sure. You know, natural stuff. Lightning. Too dry. Natural combustion. But when man arrived, it was doo-doo time for the bears and everything else. I mean, don't take me wrong. I like a good meal and a beer," he held up the bottle, "and some Jack, and hanging out in this warm tower, but something has been sapped out of me. Some sort of savage beast that was in me has been tapped and run off into the ground... I was an orphan. Did you know that?"

"I've heard the stories," Jim said.

"Yeah, well, who hasn't? It was a big fire. I was young. Some arsonists. Damn fire raged through the forest and I got separated from my mom. Dad, he'd run off. But, you know, no biggie. That's how bears do. Well, anyway, I climbed a tree like a numb nuts cause my feet got burned, and I just clung and clung to that tree. And then I seen her, my mother. She was on fire. She ran this way and that, back and forth, and I'm yelling, 'Mama,' but she's not paying attention, had her own concerns. And pretty soon she goes down and the fire licks her all over and her fur is gone and there ain't nothing but a blackened hunk of smoking bear crap left. You know what it is to see a thing like that, me being a cub?"

"I can't imagine."

"No you can't. You can't. No one can. I had a big fall too. I don't really remember it, but it left a knot on the back of my head, just over the right ear... Come here. Feel that."

Jim dutifully complied.

The bear said, "Not too hard now. That knot, that's like my Achilles heel. I'm weak there. Got to make sure I don't bump my head too good. That's no thing to live with and that's why I'm not too fond of arsonists. There are several of them, what's left of them, buried not far from here. I roam these forests and I'll tell you, I don't just report them. Now and again, I'm not doing that. Just take care of business myself. Let me tell you, slick, there's a bunch of them that'll never squat over a commode again. They're out there, their gnawed bones buried deep. You know what it's like to be on duty all the time, not to be able to hibernate, just nap. It makes a bear testy. Want a cigar?"

"Beg your pardon?"

"A cigar. I know it's funny coming from me, and after what I just told you, but, we'll be careful here in my little nest."

Jim didn't answer. The bear got up and came back with two fat, black cigars. He had boxed matches with him. He gave Jim a cigar and Jim put it in his mouth, and the bear said, "Puff gently."

Jim did and the bear lit the end with a wooden match. The bear lit his own cigar. He tossed the box of matches to Jim. "If it goes out, you can light up again. Thing about a cigar is you take your time, just enjoy it, don't get into it like a whore sucking a dick. It's done casual. Pucker your mouth like your kissing a baby."

Jim puffed on the cigar but didn't inhale. The action of it made him feel high, and not too good, a little sick even. They sat and smoked. After a long while, the bear got up and opened one of the windows, said, "Come here."

Jim went. The woods were alive with sounds, crickets, night birds, howling.

"That's as it should be. Born in the forest, living there, taking game there, dying there, becoming one with the soil. But look at me. What the fuck have I become? I'm like a goddamn circus bear."

"You do a lot of good."

"For who though? The best good I've done was catching those arsonists that are buried out there. That was some good. I'll be straight with you, Jim. I'm happy you're going to be living here. I need a buddy, and, well, tag, you're it."

"Buddy."

"You heard me. Oh, the door, it's locked, and you can't work the lock from inside, cause it's keyed, and I got the key. So don't think about going anywhere."

"That's not very buddy-like," Jim said.

The bear studied Jim for a long moment, and Jim felt himself going weak. It was as if he could see the bear's psychosis move from one eye to another, like it was changing rooms. "But, you're still my buddy, aren't you Jim?"

Jim nodded.

"Well, I'm sort of bushed, so I think I'll turn in early. Tomorrow night we'll catch up on that weenie pull."

》《

When the bear went to the bedroom and lay down, Jim lay on the couch with the blanket and pillow the bear had left for him, and listened. The bear had left the bedroom door open, and after awhile he could hear the bear snoring like a lumberjack working a saw on a log.

Jim got up and eased around the tower and found that he could open windows, but there was nowhere to go from there except straight down, and that was one booger of a drop. Jim thought of how easily the bear had killed the whore and how he admitted to killing others, and then he thought about tomorrow night's weenie pull, and he became even more nervous.

After an hour of walking about and looking, he realized there was no way out. He thought about the key, but had no idea where the bear kept it. He feared if he went in the bear's room to look, he could startle the bear and that might result in getting his head chewed off. He decided to let it go. For now. Ultimately, pulling a greased bear weenie couldn't be as bad as being headless.

Jim went back to the couch, pulled the blanket over him and almost slept.

>> <<

Next morning, Jim, who thought he would never sleep, had finally drifted off, and what awoke him was not a noise, but the smell of food cooking. Waffles.

Jim sat up slowly. A faint pink light was coming through the window. The kitchenette area of the tower was open to view, part of the bigger room, and the bear was in there wearing an apron and a big chef hat. The bear turned and saw him. The apron had a slogan on it: If Mama Ain't Happy, Ain't Nobody Happy.

The bear spotted him, gave Jim a big-fanged, wet smile. "Hey, brother, how are you? Come on in here and sit your big ass down and have one of Mr. Bear's waffles. It's so good you'll want to slap your mama."

Jim went into the kitchenette, sat at the table where the bear instructed. The bear seemed in a light and cheery mood. Coffee was on the table, a plate stacked with waffles, big strips of bacon, pats of butter and a bottle of syrup in a plastic bear modeled after Mr. Bear himself.

"Now you wrap your lips around some of this stuff, see what you think."

While Jim ate the bear regaled him with all manner of stories about his life, and most were in fact interesting, but all Jim could think about was the bear biting the head off of that hooker, and then slashing the other with a strike of his mighty paw. As Jim ate, the tasty waffles with thick syrup became wads of blood and flesh in his mouth, and he felt as if he were eating of Mr. Bear's wine and wafer, his symbolic blood and flesh, and it made Jim's skin crawl.

All it would take to end up like the whores was to make a misstep. Say something wrong. Perhaps a misinterpreted look. A hesitation at tonight's weenie pull... Oh, damn, Jim thought. The weenie pull.

"What I thought we'd do, is we'd go for a drive, dump the car. There's a ravine I know where we can run it off, and no one will see it again. Won't even know it's missing. Excuse me while I go to the shitter. I think I just got word there's been a waffle delivery called."

The bear laughed at his own joke and left the room. Jim ate a bit more of the waffle and all the bacon. He didn't want the bear to think he wasn't grateful. The beast was psychotic. Anything could set him off.

Jim got up and washed his hands at the sink, and just as he was passing into the living room, he saw the gun they had found in the car lying on a big fluffy chair. Part of it, the barrel, had slipped into the crack in the cushions. Maybe the bear had forgotten all about it, or at least didn't have it at the forefront of his mind. That was it. He'd been drunker than a Shriner's convention. He probably didn't even remember having the gun.

Jim eased over and picked up the weapon and put it under his shirt, in the small of his back. He hoped he would know how to use it. He had seen them used before. If he could get up close enough—

"Now, that was some delivery. That motherfucker probably came with a fortune cookie and six-pack of Coke. I feel ten pounds lighter. You ready, Jimbo?"

»«

In the early morning the forests were dark and beautiful and there was a slight mist and with the window of the car rolled down, it was cool and damp and the world seemed newborn. But all Jim could think about was performing a greased weenie pull and then getting his head chewed off.

Jim said, "You get rid of the car, how do we get back?"

The bear laughed. "Just like a citizen. We walk, of course."

"We've gone quite a distance."

"It'll do you good. Blow out the soot. You'll like it. Great scenery. I'm gonna show you the graves where I buried what was left of them fellows, the arsonists."

"That's all right," Jim said. "I don't need to see that."

"I want you to. It's not like I can show everyone, but my bestest bud, that's a different matter, now ain't it?"

"Well, I don't..." Jim said.

"We're going to see it."

"Sure. Okay."

Jim had a sudden revelation. Maybe there never was going to be a weenie pull, and as joyful as that perception was, the alternative was worse. The bear was going to get rid of him. Didn't want to do it in his tower. You don't shit where you eat... Well, the bear might. But the idea was you kept your place clean of problems. This wasn't just a trip to dump the car, this was a death ride. The bear was going to kill him and leave him where the arsonists were. Jim felt his butt hole clench on the car seat.

They drove up higher and the woods grew thicker and the road turned off and onto a trail. The car bumped along for some miles until the trees overwhelmed everything but the trail, and the tree limbs were so thickly connected they acted as a kind of canopy overhead. They drove in deep shadow and there were spots where the shadows were broken by light and the light played across the trail in speckles and spots and birds shot across their view like feathered bullets, and twice there were deer in sight, bounding into the forest and disappearing like wraiths as the car passed.

They came to a curve and then a sharp rise and the bear drove up the rise. The trail played out, and still he drove. He came to a spot, near the peak of the hill, where the sun broke through, stopped the car and got out. Jim got out. They walked to the highest rise of the hill, and where they stood was a clean wide swath in the trees. Weeds and grass grew there. The grass was tall and mostly yellow but brown in places.

"Spring comes," the bear said. "There will be flowers, all along that path, on up to this hill, bursting all over it. This is my forest, Jim. All the dry world used to be a forest, or nearly was, but man has cut most of it down and that's done things to all of us and I don't think in the long run much of it is good. Before man, things had a balance, know what I mean? But man.... Oh, boy. He sucks. Like that fire that burned me. Arson. Just for the fun of it. Burned down my goddamn home, Jim. I was just a cub. Little. My mother dying like that... I always feel two to three berries short of a pie."

"I'm sorry."

"Aren't they all? Sorry. Boy, that sure makes it better, don't it. Shit." The bear paused and looked over the swath of meadow. He said, "Even with there having been snow, it's dry, and when it's dry, someone starts a fire, it'll burn. The snow don't mean a thing after it melts and the thirsty ground sucks it up, considering it's mostly been dry all year. That one little snow, it ain't nothing more than whipped cream on dry cake." The bear pointed down the hill. "That swath there, it would burn like gasoline on a shag carpet. I keep an eye out for those things. I try to keep this forest safe. It's a thankless and continuous job... Sometimes, I have to leave, get a bit of recreation...like the motel room...time with a friend."

"I see."

"Do you? The graves I told you about. They're just down the hill. You see, they were bad people, but sometimes, even good people end up down there, if they know things they shouldn't, and there have been a few."

"Oh," Jim said, as if he had no idea what the bear was talking about.

"I don't make friends easily, and I may seem a little insincere. Species problems, all that. Sometimes, even people I like, well... It doesn't turn out so well for them. Know what I'm saying?"

"I...I don't think so."

"I think you do. That motel room back there, those whores. I been at this for years. I'm not a serial killer or anything. Ones I kill deserve it. The people I work for. They know how I am. They protect me. How's it gonna be an icon goes to jail? That's what I am. A fuckin' icon. So, I kinda get a free ride, someone goes missing, you know. Guys in black, ones got the helicopters and the black cars. They clean up after me. They're my homies, know what I'm saying?"

"Not exactly."

"Let me nutshell it for you: I'm pretty much immune to prosecution. But you, well...kind of a loose end. There's a patch down there with your name on it, Jimbo. I put a shovel in the car early this morning while you were sleeping. It isn't personal, Jim. I like you. I do. I know that's cold comfort, but that's how it is."

The bear paused, took off his hat and removed a small cigar from the inside hat band and struck a match and took a puff, said, "Thing is though, I can't get to liking someone too good, cause—"

The snapping sound made the bear straighten up. He was still holding his hat in his paw, and he dropped it. He almost made a turn to look at Jim, who was now standing right by him holding the automatic to the bump on the bear's noggin'. The bear's legs went out. He stumbled and fell forward and went sliding down the hill on his face and chest, a bullet nestled snuggling in his brain.

Jim took a deep breath. He went down the hill and turned the bear's head using both hands, took a good look at him. He thought the bear didn't really look like any of the cartoon versions of him, and when he was on TV he didn't look so old. Of course, he had never looked dead before. The eyes had already gone flat and he could see his dim reflection in one of them. The bear's cigar was flattened against his mouth, like a coiled worm. Jim found the bear's box of matches and was careful to use a handkerchief from the bear's pants pocket to handle it. He struck the match and set the dry grass on fire, then stuck the match between the bear's claws on his left paw. The fire gnawed patiently at the grass, whipping up enthusiasm as the wind rose. Jim wiped down the automatic with his shirt tail and put it in the bear's right paw using the handkerchief, and pushed the bear's claw through the trigger guard, and closed the bear's paw around the weapon so it looked like he had shot himself.

Jim went back up the hill. The fire licked at the grass and caught some more wind and grew wilder, and then the bear got caught up in it as well, chewing his fur and cackling over his flesh like a crazed hag. The fire licked its way down the hill, and then the wind changed and Jim saw the fire climbing up toward him.

He got in the car and started and found a place where he could back it around. It took some work, and by the time he managed it onto the narrow trail, he could see the fire in the mirror, waving its red head in his direction.

Jim drove down the hill, trying to remember the route. Behind him, the fire rose up into the trees as if it were a giant red bird spreading its wings.

"Dumb bear," he said aloud, "ain't gonna be no weenie pull now, is there?" and he drove on until the fire was a just a small bright spot in the rearview mirror, and then it was gone and there was just the tall, dark forest that the fire had yet to find.

# THE OLD MAN IN THE MOTORIZED CHAIR

**M**y grandfather, Stubble Fine, used to work for the cops, but he didn't get along with them so he quit. He opened a detective agency, but he didn't much care for that, even though he was good at it. Well, to be honest, he was great at it. But he didn't care. At heart, he's lazy.

No man in my memory has more looked forward to retirement than my grandpa. And as it turned out, he pretty much had to retire. His legs played out and he spent his days in a motorized chair, in front of the television set. His wife, my grandma, left him early on, well before he retired, and she died of some kind of disease somewhere in Florida. We never met.

On the day I'm telling you about, I was visiting his house, which is a three-bedroom that looks a lot like the three-bedrooms along his street and across from it. He and I get along well enough, considering he doesn't really like much of anyone, and hates the human race in general.

But, I get my fill of him plenty quick, and I think the feeling is mutual, though it's more about his personality than about anything I might do or say.

I was pretty close to making my escape, as it was a Saturday, and I wanted to have a nice day on the town, maybe go to the mall, see if any good-looking women were hanging around, but fate took a hand.

Grandpa was watching his favorite channel, one about reptiles and insects and animals. He loved the episodes with alligators and lions, and especially snakes. The ones where adventurers went out and showed off poisonous snakes and told you about them and handled them in precarious and irresponsible ways to show you how knowledgeable they were. Grandpa watched primarily in hopes of seeing someone bit.

So he's settled in with a snake program, waiting on another, cause it's some kind of all-day snake marathon or such, and just as I'm about to put on my coat and go out into the winter cold, the doorbell rang.

Grandpa said, "Damn it."

I went over to the kitchen window for a look. The Sheriff's car was parked at the curb, and behind it was a big black SUV splattered on the sides and all over the tires with red mud. I went to the door and opened it.

Standing there beside Jim was a young woman, who was, to put it mildly, a stunner. She looked like a movie star to me, even though her hair was a little tussled, like she had just gotten out of bed. She was wearing jeans and those tall boots with the white fluff around the tops, and she had on a well-fitting dark jacket with the same white fluff around the collar.

I invited them into the house, said, "Grandpa, it's the Sheriff."

"Oh, hell," Grandpa said.

Jim looked at me. "Cranky today?"

"Everyday," I said.

"I heard that," Grandpa said. "I got my hearing aid in."

We went over to his chair. Grandpa said, "Today is the all-day snake marathon, and I don't want to miss it."

"This is kind of important," Jim said.

"So's the snake marathon," Grandpa said. "It shows next time six months from now. I may not be here then."

I thought: Now that's silly. If you're not here, you're not gonna miss not seeing it.

Grandpa turned his head slightly, looked at me, and said, "I still want to see it."

"I didn't say anything," I said.

"Yeah, but you were smiling, like what I said was silly."

"It is," I said. "Why don't you just record it and watch it when you want?"

"Don't have a recorder."

"I bought you one for Christmas."

"That's what's in the box?"

"That would be it. I'll hook it up."

"Not today you won't."

"Well, it's still silly," I said.

"Not to me," Grandpa said. He put the TV on mute, looked at Jim, said, "Well, get on with it."

"Mr. Fine. Good to see you," Jim said, reaching out to shake hands. As he did, Grandpa sniffed, and smiled.

"Call me Stubble or Stubbs. It's not that I feel all that close to you, but Mr. Fine makes me feel more senior than I like. Besides, I see you from time to time. So we know one another."

"Very well, Stubbs—"

"Wait a minute," Grandpa said. "Never mind. Call me Mr. Fine. It sounds better coming out of your mouth."

"Okay, Mr. Fine."

"What's the problem," Grandpa said. He said it like a man who might already know the problem. But that's how he was, a know-it-all, who, much of the time, seemed in fact to actually know it all.

"This is Cindy Cornbluth," Jim said. "Her husband is missing. I had her follow me here to see if you could help us out. I know how you can figure things, how you can notice things the rest of us don't... Like... Well, you know, there was that time with the murders in the old theater."

"And all those other times," Grandpa said.

"Yes," Jim said, "and all those other times."

Cindy leaned forward and smiled a smile that would have knocked a bird out of a tree, and shook hands with Grandpa. I thought he held her hand a little too long. Before he let it go, he gave her face a good look, and when she stepped back, he gave her a good once-over. If he thought what I thought, that she was as fine a looking woman as had ever walked the earth, he didn't let on. His face looked as sour as ever.

"Give me the facts, and make it short," Grandpa said. "They got a round-up of the top ten most poisonous snakes coming on next, in about fifteen minutes"

"Jimmy... Sheriff. He can't possibly help us in fifteen minutes," Cindy said.

"That's how much time you got," Grandpa said. "You already made me miss the part about where one of the snake wranglers gets bit in the face."

"You've seen this before?" Jim asked.

"He has," I said. "But he never tapes it. Won't hook up the machine. He likes to symbolically capture the program in the wild."

"They got this one snake," Grandpa said, "bites this fool messin' with it, and they can't get its teeth out. It won't let go. The guy is going green, even as you watch."

"You enjoy that?" Jim said.

"Oh yeah," Grandpa said. "Rule of thumb. Don't mess with venomous snakes. Okay now, tell me what happened. Chop, chop."

"I woke up this morning," Cindy said, "and Bert was gone. That's my husband. I don't know where. I didn't think much of it. I thought he might be surprising me with doughnuts."

"Doughnuts?"

She nodded.

"He do that often?" Grandpa asked.

"Now and again," she said.

"So, Saturday, that's his day off?"

"Not usually. But he decided not to go into work today. He can do that when he wants. He owns his own business. Construction."

"Heard of it," Grandpa said. "Cornbluth Construction. Got some big deals lately. Saw it on the news."

"That's right," Cindy said.

"Would you say he's wealthy?" Grandpa asked. "That the two of you are wealthy?"

"He's been fortunate," Cindy said.

"So, tell me the rest of it."

"I got up this morning, he wasn't home, and I waited around until noon. Then I called the Sheriff. I was worried by then."

"Did you think he might have gone into work?"

"No. It didn't cross my mind."

Grandpa looked down at Cindy's feet. "Nice boots."

"Thanks," Cindy said, and looked at Jim perplexed. Jim smiled. He knew how Grandpa was, knew he had roundabout ways, provided he was in the mood to help at all.

Grandpa called me over, said, "Get your digital camera, go out to her car—" He paused, looked at Cindy. "I did hear right that you followed Jim over?"

"That's right," she said, "but what has that got to do with anything?"

"Maybe nothing," he said. "Get photos of the car, all around."

I found the camera and went out and took photos of the car. When I came back in, I leaned over Grandpa's shoulder and he looked at the digital photos. He took off his glasses and rubbed his eyes and sighed. He put them back on, glanced at the TV and pointed.

"That's a black mamba," Grandpa said.

"What?" Cindy said.

"The snake," Grandpa said pointing at the silent TV. "Very deadly. Hides in the grass, and then, BAM, it's got you. You're dead before you can say, 'Oh hell, I'm snake bit.'"

Grandpa said to me, "Grandson, turn up the heat."

I thought it was pretty warm, but I did as instructed.

"So, you two," Grandpa said to Cindy and Jim, "did you know each other before today?"

"Yes," Jim said. "In high school."

"Date?"

"Once or twice," Jim said. "Just a kid thing. Nothing came of it."

He looked at Cindy, and she smiled like a woman who knew she was beautiful and was a little ashamed of it, but...not really.

Grandpa nodded. "You know, the dirt around here is white. Except up on Pine Ridge Hill. The oil company did some drilling up there, and it was a bust. I heard about it on the news. They had to close it down. They say the old ground up there is unstable, that it's shifting, that a lot of it is going down the holes that were meant for oil drilling. It's like a big sink hole up there, a bunch of them actually. Saw that on the news, too."

"Okay," Jim said, "But, Mr. Fine, so what?"

"Here's the deal. Cindy has a rough place on her hand. Felt it when we shook. But I'll come back to that. She's also got red clay on her boots. The left one. I think she may have stomped some of it off, but there's still a touch on the toe, and a bit she's tracked in on the floor. So, she's been out there to the old oil site. I believe that she's got a bit of pine needle in her hair too, twisted up under the wave there, where it got caught in a tree limb."

Jim leaned over for a look. I gave it a hard look from where I was standing as well. Didn't that old codger wear glasses? How in the world had he noticed that?

"I drove up there the other day," she said. "I was looking for pine cones, to make decorations. I haven't washed my hair since then. I was hanging around the house, didn't have anywhere to go."

"Gonna spray them pine cones gold, silver?" Grandpa asked, not looking away from the TV.

"I don't know," she said. "Something like that."

"On your earlobe there's a dark spot. Noticed it when we shook hands. I'll come back to that"

Jim gave that a look too, said, "Yeah. I see it." Then, appearing puzzled, he unfastened his coat, took it off, dropped it over the back of a chair.

Grandpa grinned. "Warm, son?"

"A little," Jim said.

"Well now, Jim," Grandpa said. "I've known you a long time. Since you were a boy."

"Yes, sir."

"I believe you're a good man, but she didn't call you this morning. She lied and you let her."

"Now wait a minute," Jim said.

"When you shook hands with me I smelled her perfume on your coat. A lot of it. I don't think Sheriffs are in the habit of comforting women with missing husbands with a hug so intense it gets on their coat, and in their hair. And she called you Jimmy."

"Well, we know each other," Jim said. "And I did comfort her."

"Another thing. There's what we used to call a hickey on your neck."

Jim slapped at his neck as if a mosquito had bitten him.

"Not really. Just kidding. But here's what I think. I think you've been having an affair. If she had called the Sheriff's office to get in touch with you, and the two of you were not an item, you wouldn't have come to me right away. You were hoping it was simple and I could solve it without involving the Sheriff's Department. That's why you had her follow you in her car, so she wouldn't be in your car.

"And Mrs. Cornbluth, that smile you gave me, the one that was supposed to make me weak in the knees. That seemed out of place for the situation."

"People respond in different ways," she said.

"Yes, they do," he said. "I give you that much. Would you like to take your coat off?"

"I'm fine."

"No you're not. You're sweating. In fact, it's too hot in here. Grandson, turn down the heater, will you."

"But you just told me—"

"Cut it down," Grandpa said.

I went over and did just that.

"When you and me shook hands," Grandpa said, "there was a fresh rough spot on your palm. That's because your hands are delicate, and they held something heavy earlier today, and when you struck out with it, hitting your husband in the head with whatever you were using... A fire poker perhaps? It twisted in your hand and made that minor wound."

"That's ridiculous," Cindy said.

"It certainly is," Jim said, "Okay, Mr. Fine. Me and Cindy had a thing going, but that doesn't mean she killed her husband."

Grandpa said. "Jim, you came by her house. Just like you were supposed to. I don't mean you had anything having to do with Mr. Cornbluth, but Cindy was expecting you. You had a date with her because Bert was supposed to be at work, but when you showed for your date, she told you he had stayed home, and she hadn't been able to reach you, and now he was missing and she was worried. That it wasn't like him. Right?"

"How could you know that?" Jim said.

"I guessed a little, but all the other facts line up. After she hit her husband in the head with something or another, she wiped up quick."

"But why would I kill him?" Cindy said.

"That's between you and your husband, but if you were having an affair, it might be you weren't that fond of him, and he found out, and you didn't want to lose all that money, and thought if the body wasn't found, you'd get insurance money and no jail time. The murder was quick and spontaneous, done in anger, and afterward, because Jim was coming, you had to do on-the-spot thinking, and it was stupid thinking.

"You drove the body out to the old oil well site this morning, dumped it, drove back and cleaned the car, the house, and maybe you were cleaning yourself when Jim showed up. You had to wipe yourself down quick. But that spot of blood on your ear. You missed that. And one more thing, Mrs. Cornbluth. You're sweating. A lot. That's why I turned up the heat. To see if you'd take your coat off on your own. You didn't. That made me think you had something to hide. Like maybe the blood that splashed on you from the murder wasn't just a drop on your ear, and you didn't have time to change before Jim showed up. So, you threw a coat on over it. Was she wearing it in the house when you showed, Jim?"

Jim nodded, looked at her. He said, "Cindy. Take off your coat."

"Jim, I don't want to."

"Jim isn't asking. The Sheriff is. Take it off."

Cindy slowly removed her coat. She was wearing a gray, tight-fitting wool sweater. There were dark patches.

Grandpa said, "Those wet spots on her sweater. I think if you check them, you'll find they're blood. And if you check up at the old oil site on Pine Ridge Hill, you'll find her husband at the bottom of one of those holes. You know, they were supposed to fill those in next week. If they had, good chance that body would never have been found. That's how you got the pine straw in your hair, wasn't it? When you were draggin' Bert from the car, through the pines, to the top of the hill? And Jim, when it all comes out, that you were dallying with a married woman, while on the job... Well, I hope you keep your job."

"Yeah, me too," Jim said taking out a pair of cuffs. "Put your hands behind your back, Cindy."

"Jim. You don't have to do this. Bert found out about us—"

"Shut up! Just shut up. Put your hands behind your back. Now."

She did. He handcuffed her. She looked at Grandpa. "I hate you, you old bastard."

As they went out the front door, which I held open for them, Grandpa said, "Lots do."

Grandpa turned up the sound on the TV. Just in time. The countdown of the world's most poisonous snakes was just about to begin.

# APACHE WITCH

In the wild country where the West wind blows,
the demon of the desert comes and goes.
Dark like a shadow, a mouth full of blood,
there's nothing out there but it and the dead.

Lives in a cave near a dark red butte,
hides there by magic, in an old cavalry boot.
Released by a spell from an Apache witch,
it twists and it turns and howls like a bitch.

Lizards and coyotes, buzzards and men,
it kills and kills, again and again.
But kill it must, and each night it comes,
until a cowpoke arrives with a lamp and a gun.

The lamp is lit with oil from a dog,
and around the cowpoke's neck,
on a string of braided gut
is a dried up frog and a hickory nut.

The rifle is packed with bullets of silver and lead,
little charms buried deep in the ammo heads.
An Apache woman, the witch's daughter, the cowpoke's wife,
made it to save her husband's life.

So Apache magic meets head on.
The demon whirls with a desert song.
The cowboy fires his gun and throws his lamp.
The demon roars and the night turns damp.

Out of a cloud against a moonlit sky,
comes a rain of black lumps like a cobbler pie.
It blows and it whirls and it twists and it turns,
and when it hits the demon it smokes and it burns.

The cowpoke's magic makes the demon cry.
It even melts the damn thing's eyes.
The rain on the cowpoke is heavy and wet,
but for the demon it's the worst thing yet.

The demon becomes a twirl of smoke.
and the cowpoke laughs like it's all a joke.
On his way home he yells and he cries,
for the demon was made of his poor child's sighs.

The baby's breath stolen by a cat
that was black as the pit and little pig fat.
The Apache witch sucked the baby's soul,
because his daughter made the child in a soldier's bed roll.

So stealing a boot
and casting a spell,
the witch had wrecked vengence
so very well.

Wearing moon silver
like armor and mail,
the former soldier,
rode home to his wife.

They dried their tears and climbed in bed,
the stars at their window,
the wind at their door,
the howl of the coyote like the call of the dead.

They came together in a tearful wail,
loved one another with all their might,
tried to make a child that very night,
did what they could to set themselves right.

Back on the desert,
next day in the sun,
the Apache witch man
was dead and done.

Found at the mouth of a cave near an army boot,
the witch man was burned and wadded,
with a hole in his chest,
the demon of the desert had left its nest.

# SOLDIERIN'

They said if you went out West and joined up with the colored soldiers they'd pay you in real Yankee dollars, thirteen of them a month, feed and clothe you, and it seemed like a right smart idea since I was wanted for a lynchin'. It wasn't that I was invited to hold the rope or sing a little spiritual, I was the guest of honor on this one. They was plannin' to stretch my neck like a goozle-wrung chicken at Sunday dinner.

Thing I'd done was nothin' on purpose, but in a moment of eyeballin' while walkin' along the road on my way to cut some firewood for a nickel and a jar of jam, a white girl who was hangin' out wash bent over and pressed some serious butt up against her gingham, and a white fella, her brother, seen me take a look, and that just crawled all up in his ass and died, and he couldn't stand the stink.

Next thing I know, I'm wanted for being bold with a white girl, like maybe I'd broke into her yard and jammed my arm up her ass, but I hadn't done nothin' but what's natural, which is glance at a nice butt when it was available to me.

Now, in the livin' of my life, I've killed men and animals and made love to three Chinese women on the same night in the same bed and one of them with only one leg, and part of it wood, and I even ate some of a dead fella once when I was crossin' the mountains, though I want to rush in here and make it clear I didn't know him all that well, and we damn sure wasn't kin folks. Another thing I did was I won me a shootin' contest up Colorady way against some pretty damn famous shooters, all white boys, but them's different stories and not even akin to the one I want to tell, and I'd like to add, just like them other events, this time I'm talking about is as true as the sunset.

Pardon me. Now that I've gotten older, sometimes I find I start out to tell one story and end up tellin' another. But to get back to the one I was talkin' about... So, havin' been invited to a lynchin', I took my daddy's horse and big ole loaded six gun he kept wrapped up in an oil cloth from under the floorboards of our shack, and took off like someone had set my ass on fire. I rode that poor old horse till he was slap worn out. I had to stop over in a little place just outside of Nacogdoches and steal another one, not on account of I was a thief, but on account of I didn't want to get caught by the posse and hung and maybe have my pecker cut off and stuck in my mouth. Oh. I also took a chicken. He's no longer with me, of course, as I ate him out there on the trail.

Anyway, I left my horse for the fella I took the fresh horse and the chicken from, and I left him a busted pocket watch on top of the railing post, and then I rode out to West Texas. It took a long time for me to get there, and I had to stop and steal food and drink from creeks and make sure the horse got fed with corn I stole. After a few days I figured I'd lost them that was after me, and I changed my name as I rode along. It had been Wiliford P. Thomas, the P not standing for a thing other than P. I chose the name Nat Wiliford for myself, and practiced on saying it while I rode along. When I said it, I wanted it to come out of my mouth like it wasn't a lie.

Before I got to where I was goin', I run up against this colored fella taking a dump in the bushes, wiping his ass on leaves. If I had been a desperado, I could have shot him out from over his pile and taken his horse, cause he was deeply involved in the event, so much in fact, that I could see his eyes were crossed from where I rode up on a hill, and that was some distance.

I was glad I was downwind, and hated to interrupt, so I sat on my stolen horse until he was leaf wiping, and then I called out. "Hello, the shitter."

He looked up and grinned at me, touched his rifle lying on the ground beside him, said, "You ain't plannin' on shootin' me are you?"

"No. I thought about stealin' your horse, but it looks worse than mine, except yours is swayback and is ugly in the face."

"Yeah, and it's blind in one eye and has a knot on its back comes right through the saddle. When I left the plantation, I took that horse. Wasn't much then, and it's a lot less now."

He stood up and fastened his pants and I seen then that he was a pretty big fellow, all decked out in fresh-looking overalls and a big black hat with a feather in it. He came walkin' up the hill toward me, his wipin' hand stuck out for a shake, but I politely passed, because I thought his fingers looked a little brown.

Anyway, we struck it up pretty good, and by nightfall we found a creek, and he washed his hands in the water with some soap from his saddlebag, which made me feel a mite better. We sat and had coffee and some of his biscuits. All I could offer was some conversation, and he had plenty to give back. His name was Cullen, but he kept referrin' to himself as The Former House Nigger, as if it were a rank akin to general. He told a long story about how he got the feather for his hat, but it mostly just came down to he snuck up on a hawk sittin' on a low limb and jerked it out of its tail.

"When my master went to war against them Yankees," he said, "I went with him. I fought with him and wore me a butter-nut coat and pants, and I shot me at least a half dozen of them Yankees."

"Are you leaking brains out of your gourd?" I said. "Them rebels was holdin' us down."

"I was a house nigger, and I grew up with Mr. Gerald, and I didn't mind going to war with him. Me and him was friends. There was lots of us like that."

"Y'all must have got dropped on your head when you was young'ns."

"The Master and the older Master was all right."

"'Cept they owned you," I said.

"Maybe I was born to be owned. They always quoted somethin' like that out of the Bible."

"That ought to have been your clue, fella. My daddy always said that book has caused more misery than chains, an ill-tempered woman and a nervous dog."

"I loved young Master like a brother, truth be known. He got shot in the war, right 'tween the eyes by a musket ball, killed him deader than a goddamn tree stump. I sopped up his blood in a piece of his shirt I cut off, mailed it back home with a note on what happened. When the war was over, I stayed around the plantation for awhile, but everything come apart then, the old man and the old lady died, and I buried them out back of the place a good distance from the privy and up hill, I might add. That just left me and the Old Gentleman's dog.

"The dog was as old as death and couldn't eat so good, so I shot it, and went on out into what young Master called The Big Wide World. Then, like you, I heard the guv-ment was signing up coloreds for its man's army. I ain't no good on my own. I figured the army was for me."

"I don't like being told nothin' by nobody," I said, "but I surely love to get paid." I didn't mention I also didn't want to get killed by angry crackers and the army seemed like a good place to hide.

>><<

About three days later we rode up on the place we was looking for. Fort McKavett, between the Colorady and the Pecos rivers. It was a sight, that fort. It was big and it didn't look like nothin' I'd ever seen before. Out front was colored fellas in army blue drilling on horseback, looking sharp in the sunlight, which there was plenty of. It was hot where I come from, sticky even, but you could find a tree to get under. Out here, all you could get under was your hat, or maybe some dark cloud sailing across the face of the sun, and that might last only as long as it takes a bird to fly over.

But there I was. Fort McKavett. Full of dreams and crotch itch from long riding. Me and my new friend sat on our horses lookin' the fort over, watchin' them horse soldiers drill, and it was prideful thing to see. We rode on down in that direction.

》《

In the Commanding Officer's quarters, me and The Former House Nigger stood before a big desk with a white man behind it, name of Colonel Hatch. He had a caterpillar mustache and big sweat circles like wet moons under his arms. His eyes were aimed on a fly sitting on some papers on his desk. Way he was watchin' it, you'd have thought he was beading down on a hostile. He said, "So you boys want to sign up for the colored army. I figured that, you both being colored."

He was a sharp one, this Hatch.

I said, "I've come to sign up and be a horse rider in the Ninth Cavalry."

Hatch studied me for a moment, said, "Well, we got plenty of ridin' niggers. What we need is walkin' niggers for the goddamn infantry, and I can get you set in the right direction to hitch up with them."

I figured anything that was referred to with goddamn in front of it, wasn't the place for me.

"I reckon ain't a man here can ride better'n me," I said, "and that would be even you, Colonel, and I'm sure you are one ridin' sonofabitch, and I mean that in as fine a way as I can say it."

Hatch raised an eyebrow. "That so?"

"Yes, sir. No brag, just fact. I can ride on a horse's back, under his belly, make him lay down and make him jump, and at the end of the day, I take a likin' to him, I can diddle that horse in the ass and make him enjoy it enough to brew my coffee and bring my slippers, provided I had any. That last part about the diddlin' is just talkin', but the first part is serious."

"I figured as much," Hatch said.

"I ain't diddlin' no horses," The Former House Nigger said. "I can cook and lay out silverware. Mostly, as a Former House Nigger, I drove the buggy."

At that moment Hatch come down on that fly with his hand, and he got him too. He peeled him off his palm and flicked him on the floor. There was this colored soldier standing nearby, very stiff and alert, and he bent over, picked the fly up by a bent wing, threw it out the door and came back. Hatch wiped his palm on his pants leg. "Well," he said, "let's see how much of what you got is fact, and how much is wind."

>> <<

They had a corral nearby, and inside it, seeming to fill it up, was a big black horse that looked like he ate men and shitted out saddlebags made of their skin and bones. He put his eye right on me when I came out to the corral, and when I walked around on the other side, he spun around to keep a gander on me. Oh, he knew what I was about all right.

Hatch took hold of one corner of his mustache and played with it, turned and looked at me. "You ride that horse well as you say you can, I'll take both of you into the cavalry, and The Former House Nigger can be our cook."

"I said I could cook," The Former House Nigger said. "Didn't say I was any good."

"Well," Hatch said, "what we got now ain't even cookin'. There's just a couple fellas that boil water and put stuff in it. Mostly turnips."

I climbed up on the railing, and by this time, four colored cavalry men had caught up the horse for me. That old black beast had knocked them left and right, and it took them a full twenty minutes to get a bridle and a saddle on him, and when they come off the field, so to speak, two was limpin' like they had one foot in a ditch. One was holding his head where he had been kicked, and the other looked amazed he was alive. They had tied the mount next to the railin', and he was hoppin' up and down like a little girl with a jump rope, only a mite more vigorous.

"Go ahead and get on," Hatch said.

Having bragged myself into a hole, I had no choice.

## 》《

I wasn't lyin' when I said I was a horse rider. I was. I could buck them and make them go down on their bellies and roll on their sides, make them strut and do whatever, but this horse was as mean as home-made sin, and I could tell he had it in for me.

Soon as I was on him, he jerked his head and them reins snapped off the railing and I was clutchin' at what was left of it. The sky came down on my head as that horse leaped. Ain't no horse could leap like that, and soon me and him was trying to climb the clouds. I couldn't tell earth from heaven, cause we bucked all over that goddamn lot, and ever time that horse come down it jarred my bones from butt to skull. I come out of the saddle a few times, nearly went off the back of him, but I hung in there, tight as tick on a dog's nuts. Finally he jumped himself out and started to roll. He went down on one side, mashing my leg in the dirt, and rolled on over. Had that dirt in the corral not been tamped down and soft, giving with me, there wouldn't been nothing left of me but a sack of blood and broken bones.

Finally the horse humped a couple of sad bucks and gave out, started to trot and snort. I leaned over close to his ear and said, "You call that buckin'?" He seemed to take offense at that, and run me straight to the corral and hit the rails there with his

chest. I went sailin' off his back and landed on top of some soldiers, scatterin' them like quail.

Hatch come over and looked down on me, said, "Well, you
ain't smarter than the horse, but you can ride well enough. You
and The Former House Nigger are in with the rest of the ridin'
niggers. Trainin' starts in the morning."

》《

We drilled with the rest of the recruits up and down that
lot, and finally outside and around the fort until we was looking pretty smart. The horse they give me was that black devil I
had ridden. I named him Satan. He really wasn't as bad as I first
thought. He was worse, and you had to be at your best every time
you got on him, cause deep down in his bones he was always
thinking about killing you, and if you didn't watch it, he'd kind
of act causal, like he was watching a cloud or somethin', and
quickly turn his head and take a nip out of your leg, if he could
bend far enough to get to it.

Anyway, the months passed, and we drilled, and my buddy
cooked, and though what he cooked wasn't any good, it was better than nothin'. It was a good life as compared to being hung,
and there was some real freedom to it and some respect. I wore
my uniform proud, set my horse like I thought I was somethin'
special with a stick up its ass.

We mostly did a little patrollin', and wasn't much to it except
ridin' around lookin' for wild Indians we never did see, collectin'
our thirteen dollars at the end of the month, which was just so
much paper cause there wasn't no place to spend it. And then, one
mornin', things changed, and wasn't none of it for the better, except
The Former House Nigger managed to cook a pretty good breakfast
with perfect fat biscuits and eggs with the yolks not broke and
some bacon that wasn't burned and nobody got sick this time.

On that day Hatch mostly rode around with us, cause at the
bottom of it all, I reckon the government figured we was just

a bunch of ignorant niggers who might at any moment have a watermelon relapse and take to getting drunk and shootin' each other and maybe trying to sing a spiritual while we diddled the horses, though I had sort of been responsible for spreadin' the last part of that rumor on my first day at the fort. We was all itchin' to show we had somethin' to us that didn't have nothin' to do with no white fella ridin' around in front of us, though I'll say right up front Hatch was a good soldier who led and didn't follow, and he was polite too. I had seen him leave the circle of the fire to walk off in the dark to fart. You can't say that about just anyone. Manners out on the frontier was rare.

## » «

You'll hear from the army how we was all a crack team, but this wasn't so, at least not when they was first sayin' it. Most of the army at any time, bein' they the ridin' kind or the walkin' kind, ain't all that crack. Some of them fellas didn't know a horse's ass end from the front end, and this was pretty certain when you seen how they mounted, swinging into the stirrups, finding themselves looking at the horse's tail instead of his ears. But in time everyone got better, though I'd like to toss in, without too much immodesty, that I was the best rider of the whole damn lot. Since he'd had a good bit of experience, The Former House Nigger was the second. Hell, he'd done been in war and all, so in ways, he had more experience than any of us, and he cut a fine figure on a horse, being tall and always alert, like he might have to bring somebody a plate of something or hold a coat.

Only action we'd seen was when one of the men, named Rutherford, got into it with Prickly Pear—I didn't name him, that come from his mother—and they fought over a biscuit. While they was fightin', Colonel Hatch come over and ate it, so it was a wasted bout.

But this time I'm tellin' you about, we rode out lookin' for Indians to scare, and not seein' any we quit lookin' for what we couldn't find, and come to a little place down by a creek where it was wooded and there was a shade from a whole bunch of trees that in that part of the country was thought of as being big, and in my part of the country would have been considered scrubby. I was glad when we stopped to water the horses and take a little time to just wait. Colonel Hatch, I think truth be told, was glad to get out of that sun much as the rest of us. I don't know how he felt, being a white man and having to command a bunch of colored, but he didn't seem bothered by it a'tall, and seemed proud of us and himself, which, of course, made us all feel mighty good.

So we waited out there on the creek, and Hatch, he come over to where me and The Former House Nigger were sitting by the water, and we jumped to attention, and he said, "There's a patch of scrub oaks off the creek, scattering out there across the grass, and they ain't growin' worth a damn. Them's gonna be your concern. I'm gonna take the rest of the troop out across the ground there, see if we can pick up some deer trails. I figure ain't no one gonna mind if we pot a few and bring them back to camp. And besides, I'm bored. But we could use some firewood, and I was wantin' you fellas to get them scrubs cut down and sawed up and ready to take back to the fort. Stack them in here amongst the trees, and I'll send out some men with a wagon when we get back, and have that wood hauled back before it's good and dark. I thought we could use some oak to smoke the meat I'm plannin' on gettin'. That's why I'm the goddamn colonel. Always thinkin'."

"What if you don't get no meat?" one of the men with us said.

"Then you did some work for nothin', and I went huntin' for nothin'. But, hell, I seen them deer with my binoculars no less than five minutes ago. Big fat deer, about a half dozen of them running along. They went over the hill. I'm gonna take the rest of the troops with me in case I run into hostiles, and because I don't like to do no skinnin' of dead deer myself."

"I like to hunt," I said.

"That's some disappointin' shit for you," Colonel Hatch said. "I need you here. In fact, I put you in charge. You get bit by a snake and die, then, you, The Former House Nigger take over. I'm also gonna put Rutherford, Bill and Rice in your charge...some others. I'll take the rest of them. You get that wood cut up, you start on back to the fort and we'll send out a wagon."

"What about Indians?" Rutherford, who was nearby, said.

"You seen any Indians since you been here?" Hatch said.

"No, sir."

"Then there ain't no Indians."

"You ever see any?" Rutherford asked Hatch.

"Oh, hell yeah. Been attacked by them, and I've attacked them. There's every kind of Indian you can imagine out here from time to time. Kiowa. Apache. Comanche. And there ain't nothin' they'd like better than to have your prickly black scalps on their belts, cause they find your hair funny. They think it's like the buffalo. They call you buffalo soldiers on account of it."

"I thought it was because they thought we was brave like buffalo," I said.

"That figures," Hatch said. "You ain't seen no action for nobody to have no opinion of you. But, we ain't seen an Indian in ages, and ain't seen no sign of them today. I'm startin' to think they've done run out of this area. But, I've thought that before. And Indians, especially a Comanche or an Apache, they're hard to get a handle on. They'll get after somethin' or someone like it matters more than anything in the world, and then they'll wander off if a bird flies over and they make an omen of it."

Leaving us with them mixed thoughts on Indians and buffalo, Hatch and the rest of the men rode off, left us standing in the shade, which wasn't no bad place to be. First thing we did when they was out of sight was throw off our boots and get in the water. I finally just took all my clothes off and cleaned up pretty good with a bar of lye soap and got dressed. Then leaving the horses tied up in the trees near the creek, we took the mule and the equipment strapped on his back, carried our rifles, and went out to where them scrubs was. On the way, we cut down a couple of saplings and trimmed some limbs, and made us a kind of pull that we could fasten on to the mule. We figured we'd fill it up with wood and get the mule to drag it back to the creek, pile it and have it ready for the wagon.

Rigged up, we went to work, taking turns with the saw, two other men working hacking off limbs, one man axing the trimmed wood up so it fit good enough to load. We talked while we worked, and Rutherford said, "Them Indians, some of them is as mean as snakes. They do all kind of things to folks. Cut their eyelids off, cook them over fires, cut off their nut sacks and such. They're just awful."

"Sounds like some Southerners I know," I said.

"My Master and his family was darn good to me," The Former House Nigger said.

"They might have been good to you," Rice said, pausing at the saw, "but that still don't make you no horse, no piece of property. You a man been treated like a horse, and you too dumb to know it."

The Former House Nigger bowed up like he was about to fight. I said, "Now, don't do it. He's just talkin'. I'm in charge here, and you two get into it, I'll get it from Hatch, and I don't want that, and won't have it."

Rice tilted his hat back. His face looked dark as coffee. "I'm gonna tell you true. When I was sixteen, I cut my master's throat and raped his wife and run off to the North."

"My God," The Former House Nigger said. "That's awful."

"And I made the dog suck my dick," Rice said.

"What?" The Former House Nigger said.

"He's funnin' you,' I said.

"That part about the master's throat," Rice said, "and runnin' off to the North. I really did that. I would have raped his wife, but there wasn't any time. His dog didn't excite me none."

"You are disgustin'," The Former House Nigger said, pausing from his job of trimming limbs with a hatchet.

"Agreed," I said.

Rice chuckled, and went back to sawin' with Rutherford. He had his shirt off and the muscles in his back bunched up like prairie dogs tunnelin', and over them mounds was long, thick scars. I knew them scars. I had a few. They had been made with a whip.

Bill, who was stackin' wood, said, "Them Indians. Ain't no use hatin' them. Hatin' them for bein' what they is, is like hatin' a bush cause it's got thorns on it. Hatin' a snake cause it'll bite you. They is what they is just like we is what we is."

"And what is we?" The Former House Nigger said.

"Ain't none of us human beings no 'count. The world is just one big mess of no 'counts, so there ain't no use pickin' one brand of man or woman over the other. Ain't none of them worth a whis-tlin' fart."

"Ain't had it so good, have you, Bill?" I asked.

"I was a slave."

"We all was," I said.

"Yeah, but, I didn't take it so good. Better'n Rutherford, but not so good. I was in the northern army, right there at the end when they started lettin' colored in, and I killed and seen men killed. Ain't none of my life experience give me much of a glow about folks of any kind. I even killed buffalo just for the tongues rich folks wanted to have. We left hides and meat in the fields to rot. That was to punish the Indians. Damned ole buffalo. Ain't nothin' dumber, and I shot them for dollars and their tongues. What kind of human beings does that?"

>><<

We worked for about another hour, and then, Dog Den— again, I didn't name him—one of the other men Hatch left with us, said, "I think we got a problem."

On the other side of the creek, there was a split in the trees, and you could see through them out into the plains and you could see the hill Hatch had gone over some hours ago, and comin' running across them was a white man. He was a good distance away, but it didn't take no eagle eye to see that he was naked as a skinned rabbit, and runnin' full out, and behind him, whoopin' and have a good time, were Indians. Apache, to be right on the money, nearly as naked as the runnin' man. Four of them was on horseback, and there was six of them I could see on foot runnin' after him. My guess was they had done been at him and had set him loose to chase him like a deer for fun. I guess livin' out on the plains like they did, with nothin' but mesquite berries and what food they could kill, you had to have your fun where you could find it.

"They're funnin' him," Rutherford said, figurin' same as me.

We stood there lookin' for a moment, then I remembered we was soldiers. I got my rifle and was about to bead down, when Rutherford said, "Hell, you can't hit them from here, and neither can they shoot you. We're out of range, and Indians ain't no shots to count for."

One of the runnin' Apaches had spotted us, and he dropped to one knee and pointed his rifle at us, and when he did, Rutherford spread his arms wide, and said, "Go on, shoot, you heathen."

The Apache fired.

Rutherford was wrong. He got it right on the top of the nose and fell over with his arms still spread. When he hit the ground, The Former House Nigger said, "I reckon they been practicin'."

## 》《

We was up on a hill, so we left the mule and run down to the creek where the horses was, and waded across the little water and laid out between the trees and took aim. We opened up and it sounded like a bunch of mule skinners crackin' their whips. The air filled with smoke and there was some shots fired back at us. I looked up and seen the runnin' man was makin' right smart time, his hair and johnson flappin' as he run. But then one of the horseback Apaches rode up on him, and with this heavy knotted-looking stick he was carrying, swung and clipped the white fella along the top of the head. I seen blood jump up and the man go down and I could hear the sound of the blow so well I winced. The Apache let out a whoop and rode on past, right toward us. He stopped to beat his chest with his free hand, and when he did, I took a shot at him. I aimed for his chest, but I hit the horse square in the head and brought him down. At least I had the heathen on foot.

Now, you can say what you want about an Apache, but he is about the bravest thing there is short of a badger. This'n come runnin' right at us, all of us firin' away, and I figure he thought he had him some big magic, cause not a one of our shots hit him. It was like he come haint-like right through a wall of bullets. As he got closer, I could see he had some kind of mud paint on his chest and face, and he was whoopin' and carryin' on somethin' horrible. And then he stepped in a hole and went down. Though he was still a goodly distance from us, I could hear his ankle snap like a yanked suspender. Without meaning to, we all went, "Oooooh." It hurt us, it was so nasty soundin'.

That fall must have caused his magic to fly out of his ass, cause we all started firing at him, and this time he collected all our bullets, and was deader than a guv'ment promise before the smoke cleared.

This gave the rest of them Apache pause, and I'm sure, brave warriors or not, a few assholes puckered out there.

Them other ridin' Apaches stopped their horses and rode back until they was up on the hill, and the runnin' Indians, dropped to the ground and lay there. We popped off a few more shots, but didn't hit nothin', and then I remembered I was in charge. I said, "Hold your fire. Don't waste your bullets."

The Former House Nigger crawled over by me, said, "We showed them."

"They ain't showed yet," I said. "Them's Apache warriors. They ain't known as layabouts."

"Maybe Colonel Hatch heard all the shootin'," he said.

"They've had time to get a good distance away. They figured on us cuttin' the wood and leavin' it and goin' back to the fort. So maybe they ain't missin' us yet and didn't hear a thing."

"Dang it," The Former House Nigger said.

## 》《

I thought we might just mount up and try to ride off. We had more horses than they did, but three of them ridin' after us could still turn out bad. We had a pretty good place as we was, amongst the trees with water to drink. I decided best thing we could do was hold our position. Then that white man who had been clubbed in the head started moaning. That wasn't enough, a couple of the braves come up out of the grass and ran at his spot. We fired at them, but them Spencer single shots didn't reload as fast as them Indians could run. They come down in the tall grass where the white man had gone down, and we seen one of his legs jump up like a snake, and go back down, and the next moment came the screaming.

It went on and on. Rice crawled over to me and said, "I can't stand it. I'm gonna go out there and get him."

"No you're not," I said. "I'll do it."

"Why you?" Rice said.

"Cause I'm in charge."

"I'm goin' with you," The Former House Nigger said.

"Naw, you ain't," I said. "I get rubbed out, you're the one in charge. That's what Colonel Hatch said. I get out there a ways, you open up on them other Apache, keep 'em busier than a bear with a hive of bees."

"Hell, we can't even see them, and the riders done gone on the other side of the hill."

"Shoot where you think they ought to be, just don't send a blue whistler up my ass."

I laid my rifle on the ground, made sure my pistol was loaded, and put it back in the holster, pulled my knife, stuck it in my teeth, and crawled to my left along the side of that creek till I come to tall grass, then I worked my way in. I tried to go slow as to make the grass seem to be moved by the wind, which had picked up considerable and was helpin' my sneaky approach.

As I got closer to where the white man had gone down and the Apaches had gone after him, his yells grew somethin' terrible. I was maybe two or three feet from him. I parted the grass to take a look, seen he was lying on his side, and his throat was cut, and he was dead as he was gonna get.

Just a little beyond him, the two Apache was lying in the grass, and one of them was yellin' like he was the white man bein' tortured, and I thought, Well, if that don't beat all. I was right impressed.

Then the Apache saw me. They jumped up and come for me and I rose up quick, pulling the knife from my teeth, and one of them hit me like a cannon ball, and away we went rollin'.

A shot popped off and the other Apache did a kind of dance, about four steps, and went down holdin' his throat. Blood was flying out of him like it was a fresh-tapped spring. Me and the other buck rolled in the grass and he tried to shoot me with a pistol he was totin', but only managed to singe my hair and give me a headache and make my left ear ring.

We rolled around like a couple of doodlebugs, and then I came up on top and stabbed at him. He caught my hand. I was holding his gun hand to the ground with my left, and he had hold of my knife hand.

"Jackass," I said, like this might so wound him to the quick he'd let go. He didn't. We rolled over in the grass some more, and he got the pistol loose and put it to my head, but the cap and ball misfired, and all I got was burned some. I really called him names then. I jerked my legs up and wrapped them around his neck and pulled him back to the ground and rose up quick, between his legs, and stabbed him in the groin and the stomach, and still he wasn't finished.

I put the knife in his throat, and he gave me a look of disappointment, like he's just realized he'd left somethin' cookin' on the fire and ought to go get it, then he fell back.

I crawled over, rolled the white man on his back. They had cut his balls off and cut his stomach open and sliced his throat. He wasn't gonna come around.

>> <<

**I made it** back to the creek bank and was only shot at a few times by the Apache. My return trip was a mite brisker than the earlier one. I only got a little bit of burn from a bullet that grazed the butt of my trousers.

When I was back at the creek bank, I said, "Who made that shot on the Apache?"

"That would be me," The Former House Nigger said.

"Listen here, I don't want you callin' yourself The Former House Nigger no more. I don't want no one else callin' you that. You're a buffalo soldier, and a good'n. Rest of you men hear that?"

The men was strung out along the creek, but they heard me, and grunted at me.

"This here is Cullen. He ain't nothing but Cullen or Private Cullen, or whatever his last name is. That's what we call him. You hear that Cullen? You're a soldier, and a top soldier at that."

"That's good," Cullen said, not as moved about the event as I was. "But, thing worryin' me is the sun is goin' down."

"There's another thing," Bill said, crawlin' over close to us. "There's smoke over that hill. My guess is it ain't no cookout."

>> <<

**I figured the** source of that smoke would be where our white fella had come from, and it would be what was left of whoever he was with or the remains of a wagon or some such. The horse ridin' Apache had gone back there either to finish them off and torture them with fire or to burn a wagon down. The Apache was regular little fire starters, and since they hadn't been able to get to all of us, they was takin' their misery out on what was within reach.

As that sun went down I began to fret. I moved along the short line of our men, and decided not to space them too much, but not bunch them up either. I put us about six feet apart, and put a few at the rear as lookouts. Considerin' there weren't many of us, it was a short line, and them two in the back was an even shorter line. Hell, they wasn't no line at all. They was a couple of dots.

The night crawled on. A big frog began to bleat near me. Crickets was sawin' away. Upstairs, the black as sin heavens was lit up with stars and the half moon was way too bright.

Couple hours crawled on, and I went over to Cullen and told him to watch tight, cause I was goin' down the line and check the rear, make sure no one was sleepin' or pullin' their johnsons. I left my rifle and unsnapped my revolver holster flap, and went to check.

Bill was fine, but when I come to Rice, he was face down in the dirt. I grabbed him by the back of his collar and hoisted him up, and his head fell near off. His throat had been cut. I wheeled, snappin' my revolver into my hand. Wasn't nothin' there.

A horrible feelin' come over me. I went down the row. All them boys was dead. The Apache had been pickin' 'em off one at a time, and doin' it so careful like, the horses hadn't even noticed.

I went to the rear and found that the soldiers back there was fine. I said, "You fellas best come with me."

We moved swiftly back to Cullen and Rice, and we hadn't no more than gone a few paces, when a burst of fire cut the night. I saw an Apache shape grasp at his chest and fall back. Runnin' over, we found Cullen holding his revolver, and Bill was up waving his rifle around. "Where are they? Where the hell are they?"

"Rest of them are dead," I said.

"Ghosts," Bill said. "They're ghosts."

"What they are is sneaky," I said. "It's what them fellas do for a livin'."

By now, I had what you might call some real goddamn misgivin's, figured I hadn't reckoned right on things. I thought we'd have been safer here, but them Apache had plumb snuck up on us, wiped out three men without so much as leavin' a fart in the air. I said, "I think we better get on our horses and make a run for it."

But when we went over to get the horses, Satan, soon as I untied him, bolted and took off through the wood and disappeared. "Now that's the shits," I said.

"We'll ride double," Cullen said.

The boys was getting their horses loose, and there was a whoop, and an Apache leap-frogged over the back of one of them horses and came down on his feet with one of our own hatchets in his hand. He stuck the blade of it deep in the head of a trooper, a fella whose name I don't remember, being now in my advanced years, and not really havin' known the fella that good in the first place. There was a scramble, like startled quail. There wasn't no military drill about it. It was every sonofabitch for himself. Me and Cullen and Bill tore up the hill, cause that was the way we was facin'. We was out of the wooded area now, and the half moon was bright, and when I looked back, I could see an Apache coming up after us with a knife in his teeth. He was climbin' that hill so fast, he was damn near runnin' on all fours.

I dropped to one knee and aimed and made a good shot that sent him tumbling back down the rise. Horrible thing was, we could hear the other men in the woods down there getting hacked and shot to pieces, screamin' and a pleadin', but we knew wasn't no use in tryin' to go back down there. We was out-smarted and out-manned and out-fought.

Thing worked in our favor, was the poor old mule was still there wearing that makeshift harness and carry-along we had put him in, with the wood stacked on it. He had wandered a bit, but hadn't left the area.

Bill cut the log rig loose, and cut the packing off the mule's back, then he swung up on the beast and pulled Cullen up behind him, which showed a certain lack of respect for my leadership, which, frankly, was somethin' I could agree with.

I took hold of the mule's tail, and off we went, them ridin', and me runnin' behind holdin' to my rifle with one hand, holdin' on to the mule's tail with the other, hopin' he didn't fart or shit or pause to kick. This was an old Indian trick, one we had learned in the cavalry. You can also run alongside, you got somethin' to hang onto. Now, if the horse, or mule, decided to run full out, well you was gonna end up with a mouth full of sod, but a rider and a horse and a fella hangin', sort of lettin' himself be pulled along at a solid speed, doin' big strides, can make surprisin' time and manage not to wear too bad if his legs are strong.

When I finally chanced a look over my shoulder, I seen the Apache were comin', and not in any Sunday picnic stroll sort of way either. They was all on horseback. They had our horses to go with theirs. Except Satan. That bastard hadn't let me ride, but he hadn't let no one else ride either, so I gained a kind of respect for the bastard.

A shot cut through the night air, and didn't nothin' happen right off, but then Bill eased off the mule like a candle meltin'. The shot had gone over Cullen's shoulder and hit Bill in the back of the head. We didn't stop to check his wounds. Cullen slid forward, takin' the reins, slowed the mule a bit and stuck out his hand. I took it, and he helped me swing onto the back of the mule. There's folks don't know a mule can run right swift, it takes a mind to, but it can. They got a gait that shakes your guts, but they're pretty good runners. And they got wind and they're about three times smarter than a horse.

What they don't got is spare legs for when they step in a chuck hole, and that's what happened. It was quite a fall, and I had an idea then how that Apache had felt when his horse had gone out from under him. The fall chunked me and Cullen way off and out into the dirt, and it damn sure didn't do the mule any good.

>> <<

**On the ground,** the poor old mule kept tryin' to get up, but couldn't. He had fallen so that his back was to the Apache, and we was tossed out in the dirt, squirmin'. We crawled around so we was between his legs, and I shot him in the head with my pistol and we made a fort of him. On came them Apache. I took my rifle and laid it over the mule's side and took me a careful bead, and down went one of them. I fired again, and another hit the dirt. Cullen scuttled out from behind the mule and got hold of his rifle where it had fallen, and crawled back. He fired off a couple of shots, but wasn't as lucky as me. The Apache backed off, and at a distance they squatted down beside their horses and took pot shots at us.

The mule was still warm and he stunk. Bullets were splatterin' into his body, but none of them was comin' through, but they was lettin' out a lot of gas. Way I had it figured, them Indians would eventually surround us and we'd end up with our hair hangin' on their wickiups by mornin'. Thinkin' on this, I made an offer to shoot Cullen it looked like we was gonna be overrun.

"Well, I'd rather shoot you than shoot myself," he said.

"I guess that's a deal then," I said.

>> <<

**It was a** bright night and they could see us good, but we could see them good too. The land was flat there, and there wasn't a whole lot of creepin' up they could do without us noticin', but they could still outflank us because they outnumbered us. There was more Apache now than we had seen in the daytime; they had reinforcements; it was like a gatherin' of ants.

The Apache had run their horses all out, and now there was no water for them, so they cut the horses' throats, and lit a fire. After a while we could smell horse meat sizzlin'. The horses had been killed so that they made a ring of flesh they could hide behind, and the soft insides was a nice late supper.

"They ain't got no respect for guv-ment property," Cullen said.

I got out my knife and cut the mule's throat, and he was still fresh enough blood flowed, and we put our mouths on the cut and sucked out all we could. It tasted better than I would have figured, and it made us feel a mite better too, but with there just bein' the two of us, we didn't bother to start a fire and cook our fort.

We could hear them over there laughin' and a cuttin' up, and I figure they had them some mescal, cause after a bit they was actually singin' a white man song, "Row, row, row your boat," and we had to listen to that for a couple of hours.

"Goddamn missionaries," I said.

After a bit, one of them climbed over a dead horse and took his breech-cloth down and turned his ass to us and it winked dead-white in the moonlight, white as any Irishman's ass. I got my rifle on him, but for some reason I couldn't let the hammer down. It just didn't seem right to shoot some drunk showin' me his ass. He turned around and peed, kind of pushin' his loins out, like he was doin' a squaw, and laughed, and that was enough. I shot that sonofabitch. I was aimin' for his pecker, but I think I got him in the belly. He fell out and couple of Apache come out to get him, and Cullen shot one of them, and the one was left jumped over the dead horses and disappeared behind them.

"Bad enough they're gonna kill us," Cullen said, "but they got to act nasty too."

We laid there for awhile. Cullen said, "Maybe we ought to pray for deliverance."

"Pray in one hand, shit in the other, and see which one fills up first."

"I guess I won't pray," he said. "Or shit. Least not at the moment. You remember, that's how we met. I was—"

"I remember," I said.

»«

Well, we was waitin' for them to surround us, but like Colonel Hatch said, you can never figure an Apache. We laid there all night, and nothin' happen. I'm ashamed to say, I nodded off, and when I awoke it was good and daylight and hadn't nobody cut our throats or taken our hair.

Cullen was sittin' with his legs crossed, lookin' in the direction of the Apache. I said, "Damn, Cullen. I'm sorry. I fell out."

"I let you. They're done gone."

I sat up and looked. There was the horses, buzzards lightin' on them, and there were a few of them big ole birds on the ground eyeballin' our mule, and us. I shooed them, said, "I'll be damn. They just packed up like a circus and left."

"Guess they figured they'd lost enough men over a couple of buffalo soldiers, or maybe they saw a bird like Colonel Hatch was talkin' about, and he told them to take themselves home."

"What I figure is they were just too drunk to carry on, woke up with hangovers and went somewhere cool and shaded to sleep it off."

"Reckon so," Cullen said. Then: "Hey, you mean what you said about me bein' a top soldier and all?"

"You know it."

"You ain't a colonel or nothin', but I appreciate it. Course, I don't feel all that top right now."

"We done all we could do. It was Hatch screwed the duck. He ought not have separated us from the troop like that."

"Don't reckon he'll see it that way," Cullen said.

"I figure not," I said.

»«

We cut off chunks of meat from the mule and made a little fire and filled our bellies, then we started walkin'. It was blazin' hot, and still we walked. When nightfall come, I got nervous, thinkin' them Apache might be comin' back, and that in the long run they had just been funnin' us. But they didn't show, and we took turns sleepin' on the hard plains.

Next mornin' it was hot, and we started walkin'. My back hurt and my ass was draggin' and my feet felt like someone had cut them off. I wished we had brought some of that mule meat with us. I was so hungry I could see cornbread walkin' on the ground. Just when I was startin' to imagine pools of water and troops of soldiers dancin' with each other, I seen somethin' that was a little more substantial.

Satan.

I said to Cullen, "Do you see a big black horse?"

"You mean, Satan?"

"Yep."

"I see him."

"Did you see some dancin' soldiers?"

"Nope."

"Do you still see the horse?"

"Yep, and he looks strong and rested. I figure he found a water hole and some grass, the sonofabitch."

Satan was trottin' along, not lookin' any worse for wear. He stopped when he seen us, and I tried to whistle to him, but my mouth was so dry I might as well have been trying to whistle him up with my asshole.

I put my rifle down and started walkin' toward him, holdin' out my hand like I had a treat. I don't think he fell for that, but he dropped his head, and let me walk up on him. He wasn't saddled, as we had taken all that off when we went to cut wood, but he still had his bridle and reins. I took hold of the bridle. I swung onto his back, and then, he bucked. I went up and landed hard on the ground. My head was spinnin', and the next thing I know, that evil bastard was nuzzlin' me with his nose.

I got up and took the reins and led him over to where Cullen was leanin' on his rifle. "Down deep," he said, "I think he likes you."

» ««

We rode Satan double back to the fort, and when we got there, a cheer went up. Colonel Hatch come out and shook our hands and even hugged us. "We found what was left of you boys this mornin', and it wasn't a pretty picture. They're all missin' eyes and ballsacks and such. We figured you two had gone under with the rest of them. Was staked out on the plains somewhere with ants in your eyes. We got vengeful and started trailin' them Apache, and damn if we didn't meet them comin' back toward us, and there was a runnin' fight took us in the direction of the Pecos. We killed one, but the rest of them got away. We just come ridin' in a few minutes ahead of you."

"You'd have come straight on," Cullen said, "you'd have seen us. And we killed a lot more than one."

"That's good," Hatch said, "and we want to hear your story and Nate's soon as you get somethin' to eat and drink. We might even let you have a swallow of whisky. Course, Former House Nigger here will have to do the cookin', ain't none of us any good."

"That there's fine," I said, "But, my compadre here, he ain't The Former House Nigger. He's Private Cullen."

Colonel Hatch eyeballed me. "You don't say?"

"Yes sir, I do, even if it hair lips the United States Army."

"Hell," Hatch said. "That alone is reason to say it."

» ««

There ain't much to tell now. We said how things was, and they did some investigatin', and damn if we wasn't put in for medals. We didn't never get them, cause they was slow about given coloreds awards, and frankly, I didn't think we deserved them, not with us breakin' and runnin' the way we did, like a bunch of little girls tryin' to get in out of the rain, leavin' them men behind. But we didn't stress that part when we was tellin' our story. It would have fouled it some, and I don't think we had much choice other than what we did. We was as brave as men could be without gettin' ourselves foolishly killed.

Still, we was put in for medals, and that was somethin'. In time, Cullen made the rank of Top Soldier. It wasn't just me tellin' him no more. It come true. He become a sergeant, and would have made a good one too, but he got roarin' drunk and set fire to a dead pig and got his stripes taken and spent some time in the stockade. But that's another story.

I liked the cavalry right smart myself, and stayed on there until my time run out and I was supposed to sign up again, and would have too, had it not been for them Chinese women I told you about at the first. But again, that ain't this story. This is the one happened to me in the year of eighteen-seventy, out there on them hot West Texas plains. I will add a side note. The army let me keep Satan when I was mustered out, and I grew to like him, and he was the best horse I ever had, and me and him became friends of a sort, until eighteen-seventy-two when I had to shoot him and feed him to a dog and a woman I liked better.

# DEATH BEFORE BED

In dark cloak
and bunny slippers
I ride the country wild.

With scythe and croaker sack
I gather them up,
those shadows strong or mild.

I put them away,
and kick them some,
to quiet them down of course.

And then I carry them
quick to home,
on my wicked little horse.

Carry them fast,
like a tornado wind
where a hole in the earth awaits.

I toss them down,
I push them down,
I kick them in the ass.

Down there in the pit,
where the flames lick up,
I leave them and laugh.

# APOCALYPSE

What's that?
The apocalypse
and everyone is dead
so,
why do I hear them calling
out beyond the woods,
walking this way,
shadows
without humanity to cast them,
flowing like oil
over water and blood,
and finally
slipping quietly,
to rise slowly
underneath the crack in
my locked door.

# A STRANGE POEM

Outside on the street, I saw a strange poem
wearing nice shoes,
and pleated slacks.
Socks with dots,
baggy pants,
no hat.

We waved at each other.
I had arms.
It had words.
One of its words fell
into the storm drain
and splashed.

I laughed.
The poem chased me,
all the way home.
It's outside my window,
staring,
trying to get in.

I locked the doors.
I pulled the shades.
I went to the word processor
and wrote this down.
I looked outside my window.
The poem is gone.

Next morning,
outside,
I found its bloody tracks,
in the new
fallen
snow.

# LITTLE WORDS

struggling over words
that know more holds
and have more tricks
than i do

they will not talk to me
even though i beg
quite nicely
instead they hide

i seek
they move
always just out of
reach

i wish i had
a butterfly net
within which
i could catch one

way i feel now
the word if caught
would take a bad bad
beating

please words
do not make me talk that way
deep down
you love me

kiss kiss
pet pet
i love you words
no need for a net

still they flee
fast
and easy over the paper
unwilling to stick

i go to bed
lonely
without my little
words

# THE MAN

the man who feels
strong
loves to tell how animals die

their furry heads on walls
like friends
peeking through holes

guns like erections
line the wall
or sleep in cases

a frozen bird
on a stick
hangs in flight

pet the dogs
feed the cats
shoot a bear

the death of something
makes him
strong

his child
must have
a gun

all of nature is his
to shoot down
to smear their blood on his face

# DEAD AIR

Where are the crickets
that once chirped
and the leaping frogs

Now is the dead air
without flowers or bees
or birds

The lions are gone
the tigers
the bears

Butterflies no longer fly
but the cockroach
scuttles

Empty
Empty
Empty

# DOG
# IN WINTER

a dog
in winter
barks white clouds

from pine tree shadows
a night bird
flies

on the pond
the face of the moon
smiling

the window fogs
white
and wet

lips against glass
a cold sweet
kiss

# HIDE AND HORNS

I was recovering from some knife wounds, and was mostly healed up and hoping I wasn't gonna come up on anything that might get me all het up and cause me to tear open my cuts. I was chewin' on some jerky, riding a pretty good horse on the plains of Texas, when I seen something in the distance. I pulled my mount up and got out my long glasses and took me a look.

There was a colored fella like myself lying out there under a horse, had one leg jammed under it, and the horse was deader than a rock. The colored fella was wearing a big sombrero and a red shirt and he wasn't movin'. I figured he was dead like the horse, cause there was some buzzards circlin', and one lit down near the man and the horse and had the manner of a miner waiting for someone to ring the dinner bell. There was a little black cloud above the fella I took to be flies that was excited about soon crawling up the old boy's nose holes.

I rode on over there, and when I got near, the colored fella rolled on his side and showed me the business end of an old Sharp's fifty rifle, the hole in the barrel looked to me to be as big as a mining tunnel.

"Hold up," I said, "I ain't got nothin' agin ya."

"Yeah," he said in a voice dry as the day, "but there's them that do." He rolled over on his side again and lay the rifle across his chest. He said, "You give me any cause, I'll blow your head off."

I got down off my horse and led it over to where the fella and his dead cayuse lay. I said, "So, just restin'?"

"Me and my horse here thought we'd stop in the middle of the goddamn prairie, under the goddamn sun, and take a goddamn nap."

"Good a place as any," I said, squatting down to look the man over, "cause I don't see one spread of shade nowhere."

"And you won't for some miles."

"Course, that sombrero could cover an acre in shade."

"It does me good from time to time," he said.

I could see that the horse had a couple of bullet holes in its side, and the fella had one too, in his right shoulder. He had stuffed a rag in the hole and the rag was red, and the red shirt looked to have been a lighter color before it had sucked up all that blood.

"I ain't feelin' so good," he said.

"That would be because you got a bullet hole in you and a big old dead horse lyin' on your leg."

"And I thought he was just nappin'. I didn't want to disturb him." I bent down and looked at where the leg was trapped. The fella said, "You know, I don't know how much blood I got left in me."

"Way you look," I said, "not much. There's a town not too far from here I've heard of. Might be someone there that can do some fixin's on ya."

"That'd be right good," the fella said. "My name is Cramp, or that's what people call me anyway. I don't remember how I got the name. Something back in slave days. I think the man got my mama's belly full of me was called that, so I became Cramp too. Never knowed him. But, I got to tell you, I ain't up to a whole lot of history."

I got hold of his leg and tried to ease it out from under the horse, but that wasn't workin'.

I went back to my horse, got a little camp shovel I had when I was in the Buffalo Soldiers, and dug around Cramp's leg, said, "They call me Nat."

He said, "That diggin' is loosin' me up, but I don't know it's gonna matter. I'm startin' to feel cold."

"You've quit loosin' blood for now," I said, "otherwise, you'd already be scratchin' on heaven's door."

"Or hell's back door."

"One ta other."

I got hold of his leg and pulled, and it come free, and he made a barking sound, and I looked at him. His face was popped with sweat, and it was an older face than I'd realized, fifty or so, and it looked like an old dark withered potato. I got him under the shoulders and pulled him away and lay him down, went back to his horse and cut one of the saddlebags off with my knife, and put it under his noggin for a pillow. His sombrero had come off, and I went and got that and brought it over to him, and was about to lean it on his head, when I looked up and seen four riders comin' in the distance.

Cramp must have seen the look on my face, cause he said, "Did I mention that there's some fellas after me?"

"That didn't come up. Just said there was folks had somethin' agin you."

"That would be them. They're mad at me."

"They have a reason?"

"They don't like me."

"Are you normally likeable?"

"I'm startin' to pass out, son."

"Hang in there."

"Can't... Don't let me be buried in no lonesome ground."

He closed his eyes and lay still.

I got my long glasses and gave them a look. It was four white fellas, and one of them looked to be damn near as big as the horse he was ridin'. They all had the look of folks that would like to hang someone so they could get in the mood to do somethin' really bad. They was looking right at me, the big cracker with his hand over his eyes, studying me there in the distance.

I got hold of Cramp and dragged his big ass on the other side of the horse and stretched him out so that his head was against the saddle and his feet was stretched out toward the north, which was the direction I wanted to go. Actually, I kind of wanted to go any direction right then, and it crossed my mind that I could get on my horse and just ride off, fast as I could go, leave Cramp to the buzzards, the flies, and the ants, but havin' been partly ruint by too much good raisin', and being of too much character, it just wasn't in me. But I didn't have so much character I didn't think about it.

I went around and picked up the Sharps and looked in the saddlebag I had cut off, and found some loads in there, a whole batch of handmade shells. I studied the situation awhile, decided that when things was over there'd either be me and Cramp dead, or there would be some spare horses, so I led my nag over near where the other horse lay, grabbed his nose and pulled him down, way I had been taught in the cavalry, pulled out my pistol and shot him through the head. He kicked once and was still, and now I had me a V-shaped horse fort. It was an old trick I'd learned fightin' Indians. The other thing I'd learned was not to get too sentimental about a horse, you never knew when you might have to eat one or make a fort out of him. The one horse I'd really liked, me and a woman I cared about had eaten him, but I don't want to get side-tracked and off on that. It's a sad story and doesn't end well for any of the three of us involved.

Lying down on my belly beside Cramp, I laid out the rifle across his horse and took me a bead. A Sharps fifty, which is what Cramp's rifle was, can cover some real ground, but it takes some fine shootin' to know how to get the windage and judge the way the bullet will fall from a distance. I was a fine shooter, but that didn't stop me from worrying, especially now that they were ridin' toward me fast.

I beaded down on the big man, but another rider moved in front of him, so he became my target. I had him good in my sights, but I stopped and sucked my finger wet, stuck it up in the air and got me the pull of the wind, then I beaded again. I took a deep breath and let it out slow as I pulled the trigger. The rifle popped. I knew that from where they were, it wouldn't sound like much, and if they didn't know their business, it would seem to them I'd missed, cause it was a long damn ways.

The man I shot at was riding right along and it seemed that a lot of time passed before he threw out his hands and I seen a stream of blood leap out of his chest and he fell off his horse.

I thought: What if ole Cramp here deserves what he's gonna get? That went through my head for a moment, but then I thought, even if he does, he ought not to get it when he's about dead, least not like this by a bunch of angry peckerwoods.

They started firing at me with Winchesters, like the one on my dead horse, and the bullets fell well short. They had stopped, but they hadn't shot their horses. They had dismounted and were standing by their horses firing away, the bullets plopping well in front of me. I knew right then, them not shooting their horses, they weren't as committed as I was.

I said to myself, "You boys hold that position."

I loaded another round in the Sharps and laid it back across the dead horse and took a deep breath and cracked my neck the way I can by moving my head a little sharply, and took aim. I was feelin' frisky, so even though I should have aimed for my target's chest, I sighted a little high of his forehead and fired. The shot knocked him off his feet, causin' a puff of dust to throw up, and I figured I'd gotten him right between the peepers, though that was guess work, because all I saw were the soles of his boots comin' up.

The other two mounted up, and with the big man leading, they went back in the other direction. I popped a load after them, knocking the big man's horse out from under him, throwing the bastard for a few loops. He was on his feet quick and he got down behind the dead horse, and the other fella kept on ridin', like someone had stuck a lighted corn shuck up his horse's ass. I took a shot at him, but he kept ridin', leaning low over his horse like he was tryin' to mix himself into it.

A moment later, he was out of sight, and I turned my attentions back to the big fella.

I loaded again and raised up this time, on one knee, and shouldered the rifle and took a long deep breath, and fired. This one plopped into the dead horse. After that, I lay down behind Cramp's horse with my head barely up, and watched. The big man didn't move until the day wore down and it got near dark. He got up then and took off at a run in the other direction. I could have let him go, because it was a hard shot, it being dark and all with just some moonlight, but I was kind of worked up, them tryin' to kill me and all, so I raised up, and aimed, and fired, and got him. He went down like a three hundred pound sack of shit.

"Asshole," I said.

## »«

I wasn't sure how to go from there, or where I was goin', 'less it was that town I told Cramp about, but one thing was certain, Cramp wouldn't be going with me, least not alive. He was colder than a wedge and stiff as horse dick at breedin' time.

When I felt wasn't no one circlin' in on me, I got up and walked out a pace, carrying my Winchester with me, leavin' the Sharps, but bringin' the loads with me, lest they surprise me, come back, get hold of his rifle and pick me off from a distance.

I walked in the direction I'd seen one of the horses go, and when it was good and dark, I seen his shape outlined by the moon. I was able to cluck to him and get him to come over, not mentionin' to him I'd killed two of his kind on this day.

I rode him back to where Cramp lay, got my saddle out from under my horse, and swapped it onto the horse I'd rustled up. I got hold of Cramp and threw him over the horse. He was so stiff, he rocked there for a moment and nearly fell off. I climbed on board with the Winchester back in the boot, and the Sharps, now loaded, across my lap, and started in the direction of the town I knew was supposed to be out there, a place called Hide and Horns, if memory served me. I hadn't never been there, but I'd been told about it. Before most of the buffalo was killed out in the area, it had been a place for selling hides and horns and bones for fertilizer.

As I rode along, I didn't let myself get too sure of things. I kept my eyes open and my ears perked.

So far, I hadn't torn open any of my cuts, and I determined they had healed up good. I guess there was some things goin' my way.

>《

Hide and Horns, out there in the moonlight, looked like a place you went to shit, not a place you went to live. But there was folks there and the street was full of them, and a lot of them looked drunk. Thing was, I was still wearin' my army jacket from when I was in with the Buffalo Soldiers, and this bein' the panhandle of Texas, that blue jacket was bound to cause some former rebel to come unhitched and want to kill him a nigger. I had not removed it because of pride, but now as I neared Hide and Horns my pride was growing smaller and my feelin's about not gettin' skinned for an incident of birth was growin' larger.

I decided to ride around the street, out back of the town with my dead companion, and see what was on the far side, which is where I figured the colored would be collected, if there was any. I rode around there, taking it long and slow, and when I got to the other end, there was some shacks and a lot of tents there. No coloreds to be seen, but there was four or five Chinamen and some China girls outside next to a big fire and a boiling pot of laundry, which one of them, a young China girl was movin' around with a board. Beyond her, I could see the town proper, lit up with lanterns and such, and drunk cowboys crossin' and wanderin' around in the street like they really had some place to go.

I got off my horse and led it toward the China folk, Cramp rockin' back and forth, and when I got up close to the pot, the girl, who turned out to be a woman, only small, and beautiful in the firelight, looked at me like I'd come from hell to borrow a cup of sugar. A Chinaman walked out into the firelight with an axe. He was pretty big for a Chinaman. He said, "Do for you?"

"Not if you're plannin' on choppin' on me."

He shook his head and his pigtail slapped from side to side. "Do for you?"

"I got a fella here needs a place in the dirt."

The Chinaman, maybe not sure what I meant, or just wanting to satisfy his own curiosity, came over and took hold of Cramp's boot and pulled on it, said, "Dead nigger."

"Yeah," I said, "he won't be havin' dinner. But, I'd like some. I got Yankee dollars."

"How much dollars?"

"Enough."

"Pussy?"

"Beg your pardon."

"Sell pussy. You want?"

"Oh."

I looked around. Four of the China girls had bunched up near one of the larger tents, and they were looking at me, smiling. Two of them were right smart lookin', one was so ugly she could chase a bobcat up a tree, and there was one pretty good looker with her leg cut off at the knee. She had a wooden leg strapped on and had a crutch under her arm, and from what I could make out in the firelight, she appeared to be missin' a tooth on the far right side.

"Half a woman," the Chinaman said pointing at the wooden leg gal, "she cheaper."

"Actually, she's more than half," I said. "Way more."

"She five penny."

"Well, they are all as lovely as the next," I said, tryin' not to look at the ugly one lest I get struck by lightnin' for lyin', "but I'm gonna pass. I'm hungry."

I looked at the other one, at the wash pot. The Chinaman, figurin' I might be sizin' her up for a mattress, said: "Daughter, not sale."

"Okay," I said. "About that food?"

"Chop suey?" he said. "Cheap."

"What?"

"Chop suey," he said again.

"That'll work. Whatever that is."

"Bury dead nigger?"

"He ain't in no hurry," I said. "I'll tend to the horse and eat before I bury him."

As I was starting to remove my saddle from the horse, the Chinaman walked by the China girls, and reached out and cuffed the cripple, knocking her down. He said something in China talk. I went over and grabbed his shoulder and shoved him back, and wagged a finger at him. "Hey," I said. "Ain't no call to slap a woman around."

The Chinaman still had the axe in one hand, and he eyed me and clenched the axe a little tighter. "She go to work."

"All right," I said. "Give her time. And lighten up on that axe, or you'll wake up with it up your ass."

I reached down and picked up the crutch she had dropped, then I reached down and pulled her up and put the crutch under her arm. She smiled that missing tooth smile. She looked pretty damn good, even if she could suck a pea through that hole in her chompers with the rest of her teeth clenched.

"Chop suey," the Chinaman said to the cripple, and she limped away into a tent on her crutch.

》《

What chop suey was, was warm and delicious, though right then it might have seemed better than it really was cause I was hungry enough to eat the ass out of a dead mule and suck blood out of a chicken's eye.

I sat on my ass on the dirt floor under a tent roof and ate up and kept an eye on my Chinaman, as he had never let go of that there axe, and he had a way of lookin' at me that made me nervous. I had pulled Cramp off the horse and stretched him out on some hay that was off to the side of the tents, next to a cheap corral which was mostly dirt, wind, a frame of wood, and a spot of tarp. I unsaddled the horse and brought it some hay and water, and had a China boy curry him down. I paid for the service, and then I went in and ate.

The four whores didn't depart. They sat nearby and looked at me and giggled. The Chinaman said, "They want see black come off."

"It doesn't."

"They think you, dead nigger, painted. They not know things."

"Tell one of them they can rub my skin, see if it comes off."

The Chinaman told them somethin' in Chinese talk, and one of the girls, who now that I was closer, looked pretty young to me, came over and rubbed on my arm.

"No come off," she said.

"Not so far," I said.

"Let see dick," she said.

"Now what?"

"Let see dick."

"She want know it's black," the Chinaman said.

"She can take my word on that one, and maybe later I can show it to her in private."

"That be two bits," the Chinaman said.

"For the woman?"

He nodded. "Two bits."

I looked at the China girl, said, "What's your name?"

"Sally," she said.

"Really?"

"Sally," she said.

"They all Sally," the Chinaman said, holding the axe a little too comfortably. "You can call Polly or whatever, you buy pussy."

"I'll think that over. First things first, where's the graveyard?"

The Chinaman pointed. "Back of town, that side. No niggers."

"He's dead. What does it matter?"

"No nigger. No Chinaman."

"Well, that puts a hitch in my drawers," I said. "Promised him I'd bury him somewhere wasn't lonesome."

"Bury in pig pen, but deep. Not deep, pigs will eat him."

"No, I had something different in mind. Like a graveyard."

"White fellas, not like. Shoot black dick off."

"That wouldn't be good."

I got up and went outside and walked over to Cramp. He wasn't lookin' too good. Startin' to bloat. I got my knife and slipped it under his ribs and jabbed hard and let some of the bloat out, which was as bad air as you ever smelled. I stood over to the side while he deflated a mite.

The Chinaman had followed me out, still carrying his axe. He said, "Damn. Dead nigger smell plenty bad."

"Dead anything smells plenty bad... You think maybe you could put that axe down? You're makin' me a nervous."

"Chinaman like axe."

"I see that."

The girls had come out now.

I saddled up my horse and put poor old Cramp over the saddle again. He had loosened up some, and his head and legs hung down in a sad kind of way. I had his sombrero on the saddle horn, and I got on the horse and said, "I need to borrow a shovel and a lantern."

"Two bits," the big Chinaman said.

"I said borrow."

"Two bits."

"Shit." I dug in my pocket for two bits and gave it to him, and the one-legged whore, moving pretty good for a wooden leg and a crutch, carried the shovel and unlit lantern over to me. I reached down from the horse and took it, rode in the direction the Chinaman said the graveyard was.

>> <<

The graveyard was on a hill to the east side of the town, and I rode over there and got off the horse and lit the lantern, held it out with one hand and led the horse with the other. There was some stone markers, but mostly they was wood, and some of them was near rotted away or eaten away by bugs.

I looked until I found a place that was bare, tied up the horse to one of the wooden markers, put the lantern next to my burying spot, got the shovel off the saddle, and started to dig.

I had gotten about two feet into the ground, and about two feet wide, ready to make it six feet long, when I heard a noise and turned to see lights. Folks were comin' up the hill, and they were led by the Chinaman, still carrying his axe. The others were white folks, and they didn't look happy. Now and again, I'd like to run up against just one happy white folk.

I stuck the shovel in the dirt, left the lantern where it was, walked over and stood by my horse, cause that's where my Winchester was. I tried not to look like a man that liked being near his Winchester, but being near it gave me comfort, and of course, I had my revolver with me. It had five shots in a six-shot chamber, which is the way I carry it most of the time, lest I shoot my foot off pullin' it loose from its holster. But five shots wasn't enough for eight men, which there was, countin' the Chinaman with his axe. A couple of them were carrying shotguns, and one had a rifle. The rest had pistols on them.

When they were about twenty feet from me, they stopped walking.

The Chinaman said, "I tell him. No niggers. No Chinaman."

"You scoundrel," I said, "you rented me the shovel and the lantern."

"Make money. Not say bury nigger."

"The chink here," one of the shotgun totin' white men said, stepping forward a step, "is right. No niggers in Christian soil."

"What if he's a Christian?"

"He's still a nigger. So are you."

I was wondering how fast I could get on my horse before they rushed me. I said, "Chinaman, what problem was this of yours?"

"My town."

I thought, you asshole. Just a half hour ago you were trying to sell me pussy, sold me food and feed for my horse, and rented me a shovel and a lantern. His problem was simple, I had stopped him from slapping his property around, and now that he had my money, he was getting even. Or, from my way of lookin' at it, more than even.

"All right, gentlemen," I said. "I'll take my dead man and go."

"That there jacket," one of the men said, and my heart sank, "that's a Yankee soldier jacket."

"I was in the army, not the war," I said. "I didn't shoot at no Southerners."

"You still got on a Yankee jacket."

"I was chasin' Indians," I said, figurin' most of them wouldn't care for Indians either, and that might put me on their side a bit.

"You and them ain't got a whole lot of difference, except you can pick cotton and sing a spiritual."

"That ought to be a mark in my favor," I said.

They didn't think that was funny, and it didn't do any endearing.

"Shootin' a nigger ain't half the fun as lynchin' one," one of the charming townspeople said.

I pulled my revolver quick like and shot the closest man carryin' a shotgun, shot him right between the eyes, and then I turned and shot the other shotgunner in the side of the head, and just to make me happy, I shot the Chinaman in the chest. Bullets whizzed around me, but them fellas was already backin' down the hill. I'd learned a long time ago, you can't outshoot eight determined and brave people fair, but you can outshoot eight cowards if you get right at it and don't stop. You can't hesitate. You got to be, as I learned in the army, willin'.

I ran to the edge of the hill and popped off my last shot, and now shots were comin' back up the hill at me at a more regular pace. I grabbed my horse and took off, leavin' Cramp lyin' there. I rode on up through the cemetery and topped it out and rode down the other side as bullets whizzed around me.

I got to a clearin' and gave the horse a clear path, and it could really run. I had caught me a good one back there on the prairie, and it covered ground like a high wind. I looked back and seen that there were some lanterns waggin' back there, and then I heard horses comin', and I bent low over my pony and said, "Run, you bastard," and run he did.

We went like that, full out for a long time, and I knew if I didn't stop, the horse was gonna keel over, so I pulled up in a stand of wood and got off of him and let him blow a little. I put my hand on his heaving side and came away with it covered in salt from sweat. I heard the sound of their horses, and I hoped they didn't have no tracker amongst them, and if they did, I tried to figure that the night was on my side. Course, it would stand to reason they'd want to look in the only area where a man might hide, this little patch of woods.

I led the horse deeper in the trees, and then I led him up a little rise, which was one of the few I'd seen in this part of the country, outside of the cemetery. The trees wasn't like those in East Texas where I'd come from. They were bony lookin' and there was just this little patch standing.

I got the Sharps and the Winchester off the horse and took my saddlebag off of it, and throwed it over my shoulder. I led the horse down amongst the thickest part of the trees and looped the reins over a limb and went back to where I could see good and lay down with the Sharps. I opened the saddlebag and felt around in there for a load and opened the breech on the Sharps and slid in a round and took a deep breath and waited. They came riding up, pausing at the patch of trees, having a pretty good guess I was in there.

They was in range, though they didn't know it, not figurin' on me havin' the Sharps, and they was clutched up good. A bunch had joined them from the town, and I counted twelve. Not a very smart twelve, way they was jammed up like that, but twelve none-theless, and there wasn't no surprise goin' now. They had me treed like a possum.

After a moment, I seen one horse separate from the others, and the rider on it was sitting straight up in the saddle, stiff. He come on out away from the others and there didn't seem to be a thing cautious or worried about him.

As he closed in, I took a bead on him, and in the moonlight, as he neared, I noted he was a colored fella, and I figured they had grabbed some swamper in town and brought him with them, thinkin' he'd talk me into givin' myself up, which he couldn't. I knew how it would end if they got their hands on me, and me put-tin' a bullet in my own head was better than that.

Then I seen somethin' else. It was Cramp. He was tied up on his horse, a stick or somethin' worked into the back of the saddle, and he was bound up good so he wouldn't fall off. He had his sombrero perched on his head.

I lowered the rifle and seen that the crowd of horses behind Cramp was spreadin' out a bit. I was about to put a bead on one of them, when a white man rode out and said, "You don't come back, nigger. Stay out of our town, hear? We're gonna give you this one so you don't come back."

Well, now, I got to admit, I wasn't plannin' on goin' back for Cramp no how. I had tried to do my good deed and it hadn't worked out, so I figured the smartest thing I could do was wish him the best and ride like hell. But now, here he was. And there they were.

The horse with Cramp on it ambled right into the woods, and come up toward me like it was glad to see me. I stood up and got hold of its reins and led it behind me and tied it off on a limb and went back and lay down. I watched the white folks for awhile.

"You don't come back," the fella who'd spoken before said, and they all turned and rode back toward town.

I didn't believe they'd given up on me anymore than they'd given up on breathin'.

>><<

Way I had it reckoned, was they was gonna slow me down by givin' me Cramp to worry about, and then when they thought I figured they was gone, they was gonna get me. I knew they was worried about me, cause they had had no idea I could shoot like I could until that moment on the hill when I killed a few of them, and their snotty Chinaman too. So now, caution had set in. They were probably waiting out there until I felt safer, or got so hungry and thirsty, I had to leave out of the grove, then they was gonna spring on me like a tick on a nut sack. If I waited until daylight I could see them better, but, of course, they could see me better too, so I didn't think that was such a sterlin' plan.

I lay there and listened and was certain I could hear them ridin' in different directions, and that convinced me I was right about that they had in mind. They was gonna surround me and wait until they got their chance to shoot more holes in me than a flour sieve.

I lay there with the Sharps and strained my thinkin', and then I come up with a plan. I reloaded my revolver and went and pulled Cramp into the thickest of the trees, and there in the dark I cut him loose from that pole they had fixed up to the back of the saddle by lacin' a lariat through it, and pulled him off the horse.

Cramp stunk like a well-used outhouse and his face was startin' to wither. I put his sombrero on my head, pulled off his jacket and tossed mine across his horse. I got my guns and the things I wanted from my saddlebags, packed them up, climbed on his horse and rested my back against that pole they had tied up, put my Winchester and the Sharps across my lap, tuckin' them as close as possible, and then I clucked softly to the horse and left the other one tied back there in the trees. I had a moment of worrying about the horse, him tied and all, but I figured they'd eventually come in here after me if I managed to get away, and they'd take the horse. Thing was, though I gave the nag a thought, I was more worried about my ass than his. I tried to sit good and solid and hope anyone seein' me would think I was just that dead fella on a pony, tied to a post.

I pretty much let the horse go how he intended, except I had hold of the reins and was ready to snap them into play if a reason come up. I hadn't gone far when I seen that there were a couple of white fellas, about twenty feet apart, sittin' their horses, rifles at the ready. It was all I could do to play my part. One of the white fellas said, "There's the dead nigger. That other coon didn't want him no how."

Then the other one said somethin' that made my butt hole grab at the saddle.

"Let's see we can shoot that hat off of him."

That gave me pause.

The other one said, "Naw, we got to be quiet," even though they was about as quiet as two badgers wrestlin' in a hole.

The horse I was ridin' went between them, and it was all I could do not to put my heels to that nag and ride like hell, but I stuck to my plan. I rode right on through and nobody shot at me.

When I was out of their range, about twenty minutes, I figure, I took the reins and gave the horse a little nudge, so that he'd move out faster but not take to runnin'. I went on like that for awhile, and when I was clear enough, I put my heels to the horse and rode right on out of there, kind of gigglin' to myself and feelin' smarter than a college fella. I figured sometime come mornin', they might even get brave enough to go up there and find Cramp takin' his long nap, the other horse tied and waitin'.

》《

**The horse I** had wasn't up to snuff, and pretty soon it was limpin'. They probably knowed that was the case when they tied Cramp on it. I got off and took the reins and led it and tried to figure on a new plan. The plains out there went on and on, and pretty soon I'd have to slow down more for the horse, and maybe shoot it and eat some of it, but then I'd be on foot with miles in front of me.

I stopped leading the horse, bent down and looked at its foot. He wasn't in bad shape, but he wasn't in good ridin' shape either. I found a wash and led him down in there, and with the reins wrapped around my hand, I lay down and slept.

It was high noon when I awoke, and hotter than a rabid dog's breath. I walked the horse out of the draw, and then I did the only thing I could think to do. I started leadin' the horse back toward Hide and Horns, takin' the long way around.

**》《**

**It was night** when I come up on the town. I could see it laid out down there and there were lights from lanterns and it looked even bleaker to me now than it had at first.

I went on down there, coming up the back way, where the Chinamen were gathered. I found a little scrub bush and I tied the horse up there so he wouldn't wander into town, and then I got my saddle and guns and such, and threw the saddlebag over my shoulder and toted the saddle with the Winchester and the Sharps tied off on it, my free hand near my revolver. I walked on down into the Chinatown part, and veered toward the tent where I had seen the crippled China girl go in to make my food. I strolled in like I had good sense. It was dark in there, and I fumbled around in my pocket lookin' for a match, until I realized I was wearin' Cramp's jacket and mine was tied to the saddle I was carryin'. A light went on in the place suddenly, and I dropped the saddle and the revolver sort of hopped into my hand, but it was a lit match with a China girl face behind it. The cripple.

She was down on one knee and her nub, about waist high to me lookin' up.

I said, "I don't want no trouble."

"Black man," the cripple said.

"That's me," I said.

Then there was movement, and she was crawlin' across the floor cause she didn't have her leg strapped on. She lit a lantern and the room jumped bright, and there were all the Chinese girls. The wash pot girl and the other four, includin' the cripple.

It was a pretty big tent, but it was stuffed with all manner of stuff, includin' pallets where the girls did the rest of their work, which was haulin' all the men's folk's ashes, as they say.

"I need a good horse," I said, "and I need ya'll not to say nothin', cause I'd rather not shoot a woman. You savvy."

"Savvy," said the most beautiful of the girls, who seemed too small and delicate to be real, and far too young.

"I got Yankee dollars to pay for it, and I got my own saddle."

"We go too," the little one said.

"What?"

"We go too. Get horse. We take wagon."

"Wagon? Why don't you just bring a goddamn band and a clutch of clowns. No."

"We get horse, we go too," the cripple said.

"Damn," I said. "Listen. Tell you what. You get me a horse and I'll ride out, and then you bring the wagon along, and I'll be waitin' on you. Riders don't come with you, and I end up havin' to shoot it out, then I'll travel with you until I can get you to another town. Course, what's the difference between there and here?"

"We go back to China," said the cripple. I had come to realize the other two girls didn't speak enough English to even understand what I was sayin'. The cripple was the valedictorian of their class.

"Got news for you ladies, it's a long ride to the Pacific, and I don't think you can sail that wagon across."

"Get to San Francisco," the cripple said. "Figure from there."

"You know San Francisco?"

"We come there," the cripple said. "Think we have Chinese husbands. Big trick. We have to do big fuckin'. Not let us go. I try to go. Man shoot leg off with a shotgun, knock out a tooth."

I thought, damn, a leg ain't enough, he had to have a tooth too.

I sighed. "All right. I'll go back to what I said. I'm in a tough spot here, and you may think I'll ride away and leave you, but I try to keep my word unless there just ain't no way it can be kept. I can get out of town easier by myself, and then you can bring the wagon. But how you gonna do that? What's the excuse?"

It took them awhile to process that, talkin' to each other in Chinese, and I had to tell it different a couple times before they understood me. But it come down to me gettin' a horse, and them waitin' until daylight and sayin' they had to go out to the prairie to gather up dried buffalo shit for fires. Buffalo shit will burn pretty good, it's dried a fair amount, but it has one drawback. It smells like burning buffalo shit. Still, it'll keep a person warm.

Then again, I reckon I didn't set out to tell you this story so you could know how to warm yourself and cook with dried buffalo plops.

"You think they'll believe you?" I asked.

"We do all time," the cripple said.

"All right," I said. "That'll do. Just don't try and trick me, cause I won't like it."

"No trick," she said.

>><<

They got me a good horse, and I got rid of Cramp's jacket and put on a brown shirt the girls gave me. I put my saddle on the horse, and took my guns and rode on out. I went way out, like I told them, givin' them a kind of guide to where I planned to go.

I wasn't an entirely trustin' soul, so I actually went a little farther east than I told them, found a place where I could sit a horse down in a draw and see up over the lip of it. That way I could make sure they didn't send someone else out to get me for some payment.

It got along mornin', and I had dozed on the ground with the reins of the horse clutched in my fist, and when I awoke it was already turnin' off hotter than a stove fire.

I heard hooves movin' in my direction, and I got up and looked between that little gap in the draw and seen it was the bunch that had ridden out after me, and they was leadin' the horse I had left, and they had Cramp's body tied behind it with a long rope bound to his ankles, and they was draggin' him along face down.

At first I thought the China girls had done me in, and that this bunch was lookin' for me, and then I got it figured right. They was just now comin' in, finally snoopin' out that I had snuck off on them in the night, disguised as Cramp. I counted them. There was twelve.

Now, I tell you, I try to be practical, but lookin' out there and seein' Cramp being dragged along like that, even though I didn't know him even a little, made my blood boil. I knew all I had to do was let them ride out of sight, back to town, then I could either wait on the China girls or not. It was the way to go, and the truth of the matter was, Cramp wasn't any of my business and I didn't know what he'd done to get folks mad at him in the first place, but I knew it didn't take much when you was a colored man. It could be lookin' at a white woman, or cuttin' a surprise fart in the street, and that's all it took for you to be thought of as uppity, and if there's one thing a lot of white folks can't tolerate, it's an uppity nigger. We was supposed to know our place, and I was thinkin' on all of this, and get madder and madder, and most of my common sense began to leak out of my head like water. Without realizin' what I was doin', I got on my horse and put the reins in my teeth, put the Sharps under one arm and the Winchester under the other.

Now, they'll tell you you can't hit shit shootin' like that, and I'll tell you right off, that's mostly true, but most shooters ain't me. I've gotten so good with a gun I can shoot right smart with any kind of weapon under almost any kind of condition. That don't mean I don't miss, but I hit a lot too, and if I got a still shot, I can knock the dick off a horse fly.

I rode out and dug my heels into the horse, went to ridin' right at them, takin' them from the side. There was twelve of them, but they didn't see me until my guns barked, and the first shot with the Sharps hit one of their horses, which was an accident, I might add, and the horse went down, throwing him. I dropped the Sharps, since it just had that one load, flipped the Winchester into my right hand, and took to firin'. With four shots I killed three. They started poppin' off shots then, the ones that had figured out what was happenin', and by then I had come in amongst them. I twisted my head, and with those reins in my teeth, I made my horse twirl, and using both hands on that Winchester, I fired as fast as I could, and four more was down, and one horse was limpin' off with a bullet in his head, another unintentional, I might add.

I fired the Winchester until it was empty, and then I rode up on one of them that had fired six shots off and hadn't hit me or even come near me. He looked like he was about to scream with fear and he was snappin' the empty revolver like bullets might suddenly appear in the chambers. I swung the empty rifle and clipped him off his horse. I wheeled, and then there was a barrage of shots, and my horse went down and I went to rollin'. When I come up, I had my revolver in my hand, and I started firing, dropping two more, hittin' them both as they rode up on me. I fired at the others, not hittin' anyone else, which meant I was probably tired.

The ones that was left bolted and rode off, which was good, cause my revolver was empty.

I ran over to my dead horse and got a couple loads for the Sharps out of the saddlebags, and ran back to where I'd dropped the Sharps, scrounged around till I found it. Then I got down on a knee and loaded the Sharps and leveled it off.

They were far out now, but I took windage with a wet finger, beaded that fifty caliber, called them sonofabitches, and fired. As is often the case, it seemed like a long time before the bullet hit.

In fact, I was already startin' to reload, when one of the riders threw up his hands and went flying off. The other just kept ridin'. He was way out there, but I had the Sharps ready, and I aimed high to let the bullet drop. I fired. I got him somewhere near the back of the head and he fell off, his horse still runnin'.

I know all this makes me sound a mite godlike, but, true story. No lie. I killed everyone of them sonofabitches. It made me wonder how I'd managed to let one of them that had come up on me with Cramp get away. But, hell, even the gods nod.

But the gods don't bleed. I did. I had been hit. Didn't know it right off, but I started hurtin', and looked down at my side and seen I was bleedin'. I lay down on the ground suddenly, and closed my eyes and the sun didn't feel all that warm anymore.

>«

"You not dead," the crippled China girl said.

"No?" I said. "I feel dead, and maybe buried, but I still seem to be among the livin' Chinese."

I was lyin' under a wagon and the cripple was down there with me. I tried to sit up, but couldn't. She said, "No. Sit. Stay."

I had a dog I talked to like that. I felt my side. It was bandaged up.

"We got to go," I said. "They'll be after me."

"You all shot up," the cripple said.

"That I am," I said.

"Rest a day. Have chop suey. Pussy. Feel better."

"I'm sure. But that rest a day part, not such a good idea."

I lay for awhile anyway, not having the strength to do much else. I probably laid there much longer than I thought, but finally I woke up and crawled out from under the wagon. The other Chinese girls had pulled a tarp over the frame of the wagon, and made a kind of traveling tent out of it. They had two horses tied on the back. One of the girls was missin'. I asked the cripple about that.

"Washie girl. She stay," said the cripple. "She make good money washie clothes."

I managed to walk around and gather up my goods, saddle and saddlebags and weapons, and found the horse that had been draggin' Cramp. I cut the old boy loose and looked at him. He had asked me not to bury him out in the lonesome, but the thing was, he was lookin' pretty ripe, and I come to the conclusion I had done my best, and he wouldn't know the prairie from a place under a church pew. The girls helped me dig a hole, as they had shovels and all manner of equipment in the wagon, and I wrapped him in a blanket and put him down.

I was bleeding pretty good by the time I quit, and I had been wrong about them knife wounds being all healed up. A couple of them was leakin'. I said, "We got to get movin."

As we walked away, I looked back at Cramp's grave, said, "Sorry, Cramp. I done my best. It beats bein' dragged around till your hide comes off."

I climbed in the back of the wagon and lay down and slept while the little China girl who looked about twelve years old drove. In the back, the cripple tended me, and the other two looked on. We rode on through the day and into the night, the wagon bumpin' along, those two horses tied to the back of it, trottin' to keep up, and finally we stopped near a little run of creek, and the girls got out and made a fire from some dried buffalo shit. They fixed up some food, which was pretty good and had a lot of hot peppers in it. I didn't ask what it was, cause I couldn't identify the meat and figured I might not want to know.

Later that night, the cripple showed me how she could move around under me good as a two-legged girl, and then I had to show all of them that my pecker was black and the color didn't come off in their little nests. I showed that to all of them to be polite, and to prove I wasn't showin' no favoritism, even though I was wounded good and bleedin'. A man has to have some priorities, I always say, and if a bunch of Chinese girls beg to see your dick, you should be willin' to show it to them.

Now, them townsfolk had to have figured out their men weren't comin' back, and in time I'm sure they found them. Maybe they sent someone out after us. But if they did, we never seen them. Jumpin' ahead a bit, I should say the story about the gunfight began to spread, and since there wasn't no one livin' who'd seen it besides me, I knew the stories I heard about survivors who could tell it like it was, wasn't true in any kind of way. Thing was, the stories didn't mention I was colored. I just became a mysterious gunman, and in some of the stories I was a hero, and in others a villain. Cause of that, and some other things happened in my life, there was some dime novels written about me, basing themselves on true events at first, but not afraid to add a lie in when it made the story better, and then later, the stories was just dadgum windies. And though the stories didn't mention I was colored, they did call the books stories about The Black Rider of the Plains, and named me Deadwood Dick on account of some things happened there in Deadwood, including a shootin' contest where I shot against Buffalo Bill and Annie Oakley. But, again, that there is another story, and though it's been told a thousand times, ain't nobody told it right yet. I live long enough I plan to tell it the way it was, just like I'm tellin' you how this was.

As for me and the China girls, we rode on across that prairie for days, and when we got to the peak of the Texas panhandle, we turned northwest, across Oklahoma toward Colorady, with a plan to go on out to San Francisco so the China girls could catch a boat to China.

Now there's one more thing that's kind of interestin', and goes with this story, and if I'm lyin' I'm dyin'. When we was four or five days out, headin' up to the tip of the panhandle, we seen a scrawny horse grazin', and as we bounced the wagon closer, we seen there was a fella with his foot in the stirrup being dragged along, and even from a distance it was easy to see he was deader than a wind wagon investment.

Feelin' a bit spry, now that my wounds had had a few days to heal, I got out of the wagon and walked over and caught the horse and looked at the dead man. His boot was twisted up good in the stirrup, and he'd been dragged around for days, cause a lot of his skin had come off and ants and such had been at him. His eyes were gone and his lips had started to curl, showin' his teeth. He had a pretty large hole comin' out of his shirt on the right side of his breast, and when I seen that, it all tumbled together for me.

Back when I had found Cramp, and had a shootout with those folks who come to finish him off, one of them had got away. I had taken a shot at him, and figured I'd missed. But I hadn't. He'd just been able to ride some, and then he'd keeled over and got his foot hung in the stirrup, and his horse had been draggin' him around for damn near a week.

I worked the fella's foot out of the stirrup and let his leg drop to the ground. Tell you true, just like them other fellas I shot, I didn't have no urge to bury him and say words over him, cause buryin' someone I didn't have no feelin's for was stupid, and sayin' words that didn't seem to do nothin' but waste my breath, wasn't exactly appealin' either. I was glad he was dead, and I left him lyin' out there on the prairie with the sun on his face and ants in his ears.

His horse we took with us and fed grain the gals had in the wagon, and we fattened him up a mite, and sold him and the saddle in Amarillo, before going on up into Oklahoma, and turnin' west toward Colorady.

# THE STARS
# ARE FALLING

Befor Deel Arrowsmith came back from the dead,
he was crossing a field by late moonlight in search of
his home. His surroundings were familiar, but at the
same time different. It was as if he had left as a child
and returned as an adult to examine old property only to find
the tree swing gone, the apple tree cut down, the grass grown
high, and an outhouse erected over the mound where his best
dog was buried.

As he crossed, the dropping moon turned thin, like cheap
candy licked too long, and the sun bled through the trees. There
were spots of frost on the drooping green grass and on the taller
weeds, yellow as ripe corn. In his mind's eye he saw not the East
Texas field before him or the dark rows of oaks and pines beyond
it, or even the clay path that twisted across the field toward the
trees like a ribbon of blood.

He saw a field in France where there was a long, deep trench,
and in the trench were bloodied bodies, some of them missing
limbs and with bits of brains scattered about like spilled oatmeal.
The air filled with the stinging stench of rotting meat and wafting

gun smoke, the residue of poison gas, and the buzz of flies. The back of his throat tasted of burning copper. His stomach was a knot. The trees were like the shadowy shades of soldiers charging toward him, and for a moment, he thought to meet their charge, even though he no longer carried a gun.

He closed his eyes, breathed deeply, shook his head. When he opened them the stench had passed and his nostrils filled with the nip of early morning. The last of the moon faded like a melting snowflake. Puffy white clouds sailed along the heavens and light tripped across the tops of the trees, fell between them, made shadows run low along the trunks and across the ground. The sky turned light blue and the frost dried off the drooping grass and it sprang to attention. Birds began to sing. Grasshoppers began to jump.

He continued down the path that crossed the field and split the trees. As he went, he tried to remember exactly where his house was and how it looked and how it smelled, and most important, how he felt when he was inside it. He tried to remember his wife and how she looked and how he felt when he was inside her, and all he could find in the back of his mind was a cipher of a woman younger than he was in a long, colorless dress in a house with three rooms. He couldn't even remember her nakedness, the shape of her breasts and the length of her legs. It was as if they had met only once, and in passing.

When he came through the trees and out on the other side, the field was there as it should be, and it was full of bright blue and yellow flowers. Once it had been filled with tall corn and green bursts of beans and peas. It hadn't been plowed now in years, most likely since he left. He followed the trail and trudged toward his house. It stood where he had left it. It had not improved with age. The chimney was black at the top and the unpainted lumber was stripping like shedding snakeskin. He had cut the trees and split them and made the lumber for the house, and like everything else he had seen since he had returned, it was smaller than he remembered. Behind it was the smokehouse he had made of logs, and far out to the left was the outhouse he had built. He had read many a magazine there while having his morning constitutional.

Out front, near the well, which had been built up with stones and now had a roof over it supported on four stout poles, was a young boy. He knew immediately it was his son. The boy was probably eight. He had been four years old when Deel had left to fight in the Great War, sailed across the vast dark ocean. The boy had a bucket in his hand, held by the handle. He set it down and raced toward the house, yelling something Deel couldn't define.

A moment later she came out of the house and his memory filled up. He kept walking, and the closer he came to her, standing framed in the doorway, the tighter his heart felt. She was blond and tall and lean and dressed in a light-colored dress on which were printed flowers much duller than those in the field. But her face was brighter than the sun, and he knew now how she looked naked and in bed, and all that had been lost came back to him, and he knew he was home again.

When he was ten feet away the boy, frightened, grabbed his mother and held her, and she said, "Deel, is that you?"

He stopped and stood, and said nothing. He just looked at her, drinking her in like a cool beer. Finally he said, "Worn and tired, but me."

"I thought…"

"I know…but I'm back, Mary Lou."

>> <<

They sat stiffly at the kitchen table. Deel had a plate in front of him and he had eaten the beans that had been on it. The front door was open and they could see out and past the well and into the flower-covered field. The window across the way was open too, and there was a light breeze ruffling the edges of the pulled-back curtains framing it. Deel had the sensation he'd had before when crossing the field and passing through the trees, and when he had first seen the outside of the house. And now, inside, the roof felt too low and the room was too small and the walls were too close. It was all too small.

But there was Mary Lou. She sat across the table from him. Her face was clean of lines and her shoulders were as narrow as the boy's. Her eyes were bright, like the blue flowers in the field.

The boy, Winston, was to his left, but he had pulled his chair close to his mother. The boy studied him carefully, and in turn, Deel studied the boy. Deel could see Mary Lou in him, and nothing of himself.

"Have I changed that much?" Deel said, in response to the way they were looking at him. Both of them had their hands in their laps, as if he might leap across the table at any moment and bite them.

"You're very thin," Mary Lou said.

"I was too heavy when I left. I'm too skinny now. Soon I hope to be just right." He tried to smile, but the smile dripped off. He took a deep breath. "So, how you been?"

"Been?"

"Yeah. You know. How you been?"

"Oh. Fine," she said. "Good. I been good."

"The boy?"

"He's fine."

"Does he talk?"

"Sure he talks. Say hello to your daddy, Winston."

The boy didn't speak.

"Say hello," his mother said.

The boy didn't respond.

"That's all right," Deel said. "It's been a while. He doesn't remember me. It's only natural."

"You joined up through Canada?"

"Like I said I would."

"I couldn't be sure," she said.

"I know. I got in with the Americans, a year or so back. It didn't matter who I was with. It was bad."

"I see," she said, but Deel could tell she didn't see at all. And he didn't blame her. He had been caught up in the enthusiasm of war and adventure, gone up to Canada and got in on it, left his family in the lurch, thinking life was passing him by and he was missing out. Life had been right here and he hadn't even recognized it.

Mary Lou stood up and shuffled around the table and heaped fresh beans onto his plate and went to the oven and brought back cornbread and put it next to the beans. He watched her every move. Her hair was a little sweaty on her forehead and it clung there, like wet hay.

"How old are you now?" he asked her.

"How old?" she said, returning to her spot at the table. "Deel, you know how old I am. I'm twenty-eight, older than when you left."

"I'm ashamed to say it, but I've forgotten your birthday. I've forgotten his. I don't hardly know how old I am."

She told him the dates of their births.

"I'll be," he said. "I don't remember any of that."

"I...I thought you were dead."

She had said it several times since he had come home. He said, "I'm still not dead, Mary Lou. I'm in the flesh."

"You are. You certainly are."

She didn't eat what was on her plate. She just sat there looking at it, as if it might transform.

Deel said, "Who fixed the well, built the roof over it?"

"Tom Smites," she said.

"Tom? He's a kid."

"Not anymore," she said. "He was eighteen when you left. He wasn't any kid then, not really."

"I reckon not," Deel said.

## 》《

After dinner, she gave him his pipe the way she used to, and he found a cane rocker that he didn't remember being there before, took it outside and sat and looked toward the trees and smoked his pipe and rocked.

He was thinking of then and he was thinking of now and he was thinking of later, when it would be nighttime and he would go to bed, and he wasn't certain how to approach the matter. She was his wife, but he hadn't been with her for years, and now he was home, and he wanted it to be like before, but he didn't really remember how it was before. He knew how to do what he wanted to do, but he didn't know how to make it love. He feared she would feel that he was like a mangy cat that had come in through the window to lie there and expected petting.

He sat and smoked and thought and rocked.

The boy came out of the house and stood to the side and watched him.

The boy had the gold hair of his mother and he was built sturdy for a boy so young. He had a bit of a birthmark in front of his right ear, on the jawline, like a little strawberry. Deel didn't remember that. The boy had been a baby, of course, but he didn't remember that at all. Then again, he couldn't remember a lot of things, except for the things he didn't want to remember. Those things he remembered. And Mary Lou's skin. That he remembered. How soft it was to the touch, like butter.

"Do you remember me, boy?" Deel asked.

"No."

"Not at all?"

"No."

"Course not. You were very young. Has your mother told you about me?"

"Not really."

"Nothing."

"She said you got killed in the war."

"I see... Well, I didn't."

Deel turned and looked back through the open door. He could see Mary Lou at the washbasin pouring water into the wash pan, water she had heated on the stove. It steamed as she poured. He thought then he should have brought wood for her to make the fire. He should have helped make the fire and heat the water. But being close to her made him nervous. The boy made him nervous.

"You going to school?" he asked the boy.

"School burned down. Tom teaches me some readin' and writin' and cipherin'. He went eight years to school."

"You ever go fishin'?"

"Just with Tom. He takes me fishin' and huntin' now and then."

"He ever show you how to make a bow and arrow?"

"No."

"No, sir," Deel said. "You say, no, sir."

"What's that?"

"Say yes, sir or no, sir. Not yes and no. It's rude."

The boy dipped his head and moved a foot along the ground, piling up dirt.

"I ain't gettin' on you none," Deel said. "I'm just tellin' you that's how it's done. That's how I do if it's someone older than me. I say no, sir and yes, sir. Understand, son?"

The boy nodded.

"And what do you say?"

"Yes, sir."

"Good. Manners are important. You got to have manners. A boy can't go through life without manners. You can read and write some, and you got to cipher to protect your money. But you got to have manners too."

"Yes, sir."

"There you go... About that bow and arrow. He never taught you that, huh?"

"No, sir."

"Well, that will be our plan. I'll show you how to do it. An old Cherokee taught me how. It ain't as easy as it might sound, not to make a good one. And then to be good enough to hit somethin' with it, that's a whole nuther story."

"Why would you do all that when you got a gun?"

"I guess you wouldn't need to. It's just fun, and huntin' with one is real sportin', compared to a gun. And right now, I ain't all that fond of guns."

"I like guns."

"Nothin' wrong with that. But a gun don't like you, and it don't love you back. Never give too much attention or affection to somethin' that can't return it."

"Yes, sir."

The boy, of course, had no idea what he was talking about. Deel was uncertain he knew himself what he was talking about. He turned and looked back through the door. Mary Lou was at the pan, washing the dishes; when she scrubbed, her ass shook a little, and in that moment, Deel felt, for the first time, like a man alive.

》《

That night the bed seemed small. He lay on his back with his hands crossed across his lower stomach, wearing his faded red union suit, which had been ragged when he left, and had in his absence been attacked by moths. It was ready to come apart. The window next to the bed was open and the breeze that came through was cool. Mary Lou lay beside him. She wore a long white nightgown that had been patched with a variety of colored cloth patches. Her hair was undone and it was long. It had been long when he left. He wondered how often she had cut it, and how much time it had taken each time to grow back.

"I reckon it's been a while," he said.

"That's all right," she said.

"I'm not sayin' I can't, or I won't, just sayin' I don't know I'm ready."

"It's okay."

"You been lonely?"

"I have Winston."

"He's grown a lot. He must be company."

"He is."

"He looks some like you."

"Some."

Deel stretched out his hand without looking at her and laid it across her stomach. "You're still like a girl," he said. "Had a child, and you're still like a girl... You know why I asked how old you was?"

"'Cause you didn't remember."

"Well, yeah, there was that. But on account of you don't look none different at all."

"I got a mirror. It ain't much of one, but it don't make me look younger."

"You look just the same."

"Right now, any woman might look good to you." After she said it, she caught herself. "I didn't mean it that way. I just meant you been gone a long time... In Europe, they got pretty women, I hear."

"Some are, some ain't. Ain't none of them pretty as you."

"You ever...you know?"

"What?"

"You know... While you was over there."

"Oh... Reckon I did. Couple of times. I didn't know for sure I was comin' home. There wasn't nothin' to it. I didn't mean nothin' by it. It was like filling a hungry belly, nothin' more."

She was quiet for a long time. Then she said, "It's okay."

He thought to ask her a similar question, but couldn't. He eased over to her. She remained still. She was as stiff as a corpse. He knew. He had been forced at times to lie down among them. Once, moving through a town in France with his fellow soldiers, he had come upon a woman lying dead between two trees. There wasn't a wound on her. She was young. Dark haired. She looked as if she had lain down for a nap. He reached down and touched her. She was still warm.

One of his comrades, a soldier, had suggested they all take turns mounting her before she got cold. It was a joke, but Deel had pointed his rifle at him and run him off. Later, in the trenches he had been side by side with the same man, a fellow from Wisconsin, who like him had joined the Great War by means of Canada. They had made their peace, and the Wisconsin fellow told him it was a poor joke he'd made, and not to hold it against him, and Deel said it was all right, and then they took positions next to each other and talked a bit about home and waited for the war to come. During the battle, wearing gas masks and firing rifles, the fellow from Wisconsin had caught a round and it had knocked him down. A moment later the battle had ceased, at least for the moment.

Deel bent over him, lifted his mask, and then the man's head. The man said, "My mama won't never see me again."

"You're gonna be okay," Deel said, but saw that half the man's head was missing. How in hell was he talking? Why wasn't he dead? His brain was leaking out.

"I got a letter inside my shirt. Tell Mama I love her... Oh, my god, look there. The stars are falling."

Deel, responding to the distant gaze of his downed companion, turned and looked up. The stars were bright and stuck in place. There was an explosion of cannon fire and the ground shook and the sky lit up bright red; the redness clung to the air like a veil. When Deel looked back at the fellow, the man's eyes were still open, but he was gone.

Deel reached inside the man's jacket and found the letter. He realized then that the man had also taken a round in the chest, because the letter was dark with blood. Deel tried to unfold it, but it was so damp with gore it fell apart. There was nothing to deliver to anyone. Deel couldn't even remember the man's name. It had gone in one ear and out the other. And now he was gone, his last words being, "The stars are falling."

While he was holding the boy's head, an officer came walking down the trench holding a pistol. His face was darkened with gunpowder and his eyes were bright in the night and he looked at Deel, said, "There's got to be some purpose to all of it, son. Some purpose," and then he walked on down the line.

Deel thought of that night and that death, and then he thought of the dead woman again. He wondered what had happened to her body. They had had to leave her there, between the two trees. Had someone buried her? Had she rotted there? Had the ants and the elements taken her away? He had dreams of lying down beside her, there in the field. Just lying there, drifting away with her into the void.

Deel felt now as if he were lying beside that dead woman, blond instead of dark haired, but no more alive than the woman between the trees.

"Maybe we ought to just sleep tonight," Mary Lou said, startling him. "We can let things take their course. It ain't nothin' to make nothin' out of."

He moved his hand away from her. He said, "That'll be all right. Of course."

She rolled on her side, away from him. He lay on top of the covers with his hands against his lower belly and looked at the log rafters.

## 》《

A couple of days and nights went by without her warming to him, but he found sleeping with her to be the best part of his life. He liked her sweet smell and he liked to listen to her breathe. When she was deep asleep, he would turn slightly, and carefully, and rise up on one elbow and look at her shape in the dark. His homecoming had not been what he had hoped for or expected, but in those moments when he looked at her in the dark, he was certain it was better than what had gone before for nearly four horrible years.

The next few days led to him taking the boy into the woods and finding the right wood for a bow. He chopped down a bois d'arc tree and showed the boy how to trim it with an axe, how to cut the wood out of it for a bow, how to cure it with a fire that was mostly smoke. They spent a long time at it, but if the boy enjoyed what he was learning, he never let on. He kept his feelings close to the heart and talked less than his mother. The boy always seemed some yards away, even when standing right next to him.

Deel built the bow for the boy and strung it with strong cord and showed him how to find the right wood for arrows and how to collect feathers from a bird's nest and how to feather the shafts. It took almost a week to make the bow, and another week to dry it and to make the arrows. The rest of the time Deel looked out at what had once been a plowed field and was now twenty-five acres of flowers with a few little trees beginning to grow, twisting up among the flowers. He tried to imagine the field covered in corn.

Deel used an axe to clear the new trees, and that afternoon, at the dinner table, he asked Mary Lou what had happened to the mule.

"Died," Mary Lou said. "She was old when you left, and she just got older. We ate it when it died."

"Waste not, want not," Deel said.

"Way we saw it," she said.

"You ain't been farmin', how'd you make it?"

"Tom brought us some goods now and then, fish he caught, vegetables from his place. A squirrel or two. We raised a hog and smoked the meat, had our own garden."

"How are Tom's parents?"

"His father drank himself to death and his mother just up and died."

Deel nodded. "She was always sickly, and her husband was a lot older than her... I'm older than you. But not by that much. He was what? Fifteen years? I'm... Well, let me see. I'm ten."

She didn't respond. He had hoped for some kind of confirmation that his ten-year gap was nothing, that it was okay. But she said nothing.

"I'm glad Tom was around," Deel said.

"He was a help," she said.

After a while, Deel said, "Things are gonna change. You ain't got to take no one's charity no more. Tomorrow, I'm gonna go into town, see I can buy some seed, and find a mule. I got some muster-out pay. It ain't much, but it's enough to get us started. Winston here goes in with me, we might see we can get him some candy of some sort."

"I like peppermint," the boy said.

"There you go," Deel said.

"You ought not do that so soon back," Mary Lou said. "There's still time before the fall plantin'. You should hunt like you used to, or fish for a few days... You could take Winston here with you. You deserve time off."

"Guess another couple of days ain't gonna hurt nothin'. We could all use some time gettin' reacquainted."

>><<

Next afternoon when Deel came back from the creek with Winston, they had a couple of fish on a wet cord, and Winston carried them slung over his back so that they dangled down like ornaments and made his shirt damp. They were small but good perch and the boy had caught them, and in the process, shown the first real excitement Deel had seen from him. The sunlight played over their scales as they bounced against Winston's back. Deel, walking slightly behind Winston, watched the fish carefully. He watched them slowly dying, out of the water, gasping for air. He couldn't help but want to take them back to the creek and let them go. He had seen injured men gasp like that, on the field, in the trenches. They had seemed like fish that only needed to be put in water.

As they neared the house, Deel saw a rider coming their way, and he saw Mary Lou walking out from the house to meet him.

Mary Lou went up to the man and the man leaned out of the saddle, and they spoke, and then Mary Lou took hold of the saddle with one hand and walked with the horse toward the house. When she saw Deel and Winston coming, she let go of the saddle and walked beside the horse. The man on the horse was tall and lean with black hair that hung down to his shoulders. It was like a waterfall of ink tumbling out from under his slouched, gray hat.

As they came closer together, the man on the horse raised his hand in greeting. At that moment the boy yelled out, "Tom!" and darted across the field toward the horse, the fish flapping.

**》《**

They sat at the kitchen table. Deel and Mary Lou and Winston and Tom Smites. Tom's mother had been half Chickasaw, and he seemed to have gathered up all her coloring, along with his Swedish father's great height and broad build. He looked like some kind of forest god. His hair hung over the sides of his face, and his skin was walnut colored and smooth and he had balanced features and big hands and feet. He had his hat on his knee.

The boy sat very close to Tom. Mary Lou sat at the table, her hands out in front of her, resting on the planks. She had her head turned toward Tom.

Deel said, "I got to thank you for helpin' my family out."

"Ain't nothin' to thank. You used to take me huntin' and fishin' all the time. My daddy didn't do that sort of thing. He was a farmer and a hog raiser and a drunk. You done good by me."

"Thanks again for helpin'."

"I wanted to help out. Didn't have no trouble doin' it."

"You got a family of your own now, I reckon."

"Not yet. I break horses and run me a few cows and hogs and chickens, grow me a pretty good-size garden, but I ain't growin' a family. Not yet. I hear from Mary Lou you need a plow mule and some seed."

Deel looked at her. She had told him all that in the short time she had walked beside his horse. He wasn't sure how he felt about that. He wasn't sure he wanted anyone to know what he needed or didn't need.

"Yeah. I want to buy a mule and some seed."

"Well, now. I got a horse that's broke to plow. He ain't as good as a mule, but I could let him go cheap, real cheap. And I got more seed than I know what to do with. It would save you a trip into town."

"I sort of thought I might like to go to town," Deel said.

"Yeah, well, sure. But I can get those things for you."

"I wanted to take Winston here to the store and get him some candy."

Tom grinned. "Now, that is a good idea, but so happens, I was in town this mornin', and—"

Tom produced a brown paper from his shirt pocket and laid it out on the table and carefully pulled the paper loose, revealing two short pieces of peppermint.

Winston looked at Tom. "Is that for me?"

"It is."

"You just take one now, Winston, and have it after dinner," Mary Lou said. "You save that other piece for tomorrow. It'll give you somethin' to look forward to."

"That was mighty nice of you, Tom," Deel said.

"You should stay for lunch," Mary Lou said. "Deel and Winston caught a couple of fish, and I got some potatoes. I can fry them up."

"Why that's a nice offer," Tom said. "And on account of it, I'll clean the fish."

>«

The next few days passed with Tom coming out to bring the horse and the seed, and coming back the next day with some plow parts Deel needed. Deel began to think he would never get to town, and now he wasn't so sure he wanted to go. Tom was far more comfortable with his family than he was and he was jealous of that and wanted to stay with them and find his place. Tom and Mary Lou talked about all manner of things, and quite comfortably, and the boy had lost all interest in the bow. In fact, Deel had found it and the arrows out under a tree near where the woods firmed up. He took it and put it in the smokehouse. The air was dry in there and it would cure better, though he was uncertain the boy would ever have anything to do with it.

Deel plowed a half-dozen acres of the flowers under, and the next day Tom came out with a wagonload of cured chicken shit, and helped him shovel it across the broken ground. Deel plowed it under and Tom helped Deel plant peas and beans for the fall crop, some hills of yellow crookneck squash, and a few mounds of watermelon and cantaloupe seed.

That evening they were sitting out in front of the house, Deel in the cane rocker and Tom in a kitchen chair. The boy sat on the ground near Tom and twisted a stick in the dirt. The only light came from the open door of the house, from the lamp inside. When Deel looked over his shoulder, he saw Mary Lou at the washbasin again, doing the dishes, wiggling her ass. Tom looked in that direction once, then looked at Deel, then looked away at the sky, as if memorizing the positions of the stars.

Tom said, "You and me ain't been huntin' since well before you left."

"You came around a lot then, didn't you?" Deel said.

Tom nodded. "I always felt better here than at home. Mama and Daddy fought all the time."

"I'm sorry about your parents."

"Well," Tom said, "everyone's got a time to die, you know. It can be in all kinds of ways, but sometimes it's just time and you just got to embrace it."

"I reckon that's true."

"What say you and me go huntin'?" Tom said. "I ain't had any possum meat in ages."

"I never did like possum," Deel said. "Too greasy."

"You ain't fixed 'em right. That's one thing I can do, fix up a possum good. Course, best way is catch one and pen it and feed it corn for a week or so, then kill it. Meat's better that way, firmer. But I'd settle for shootin' one, showin' you how to get rid of that gamey taste with some vinegar and such, cook it up with some sweet potatoes. I got more sweet potatoes than I know what to do with."

"Deel likes sweet potatoes," Mary Lou said.

Deel turned. She stood in the doorway drying her hands on a dish towel. She said, "That ought to be a good idea, Deel. Goin' huntin'. I wouldn't mind learnin' how to cook up a possum right. You and Tom ought to go, like the old days."

"I ain't had no sweet potatoes in years," Deel said.

"All the more reason," Tom said.

The boy said, "I want to go."

"That'd be all right," Tom said, "but you know, I think this time I'd like for just me and Deel to go. When I was a kid, he taught me about them woods, and I'd like to go with him, for old time's sake. That all right with you, Winston?"

Winston didn't act like it was all right, but he said, "I guess."

## »«

That night Deel lay beside Mary Lou and said, "I like Tom, but I was thinkin' maybe we could somehow get it so he don't come around so much."

"Oh?"

"I know Winston looks up to him, and I don't mind that, but I need to get to know Winston again... Hell, I didn't ever know him. And I need to get to know you... I owe you some time, Mary Lou. The right kind of time."

"I don't know what you're talkin' about, Deel. The right kind of time?"

Deel thought for a while, tried to find the right phrasing. He knew what he felt, but saying it was a different matter. "I know you ended up with me because I seemed better than some was askin'. Turned out I wasn't quite the catch you thought. But we got to find what we need, Mary Lou."

"What we need?"

"Love. We ain't never found love."

She lay silent.

"I just think," Deel said, "we ought to have our own time together before we start havin' Tom around so much. You understand what I'm sayin', right?"

"I guess so."

"I don't even feel like I'm proper home yet. I ain't been to town or told nobody I'm back."

"Who you missin'?"

Deel thought about that for a long time. "Ain't nobody but you and Winston that I missed, but I need to get some things back to normal... I need to make connections so I can set up some credit at the store, maybe some farm trade for things we need next year. But mostly, I just want to be here with you so we can talk. You and Tom talk a lot. I wish we could talk like that. We need to learn how to talk."

"Tom's easy to talk to. He's a talker. He can talk about anything and make it seem like somethin', but when he's through, he ain't said nothin'... You never was a talker before, Deel, so why now?"

"I want to hear what you got to say, and I want you to hear what I got to say, even if we ain't talkin' about nothin' but seed catalogs or pass the beans, or I need some more firewood or stop snoring. Most anything that's got normal about it. So, thing is, I don't want Tom around so much. I want us to have some time with just you and me and Winston, that's all I'm sayin'."

Deel felt the bed move. He turned to look, and in the dark he saw that Mary Lou was pulling her gown up above her breasts. Her pubic hair looked thick in the dark and her breasts were full and round and inviting.

She said, "Maybe tonight we could get started on knowing each other better."

His mouth was dry. All he could say was, "All right."

His hands trembled as he unbuttoned his union suit at the crotch and she spread her legs and he climbed on top of her. It only took a moment before he exploded.

"Oh, God," he said, and collapsed on her, trying to support his weight on his elbows.

"How was that?" she said. "I feel all right?"

"Fine, but I got done too quick. Oh, girl, it's been so long. I'm sorry."

"That's all right. It don't mean nothin'." She patted him stiffly on the back and then twisted a little so that he'd know she wanted him off her.

"I could do better," he said.

"Tomorrow night."

"Me and Tom, we're huntin' tomorrow night. He's bringin' a dog, and we're gettin' a possum."

"That's right... Night after."

"All right, then," Deel said. "All right, then."

He lay back on the bed and buttoned himself up and tried to decide if he felt better or worse. There had been relief, but no fire. She might as well have been a hole in the mattress.

》《

Tom brought a bitch dog with him and a .22 rifle and a croaker sack. Deel gathered up his double barrel from out of the closet and took it out of its leather sheath coated in oil and found it to be in very good condition. He brought it and a sling bag of shells outside. The shells were old, but he had no cause to doubt their ability. They had been stored along with the gun, dry and contained.

The sky was clear and the stars were out and the moon looked like a carved chunk of fresh lye soap, but it was bright, so bright you could see the ground clearly. The boy was in bed, and Deel and Tom and Mary Lou stood out in front of the house and looked at the night.

Mary Lou said to Tom, "You watch after him, Tom."

"I will," Tom said.

"Make sure he's taken care of," she said.

"I'll take care of him."

Deel and Tom had just started walking toward the woods when they were distracted by a shadow. An owl came diving down toward the field. They saw the bird scoop up a fat mouse and fly away with it. The dog chased the owl's shadow as it cruised along the ground.

As they watched the owl climb into the bright sky and fly toward the woods, Tom said, "Ain't nothin' certain in life, is it?"

"Especially if you're a mouse," Deel said.

"Life can be cruel," Tom said.

"Wasn't no cruelty in that," Deel said. "That was survival. The owl was hungry. Men ain't like that. They ain't like other things, 'cept maybe ants."

"Ants?"

"Ants and man make war 'cause they can. Man makes all kinds of proclamations and speeches and gives reasons and such, but at the bottom of it, we just do it 'cause we want to and can."

"That's a hard way to talk," Tom said.

"Man ain't happy till he kills everything in his path and cuts down everything that grows. He sees something wild and beautiful and wants to hold it down and stab it, punish it 'cause it's wild. Beauty draws him to it, and then he kills it."

"Deel, you got some strange thinkin'," Tom said.

"Reckon I do."

"We're gonna kill so as to have somethin' to eat, but unlike the owl, we ain't eatin' no mouse. We're having us a big, fat possum and we're gonna cook it with sweet potatoes."

They watched as the dog ran on ahead of them, into the dark line of the trees.

»«

When they got to the edge of the woods the shadows of the trees fell over them, and then they were inside the woods, and it was dark in places with gaps of light where the limbs were thin.

They moved toward the gaps and found a trail and walked down it. As they went, the light faded, and Deel looked up. A dark cloud had blown in.

Tom said, "Hell, looks like it's gonna rain. That came out of nowhere."

"It's a runnin' rain," Deel said. "It'll blow in and spit water and blow out before you can find a place to get dry."

"Think so?"

"Yeah. I seen rain aplenty, and one comes up like this, it's traveling through. That cloud will cry its eyes out and move on, promise you. It ain't even got no lightnin' with it."

As if in response to Deel's words it began to rain. No lightning and no thunder, but the wind picked up and the rain was thick and cold.

"I know a good place ahead," Tom said. "We can get under a tree there, and there's a log to sit on. I even killed a couple possums there."

They found the log under the tree, sat down and waited. The tree was an oak and it was old and big and had broad limbs and thick leaves that spread out like a canvas. The leaves kept Deel and Tom almost dry.

"That dog's done gone off deep in the woods," Deel said, and laid the shotgun against the log and put his hands on his knees.

"He gets a possum, you'll hear him. He sounds like a trumpet."

Tom shifted the .22 across his lap and looked at Deel, who was lost in thought. "Sometimes," Deel said, "when we was over there, it would rain, and we'd be in trenches, waiting for somethin' to happen, and the trenches would flood with water, and there was big ole rats that would swim in it, and we was so hungry from time to time, we killed them and ate them."

"Rats?"

"They're same as squirrels. They don't taste as good, though. But a squirrel ain't nothin' but a tree rat."

"Yeah? You sure?"

"I am."

Tom shifted on the log, and when he did Deel turned toward him. Tom still had the .22 lying across his lap, but when Deel looked, the barrel was raised in his direction. Deel started to say somethin', like, "Hey, watch what you're doin'," but in that instant he knew what he should have known all along. Tom was going to kill him. He had always planned to kill him. From the day Mary Lou had met him in the field on horseback, they were anticipating the rattle of his dead bones. It's why they had kept him from town. He was already thought dead, and if no one thought different, there was no crime to consider.

"I knew and I didn't know," Deel said.

"I got to, Deel. It ain't nothin' personal. I like you fine. You been good to me. But I got to do it. She's worth me doin' somethin' like this... Ain't no use reaching for that shotgun, I got you sighted; twenty-two ain't much, but it's enough."

"Winston," Deel said, "he ain't my boy, is he?"

"No."

"He's got a birthmark on his face, and I remember now when you was younger, I seen that same birthmark. I forgot but now I remember. It's under your hair, ain't it?"

Tom didn't say anything. He had scooted back on the log. This put him out from under the edge of the oak canopy, and the rain was washing over his hat and plastering his long hair to the sides of his face.

"You was with my wife back then, when you was eighteen, and I didn't even suspect it," Deel said, and smiled as if he thought there was humor in it. "I figured you for a big kid and nothin' more."

"You're too old for her," Tom said, sighting down the rifle. "And you didn't never give her no real attention. I been with her mostly since you left. I just happened to be gone when you come home. Hell, Deel, I got clothes in the trunk there, and you didn't even see 'em. You might know the weather, but you damn sure don't know women, and you don't know men."

"I don't want to know them, so sometimes I don't know what I know. And men and women, they ain't all that different... You ever killed a man, Tom?"

"You'll be my first."

Deel looked at Tom, who was looking at him along the length of the .22.

"It ain't no easy thing to live with, even if you don't know the man," Deel said. "Me, I killed plenty. They come to see me when I close my eyes. Them I actually seen die, and them I imagined died."

"Don't give me no booger stories. I don't reckon you're gonna come see me when you're dead. I don't reckon that at all."

It had grown dark because of the rain, and Tom's shape was just a shape. Deel couldn't see his features.

"Tom—"

The .22 barked. The bullet struck Deel in the head. He tumbled over the log and fell where there was rain in his face. He thought just before he dropped down into darkness: It's so cool and clean.

### 〉〈

Deel looked over the edge of the trench where there was a slab of metal with a slot to look through. All he could see was darkness except when the lightning ripped a strip in the sky and the countryside lit up. Thunder banged so loudly he couldn't tell the difference between it and cannonfire, which was also banging away, dropping great explosions near the breastworks and into the zigzagging trench, throwing men left and right like dolls.

Then he saw shapes. They moved across the field like a column of ghosts. In one great run they came, closer and closer. He poked his rifle through the slot and took half-ass aim and then the command came and he fired. Machine guns began to burp. The field lit up with their constant red pops. The shapes began to fall. The faces of those in front of the rushing line brightened when the machine guns snapped, making their features devil red. When the lightning flashed they seemed to vibrate across the field. The cannons roared and thunder rumbled and the machine guns coughed and the rifles cracked and men screamed.

Then the remainder of the Germans were across the field and over the trench ramifications and down into the trenches themselves. Hand-to-hand fighting began. Deel fought with his bayonet. He jabbed at a German soldier so small his shoulders failed to fill out his uniform. As the German hung on the thrust of Deel's blade, clutched at the rifle barrel, flares blazed along the length of the trench, and in that moment Deel saw the soldier's chin had bits of blond fuzz on it. The expression the kid wore was that of someone who had just realized this was not a glorious game after all.

And then Deel coughed.

He coughed and began to choke. He tried to lift up, but couldn't, at first. Then he sat up and the mud dripped off him and the rain pounded him. He spat dirt from his mouth and gasped at the air. The rain washed his face clean and pushed his hair down over his forehead. He was uncertain how long he sat there in the rain, but in time, the rain stopped. His head hurt. He lifted his hand to it and came away with his fingers covered in blood. He felt again, pushing his hair aside. There was a groove across his forehead. The shot hadn't hit him solid; it had cut a path across the front of his head. He had bled a lot, but now the bleeding had stopped. The mud in the grave had filled the wound and plugged it. The shallow grave had most likely been dug earlier in the day. It had all been planned out, but the rain was unexpected. The rain made the dirt damp, and in the dark Tom had not covered him well enough. Not deep enough. Not firm enough. And his nose was free. He could breathe. The ground was soft and it couldn't hold him. He had merely sat up and the dirt had fallen aside.

Deel tried to pull himself out of the grave, but was too weak, so he twisted in the loose dirt and lay with his face against the ground. When he was strong enough to lift his head, the rain had passed, the clouds had sailed away, and the moon was bright.

Deel worked himself out of the grave and crawled across the ground toward the log where he and Tom had sat. His shotgun was lying behind the log where it had fallen. Tom had either forgotten the gun or didn't care. Deel was too weak to pick it up.

Deel managed himself onto the log and sat there, his head held down, watching the ground. As he did, a snake crawled over his boots and twisted its way into the darkness of the woods. Deel reached down and picked up the shotgun. It was damp and cold. He opened it and the shells popped out. He didn't try to find them in the dark. He lifted the barrel, poked it toward the moonlight, and looked through it. Clear. No dirt in the barrels. He didn't try to find the two shells that had popped free. He loaded two fresh ones from his ammo bag. He took a deep breath. He picked up some damp leaves and pressed them against the wound and they stuck. He stood up. He staggered toward his house, the blood-stuck leaves decorating his forehead as if he were some kind of forest god.

>《

It was not long before the stagger became a walk. Deel broke free of the woods and onto the path that crossed the field. With the rain gone it was bright again and a light wind had begun to blow. The earth smelled rich, the way it had that night in France when it rained and the lightning flashed and the soldiers came and the damp smell of the earth blended with the biting smell of gunpowder and the odor of death.

He walked until he could see the house, dark like blight in the center of the field. The house appeared extremely small then, smaller than before; it was as if all that had ever mattered to him continued to shrink. The bitch dog came out to meet him but he ignored her. She slunk off and trotted toward the trees he had left behind.

He came to the door, and then his foot was kicking against it. The door cracked and creaked and slammed loudly backward.

Then Deel was inside, walking fast. He came to the bedroom door, and it was open. He went through. The window was up and the room was full of moonlight, so brilliant he could see clearly, and what he saw was Tom and Mary Lou lying together in mid-act, and in that moment he thought of his brief time with her and how she had let him have her so as not to talk about Tom anymore. He thought about how she had given herself to protect what she had with Tom. Something moved inside Deel and he recognized it as the core of what man was. He stared at them and they saw him and froze in action. Mary Lou said, "No," and Tom leaped up from between her legs, all the way to his feet. Naked as nature, he stood for a moment in the middle of the bed, and then plunged through the open window like a fox down a hole. Deel raised the shotgun and fired and took out part of the windowsill, but Tom was out and away. Mary Lou screamed. She threw her legs to the side of the bed and made as if to stand, but couldn't. Her legs were too weak. She sat back down and started yelling his name. Something called from deep inside Deel, a long call, deep and dark and certain. A bloody leaf dripped off his forehead. He raised the shotgun and fired. The shot tore into her breast and knocked her sliding across the bed, pushing the back of her head against the wall beneath the window.

Deel stood looking at her. Her eyes were open, her mouth slightly parted. He watched her hair and the sheets turn dark.

He broke open the shotgun and reloaded the double barrel from his ammo sack and went to the door across the way, the door to the small room that was the boy's. He kicked it open. When he came in, the boy, wearing his nightshirt, was crawling through the window. He shot at him, but the best he might have done was riddle the bottom of his feet with pellets. Like his father, Winston was quick through a hole.

Deel stepped briskly to the open window and looked out. The boy was crossing the moonlit field like a jackrabbit, running toward a dark stretch of woods in the direction of town. Deel climbed through the window and began to stride after the boy. And then he saw Tom. Tom was off to the right, running toward where there used to be a deep ravine and a blackberry growth. Deel went after him. He began to trot. He could imagine himself with the other soldiers crossing a field, waiting for a bullet to end it all.

Deel began to close in. Being barefoot was working against Tom. He was limping. Deel thought that Tom's feet were most likely full of grass burrs and were wounded by stones. Tom's moon shadow stumbled and rose, as if it were his soul trying to separate itself from its host.

The ravine and the blackberry bushes were still there. Tom came to the ravine, found a break in the vines, and went over the side of it and down. Deel came shortly after, dropped into the ravine. It was damp there and smelled fresh from the recent rain. Deel saw Tom scrambling up the other side of the ravine, into the dark rise of blackberry bushes on the far side. He strode after him, and when he came to the spot where Tom had gone, he saw Tom was hung in the berry vines. The vines had twisted around his arms and head and they held him as surely as if he were nailed there. The more Tom struggled, the harder the thorns bit and the better the vines held him. Tom twisted and rolled and soon he was facing in the direction of Deel, hanging just above him on the bank of the ravine, supported by the blackberry vines, one arm outstretched, the other pinned against his abdomen, wrapped up like a Christmas present from nature, a gift to what man and the ants liked to do best. He was breathing heavily.

Deel turned his head slightly, like a dog trying to distinguish what it sees. "You're a bad shot."

"Ain't no cause to do this, Deel."

"It's not a matter of cause. It's the way of man," Deel said.

"What in hell you talkin' about, Deel? I'm askin' you, I'm beggin' you, don't kill me. She was the one talked me into it. She thought you were dead, long dead. She wanted it like it was when it was just me and her."

Deel took a deep breath and tried to taste the air. It had tasted so clean a moment ago, but now it was bitter.

"The boy got away," Deel said.

"Go after him, you want, but don't kill me."

A smile moved across Deel's face. "Even the little ones grow up to be men."

"You ain't makin' no sense, Deel. You ain't right."

"Ain't none of us right," Deel said.

Deel raised the shotgun and fired. Tom's head went away and the body drooped in the clutch of the vines and hung over the edge of the ravine.

》《

The boy was quick, much faster than his father. Deel had covered a lot of ground in search of him, and he could read the boy's sign in the moonlight, see where the grass was pushed down, see bare footprints in the damp dirt, but the boy had long reached the woods, and maybe the town beyond. He knew that. It didn't matter anymore.

He moved away from the woods and back to the field until he came to Pancake Rocks. They were flat, round chunks of sandstone piled on top of one another and they looked like a huge stack of pancakes. He had forgotten all about them. He went to them and stopped and looked at the top edge of the pancake stones. It was twenty feet from ground to top. He remembered that from when he was a boy. His daddy told him, "That there is twenty feet from top to bottom. A Spartan boy could climb that and reach the top in three minutes. I can climb it and reach the top in three minutes. Let's see what you can do."

He had never reached the top in three minutes, though he had tried time after time. It had been important to his father for some reason, some human reason, and he had forgotten all about it until now.

Deel leaned the shotgun against the stones and slipped off his boots and took off his clothes. He tore his shirt and made a strap for the gun, and slung it over his bare shoulder and took up the ammo bag and tossed it over his other shoulder, and began to climb. He made it to the top. He didn't know how long it had taken him, but he guessed it had been only about three minutes. He stood on top of Pancake Rocks and looked out at the night. He could see his house from there. He sat cross-legged on the rocks and stretched the shotgun over his thighs. He looked up at the sky. The stars were bright and the space between them was as deep as forever. If man could, he would tear the stars down, thought Deel.

Deel sat and wondered how late it was. The moon had moved, but not so much as to pull up the sun. Deel felt as if he had been sitting there for days. He nodded off now and then, and in the dream he was an ant, one of many ants, and he was moving toward a hole in the ground from which came smoke and sparks of fire. He marched with the ants toward the hole, and then into the hole they went, one at a time. Just before it was his turn, he saw the ants in front of him turn to black crisps in the fire, and he marched after them, hurrying for his turn, then he awoke and looked across the moonlit field.

He saw, coming from the direction of his house, a rider. The horse looked like a large dog because the rider was so big. He hadn't seen the man in years, but he knew who he was immediately. Lobo Collins. He had been sheriff of the county when he had left for war. He watched as Lobo rode toward him. He had no thoughts about it. He just watched.

Well out of range of Deel's shotgun, Lobo stopped and got off his horse and pulled a rifle out of the saddle boot.

"Deel," Lobo called. "It's Sheriff Lobo Collins."

Lobo's voice moved across the field loud and clear. It was as if they were sitting beside each other. The light was so good he could see Lobo's mustache clearly, drooping over the corners of his mouth.

"Your boy come told me what happened."

"He ain't my boy, Lobo."

"Everybody knowed that but you, but wasn't no cause to do what you did. I been up to the house, and I found Tom in the ravine."

"They're still dead, I assume."

"You ought not done it, but she was your wife, and he was messin' with her, so you got some cause, and a jury might see it that way. That's something to think about, Deel. It could work out for you."

"He shot me," Deel said.

"Well now, that makes it even more different. Why don't you put down that gun, and you and me go back to town and see how we can work things out."

"I was dead before he shot me."

"What?" Lobo said. Lobo had dropped down on one knee. He had the Winchester across that knee and with his other hand he held the bridle of his horse.

Deel raised the shotgun and set the stock firmly against the stone, the barrel pointing skyward.

"You're way out of range up there," Lobo said. "That shotgun ain't gonna reach me, but I can reach you, and I can put one in a fly's asshole from here to the moon."

Deel stood up. "I can't reach you, then I reckon I got to get me a wee bit closer."

Lobo stood up and dropped the horse's reins. The horse didn't move. "Now don't be a damn fool, Deel."

Deel slung the shotgun's makeshift strap over his shoulder and started climbing down the back of the stones, where Lobo couldn't see him. He came down quicker than he had gone up, and he didn't even feel where the stones had torn his naked knees and feet.

When Deel came around the side of the stone, Lobo had moved only slightly, away from his horse, and he was standing with the Winchester held down by his side. He was watching as Deel advanced, naked and committed. Lobo said, "Ain't no sense in this, Deel. I ain't seen you in years, and now I'm gonna get my best look at you down the length of a Winchester. Ain't no sense in it."

"There ain't no sense to nothin'," Deel said, and walked faster, pulling the strapped shotgun off his shoulder.

Lobo backed up a little, then raised the Winchester to his shoulder, said, "Last warnin', Deel."

Deel didn't stop. He pulled the shotgun stock to his hip and let it rip. The shot went wide and fell across the grass like hail, some twenty feet in front of Lobo. And then Lobo fired.

Deel thought someone had shoved him. It felt that way. That someone had walked up unseen beside him and had shoved him on the shoulder. Next thing he knew he was lying on the ground looking up at the stars. He felt pain, but not like the pain he had felt when he realized what he was.

A moment later the shotgun was pulled from his hand, and then Lobo was kneeling down next to him with the Winchester in one hand and the shotgun in the other.

"I done killed you, Deel."

"No," Deel said, spitting up blood. "I ain't alive to kill."

"I think I clipped a lung," Lobo said, as if proud of his marksmanship. "You ought not done what you done. It's good that boy got away. He ain't no cause of nothin'."

"He just ain't had his turn."

Deel's chest was filling up with blood. It was as if someone had put a funnel in his mouth and poured it into him. He tried to say something more, but it wouldn't come out. There was only a cough and some blood; it splattered warm on his chest. Lobo put the weapons down and picked up Deel's head and laid it across one of his thighs so he wasn't choking so much.

"You got a last words, Deel?"

"Look there," Deel said.

Deel's eyes had lifted to the heavens, and Lobo looked. What he saw was the night and the moon and the stars. "Look there. You see it?" Deel said. "The stars are fallin'."

Lobo said, "Ain't nothin' fallin', Deel," but when he looked back down, Deel was gone.

# THE METAL MEN OF MARS

(An authorized John Carter of Mars story)

I suppose some will think it unusual that mere boredom might lead a person on a quest where one's life can become at stake, but I am the sort of individual who prefers the sound of combat and the sight of blood to the peace of Helium's court and the finery of its decorations. Perhaps this is not something to be proud of, but it is in fact my nature, and I honestly admit it.

Certainly, as Jeddak of Helium, I have responsibilities at the court, but there are times when even my beloved and incomparable Dejah Thoris can sympathize with my restlessness, as she has been raised in a warrior culture and has been known to wield a sword herself. She knows when she needs to encourage me to venture forth and find adventure, lest my restlessness and boredom become like some kind of household plague.

Of course, she realizes I may be putting my life on the line, but then again, that is my nature. I am a fighting man. I find that from time to time I must seek out places where adventure still exists, and then, confronted by peril, I take my sword in hand. Of course, there are no guarantees of adventure, and even an adventurous journey may not involve swordplay, but on Barsoom it can be as readily anticipated as one might expect the regular rising and setting of the sun.

Such was the situation as I reclined on our bedroom couch and tried to look interested in what I was seeing out the open window, which was a flat blue, cloudless sky.

Dejah Thoris smiled at me, and that smile was almost enough to destroy my wanderlust, but not quite. She is beyond gorgeous; a raven-haired, red-skinned beauty whose perfectly oval face could belong to a goddess. Her lack of clothing, which is the Martian custom, seems as natural as the heat of the sun. For that matter, there are no clothes or ornaments that can enhance her shape. You can not improve perfection.

"Are you bored, my love?" she asked.

"No," I said. "I am fine."

"You are not," she said, and her lips became pouty. "You should know better than to lie to me."

I came to my feet, took hold of her, and pulled her to me and kissed her. "Of course. No one knows me better. Forgive me."

She studied me for a moment, kissed me and said, "For you to be better company, my prince, I suggest you put on your sword harness and take leave of the palace for a while. I will not take it personally. I know your nature. But I will expect you to come back sound and whole."

I hesitated, started to say that I was fine and secure where I was, that I didn't need to leave, to run about in search of adventure. That she was all I needed. But I knew it was useless. She knew me. And I knew myself.

She touched my chest with her hand.

"Just don't be gone too long," she said.

》《

I arranged for a small two-seater flyer. Dressed in my weapons harness, which held a long needle sword that is common to Barsoom, as well as a slim dagger, I prepared for departure. Into the flyer I loaded a bit of provisions, including sleeping silks for long Martian nights. I kissed my love goodbye, and climbed on board the moored flyer as it floated outside the balcony where Dejah Thoris and I resided.

Dejah Thoris stood watching as I slipped into the seat at the controls of the flyer, and then smiling and waving to me as if I were about to depart for nothing more than a day's picnic, she turned and went down the stairs and into our quarters. Had she shown me one tear, I would have climbed out of the flyer and canceled my plans immediately. But since she had not, I loosed the mooring ropes from where the craft was docked to the balcony, and allowed it to float upward. Then I took to the controls and directed the ship toward the great Martian desert.

Soon I was flying over it, looking down at the yellow moss-like vegetation that runs on for miles. I had no real direction in mind, and decided to veer slightly to the east. Then I gave the flyer its full throttle and hoped something new and interesting lay before me.

》《

I suppose I had been out from Helium for a Martian two weeks or so, and though I had been engaged in a few interesting activities, I hesitate to call any of them adventures. I had spent nights with the craft moored in the air, an anchor dropped to hold it to the ground, while it floated above like a magic carpet; it was a sensation I never failed to enjoy and marvel at. For mooring, I would try to pick a spot where the ground was low and I could be concealed to some degree by hills or desert valley walls. The flyer could be drawn to the ground, but this method of floating a hundred feet in the air, held fast to the ground by the anchor rope, was quite satisfying. The craft was small, but there was a sleeping cubicle, open to the sky. I removed my weapon harness, laid it beside me, and crawled under my sleeping silks and stretched out to sleep.

After two weeks my plan to find adventure had worn thin, and I was set to start back toward Helium and Dejah Thoris on the morning. As I closed my eyes, I thought of her, and was forming her features in my mind, when my flying craft was struck by a terrific impact.

The blow shook me out of my silks, and the next moment I was dangling in the air, clutching at whatever I could grab, as the flyer tilted on its side and began to gradually turn toward the ground. As I clung, the vessel flipped upside down, and I could hear a hissing sound that told me the flyer had lost its peculiar fuel and was about to crash to the desert with me under it.

The Martian atmosphere gave my Earthly muscles a strength not given to those born on the red planet, and it allowed me to swing my body far and free, as the flyer—now falling rapidly—crashed toward the sward. Still, it was a close call, and I was able to swing out from under the flyer only instants before it smashed the ground. As I tumbled along the desert soil beneath the two Martian moons, I glimpsed the flying machine cracking into a half dozen pieces, tossing debris—including my weapon harness—onto the mossy landscape.

Glancing upward, I saw that the author of the flyer's destruction had turned its attention toward me. It was a great golden bird, unlike anything I had ever seen. It was four times the size of my flyer. As I got a better look, its resemblance to a bird evaporated. It looked more like a huge winged dragon, its coating of scales glinting gold in the moonlight. From its tooth-filled mouth, and easing out from under its scales, came the hiss of steam. With a sound akin to that of a creaking door, it dove at top speed toward me.

》《

I practically galloped like a horse toward my weapon harness, and had just laid my hands on it and withdrawn my sword, when I glanced up and saw what I first thought was my reflection in the golden dragon's great black eyes.

But what I saw was not my reflection, but the moonlit silhouettes of figures behind those massive dark eyes. They were mere shapes, like shadows, and I realized in that moment that the golden dragon was not a creature at all: It was a flying machine, something I should have realized immediately as it had not flapped its wings once, but had been moving rapidly about the sky without any obvious means of locomotion.

It dove, and as it came toward me, I instinctively slashed at one of its massive black eyes. I had the satisfaction of hearing it crack just before I dropped to my belly on the sward, and I felt the air from the contraption as it passed above me like an ominous storm cloud, perhaps as close as six inches.

It doesn't suit me to lie facedown with a mouth full of dirt, as it hurts my pride. I sprang to my feet and wheeled to see that the flying machine was still low to the ground, cruising slowly, puffing steam from under its metal scales. I leapt at it, and the Martian gravity gave my Earthly muscles tremendous spring; it was almost like flying. I grabbed at the dragon's tail, which was in fact a kind of rudder, and clung to it as it rose higher and wheeled, no doubt with an intent to turn back and find me.

I grinned as I imagined their surprise at my disappearance. I hugged the tail rudder with both arms without dropping my sword, and pulled. The dragon wobbled. I yanked at it, and a piece of the tail rudder came loose with a groan. I fell backward and hit the ground with tremendous impact; I wasn't that high up, but still, it was quite a fall.

As I lay on the ground, trying to regain the air that had been knocked out of me, I saw the craft was veering wildly. It smacked the ground and threw up chunks of desert, then skidded, bounced skyward again, then came back down, nose first. It struck with tremendous impact. There was a rending sound, like a pot and pan salesman tumbling downhill with his wares, and then the dragon flipped nose over tail and slammed against the desert and came apart in an explosion of white steam and flying metal scales and clockwork innards.

Out of anger and pure chance, I had wrecked the great flying machine.

>> <<

Crawling out of the debris were two of the most peculiar men I had ever seen. They, like the dragon, were golden in color and scaled. White vapor hissed from beneath their metallic scales, and from between their teeth and out of their nostrils. They were moving about on their knees, clanking like knights in armor, their swords dragging in their harnesses across the ground.

Gradually, one of them rose to his feet and looked in my direction; his face was a shiny shield of gold with a broad, unmoving mouth and a long nose that looked like a small piece of folded gold paper. Steam continued to hiss out of his face and from beneath his scales.

The other one crawled a few feet, rolled over on his back, and moved his legs and arms like a turtle turned onto its shell...and then ceased to move at all.

The one standing drew his sword, a heavy-looking thing, and with a burst of steam from his mouth and nose, came running in my direction. When confronted by an enemy with a sword, I do not allow myself to become overconfident. Anything can go wrong at anytime with anyone. But for the most part, when a warrior draws his sword to engage me, I can count on the fact that I will be the better duelist; this is not brag, this is the voice of experience. Not only am I a skilled swordsman, but I have tremendously enhanced agility and strength on my side, all of it due to my Earthly muscles combined with the lighter Martian gravity.

On the armored warrior came, and within an instant we crossed swords. We flicked blades about, wove patterns that we were each able to parry or avoid. But now I understood his method. He was good, but I brought my unique speed and agility into play. An instant later, I was easily outdueling him, but even though my thin blade crisscrossed his armor, leaving scratch marks, I couldn't penetrate it. My opponent's armor was hard and light and durable. No matter what my skill, no matter how much of an advantage I had due to my Earthly muscles, eventually, if I couldn't wound him, he would tire me out.

He lunged and I ducked and put my shoulder into him as I rose up and knocked him back with such force that he hit on his head and flipped over backward. I was on him then, but he surprised me by rolling and coming to his feet, swinging his weapon. I parried his strike close to the hilt of my weapon, drew my short blade with my free hand at the same time, stepped in and stuck it into the eye slot in his helmet.

It was a quick lunge and a withdrawal. He stumbled back, and steam wheezed out of the eye slot and even more furiously from out of his mouth and nose, as well as from beneath his armor's scales. He wobbled and fell to the ground with a clatter.

No sooner had I delighted in my conquest than I realized there had been others in the wreckage, concealed, and I had made the amateur mistake of assuming there had been only two. They had obviously been trapped in the wreckage, and had freed themselves while I was preoccupied. I sensed them behind me and turned. Two were right on top of me and two more were crawling from the remains of the craft. I had only a quick glimpse, for the next thing I knew a sword hilt struck me on the forehead and I took a long leap into blackness.

>《

I do not know how long I was out, but it was still night when I awoke. I was being carried on a piece of the flying dragon wreckage, a large scale. I was bound to it by stout rope and my weapon harness was gone. I did not open my eyes completely, but kept them hooded, and glancing toward my feet, saw that one of the armored men was walking before me, his arms held behind his back, clutching the wreckage I was strapped to as he walked. His scales breathed steam as he walked. It was easy to conclude another bearer was at my head, supporting that end, and I was being borne slowly across the Martian desert.

After a moment, I discarded all pretenses and opened my eyes fully to see that the other two were walking nearby. The fact they had not killed me when they had the chance, especially after I had been responsible for killing two of their own and destroying their craft, meant they had other ideas for me; I doubted they were pleasant.

The moonlight was bright enough that I could see that the landscape had changed, and that we were slowly and gradually descending into a valley. The foliage that grew on either side of the trail we were using was unlike any I had seen on Mars, though even in the moonlight, there was much I could not determine. But it was tall foliage for Mars, and some of it bore berries and fruit. I had the impression the growth was of many colors, though at night this was merely a guess made according to variation in shading.

Down we went, my captors jarring me along. I felt considerably low, not only due to my situation, but because I had allowed myself to fall into it. I might have defended myself adequately with my sword, but I had been so engaged with the one warrior, I had not expected the others. I thought of Dejah Thoris, and wondered if I would ever see her again. Then that thought passed. I would have it no other way. All that mattered was I was alive. As long as I was alive, there was hope.

"I still live," I said to the heavens, and it startled my wardens enough that they stumbled, nearly dropping me.

We traveled like this for days, and the only time I was released was to be watered and fed some unidentifiable gruel and to make my toilet. Unarmed or not, I might have made a good fight had the blow to my head not been so severe. Fact was, I welcomed the moment when I was tied down again and carried. Standing up for too long made me dizzy and my head felt as if a herd of thoats were riding at full gallop across it.

I will dispense with the details of the days it took us to arrive at our destination, but to sum it up, we kept slowly descending into the valley, and as we did the vegetation became thicker and more unique.

During the day we camped, and began our travels just before night. I never saw my captors lie down and sleep, but as morning came they would check to make sure I was well secured. Then they would sit near the scale on which I was bound, and rest, though I never thought of them as tired in the normal manner, but more worn-down as if they were short on fuel. For that matter, I never saw them eat or drink water. After several hours, they seemed to have built up the steam that was inside their armor, for it began to puff more vigorously, and the steam itself became white as snowfall. I tried speaking to them a few times, but it was useless. I might as well have been speaking to a Yankee politician for all the attention they paid.

After a few days, the valley changed. There was a great over-hang of rock, and beneath the overhang were shadows so thick you could have shaved chunks out of them with a sword. Into the shadows we went. My captors, with their catlike vision, or batlike radar, were easily capable of traversing the path that was unseen to me. Even time didn't allow my eyes to adjust. I could hear their armored feet on the trail, the hiss of steam that came from their bodies. I could feel the warmth of that steam in the air. I could tell that the trail was slanting, but as for sight, there was only darkness.

It seemed that we went like that for days, but there was no way to measure or even estimate time. Finally the shadows soft-ened and we were inside a cavern that linked to other caverns, like vast rooms in the house of a god. It was lit up by illumina-tion that came from a yellow moss that grew along the walls and coated the high rocky ceilings from which dangled stalactites. The light was soft and constant; a golden mist.

If that wasn't surprising enough, there was running water; something as rare on Mars as common sense is to all the creatures of the universe. It ran in creeks throughout the cavern and there was thick brush near the water and short, twisted, but vibrant trees flushed with green leaves. It was evident that the moss not only provided a kind of light, but other essentials to life, same as the sun. There was a cool wind lightly blowing and the leaves on the trees shook gently and made a sound like someone walking on crumpled paper.

Eventually, we came to our destination, and when we did I was lifted upright, like an insect pinned to a board, and carried that way by the two warriors gripping the back of the scale. The others followed. Then I saw something that made my eyes nearly pop from my head.

It was a city of rising gold spires and clockwork machines that caused ramps to run from one building to another. The ramps moved and switched to new locations with amazing timing; it all came about with clicking and clucking sounds of metal snapping together, unseen machinery winding and twisting and puffing out steam through all manner of shafts and man-made crevices. There were wagons on the ramps, puffing vapor, running by means of silent motors, gliding on smooth rolling wheels. There were armored warriors walking across the ramps, blowing white fog from their faces and from beneath their scales like teakettles about to boil. The wind I felt was made by enormous fans supported on pedestals.

The buildings and their spires rose up high, but not to the roof of the caverns, which I now realized were higher than I first thought. There were vast windows at the tops of the buildings; they were colored blue and yellow, orange and white, and gave the impression of not being made of glass, but of some transparent stone.

Dragon crafts, large and small, flittered about in the heights. It was a kind of fairy-tale place; a vast contrast from the desert world above.

The most spectacular construction was a compound, gold in color, tall and vast, surrounded by high walls and with higher spires inside. The gold gates that led into the compound were spread wide on either side. Steam rose out of the construction, giving it the appearance of something smoldering and soon to be on fire. Before the vast gates was a wide moat of water. The water was dark as sewage, and little crystalline things shaped like fish swam in it and rose up from time to time to show long, brown teeth.

A drawbridge lowered with a mild squeak, like a sleepy mouse having a bad dream. As it lowered, steam came from the gear work and filled the air to such an extent that I coughed. They carried me across the drawbridge and into the inner workings of the citadel, out of the fairy tale and into a house of horrors.

## 》《

For a moment we were on streets of gold stone. Then we veered left and came to a dark mouthlike opening in the ground. Steam gasped loudly from the opening, like an old man choking on cigar smoke. There was a ramp that descended into the gap, and my bearers carried me down it. The light in the hole was not bright. There was no glowing moss. Small lamps hung in spots along the wall and emitted heavy orange flames that provided little illumination; the light wrestled with the cotton-thick steam and neither was a clear winner.

In considerable contrast to above, with its near-silent clock-work and slight hissing, it was loud in the hole. There was banging and booming and screaming that made the hair on the back of my neck prick.

As we terminated the ramp and came to walk on firm ground, the sounds grew louder. We passed Red Martians, men and women, strapped to machines that were slowly stripping their flesh off in long, bloody bands. Other machines screwed the tops of their heads off like jar lids. This was followed by clawed devices that dipped into the skull cavity and snapped out the brain and dunked it into an oily blue liquid in a vat. Inside the vat the liquid spun about in fast whirls. The brains came apart like old cabbages left too long in the ground. More machines groaned and hissed and clawed and yanked the victims' bones loose. Viscera was removed. All of this was accompanied by the screams of the dying. When the sufferers were harvested of their bodily parts, a conveyer brought fresh meat along; Red Martians struggling in their straps, gliding inevitably toward their fate. And all the time, below them were the armored warriors, their steam-puffing faces lifted upward, holding long rods to assist the conveyer that was bringing the sufferers along, dangling above the metal men like ripe fruit ready for the picking.

》《

The cage where they put me was deep in the bowels of the caverns, below the machines. There were a large number of cages, and they were filled mostly with Red Martians, though there were also a few fifteen-foot-tall, four-armed, green-skinned Tharks, their boarlike tusks wet and shiny.

The armored warriors opened a cage, and the two gold warriors, who had followed my bearers, sprang forward and shoved those who tried to escape back inside. I was unbound and pushed in to join them. They slammed the barred gate and locked it with a key. Men and women in the cage grabbed at the bars and tried uselessly to pull them loose. They yelled foul epithets at our captors.

I wandered to the far side of our prison, which was a solid wall, and slid down to sit with my back to it. Though I was weak, and in pain, I tried to observe my circumstances, attempted to formulate a plan of escape.

One Red man came forward and stood over me. He said, "John Carter, Jeddak of Helium."

I looked up in surprise. "You know me?"

"I do, for I was once a soldier of Helium. My name is Farr Larvis."

I managed to stand, wobbling only slightly. I reached out and clasped his shoulder. "I regret I didn't recognize you, but I know your name. You are well respected in Helium."

"Was respected," he said.

"We wondered what happened to your patrol," I said. "We searched for days."

Farr Larvis was a name well-known in Helium: a general of some renown who had fought well for our great city. During one of our many conflicts with the Green Men of Mars, he and a clutch of warriors had been sent to protect citizens on the outskirts of the city from Thark invaders. The invaders had been driven back, Farr Larvis and his men pursuing on their thoats. After that, they had not been heard of again. Search parties were sent out, and for weeks they were sought, without so much as a trace.

"We chased the Tharks," Farr Larvis said, "and finally met them in final combat. We lost many men, but in the end prevailed. Those of us who remained prepared to return to Helium. But one night we made our camp and the gold ones came in their great winged beasts. They came to us silently and dropped nets, and before we could put up a fight, hoisted us up inside the bellies of their beasts. We were brought here. I regret to inform you, John Carter, that of my soldiers, I and two others are all that remain. The rest have become one with the machine."

He pointed the survivors out to me in the crowd.

I clasped his shoulder again. "I know you fought well. I am weak. I must sit."

We both sat and talked while the other Red Martians wandered about the cell, some moaning and crying, others merely standing like cattle waiting their turn in the slaughterhouse line. Farr Larvis's two soldiers sat against the bars, not moving, waiting. If they were frightened, it didn't show in their eyes.

"The gold men, they are not men at all," Farr Larvis told me.

"Machines?" I said.

"You would think, but no. They are neither man nor machine, but both. They are made up of body parts and cogs and wheels and puffs of steam. And most importantly, the very spirits of the living. Odar Rukk is responsible."

"And who and what is he?" I asked.

"His ancestors are from the far north, the rare area where there is ice and snow. They were a wicked race, according to Odar Rukk, fueled by the needs of the flesh. They were warlike, destroying every tribe within their range."

"Odar Rukk told you this personally?"

"He speaks to us all," said Farr Larvis. "There are constant messages spilled out over speakers. They tell his history, they tell his plans. They explain our fate, and how we are supposed to accept it. According to him, in one night there came a great melting in the north, and the snow and much of the ice collapsed. Their race was lost, except for those driven underground. These were people who found a chamber that led down into the earth. It was warmer there, and they survived because the walls were covered in moss that gave heat and light. There were wild plants and wild animals, and the melting ice and snow leaked down into the world and formed lakes and creeks and rivers. In time these people populated all of the underground. They found gold. They discovered hissing vats of volcanic release; it's the power source for most of what occurs here. They built this city.

"But in time, the time of Odar Rukk, the people began to return to their old ways. The ways that led to their destruction by the gods. And Odar Rukk, a scientist who helped devise the way this city works, decided, along with idealistic volunteers, that there was a need for a new and better world. Gradually, he changed these volunteers into these gold warriors, and then they captured the others and changed them. The goal was to eliminate the needs of people, and to make them machinelike."

"All of them under his control?" I said.

"Correct," Farr Larvis said. "Ah, here comes the voice."

And so it came: Odar Rukk's voice floating out from wall speakers and filling the chambers like water. It was a thin voice, but clear, and he spoke for hours and hours, explained how we were all part of a new future, that we should submit, and that soon all our needs, all our desires for greed and romance and success and war, would be behind us. We would be blended in blood and bone and spirit. We would be collectively part of the greatest race that Barsoom had ever known. And soon the gold ones would spread out far and wide, crunching all Martians beneath their steam-powered plans.

## 》《

I do not know how long we waited there in the cell, but every day the gold ones came and brought us food, which was some kind of gruel. They gave us water and we made our toilet where we could. And then came the day when the speakers did not speak. Odar Rukk's voice did not drone. There was only silence, except for the moaning and crying from the captives.

"The gold ones come today," Farr Larvis said. "On the day of Complete Silence. They take the people away and they do not come back."

"I suggest, then, that we do not let them take us easily," I said. "We must fight. And if they should carry us away, we should fight still."

"If it is at all possible," Farr Larvis said, "I will fight to the bitter end. I will fight until the machines take me apart."

"It is all we can do," I said. "And sometimes, that is enough."

True to Farr Larvis's word, they came. There were many of them, and they marched in time in single file. They brought a gold key and snicked it in the cell lock. They entered the cell, and the moans and cries of the Red Martians rose up.

"Silence," Farr Larvis yelled. "Do not give them the satisfaction."

But they did not go silent.

The gold ones came in with short little sticks that gave off shocks. I fought them, because I knew nothing other than to fight. They came and I knocked them down with my fist, their armor crunching beneath my Earthly strength. There were too many, however, and finally I went down beneath their shocks. My hands were bound quickly with rope in front of me, and I was lifted up.

Farr Larvis fought well, and so did his two men, but they took them, and all the others, and carried them away.

Along the narrow path between the cells we went, in their clutches, and then a curious thing happened. The half a dozen gold ones carrying me, giving me intermittent shocks with their stinging rods, veered off and took me away from the mass being driven toward the Meat Rooms, as Farr Larvis called them: the place of annihilation.

I was being separated from the others, carried toward some separate fate.

Farr Larvis called out: "Good-bye, John Carter."

"Remember," I said back. "We still live."

》《

They hauled me into a colossal room which was really a cavern. The walls sweated gooey liquid gold, thick as glowing honey. There were clear tubes running along the ceiling and they were full of the yellow liquid. In spots the tubes leaked, and the fluid dripped from the leaks and fell in splotches like golden bird droppings to the ground. The air in the room was heavily misted with gold. It gave the illusion that we were like flies struggling through amber. There was a cool wet wind flowing through the cavern, its temperature just short of being cold.

I was carried forward to where a domed building could be seen at the peak of a pyramid of steps. On the top of the dome was an immense orb made of transparent stone, and it was full of the golden elixir. It popped and bubbled and splattered against the globe. Up we went, and finally, after giving me a series of shocks to make sure my resistance was lowered, they laid me on the ground and stood around me, waited, looked up at the dome and globe.

A part of the dome's wall lowered with the expected hiss of steam. A multi-wheeled machine rolled out, and in it sat an obese, naked, red-skinned man with a misshapen skull. The skull was bare except for a few strands of gray hair that floated above it in the gold-tinted wind, wriggling like albino roach antennae. The eyes in the skull were dark and beady and rheumy; one of them had a mind of its own, wandering first up, and then down, then left to right. His massive belly looked ready to pop, like an overripe pomegranate. He was without legs. In fact, from his lower torso on, he was machine. Hoses and wires ran from the wheeled conveyance to the back of his head, and when he breathed, steam issued from his mouth and nose like a snorting dragon. His long, skeletal fingers rested on the arms of the chair, in easy reach of a series of buttons and switches and levers and dials. Off of the chair trailed transparent tubes pulsing with the gold fluid, and red and blue and green and yellow wires. All of this twisted back behind him, along the ramp, and into the dome, and I could see where the wires and hoses curled upward toward the globe. All of this ran out from the globe and into the wall behind it.

Having recovered somewhat from the electrical shocks, I slowly stood up. Two of the gold men moved toward me.

"Leave him," said the man, who I knew to be Odar Rukk. I had heard his voice many times over the speakers in the walls. "Leave him be."

He fixed his good eye on me. "Your name?"

I pushed out my chest and stuck out my chin. "John Carter, Warlord of Mars."

"Ah, that obviously means something to you, but it means nothing to me. Do you know who I am?"

"A madman named Odar Rukk."

He smiled, and the smile was a glint of metal teeth and hissing steam. "Yes, I am Odar Rukk, and I may be the only sane man on Barsoom."

"I would not put that up for a vote," I said.

"Oh, I don't know. My golden army would agree."

"They neither agree or disagree," I said. "They blindly obey."

"As do all armies."

"Armies and men fight for beliefs and for purpose."

"Oh. You titled yourself Warlord of Mars. Do you not enjoy battle? War?"

I said nothing. He had spoken the truth. It was not all about ideals.

"I brought you here because my golden warriors have been recording in their memory cells all that they saw you do. They know you single-handedly brought down my flying machine, destroyed one of their kind in the crash, another with your swordsmanship. Those events they recorded in their heads and now those events are in my head."

Odar Rukk paused to tap his skull with the tip of his index finger.

"They brought those images to me, and with but a twist of a dial and the flick of a switch, they come into my head and I see what they have seen. They showed me a man who could do extraordinary things. Before I take those things from you, tell me, John Carter, Warlord of Mars, why are you so different?"

"I am from Earth. The gravity is heavier there. It makes me stronger here. And most importantly, I do what I do because I am who I am. John Carter, formerly of a place called Virginia."

"You, John Carter, will be my personal fuel. I will suck out your spirit and your abilities and into me directly they will go."

"You will still be you. Not me."

"I do not wish to be you, John Carter. I wish to take away your spirit, your powers. I will use them to live longer yet. I will use them to change this planet for the better. Soon, I will spread our empire. I will take away the insignificant needs of men and women. I will eliminate hunger and fear and war, all the negative aspects."

"Except for yourself," I said. "You remain very manlike."

Odar Rukk smiled that steamy, gleaming smile again. "Someone must rule. Someone must control. There must be one mind that oversees and does not merely respond. That is my burden."

"What you have done here is nothing more than an exercise in vanity," I said.

"Have it your way," he said. "But soon your strength, your will, shall be contained inside of me, and I will be stronger than before. When I saw what you could do, your uniqueness, I decided it would be all mine. Not spread out among the others. But all mine."

"Being unique somewhat spoils your vision of everyone and everything being alike, does it not?"

"I have no need to argue, John Carter," he said. "I have the power here, not you. And in moments, when you are strapped in and sucked out and all those abilities are pumped into me, you will cease to exist, and I will be stronger."

The shocks had worn off, and the ropes they had tied me with had loosened. They had not been tied that well to begin with, but still, they were sufficient to hold me. No matter. I had decided I would give my life dearly before I let this monster take away my spirit, my abilities, my blood and bones and flesh.

And then, when I was on the verge of hurling myself at Odar Rukk, knocking him out of his chair with my body, with the intent of trying to bite his throat out, there was an unexpected change of situation.

>《

There was a noise beyond our cavern, a noise that echoed into our huge chamber and clamored about the walls like a series of great metal butterflies clanging against the walls. It was the sound of conflict from beyond our cavern. Somehow, I knew it was Farr Larvis and his two warriors. They were managing to put up a last hard fight.

In that moment, with Odar Rukk's head twisting about, trying to find the source of the sound, the gold ones having turned their attention to the back of the cave, I jumped toward the nearest gold one, grabbed his sword with my bound hands, and pulled it from its sheath. I sliced at him, catching him beneath the helmet and slicing his head off his shoulders. There was a spurt of gold liquid from his neck, a spark from a batch of severed wires, and he went down.

I managed to twist the sword in my hand and cut my rope and free my hands. Then I turned as they came at me. I wove my sword like a tapestry of steel. Poking through eye slots, slicing under the helmets, taking off heads, chopping legs and arms free at joint connections where the armor was thinnest.

I spun about for a look, saw Odar Rukk had wheeled his machine about and was darting up the ramp, back into the dome. Already the ramp was rising. Soon he would be safe inside. I leapt. My Earthly muscles saved me again, for the horde of gold men were about to be on me, thick as a cluster of grapes, and even with all my skill, I could not have fought them all. I landed on the ramp. It was continuing to lift, and it unsettled my footing. I started to slide after Odar Rukk, who had already driven himself inside the dome.

When the door clamped shut, I was in a large room with Odar Rukk. He had turned himself about in the chair, the hoses and wires fastened to the back of it twisted with him. I saw at a glance that the walls were lined with darkened bodies, both Red folk and Green Men. They hung like flies in webs, but the webs were wires and hoses and metal clamps. This was undoubtedly Odar Rukk's power source, something he had planned for me to become a part of.

"This is your day of reckoning, Odar Rukk," I said.

From somewhere he produced a pistol and fired. The handguns of Barsoom are notoriously inaccurate, as well as few and far between, but the shot had been a close one. I leapt away. The gun blasted again, and its beam came closer still. I threw my sword and had the satisfaction of seeing it go deep into his shoulder. His gun hand wavered.

Leaping again, I drove both my feet in front of me. I hit Odar Rukk in the chest with tremendous impact. The blow knocked him and his attached machine chair backward, tipping it over. Odar Rukk skidded across the floor. The part of him that was machine threw up sparks. Hoses came unclamped, spewed gold fluid. Wires came loose and popped with electric current. Odar Rukk screamed.

I hustled to my feet and sprang toward him to administer a death blow, but it was unnecessary. The hoses and wires had been his arteries, his life force, and now they were undone. Odar Rukk's body came free of the chair connection with a snick, and he slipped from it, revealing the bottom of his torso, a scarred and cauterized mess with wire and hose connections, now severed. The fat belly burst open and revealed not only blood and organs, but gears and wheels and tangles of wires and hoses. His flesh went dark and fell from his skull and his eyes sank in his head like fishing sinkers. A moment later, he was nothing more than a piece of fragmented machine and rotten flesh and yellow bones.

I recovered his firearm, cut some of the wire from the machine-man loose with my sword, used it to make a belt, and stuck the pistol between it and my flesh. I recovered my sword.

Outside of the locked dome, I could hear the clatter of battle. Farr Larvis had been more successful than I expected. But even if he had put together an army, the metal men would soon make short work of them.

I looked up at the pulsing globe that rose through the top of the dome. I jumped and grabbed the side of the dome, in a place where my hands could best take purchase, and clambered up rapidly to the globe, my sword in my teeth.

Finally I came to the rim below the globe. There was a metal rim there, and it was wide enough for me to stand on it. I took hold of my sword, and with all my strength, I struck.

The blow was hard, but the structure, which I was now certain was some form of transparent stone, withstood it. I withdrew the pistol and fired. The blast needled a hole in the dome and a spurt of gold liquid nearly hit me in the face. I moved to the side and it gushed out at a tremendous rate. I fired again. Another hole appeared and more of the gold goo leapt free. The globe cracked slightly, then terrifically, generating a web of cracks throughout. Then it exploded and the fluid blew out of it like a massive ocean wave. It washed me away, slamming me into the far wall. I went under, losing the pistol and sword. I tried my best to swim. Something, perhaps a fragment of the globe, struck my head and I went out.

〉〈

When I awoke, I was outside the dome, which had collapsed like wet paper. I was lying on my back, my head being lifted up by a smiling Farr Larvis.

"When you broke the globe, it caused the gold men to collapse. It was their life source."

"And Odar Rukk's," I said.

"It was a good thing," Farr Larvis said. "The revolt I led was not doing too well. It was exactly at the right moment, John Carter. Though we were nearly all washed away. Including you."

I grinned at him. "We still live."

〉〈

There isn't much left to tell.

Simply put, all of us who had survived gathered up weapons and started out as the machinery that Odar Rukk had invented gradually ceased to work. The drawbridge was down. All the gates throughout the underground city had sprung open, and had hissed out the last of their steam. The gold ones were lying about like uneven pavement stones.

We found water containers and filled them. We tore moss from the walls and used it for light, made our way up the long path out. After much time, we came to the surface. We gathered up fruit and such things as we thought we could eat on our journey, and then we climbed higher out of the green valley until we stood happily on the warm desert sand.

It was a long trip home, and there were minor adventures, but nothing worth mentioning. Eventually we came within sight of Helium, and I paused and stood before the group, which was of significant size, and swore allegiance to them as Jeddak of Helium, and in return they swore the same to me.

Then we started the last leg of our journey, and as we went, I thought of Dejah Thoris, and how so very soon she would be in my arms again.

# MORNING, NOON, AND NIGHT

**B**illy was walking in the woods just before noon, throwing his large blade pocketknife at the ground, sticking it through leaves. He liked the woods, and since his father liked to drink all day Saturday at the Dew Drop Inn, there really wasn't much to do at home since his father had hocked the TV set for beer money and Billy's mother was dead.

The fall woods smelled good though, and Billy pulled his knife from the ground and took out a handkerchief and rubbed the blade clean of dirt and told himself he would oil it when he got home. He folded it up and put it in his pocket and put his handkerchief back.

He walked till he came to the huge oak he thought of as his tree. He had read a story about Robin Hood once, and in the story Robin and his men met under a big oak tree in Sherwood Forest, and sometimes he liked to pretend he was Robin Hood. The tree was easy to climb too, with a limb you jumped up and grabbed, and then well spaced limbs that went up amongst easy-to-climb boughs.

He had once jumped from near the top of the oak to the sweet gum tree next to it, and had climbed down from there, so he liked to go up the oak and down the sweet gum when he came to the woods. The sweet gum wasn't as easy to climb up, but for some reason, it was easy to climb down.

Billy was thinking about that when he heard something in the woods. He went toward a cluster of brush and looked through it and saw a deer running right toward him. The deer was probably a good hundred yards away, in a lightning-burned-out clearing, and it was running fast and frantic. It dodged to the left, and then to the right, and then it stumbled, and the air around the deer seemed to wobble, and there was a man running alongside the deer, just as fast as the deer ran. He hadn't been there one minute before, and then the air had wavered and he had appeared. He had been invisible. The man grabbed the deer by the neck and brought it down and clenched it tight, as if in a grappling choke.

Billy let out a gasp as the man's mouth came down on the deer's neck; it went way wide, and Billy could see rows of needle-like teeth biting into the deer. Without meaning to, Billy let out another gasp and backed up, and through the brush he could see that the man had heard him. The man shifted his eyes without letting his mouth slip off the deer, and Billy could hear the man sucking at the deer's throat. He could see blood seeping out onto the deer's neck and onto the ground.

The man ripped the deer's throat out with a jerk of his head. He stood up and wiped his bloody mouth on a plaid shirt sleeve, moved his head from side to side like a cobra watching its prey.

Billy ran to the oak and jumped up and grabbed the limb and climbed fast.

He could hear the man stomping through the brush, and when Billy looked down, the man was already under the tree. He couldn't believe how fast the man could run.

The man looked up, moved his head around to find a spot through the limbs and dying brown and gold leaves, find a spot where he could get a good look at Billy.

"Reckon you seen what I did to that deer, didn't you?" the man said, his words a little muffled due to the mouthful of teeth.

Since the man's face and shirt were covered in blood, Billy felt this wasn't a question that needed answering. As he watched, the man flexed his lips and wriggled his jaw and the teeth in his mouth disappeared inside his gums, and all that could be seen now was a top and bottom row of normal teeth.

"You ain't got no cause to be scared none," the man said. "Why don't you come down so you and me can talk."

Billy didn't budge.

"You know," said the man. "I can come up there after you."

Billy thought: well come on, and I'll jump to the sweet gum and hit the ground and be gone. Then he thought about how fast he had seen the man running. First he was invisible, and then he was running. Billy decided he wouldn't have much chance of outrunning him.

"I could fix it so you could do the same thing I can," the man said. "You come down, and I'll show you."

Billy didn't offer to come down.

"Well, I can fix you the same. You know, so you can be invisible or run real fast."

"I don't want to run no deer down in the woods and bite its neck and suck its blood."

"It's messy, I admit. But one thing happens when you get the change, you don't care much for grilled steak and taters. You like it raw and you like it wet, and you like to take it down alive. It tastes better than you could ever imagine."

"I'll just have to imagine," Billy said.

The man looked up and smiled. His mouth was coated in gore, and it made Billy sick to look at him.

"I don't want no one tellin' about me," the man said. "What can I do?"

"I ain't gonna say nothin'," Billy said. "'sides, who's gonna believe me?"

The man nodded. "You got you a point there, but the thing is, I can't take no chances. If you're deader than last Christmas, I ain't got to worry about you sayin' a thing."

"So you was lyin' when you said you'd show me how to do what you do?"

"Reckon I was. But I could still show you. I don't have to kill you."

"I don't trust you," Billy said.

"I wouldn't trust me neither, but I don't know you got no choice."

"I'm up in this here tree, and you're down there standin' on the ground."

"There's an old sayin' about how some fellas would rather climb a tree and tell a lie than stand on the ground and tell the truth. That could be me. But if I have to come up there after you, you can count on bein' dead. Ain't nobody gonna find you when I get through. I can suck out your blood and insides and suck until your bones turn to liquid, suck until your teeth turns the same and your skin shrivels up and there ain't no more left than enough to fold up like a handkerchief and put in my pocket. Then, when I get the sniffles, I'll blow my nose on you."

"You want me, you got to climb up after me."

"I might just do that, but you know, I don't have to. I'm special. You ain't special, but I am. My daddy, he always told me I wasn't worth the gun powder to blow me up, but he was wrong. I got me some abilities. I don't know how I come by them, but I found I had them, morning, noon and night. I can turn invisible when the sun breaks day. I can be like that all mornin' long, and then just before noon it starts to go away. But I can run fast then, and I can keep right on doin' that for a long time, and then when it gets night, I can jump like a kangaroo. Higher than a kangaroo. It comes night, I don't have to climb up there. I can jump up there and get you. I can do other things too."

"Jump?"

"Oh yeah. Way high."

"How come you're so special?" Billy asked. "How come you got these powers and I ain't and nobody else ain't?"

"I was born with them, but didn't know about them. They kicked in when I was twenty-five. I'm thirty now. I've got so I know how they work. When they first kicked in, I didn't know what to think. Early in the morning, I turned invisible. I got used to that, I tried stealin' things, but the things I touched weren't invisible, and folks would see them move, and I had drop them and run. So, I made me a little money doin' magic acts. Goin' invisible, and then walkin' around and movin' things. But I had to do it in the mornin'. Come noon, or thereabouts, my speed come on me then, and it overlapped with the invisibility for a few minutes, and then what I could do was run real fast. I'd snatch purses, and there weren't no one could catch me. I can run faster than that deer, for instance. I can outrun one of them African cats, them spotted ones. I ain't tried it, but I know I can. When I'm like this, ain't nobody can catch me that's on the ground."

"On the ground?" Billy said.

The man looked up. "You caught that, huh? Yeah, I climb up there I lose my runnin' powers cause I ain't in touch with the ground. And I get weak. Real weak. At least during the time the runnin' is on me. So climbin' a tree, it's a bother. But way I figure it, it don't matter. You got to come down eventually, and when it comes night, runnin' power goes away till the next day. Then I got the jumpin' power and such."

"What about all them teeth?" Billy asked.

The man wiggled his mouth and popped his jaw and spread his lips way too wide and tapped his now-needle teeth with the tip of a finger. "They're real strong, and they got hollows in them so I can suck blood. I can kill with them. I can eat with them. And if I got the time I can do what I said before, suck you flat and small."

Another moving of the jaw and the teeth shrunk and disappeared inside his mouth. Billy wondered where the teeth went. Were they inside his head? How the hell could anyone do that?

"I got my powers, I got the teeth. I can will them at any time. Ain't no time of day they won't work. And the thing I found, I

crave blood. Lots of it. It's a need that kicked in when the pow-
ers did. One time, I went without blood, and I didn't have no
powers durin' that time. The powers feed off blood. You see, like
I told you, I'm special. I was born this way. I don't know how.
My father and mother weren't this way. But I am. It's a gift.
Maybe from the devil. Maybe from some other god than the one
Christians worship. Maybe it's what they call DNA, and mine,
for whatever reason, is all messed up. It don't matter. I am what
I am, and you are who you are, my nighttime snack."

"You're just tellin' me the same stuff over again."

"It's a way to fill the time," the man said.

Billy sat up in the tree and watched the man, who ran out of
talking and went to sit in the shade under the sweet gum. The
day eased along, and Billy found that he was nodding. He startled awake a couple of times, grabbed at limbs and saved himself
from falling. The second time he did that, he noticed it had just
turned night. The dark had slipped in quick like a snake, all soft
and shadowy and with a rising partial moon seemingly dropping
down to nest in the trees.

The man was no longer under the sweet gum. He was standing
under the oak, looking up, showing his teeth in the moonlight;
the silver gleam of the light on the round spittle pops on his teeth
looked like miniature pearls.

Without seeming to flex, the man leaped and was halfway up
the tree. Billy turned and fled along a limb, swung to another,
and was about to leap from the oak to the sweet gum, when the
man laid a hand on his shoulder and spun him. Somehow, Billy
managed not to fall off the limb, but it didn't matter much. The
man had hold of him, and now they were facing one another. The
man's teeth were wet and shiny in the moonlight and his breath
was as putrid as a sewer.

"I think," said the man, "I'm what some people call vampires.
I don't know what I am, but the blood you got in your body, I can
hear it. I can hear it runnin' through your veins. I can hear your
heart beatin' like a tom-tom."

The man was playing with him. Billy realized that and let his hand slip to his pocket and brought out his knife and flicked the blade open with a twist of his wrist and brought it up under the arm the man was using to grasp him by the neck. He brought the blade into the man's armpit as hard as he could, and when he felt it go in, deep, he twisted. A stream of blood, dark as oil, spurted out of the armpit, and the man made a noise like someone swallowing a rock. The grip on Billy's throat went limp, and the man grabbed at a limb with his good arm, but the blood poured out of the wound so fast it was as if the man were an open oil can turned upside down.

The man's head dipped, and then, without so much as a grunt, he fell from the tree, bounced against a limb, and smacked the ground right on top of his head. His neck twisted and there was a noise like dog biting into a chicken bone. The man sort of stood on his bent neck for a moment, and then his legs lowered to the ground slowly, and he rolled over on his side.

For a long moment Billy just looked at the unmoving man. Finally, he took out his handkerchief and wiped the knife clean as possible. He dropped the cloth from the tree and it floated down and landed on the man like a leaf.

Billy folded up his knife and slipped it back in his pocket. He didn't want to go down the oak. He didn't want to be near the strange man, dead or not. He climbed along the oak and made the transition to the sweet gum, and climbed down from there.

Looking back, he saw the man was still lying on the ground, not moving.

Billy bolted for home.

When Billy got home his father's car was still gone and the house was dark and empty. Billy thought about what had happened, and realized he had killed a man. He didn't know how to feel about it. Was it really a man? Certainly it was self defense.

Billy unlocked the house and went in and locked the door back. He walked around nervously for awhile, going from room to room. He sat in the dark and waited on his father, but he didn't show. He was probably good and drunk now, and the only way he was coming home was if someone brought him, or he came home with the woman he had been seeing. The one with the tall hairdo.

Billy finally got up and went in the kitchen and looked at the time. Ten p.m. He opened up the refrigerator and got out the milk and poured a glass and got two slices of almost stale bread and lathered them with mayonnaise and made a sandwich of that. He ended up eating two of the sandwiches and drinking another glass of milk.

He sat in the kitchen for a long time and waited, but his father didn't come home. If he did, Billy thought he might get a beating out of the arrival, and that wasn't good, but tonight, the whole idea of a beating from a drunk father was a better thing to think about than the needle-toothed man who could turn invisible in the mornings, run fast at noon, and jump high at night.

But his old man didn't arrive. Billy went to his bedroom and made sure the window was locked. The curtains were pulled shut. He went to bed. For a long time he couldn't sleep. He kept playing the events of the day over and over in his mind, seeing the man waver in the air and then running alongside the deer. He remembered how fast he ran, the story he told, and then he remembered him jumping high and how it had felt when he shoved the sharp knife into the man's armpit.

Eventually, he drifted off. Once, during the night, he thought he heard his father come in, but now he was too deep down in the well of sleep to be certain, and didn't move. At least not right away. But he heard something crash, and he got up and got his flashlight from the bedside drawer and went out in the hall. The front door was wide open, and his father was lying on the floor where he had passed out.

Billy went over and tried to wake him, but he didn't wake. He turned on the light, but it didn't come on. Billy stepped out on the porch with the flashlight and looked left, and then looked right. He thought he saw something move around the edge of the house, but it was a fleeting glimpse and could have been most anything. He noticed that the wires that connected from the electric post to the box on the side of the house were snapped off. He thought maybe a limb had broken off a tree and fallen on it, but he couldn't see a limb. He could see his father's car in the drive. He had been stupid and driven home drunk without the lady with the tall hair.

Billy heard a noise somewhere, something breaking, but it was faint and unrecognizable. He listened for a moment, but he didn't hear anything else, determined it was nothing. Maybe an animal, moving around the edge of the house, knocking over one of the old outside flower pots his mother had had, now empty of flowers, but still stuffed with dirt.

He decided he'd get a pillow and blanket for his father, and leave him right there on the floor. He closed and locked the door, and when he turned, he slipped and fell. He got up and felt something on his hands. He shined the flashlight on his left hand. It was covered in something wet and dark and sticky. Blood.

Billy kneeled down by his father and looked closely and saw that his throat was ripped. He hadn't noticed it before, the way he had been laying, but now he saw it.

"Oh, my," Billy said. "Daddy."

Flashing the light around, Billy looked to see if he might see the needle-toothed man, but there was nothing. He didn't know how the needle-toothed man had survived, but Billy knew then that he had. Billy wanted him then. He wanted to stick him with a knife again. He got a large butcher knife from the rack beside the sink and went through the house carefully, and ended up in his bedroom. He saw something lying on the bed. Something small and square. He went over to look at it, holding the knife at ready in one hand, the flashlight in the other.

It was his handkerchief. The one he had used in the woods to clean his knife. And now he realized something. The curtains were pulled back and the window had been broken out and lifted up. That had been the noise he heard when he was on the porch.

The needle-toothed man must have caught his father as he came in, and then he had torn out the electrical wires and knocked out the window to the bedroom.

Billy had felt brave before with the knife, and mad from what had happened to his father, but now he felt a lot less brave, and the open window looked like a hatch through which he could leap and escape. He darted for it, but a shadow moved, and the shadow got hold of him, and the shadow was large and flickering, like a bat. The next thing Billy knew he was pushed back on the bed and the shadow was holding him down. The shadow had some shape, and in a moment it had more shape. The moonlight from the window was in the room and he could see that the shadow was no longer a shadow at all, but the needle-toothed man, and that his neck was so badly busted from the fall his head lay on his chest like a growth. The needle-toothed man was showing all his teeth and his eyes were wet and flashing, and he was stripped of all clothing, naked as a jaybird, and there were bones sticking through his chest and abdomen.

The teeth in the twisted head smiled wide. The man said, "And after midnight, I can turn to shadows and flow across the earth with the wind, and if I get dead, and I been dead before, several times, I don't stay that way. I come back, and I can always find my killer. So, I'm back, and I've found you."

Billy tried to move, tried to stab the man with his butcher knife, but the needle-toothed man had hold of his hand and his grip was strong.

Then the man jutted forward, and the crooked hanging head snapped at Billy's jugular. Billy felt warm and wet, as if he were falling down quickly and sadly into a deep dark grotto with no bottom. But before he was gone, he could hear the man with the needle teeth sucking at him, sucking like a pig at trough, sucking out everything he was or might ever have been, sucking it out of him with those needle-sharp teeth.

# SANTA AT
# THE CAFÉ

**W**hen Santa came into the café, he had the fake beard pulled off his chin and it hung down on his chest. He had his Santa hat folded and stuck through the big black belt around his waist. His hair was red, so it was a sharp contrast to the rest of his outfit.

No one took much notice of him, as the city was full of Santas this time of year, but the middle-aged man behind the counter, a big guy wearing a food-stained white shirt, lifted his hand and waved.

Santa waved back. It was their usual greeting.

Santa took a seat at a booth in the rear, sat down with a sigh and took a look around. The place was packed, as it always was this time of night, and with it being Christmas Eve, and with many eateries shutting down early tonight, it was a natural gathering spot. He felt lucky to have found an empty booth. There were still dishes left on it from the last customer.

A young woman, who looked as if she might be one cup of coffee short of her hair starting to crawl, came over and sat down across from him. She said, "Do you mind?"

He did mind. Or he would have normally, but she wasn't bad looking. She was thin-faced and nicely built with eyes that drooped slightly, as if she might drop off to sleep at any moment. She had a wide mouth full of nice teeth. She had on blue jeans and a sweater and a heavy coat. She had a huge cloth purse with a long shoulder strap.

She said, "There are only a few seats."

"Sure," he said. "Sure, go ahead."

She took off her coat and sat down.

"You work the department store?" she asked.

"Yeah. I got off a few minutes ago."

"Don't see many thin, red-headed Santas," she said.

"Well, at the store, I got this pillow, you see, and I put it under the suit. I finish for the night, I put the pillow back. It don't belong to me, it belongs to the store. The suit, that's mine though. I do this every Christmas. You can make pretty good, you work it right."

"Yeah, how's that?"

"I do it for a couple weeks before Christmas, and if there are enough kids sitting on my lap, and they feel like they're bringing in some business, they like to toss a little extra my way. I mean, you can't live on what I make, but it's a nice enough slice of cheese."

While they talked, a man came over and gathered up the dishes, came back with a rag and wiped their table, and was gone as swiftly and silently as he had come.

The waitress, wearing a striped uniform the colors of a candy cane, arrived. She walked like her feet hurt and there was nothing to go home to. She wore a bright green sprig of plastic mistletoe on her blouse. For all the Christmas spirit she showed, it might as well have been poison ivy.

The young woman ordered coffee. Santa ordered steak and eggs and a side of wheat toast and a glass of milk.

When the waitress left, Santa said, "You ought to eat something, kid. You look like maybe you been holding back on that a bit."

"Just cutting calories."

He studied her for a moment.

"Okay," she said, withering under his gaze. "I'm short on money. I'm not doing so good lately."

"Let me help you out. I'll buy you something."

"I'm fine. Thanks. But I'm fine."

"Really. Let me. No obligations."

"None," she said.

"None," he said.

"I don't want you to think I'm trying to work you, that that's why I sat here."

"I don't think that," he said, and then he thought, you know, maybe that's exactly what she did.

But he didn't care.

Santa caught the waitress's eye and called her over.

She came with less enthusiasm than before, which wasn't something Santa thought she could do, and took the woman's order, and went away.

"What's your name?" asked Santa.

"Mary. What's yours?"

"Hell, tonight, just call me Santa. I'm buying you a late dinner. Or early breakfast, whatever you want to call it."

They talked a little, and Santa liked the talk. The food came, and when it did he removed the beard and folded it up and pushed it into his belt on the opposite side of his Santa hat.

While they were eating, he saw that the crowd was thinning. That's the way it was. Business hit hard, and then went away. He had taken note the last two weeks. Every night after work he'd come here to eat and watch the crowd. It was entertaining.

He and the young woman finished eating, and Santa looked up and saw a nervous young man come in. Very nervous. He had sweat beads on his forehead the size of witch warts. He sat down and shifted in his seat and touched something inside his coat. The waitress came over and the man ordered.

Santa kept his eye on him. He had seen the type before. Fact was, the nervous man made him nervous. The young woman noticed the nervous man as well.

"He don't seem right," she said.

"No. No he doesn't."

"Place like this," she said, "it'll fool you. There's lots of money made here. For a greasy spoon it maybe makes as much as Bloomingdale's."

"I doubt that," said Santa.

"All right, that's an exaggeration, but you got think, way customers come and go, it does all right."

"I figure you're right."

After awhile, the customers thinned. There were half a dozen people left. A few came and went, picking up coffee, but that was it. Santa looked at his watch. 2 a.m.

"You got a home to go to," the young woman asked Santa.

"Yeah, but I been there before."

"No wife?"

"No dog. No cat. Not much of anything but four walls and pretty good couch to sleep on."

"No bed?"

"No bed."

"What do you do when you're not Santa?"

"These days, I don't do much of anything. I lost my job a while back."

"What did you do?"

"Short order cook... Hell, look there."

She turned to look, the nervous man was up and he pulled a gun out from under his coat just as the waitress was approaching his booth. For no reason at all, he struck out and hit her on the side of the neck, dropped her and the coffee pot she was carrying to the floor. The pot was hard plastic and it rolled, spilling coffee all over the place. The waitress lay on the floor, not moving.

The man pointed the gun at the man behind the counter. "Give me the money. All of it."

"Hey now," said the man behind the counter, "you don't want to do this."

"Yeah," said the nervous man, "I do."

"All right, take it easy." The counter man looked at Santa, like maybe he had some magic that would help. Santa didn't move. The girl didn't move. The well-dressed man at the bar turned slightly on his stool.

The nervous man pointed his gun at the well-dressed man. "I say don't move, that means you too. You too over there, Santa and the chick. Freeze up."

Everyone was still, except the counter man. He started unloading the money from the register, sticking it in a to-go sack.

"Come on," said the nervous man, shaking a little. "Hurry. Don't try and hold back."

"Ain't my money," said the counter man. "You can have it. I don't want to get shot over money."

The counter man was stuffing the money in a big take-away sack. There was a lot of it.

When he was almost finished with the stuffing, the nervous man came closer to the counter. The well-dressed man hardly seemed to move, but move he did, and there was a gun in his hand and he said, "Now hold up. I'm a cop."

The nervous man didn't hold up. He turned with his gun and the cop fired his. The nervous man staggered and sat down on the floor, got part of the way up, then staggered and fell over one of the tables at a booth. He bled on the table and the blood ran down into the coffee the waitress had dropped.

The well-dressed man got up and leaned slightly over the counter, said, "Actually, I ain't no cop. I want the money."

"Not a cop?" said the counter man.

"Naw. But I thought it might stop him. I didn't want to kill nobody. Just planned on the money."

The counter man gave him the bag and the man who was not a cop walked briskly out the door and left.

》《

**Cops came, and** Santa and the young woman and the counter man gave their statements, told how two crooks had got into it, and how one of them was dead and the other had walked away with about two thousand dollars in a to-go bag.

It took about an hour for the interviews, then the dead man's body was carried away, and the waitress, who had come to with a headache, told the man behind the counter she quit. She went out and got a taxi. The man behind the counter got a mop and a bucket and pushed it out to wipe up the blood and coffee.

Santa and the young woman were still there. The counter man told them they could have free coffee.

"I'm gonna close it," said the counter man, when they had their Styrofoam cups of coffee.

Santa and the young woman went out.

"That was some night," she said.

"Yeah," Santa said. "Some night."

She caught a cab after a long wait with Santa standing beside her at the curb. Santa opened the door and watched her get in and saw the taxi drive off. Santa sighed. She was one fine looking girl. A little skinny, but fine just the same.

Santa went back to the diner and tugged on the door. It was locked. He knocked.

The counter man came over and let him in and locked the door.

"Damn," said the counter man. "How about that?"

"Yeah," said Santa. "How about it?"

"Makes it easier, don't it?"

"Yeah, easier."

"Come on," said the counter man. They went back behind the counter and into a little office. The counter man moved a bad still life painting on the wall and there was a safe behind it.

As he turned the dial, the counter man said, "This way, no one will be looking for you or thinking of me. It's better this way, way things worked out."

"It's one hell of a coincidence."

"I was worried. I figured you took the money at gunpoint, they might think I had something to do with it."

"You do."

The counter man talked while he turned the dials on the safe.

"I know. But this way, you don't even have to be a fake robber. We just split it. It works out good, man. I told the police the robber got all we had. All of it. I didn't mention the safe. Boss asks, I'll tell him it was all out. I hadn't put it in the safe yet. Meant to, but got swamped. But I put it in all right. It was safe. All the guy got was the till. You and me, we're gonna split twenty thousand dollars tonight, and the cops, they're looking for a well-dressed man who pretended to be a cop and got away with a few thousand. They think he got it all. It's sweet."

"Yeah," Santa said, "that's sweet all right."

They split the money and the counter man put his in a take-away bag, and Santa put his inside his Santa suit. It just made him look a little fat.

They went out of the café and the counter man locked the door.

Walking around the corner, the counter man said, "You parked in the same lot?"

"No. I didn't come by car."

"No?"

"No," said Santa. And then the counter man got it. They were at a dark intersection near an alley. No one was in the alley. Santa pulled a gun from one of his big pockets and pointed it at the counter man.

"Come on, man," said the counter man. "You and me, we been friends since you was a fry cook, back over at the Junction Café."

"I knew you from there," Santa said. "But friends, not so much."

"For god's sake," the counter man, said, "it's Christmas Eve."

"Merry Christmas, then," Santa said, and shot the counter man in the head with his little pistol. It hardly made more than a pop.

Santa picked up the dropped take-away bag and put it inside his suit. Now he really looked like Santa. He put on the beard and the hat and shoved the pistol in his pocket.

He walked smartly back toward the café. He had to pass it on his way to the subway. When he was almost there, he realized there was someone pacing him on the sidewalk across the street. It was dark back where he had been, but now as he neared the café there was light. He could see who was there. Walking on the opposite side of the street was the young woman.

He stopped and turned and looked at her as she crossed the street.

"I decided I didn't want to go home," she said. "You think maybe you could show me your place?"

"My couch?" he said.

"Sure, I can stand it if you can."

"You just been waiting on me?"

"I drove down a piece, changed my mind and walked back. I thought I might catch you."

"That was a long shot."

"Yep. But here you are."

Santa smiled. It was some night. Money, a profitable dissolution of a partnership, and now this fine looking dame. "All right," he said.

She patted his belly.

"You put on weight since I seen you last, what, thirty minutes ago?"

"I got a takeout order with me. Something for tomorrow."

"Under your coat?"

"Yeah, under my coat."

She smiled, and he smiled, and then he quit smiling. She had a gun in her hand. It came out of her big purse as smooth as a samurai drawing a sword.

"I got to say it, just got to let you know that I know your type," she said, "cause I'm the same type. I saw you watching the counter man count that money. I could see it in your eyes, what you had planned, though I didn't know the counter man was in on it. That was something else. There I was, thinking how I can hang in there until everyone leaves, because, you see, I got plans myself. Then that nervous man came in, and the other guy, the well-dressed fellow, that was some coincidence. When all that happened, I was glad to leave. As I was driving away in the taxi, I looked back, saw you go back to the diner. I thought that was suspicious, cause you see, I'm the suspicious type. I had the taxi stop. I walked back and hid in the shadows. Saw the two of you come out. I followed, carefully. I'm like a cat, I want to be. I saw you shoot the counter man, take his share. Guess what, it all fell together then, what went on. Now, I'm gonna take both your shares. That's what I call a real Christmas surprise and one hell of a present for me. I mean, come on, you're Santa. You got to want me to have a good Christmas, right?"

"Now, wait a minute," Santa said, easing his hand toward his pocket for the gun.

He didn't make it. A bullet parted his beard and hit him in the neck and he went back and leaned against the diner wall.

She popped him again. This time in the head.

Santa sat down hard. His hat fell off.

She opened up his coat and got the money. It was a lot of money. She put the gun away, stuffed the money that was loose inside his suit into her huge cloth purse. She picked up the to-go bag. Someone saw it, it could be a bag of sandwiches, a bag of doughnuts. It could be most anything.

"Merry Christmas," she said to Santa's corpse, and crossed the street and started toward the lights and the subway, and a short ride home.

# WHAT HAPPENED
# TO ME

**I** wish I had a story to tell, but I don't.

Not like all of you, and being last to go after all those fine stories is a toughie. I can't make things up like you people, and I'm impressed. So, all I can do is do my best, and admit right up front that this isn't a story, and therefore may be a bit pedestrian because it's something that actually happened to me.

I suppose you could say it's a kind of haunted house story, except it's not a story, and took place many years ago and ends with a not altogether satisfying explanation, if it is an explanation at all. But it does end with a death, I'm sad to say, and some of the things I saw disturb me even now, and I suppose they will do so until the end of my days.

It would be an almost classic story in a way, if it were fiction.

But it's not. It happened, and I'm not going to add any frills, just tell it to the best of my memory, as accurately as I can, and you can judge its worth as my offering for the night.

When I was a young college student attending Stephen F. Austin University, I was poor as the proverbial church mouse. A friend of mine, Clifford, who I called Cliff, was poor too, as was another friend, William, who did not go by Bill. Always William. He was adamant about it.

We decided that the only way we could attend college was to find a place with as cheap a rent as possible, with enough room for three, and go into it together. What we all had to live on were student loans, and they were not large, and after we paid for tuition and books, there was very little to survive on for a semester.

I forget how we came about knowing of the place now, but as it happened we found a house—and get this, because it will be hard to believe in this day and time—but we found a house where the rent was thirty-five dollars a month, split three ways.

Admittedly, thirty-five dollars in those days was worth more than thirty-five dollars now, but it was still very reasonable for us, split up like that.

East Texas, even in winter, is generally a warm place. But this winter I'm talking about was unusually cold, at least it was for a while, and considering the house we were about to rent was without gas heat, only fireplaces, it seemed even colder.

After renting the house, Cliff and I had other matters to attend to in our hometown of Tyler, and couldn't be there on the day our rent began. But William could be. His plan was to stay there and we would catch up with him the next day.

Cliff and I drove down together from Tyler in that rare and bad weather I mentioned, and by the time we arrived at the house the next afternoon, the wind was blowing sleet. As we pulled in we were surprised to see that William's car wasn't in the drive.

We were even more surprised to find a note tacked to the door. It was on a piece of notebook paper and said simply: I'VE DECIDED TO GO TO KILGORE COLLEGE.

This was out of the blue, and immediately eliminated one-third of our income as far as rent went, but as I said, it wasn't a terrible rent we were expected to pay, so we could bear it. The main thing was we were surprised that he had bailed out on our plans, and had explained himself so thinly with that note.

These days, to find out more, you would pop open your cell phone and give him a call, but then there were no cell phones, and for that matter, the house didn't have any kind of phone, and, frankly, the electricity out that far, especially during weather of the sort we were having, was iffy with all that ice hanging from the lines.

After cussing our partner, we entered the house and found that his bedroll—for there were no beds at this point, and only limited furniture—was still there, stretched out in front of the fireplace. There was no fire, but we could see where there had been a recent one, built by William, no doubt, and after discovering that not only had William left his bedroll on the floor, we found he had left a number of other items, including a grocery sack of food, most of it canned goods.

But, let me jump ahead in my story a little, saying that we got over his departure quickly, and that for the first two days things were fine. We were there very little, since we began attending classes. On the weekend we went home to load furniture in a rented van to deliver to the house.

In no time at all we were settled in, and also in no time at all we began to feel uncomfortable. It was nothing radical, and I can't say that I remember being scared, early on that is, but that I did feel discomfort. It was akin to the sensation of thinking someone was peeking in a window at you. And as there were no curtains on the windows at the time, I thought this was most likely a natural sensation of being exposed, though where we were located we could have pretty much gone naked and no one would have noticed.

There were also minor things, such as thinking we had heard sounds, but when we discussed it, we were unable to adequately describe what it was we had heard. One of the more uncomfortable places in the house was the dog run. The house was divided by a long hallway that went from the front porch to the back porch. The front porch was long and ran right and left to the door, but the back porch extended out from the back door on the same path as the dog run hall. Both porches were roofed over and were wide and solidly built, though the back porch creaked whenever you stepped on it.

The dog run hallway, however, was what was most uncomfortable. We assumed this was due to it being separate of the rest of the house, and therefore devoid of heat. Anytime we entered it, it was not only cold, it was foul, as if a dead cat were somewhere within the walls. And the first few nights, when we slept on the floor in the living room, I had the most miserable sensation that something was moving about in the hallway, though I can't say as I remember hearing anything at all. Just this feeling that something was out there, pausing at the closed door that led to the living room. The way those old houses worked, was the front and back door were locked, but as an extra precaution, the door to the hallway could be locked as well from either side of the house; what you had was essentially two houses separated, and yet connected, by a hallway that ran between them and connected to the porches. After the first night, I took to locking the one connected to the living room.

I remember Cliff seeing me do it, and expecting him to laugh or chide me for my extra caution. But he didn't. He merely looked away and went about his business, which gave me the impression that he had the same concerns that I had.

Now, keep in mind, because I know more about what happened later, I'm certainly overselling this aspect of the house, at least early on. I'm merely trying to explain that the two of us were a bit prickly, if not frightened, or even concerned. I thought, as I'm confident Cliff did, it was due primarily to the isolated location, the age of the house, which surely provided noises to which we were unfamiliar, and the fact that we were unaccustomed to being there.

It seemed to me that once we got curtains, odds and ends, our own rooms chosen, that things would be considerably more homey, and this proved to be the case.

At least for a time.

Now, there was another matter. I thought little of it at first, but early on, after we had assigned bedrooms, when the furniture was placed, I had begun to have uneasy dreams; a serial dream actually. You know the sort, where you dream it each night, but it changes slightly.

I would feel myself lying in bed, slowly coming awake, and when I would awake, it would still be dark. Each night I saw a shadow at the window, like a tree limb with branches, handlike, but much larger than a hand. I would see the shadow curl its 'fingers,' then flex out, as if stretching, and touch the window, and with little effort, lift it.

On one occasion the last part of the dream had been of those wooden-like fingers stalking across the floor, attached to a long branch, an arm if you will, and the fingers had taken hold of my blanket at the foot of my bed and began to pull.

And then I came awake.

This time, as before, there was no branch, and the window was shut. But the blanket that had covered my feet was on the floor in a heap.

This, of course, was easy enough to explain, and I came to the conclusion that during the dream, in fear, I had kicked at my blanket and caused it to come free of the bed and fall on the floor. It was a reasonable explanation, and I accepted it as truth without due consideration.

It seemed so logical.

I also determined that to have peace of mind, I would inspect the windows, to make sure they were fastened tight. I had checked them when we first moved in and found them stuck, as if the window frame had been painted and pushed down before drying, causing it to stick. But when I examined the window I had dreamed about, it was unlocked and no longer stuck. It lifted easily.

It is also of importance to note there wasn't a tree near the window, so the idea that I might have half-awakened and saw the shadow of a tree limb and its branches against the glass was immediately dismissed. I came to the conclusion that it had been less stuck than previously thought, and I had been mistaken about the lock; in other words, human error.

On a day when Cliff had class and I had none, I went out to the barn behind the old house and looked for a hammer and nails to seal that window shut. I knew if I were to sleep in the room comfortably, even if I was only taking care of psychological worries, I would have to seal the window more securely.

The barn was a dusty affair and both sides of it were festooned with all manner of horse-drawn accouterments: horse collars and bridles and back bands and the like for pulling plows. The plows themselves were there, rusted over. There was a big cedar trunk as well, and I looked in there first. It was chock-full of junk, including children's toys and a large notebook that I opened. Inside it were a child's drawings. They were of the usual thing, a house with a family. The drawing was done in what I supposed was crayon, or something like it, and it had a blue sky and yellow sun, and dark stick-like figures of a woman and a man.

There was a drawing of a child, placed somewhat at an angle between them, as if the child were falling over, and there was a shadow drawn for the child, but none for the parents. The shadow was crude, but very interestingly drawn nonetheless. There were quite a few other paintings as well, including one of the night sky and what looked like a line of crudely drawn trees. There were other paintings of trees and what I concluded was the barn I was in, and I reached the obvious conclusion that they were the drawings of a very young child. There were quite a few of these drawings, varying only in the fact that in each drawing the trees were closer to the house.

I closed up the notebook, put it back, and went rummaging about the barn looking for that hammer and nails, and finally found them. The nails were in a paper bag and they were an assortment of lengths.

Back in my bedroom, I picked through the bag until I found four long, thin nails, and used those and my hammer to firmly nail the window shut. There was a part of me that felt idiotic about doing it, but I can say truthfully, that after I had fastened those windows down tight, I felt significantly better than before.

Early afternoon, after class, Cliff drove back to the house and announced he was going home for the weekend, hoping to borrow a bit of money from his parents. I wished him luck, but at the bottom of it all I felt abandoned, as if I had been set adrift on a stormy sea. I'll tell you another thing. I think he too was having discomfort with the house, and had decided to get away from it for awhile. This only added to my discomfort. These concerns soon took a backseat as I decided to stay and study for a history exam.

I sat on the couch in the main room—the one we had begun to call the living room—and studied for my test. I had the books spread out beside me on the couch, and there was plenty of light through the windows, and I was deep into the American Revolution, when a shadow passed over me, darkening the room considerably, and giving me a chill that went beyond the winter weather outside.

I got up and stoked the fireplace, built up the fire, but it did little to heat me up. I pulled on my coat, returned to the couch, but the shadow had swollen to fill the room. The shadow seemed to be nothing more than a reflection of the outside weather seeping in. Clouds had moved to cover the sun. I went to the window to look out, pulled aside the curtains, and saw that it was quite dark for midday. I could hear thunder rumbling in the background, and saw a flash of lightning snap out over the thick forest across the road from our rental, giving the trees the brief impression of having been drawn with a piece of charcoal instead of by the hand of nature.

I went back and sat on the couch and turned on a lamp beside it, and began to study again. A short time later, I heard a scratching sound, and then I had what I can only refer to as an impression. A feeling something was on the porch. It was a primitive sensation, something I assume our prehistoric ancestors might have experienced regularly, the feeling that something predatory was near, even if it was unseen, and that it was necessary to be alert.

I glanced toward the row of windows that looked out over the porch. Curtains covered them now, and it would have been necessary for me to go over and pull them back to take a look outside. But I just couldn't make myself do it, so sure was I that something was on the porch, and that there was something to fear about it being there. And then I heard the porch floor creak. The clouds shifted and it grew darker yet behind the curtains. They were white curtains, but thick. I couldn't see clearly through them, but I could see enough to determine light or dark, and now I saw there was a spot, a shape that had moved in front of one of the windows, and I swear, it seemed as if it were leaning forward as if to try and peek through the windows and the curtains.

I sat there, frozen to the spot. The shadow, which was human in shape, also reminded me of a willow tree, the arms like limbs, the long fingers like branches; it was the thing from my dream, and it swayed with the wind… I must stop here, for to be honest, I can't fully describe it. I'm uncertain how much of what I'm describing is how it actually looked, and how much of it was me having an impression of something I couldn't really see accurately. I know no better way to explain or to describe it than how I have.

The shape moved, and I heard the boards on the porch squeak, and then…I swear to all I know to be true, the door off the front porch opened. I was certain I had locked it, as well as the door to the other end of the dog run, but I was equally certain that I heard it open.

Now I knew someone was out there. It was someone who had arrived with the rain, and not by car. And even as I thought this, I heard the screen door move, and then the screen door and the front door slammed shut in rapid succession.

I glanced toward the door that led out into the dog run hall, and without really thinking about it, I stepped quickly there and turned the latch. A moment later, as I stood at the door, I heard what can only be described as...breathing. The door was generating tremendous cold, and I felt a chill run all the way down my spine. Someone, or something, was standing just outside that door and they were causing the door to turn cold.

The door knob started to twist, very slowly.

In case you're unclear, I will explain once again that the house was like two houses, divided by that dog run, and that meant that the only way into the house was through the doors on either end of the hallway, with the exception of a back door that led out onto the back porch from the kitchen. Forgive me for repeating this, but it's essential that you understand this so as to appreciate my situation at the time.

That thought occurred to me, about the kitchen door, and as it did, I stepped back and turned and walked gently through the living room toward that door, which was at the rear of the house on the same side as the living room.

I heard movement back in the dog run, and I knew that whoever, or whatever, was there had realized my plan and was rushing toward the kitchen door. My intent was to lock it, for I knew it to be unlocked, and if whatever was in the dog run made it through the hall, out the back door, and onto the back porch, he/she/it might beat me there.

I broke in a blind panic and ran for it. I heard the door to the back porch—general door and screen door—open and slam, in spite of it supposedly being locked.

I glanced to my right as I ran. There were a series of windows against the dining room that viewed out onto the long back porch. I had to pass through the dining room to end up in the kitchen. As I hurried, I glimpsed through those windows. The curtains were pulled back and my view was clear, and I saw the same dark, willow tree shape I had seen on the front porch. But now it was twisting and flowing in a manner that is impossible to describe. But I knew one thing for certain, even if all I had was a glimpse, whatever was out there was most certainly not human.

I made it to the back door and twisted the lock, and immediately the knob turned violently, and then the door began to shake, and there was a moaning like something big and wounded dying out there on the porch. That door shook and shook. I thought it would never end. I heard the wood screech and give a little, and I was absolutely positive that it was about to break and fall apart, that I would then be at the mercy of the thing.

And then, it was over.

The door quit shaking, and the air, which I now realized was cold throughout the house, warmed immediately. The rain was starting to come down, and I could hear thunder and lightning, but I knew as certain as I was standing there, that whatever had been out there, was now gone. It was the kind of thing you could sense.

As an added note, when I had the nerve, I unlocked the door from the living room to the dog run, stepped into the hallway and looked about. Nothing was there, and to make things even more disconcerting, both doors to the dog run were still locked.

Before night settled in solid, I was brave enough to go to my bedroom to gather up bedclothes to sleep on the couch. I found that side of the house, where my bedroom was, incredibly cold. Though I didn't have the impression anything was there, I had an overwhelming feeling that something had been there, and that that side of the house was more its domain. In my bedroom, I grabbed a pillow and some blankets, noted that the window I had nailed down had been lifted, and that the tips of the nails I had driven through the wood stuck out at the bottom like weak little teeth.

I closed the window and locked it, as if it mattered, and with my pillow and blankets left the room. That night I slept on the couch, but not comfortably. Nothing else happened.

That I was aware of.

**〉《**

The first thing I suppose you might think is if there was something actually wrong with that house, what was its history? I thought of that, and I must also pause here to say that I never in my life have believed in ghosts, and oddly, I'm not sure I do now. Not in the way that some people might think of them. But I took it on myself to visit with the lady who had rented the house to us.

It was Saturday morning, and the moment I awoke, I went to town, dropped by to see her. She had an office on North Street where she handled dozens of rentals. She was a big, middle-aged woman who looked as if she could wrestle a steer to the ground and make it recite poetry. Something I was assured by people around town she had actually done, minus the poetry part. I asked her if there had been unusual experiences reported in the house.

She laughed at me. "You mean ghosts?"

"Unusual things," I said.

"No. Until about six months ago the only thing in that old house was hay. I kept it stocked there, like a barn. No one but you and your friend have rented that house ever. I bought that property thirty years ago from the Wright family. You two are the first renters."

"Is there anything curious about the Wrights?" I asked.

"Yes; they are all very successful and there are no drunkards in the family," she said. "But as for ghosts, or murders, or ancient disturbed graveyards...nothing to my knowledge. Matilda is the only one alive. She was the youngest child of the family, and she's young no more. She was a famous artist of sorts. At least, she was famous around here. She's up in the Mud Creek Rest Home now, and no doubt that's where she'll finish things off."

I don't know if it was our landlady's intent to make me feel foolish, but she did. I had not directly asked about ghostly activities, but she certainly understood that this was exactly what I was alluding to, and had found the whole thing amusing.

I drove home, stopping by the mailbox across the dirt road from our house. It was rare I received any mail, outside of a few bills, but inside was a note from Cliff. It wasn't a letter. It hadn't been mailed. It was a note he had left there for me.

Its content was simple. He wasn't coming back. He had dropped out of college and was thinking of starting next semester at a junior college in Tyler. There was a P.S. written at the bottom of the note. It read: 'There's also the house. It makes me uncomfortable. It might be a good idea for you to leave.'

That was it. I concluded he too had had experiences, but had never elaborated. My guess was he had driven home, felt better being away from the house, and determined not to come back, except to the mailbox to leave me a note. He had driven all the way, which was a good two-hour drive, to deliver that note, not waiting to send it by mail, and not waiting until I was home, therefore avoiding having to re-enter the house. As I considered that, I decided that what was even more likely was he intended to return, but once he arrived, just couldn't go inside again, and had written the note in his car and left it for me in the mailbox.

Of course, that should have been it for me. I should have grabbed what mattered to me and hauled out of there, but the truth is, even with two of my roommates gone, I could still better afford the rent there than somewhere else, and I really needed to continue with the semester. If I dropped out, I would lose my tuition. With that very earthly consideration to deal with, I decided that most of what had happened had been in my imagination. It was a decision based on necessity, not common sense, but there you have it. I was determined not to believe what my own senses had revealed to me.

At night, though, I felt differently. I felt trapped, fearful of stepping out into that dog run. I was also equally determined not to believe that the thing had opened locked doors and had paused at the one to the living room, and had not opened it. I couldn't explain that, nor could I explain that I could lock it out from the kitchen, yet it had free run of the porches, and the dog run, and, as I was to discover the next morning, the other side of the house.

》《

I had learned to fear the night and any dark days due to rain. Because of that, I always hurried home before dark, and I had learned that as night came the house became colder on the bedroom side. Because of that, I had taken to permanently sleeping on the couch in the living room, and due to that choice, I had not really visited the other side of the residence since Cliff left. In fact, it seemed, with him gone, the atmosphere of dread had compounded, and was focused now on one person. Me.

But the mornings always seemed brighter and less fearful, and it continued that way until late afternoon when the ambiance of the house shifted to a darker and more oppressive tone. It also seemed activated by any grim change in the weather. The ice storms had melted out, but the winter was still unseasonably cold and subject to shifts in temperature and sudden outbursts of rain. When that occurred, no matter what time of day, the feelings of dread mounted. Because of that, I was glad I was gone most of the time, and on Wednesdays, when I had a late class, I was at my most nervous on returning. I parked as close to the porch as possible and entered the house rapidly and made my way to the living room, and locked myself inside. The back door from the kitchen to the porch I never unlocked.

But, I was telling you of the morning I went to the other side of the dog run to examine that side of the house. In Cliff's bedroom I saw that all of his abandoned belongings—his books, his clothes—were strewn everywhere, the clothes ripped to fragments, pages torn from books. I was shocked to discover the entire room looked as if an angry burglar had been through it. That was my first thought, actually, or vandals, until I saw that the bed clothes in my bedroom had been ripped from the bed and piled at the end of it in a shape. That's the only way I know how to explain it. Somehow, those blankets had been twisted in such a way as to make a kind of teepee, but one that had no opening into which to crawl; a twisted cone the height of my shoulders. The sheets were ripped in strips and thrown around the room and the glass was knocked out of all the windows. My mattress had been ripped apart and the stuffing was tossed about as if a fox had had its way with a chicken.

When I breathed my breath frosted. This made sense as the outside weather had been let inside, but I had the feeling that the air was not cold from natural atmospheric occurrences. Still, I didn't feel that odd impression of something being in the room or nearby; the cold was more like the residue of something having passed through.

》《

This should have been my absolute cue to pack up, but at this point, to tell it as truthful as I can—I was mad. The idea of being forced out of the house, and the idea of having to pay money I didn't really have for a different place to live, or to consider moving home and losing my tuition loan, was more than I could bear.

I locked the door to the ravaged side of the house as I came out, and then I made sure both ends of the dog run were locked. I followed that by entering the living room side of the house and locking that door. I pulled all the curtains across the windows, and even went as far as to take some of the spare blankets I had moved into that room a few days back, and hung them over the curtain rods in such a way to secure myself from the sight of anything on the porch. I concluded if I couldn't see it, I would be less fearful of it.

I took some peanut butter and a loaf of bread, a plate and a knife to spread it with, and carried it into the living room, followed a moment later with a glass and a gallon of milk from the refrigerator. I closed the door from the living room to the dining room and locked it. I determined I was going to make that room my sanctuary this night.

I didn't have a television or a radio, not in that old house. There were actually only a few electrical outlets available. It had never been fully transitioned from farm house to modern home.

There was a little bathroom off the living room, a kind of guest bath that had once been a closet. It was large enough for a toilet, a sink, and a shower. I took a shower and dressed in comfortable clothes I had laid out, as I had already moved all of my major possessions into the living room, and then I prepared myself a peanut butter sandwich, had a glass of milk and, sitting on the couch with an end table lamp at my elbow, began taking a crack at my studies.

As the teacher had cancelled her class for that day, there was no need to leave the house, and I decided not to. Instead, I planned to direct myself to my studies. The house had already taken up far too much of my attention, and to be honest, even at this point I thought that what I might be dealing with were vandals, and that tomorrow, when I went into town, I would file a police report. Mostly, I tried not to think about the other side of the house, and instead concentrate my efforts on my studies.

This went well throughout the day, until late afternoon. I had by this time become a bit more confident—fool's confidence—and I chose to unlock the door from the living room to the dining room and to make my way to the kitchen to see if I might find something more appetizing for dinner than a peanut butter sandwich. As I reached the kitchen I noticed a curious thing; the hinges on the door to the porch were losing their screws; they were twisting slowly from the hinge. One of them fell to the floor with a small clatter. The hair on the back of my neck spiked up.

I observed this for a moment, until another screw began to move, and then I will admit quite freely, I broke and ran for the living room, closed the door—quietly, lest I somehow aggravate whatever was out on the back porch further—and locked it. I picked up a poker from the fireplace and moved to the couch. After awhile I heard a noise, and I knew immediately what it was. The back door had fallen off its hinges and there was nothing the lock could do for it; the door had dropped into the kitchen, and if that wasn't enough, there was something moving in there now, and even two rooms away, I could hear it breathe.

The breathing became louder as it moved through the house, toward the living room. I gripped the poker so hard I tore the skin on my palm. And then it was at the door connecting the living room to the dining room. I could hear it breathing, and there was a shadow at the bottom of the door where there was a thin crack. The shadow remained for a long time, and then it shifted, and I swear to you that the next thing I saw was a long finger, or what looked somewhat like a finger, slide under that gap in the door and run along its length, wiggling, as if feeling the temperature of the room, which had become almost unbearably cold. Then I saw it wasn't a finger at all, but a limb, or a thin, knobby branch. It clutched at the bottom of the door frame, and then more fingers appeared, and more, until there were far more woody fingers than could be part of a human being, and they began to pull at the bottom of the door. The door moved; it heaved, but after a long fearful moment, it held.

There was a sudden yanking and then a screech so strange and so loud I almost thought I would faint. This was followed by a rush of wind, an appearance of light at the bottom of the door—the artificial light of the dining room bulb—and then there was a popping sound and the light was gone. This was followed by banging and what was obviously the clattering of pots and pans.

And then everything was still and silent and the room warmed up.

I didn't leave the living room until the morning was so bright it bled through the blankets. I unlocked the living room door and made my way through the dining room and kitchen. They were a wreck. The dining room table was flattened and chairs had been thrown through the windows that led to the porch. In the kitchen, pots and pans were tossed about, along with flour and sugar, and there were broken plates and glasses. Some of the plastic glasses I had collected from fast food places to supplement my dishes had been ripped apart as easily as you might tear wet newspaper.

I had a class that morning, and a test, but they were the furthest things from my mind. I drove into town. I went straight for the Mud Creek Rest Home.

》《

Mud Creek Rest Home actually turned out to be Mud Creek Retirement Home. It was a community home where the elderly could have their own rooms and shared facilities. It was very nice, actually. I found out which room was Matilda Wright's. When I came to her door, it was open and there was bright sunlight pouring through her windows and the room was stuffed fat with easels and paints and paintings. Matilda, who I had somehow expected to look ancient and be confined to her bed or a wheelchair, was standing at one of the many easels, painting. What she was painting was a large multi-colored flower, unlike any flower that actually existed was my guess, and the rest of the paintings were of beautiful, but twisted trees and rivers, all nature paintings.

Matilda was so deeply into her work I hesitated to interrupt her. She was a tall lean woman, and quite attractive for someone I had to guess was in her late seventies. She had her hair dyed blond, and her face, though creased with wrinkles, looked lively, or at least the side of it I could see. She was actually quite beautiful for a woman of her age, and I could imagine that even twenty years earlier she must have turned quite a few heads. She was wearing a paint-splattered, over-sized shirt and blue jeans, white canvas shoes dotted with paint. She didn't look like a woman who would know about weird things that crept up on the porch where she once lived.

Finally, I knocked. She turned, slightly startled, and saw me. Her face lit up and she said, "Yes?"

"Miss Wright?" I said, not entering the room.

"Actually, it's 'Mrs,' but my husband is long dead. I prefer Matilda. Do I know you?"

I shook my head. "No, ma'am. I live in what used to be your family home, or so I'm told. Would it be all right if I came in and spoke with you?"

"By all means," she said.

She hustled to lift a box of paints out of a chair and offered it to me. I took the seat and she sat on her bed and looked at me. "You live in my old house?"

"I do."

"How interesting. I think about it often. It's where I grew up."

I nodded. "I wanted to ask you a few questions about it. They might seem like silly questions."

"By all means, ask."

It turned out I didn't so much as ask her a question, but broke down and told her all that had happened since I had lived there. I felt, as I feel now speaking to you about these events, a little silly. But I couldn't stop telling her all that had occurred, and she didn't once interrupt me. When I finished, I asked the actual question. "Did anything odd ever occur while you and your family lived there?"

"Nothing of that nature, no. And my family and I were very happy there."

This was a disappointing answer, and I'm sure my face showed it. I said, "I don't know what difference it would make if I knew what's responsible for what goes on there, but I keep thinking if I knew something, then maybe it would make a difference. Though, now that I say that aloud, I can't imagine what it would be."

Matilda looked at me for a moment, as if measuring my character. "I didn't say there was nothing odd that ever happened there."

My ears pricked.

"I said there was nothing of the nature you describe, and that we were happy there."

"Then there was something?"

"Quite different than what you describe. I had an invisible friend."

I was immediately disappointed. "So did I, when I was very young," I said. "Lots of children do."

"That's true," she said. "The thing is, well...shall I take some time to explain?"

"Yes, ma'am, that's why I came."

"When I was very young and we lived in that house, we owned a large amount of acreage. I don't know how much of that is left."

"Ten acres and the house and barn," I said.

She nodded. "It was a hundred acres then. Right behind the barn there were woods."

"There still are."

"The woods were thick, and I often went there to play. And one day I came upon a grove of trees. It's impossible to describe how surprising this was, because they weren't just trees. Here I was in the middle of a forest, quite comfortable walking about, and I came upon what can only be described as a kind of grove. It was broken apart from the thickness of the woods, and there were a number of trees that were clutched together, but they were not like any of the other trees. They were thick limbed, and they didn't grow very high, and they were amazing in the way their boughs twisted, and underneath them it was cool and pleasant. None of the other trees were near them. There was instead a field of flowers, blue bonnets, and they were the buffer between the grove and the other trees. I would suspect that the grove was surrounded by two acres of those flowers.

"The trees appeared very ancient, though I can't say that I knew that at the time; I say that in retrospect. For me then, they were merely odd and beautiful. Thinking back, they seemed to me to be among the first trees to ever grow on the earth. They had not aged like other trees, or grown high, but they were thick, and their bark was soft to the touch.

"I sat under those trees and took a rest, and as I did, a little girl stepped out from between them and looked at me."

"A little girl?"

"Yes. She hadn't a stitch on, but she seemed comfortable with that. She told me her name was Elizabeth. That's my middle name, young man, Elizabeth, so there was a kind of small bond immediately. And here's the interesting part. She looked just like me."

"Your imaginary friend?"

She didn't respond to my remark, she just continued talking. "She was very pleasant. She and I began to talk, and it was amazing. We had so much in common, and pretty soon we were playing together. She wouldn't leave the grove of trees, however, and stayed under their shadow. That was all right. I liked it there, and the grove was large enough to give us plenty of shadow to play under. It was hard for me to tear my way free of her and go home, but night was coming. I became aware of it suddenly, and wanted to go home. I was, as I said, comfortable in the woods, but I knew I wouldn't be comfortable there if night came, as it was easy to get lost, so I told her goodbye. She begged me to stay, but I told her I couldn't, but that I would be back as soon as possible. She finally relented, and as I was about to leave, she stepped between a gap in two of the trees, and was gone. I looked, but there was nothing there but the trees.

"Young as I was, nine or ten years old; I don't remember exactly. But young as I was, I accepted all of this freely. I went home and told my mother that I had met a girl in the forest and that we had played together, and that the little girl didn't wear clothes and had disappeared inside some odd trees.

"Mother laughed at this, and thought I was playing, and didn't take alarm at the matter. I went back the next morning, and Elizabeth was there, but this time she wore clothes. The ones I had worn the day before. Or clothes that were like them. We played that day and it was even more fun than the day before. I don't remember what we played, but there were no girl games of tea and pretending to be married. None of that. Chase, I suppose. I don't remember, but by midday I grew hungry and went home. Elizabeth was pouty about it, but I assured her I would be back after eating, and that's exactly what I did. But when night came and I started home, she decided to go with me. As I had played past the time I should have, I was growing frightened of the forest, and I was glad to have Elizabeth as a companion.

"As we went through the woods, I heard my mother calling, and I hastened to reach her. Elizabeth held my hand as we went, and finally when we arrived in the yard, there was my mother, in her apron, worried looking. When she saw me she ran to me and scolded me. I still had hold of Elizabeth's hand. I introduced her to my mother, and my mother smiled, and said, 'So this is your imaginary friend.'

"It was obvious she saw no one and was humoring me. But Elizabeth was there. To shorten this up, she stayed with me for several years, or at least she was with me nights. During the day she told me that she went back to the grove. When I came home from school, after supper, when it began to turn dark, or sometimes on rainy days, she would be in my room, waiting. We had wonderful times together. I finally quit trying to convince my mother Elizabeth was real. This had eventually resulted in me being sent to a doctor—not a therapist, I might add, as there were none available then, least not that we knew of—and frankly, I had come to the conclusion she was not real at all. But, I didn't dismiss her from my memory. I enjoyed having her around, even if I aged and she did not. In fact, she never changed or changed clothes from the day she walked out of the forest with me. Then, all of a sudden, I was twelve and we were moving.

"Elizabeth was very confused. We had a long talk about it, but she didn't understand. I invited her to move with us, but she said she couldn't. That she had to stay near the grove. And then we moved, and that was it. No more Elizabeth. I came to the conclusion that moving had been an excuse for me to cut the bonds to this imaginary friend I had invented, and though we always had good times together, when she was no longer there, I felt a strange sense of relief. Elizabeth is the only thing odd that I know of that ever happened in that house."

I looked around the room, and back at Matilda. "So many of your paintings are of flowers and trees. Especially trees."

"I like nature," Matilda said. "But that grove...I have spent my life trying to duplicate those trees. Here's something odd. After the night Elizabeth came home with me, I began to paint. It was an obsession. I painted for one reason and one reason alone, and that was to somehow put the images of those trees on paper. Oh, I painted other things, of course, but I always came back to them, and in time, I became known for them, and they became a large part of my career as a painter."

"Did you ever paint Elizabeth?" I asked.

Matilda shook her head. "No. There was no need. I knew what she looked like. She looked like me when I was a child. But where she came from, that intrigued me."

"I think I saw some of your early drawings in the barn," I said.

"Really?"

"Perhaps, or one of your siblings."

"I had two brothers," she said. "To the best of my knowledge they didn't paint or draw."

I sat for a moment, thinking about Matilda's invisible friend, but there was nothing in that story that told me much.

"May I have a look at the old homestead?" Matilda asked.

This took me by surprise.

"Of course, but after what I told you about the house...are you sure?"

"You said it only happened at night and on dark days," she said. She nodded her head toward the blinds and the harsh light seeping in. "It's still very much day and there doesn't seem to be a cloud in the sky."

"Certainly," I said. "I can drive you out for a look, and then I'll drive you back."

Though I had gone in to see Matilda with high hopes—even though I was uncertain what I was hoping for—I was leaving with less enthusiasm. I was in fact thinking I would take her to see the homestead, bring her back, and then use a bit of my fading bank account to stay at a cheap motel. And then, the next morning, I was going to concede defeat. I had already missed a major test to hear about Matilda's imaginary friend. It was time to dissolve my old plan and start thinking of another, as had my erstwhile roommates.

>> <<

It was cold outside, but there was no wind blowing and there was plenty of sunlight, so it wasn't unpleasant. Matilda was dressed in a lined leather coat and wore a kind of cloth hat that made her look like the cutest grandmother that ever lived.

She walked briskly, as if she was twenty years younger, and climbed into my wreck of a car without comment, or any obvious examination, and we were off. It was as if we had known each other for years.

When we arrived at the house, the first thing Matilda wanted to do was see the old drawings I had told her about. Out at the barn I found them and showed them to her. She smiled. "Yes, these are mine. Interesting. You'll note that my brothers are not in the drawings."

I smiled and she laughed.

"This one," she said touching the one with the shadow, "is Elizabeth. It feels odd looking at this, now. I drew Elizabeth like a shadow, my shadow. How unusual for me to see her that way. I had totally forgotten about this."

"You should take those with you," I said.

"I will," she said. "I'll leave them here for now, but when you take me back, I'll bring them. Would you like to see the grove?"

I hadn't the slightest interest, actually, but I was trying to be polite, and to tell you true, I was glad to have company after all I had been through.

"Certainly," I said.

Matilda led the way. The woods were thick, but there was an animal path through them, and we followed it. It was narrow and a little muddy from the rains of the day before, but the walk felt good in the cool winter air.

There wasn't a true trail, and it appeared even the animals were no longer using it, as it was overgrown and hard to follow, I felt certain Matilda would give up shortly, but she didn't. She moved like a squirrel. Far better than I did. The woods were thick on either side of us, and there were an amazing number of brightly colored birds flittering about from tree to tree, singing their songs.

Finally, the trail came out in a clearing, and in the center of the clearing were the trees. They were as Matilda had said. Strange. But I saw them with less warmth than she had depicted them. There were a large number of them. They were squatty in construction, and the limbs had a twisted look. I swear to you, a few of the limbs were actually knotted. The leaves that grew on the trees were black and chunky. The bark had fallen off of them in a number of places; the only way I truly know to describe those trees is to say they appeared cancerous. The clearing around them wasn't spotted with blue bonnets, or any kind of flower, but instead yellow weeds grew knee high on all sides. There were no birds singing now. There were no birds in sight.

"My God," Matilda said. "They have aged so. They look so...sad."

I couldn't disagree with this assessment, and actually, when I think about it, it's a far better description than my saying they were cancerous-looking. 'Sad' is exactly the word, and now that I remember that, and tell it to you, I have to emphasize that no other word would be as accurate.

We walked toward the trees, and as we did I heard them shift. It was not the wind that did it, and I didn't actually see movement, but there was a sound akin to ancient lumber being stepped upon by a large man. Had I not felt I was in some way there to protect Matilda, I would have turned around then and gone back. But she was like a juggernaut. She walked into the shadows beneath the grove of trees. The leaves rustled. The limbs creaked.

Matilda bent down and picked up a chunk of bark lying on the ground and examined it. She dropped it, touched one of the trees. There came that creaking sound, but I swear to you no limbs moved and no wind blew.

"They have suffered so," she said. "Elizabeth, are you there?"

The limbs began to move and thrash about, and one of them stretched long, swept low, and knocked me off my feet. I tried to get up, but the limbs came thrashing down on me like whips.

"Come on," Matilda said. "Come on."

Next thing I knew, she had helped me to my feet, and we were both running. Matilda, in spite of her age, ran spryly, at least until we were away from the grove and back on the trail. She had to stop then and catch her breath. Her face was red and she coughed a few times, leaning one hand against a pine to hold herself up.

I felt like an absolute fool having let her talk me into taking her out into the woods to see a grove of trees, and now that we had seen them, I felt not only like an idiot, but like a very frightened idiot. If there was, anywhere in the back of my mind, an urge to stay on and deal with this odd problem, it was now gone. I wanted one thing, and one thing only. To leave that house and that property.

》《

Matilda moved slowly after that, one arm around my neck as we walked. By the time we made the house she had grown weak, and insisted on going inside. I was ready to put her in the car and leave, but as it was still light, and we were away from that infernal grove, I waltzed her inside and let her stretch out on the couch. After a few minutes she felt better, but she didn't move. I fetched her a glass of water and sat it on the end table, but she didn't touch it.

"Elizabeth, she was there," she said.

"I didn't see her," I said.

"Which would be why I called her an invisible friend," Matilda said. "Actually, I couldn't see her either, but I could sense her."

"What I sense is a change in my plans," I said. "I'm going to leave this house like my comrades, and not come back."

Matilda ignored me. "The trees, they reflect Elizabeth's mental state."

I sat down in a chair and put my hands on my knees and listened.

"I don't know exactly how all this has happened," she said. "But I never truly doubted that she was real, and invisible to others, in spite of what I said earlier. I realize now I lied to you. It was an unintentional lie, but it was a lie. I always felt, on some level, that she was real and invisible. Or refused to reveal herself to others. I can't say. But when we left here I had a feeling not only of sadness and loss, but one of euphoria. It was as if I knew somewhere inside of Elizabeth was something dark, just waiting to take control."

"But how could this be?" I said.

Matilda sat up slowly. "I don't know. I think it may be that Elizabeth is like those spirits of old. That the grove is one of a handful left that hasn't been chopped down and plowed under. Groves like that had to exist all over the world at one time. I don't know any other way to explain it. Trees like those, they're the homes for something that is unworldly."

"You're telling me," I said.

"I remember reading about nymphs in Greek mythology. Some of them were sacred to a particular stream, or lake, or grove."

"You think she's a nymph?"

"An elemental," she said. "One of the last ones left. One of the ones that is connected to the earth when it was raw and new. One of the ones that has survived. I have been thinking about this for years. I've wanted to come back here for years, but didn't for one simple reason. I was afraid I might be right. That Elizabeth might be real. And that she might be angry."

"How could you know that?"

Matilda shook her head. "I don't know. But I always thought there was something dark in Elizabeth, and that it was just waiting to get out. And as I said, I was glad to move away. She was my friend, but I was glad to leave her."

"I think we both should leave her," I said. "I admit defeat."

"Would you consider staying?" Matilda said. "Just one more night?"

"Why would I do that?"

"So I can see her," she said.

"Why would you want to do that?"

"I feel as if I owe her," she said. "I feel somehow responsible for how angry she has become."

"Why didn't she show herself in the grove?" I said.

"The trees were her," Matilda said. "But this house, where she and I were happy, this is her focal point now. She wants you out."

"And I'm more than willing to go," I said.

"Will you stay?"

Until moments before I had been ready to grab a few things, stick them in the car, and drive Matilda back to the retirement home, and drive myself back to my parents' house, but she was convincing.

I gave her a tour of the wrecked house, and even managed to put the kitchen door back in place while Matilda twisted the screws through the holes in the hinges. Then I made us a sandwich of peanut butter, and we sat at the dining room table and ate. About us was the carnage of the night before.

I said, "Why didn't she come in the living room?"

"If I understand what you've told me," Matilda said, "the opposite side of the house is where she's strongest, and that's because that's where she and I played. The back bedroom was mine. She feels comfortable there, as if she belongs. This side was where the family congregated, and she preferred the privacy of the other side of the house. My parents had a bedroom there, and there was my bedroom, but my guess is she associates that side with me, and this side with the family. And another guess is that this is the heart of the house. The part that is most powerful."

"That's two guesses," I said.

"You have me there," Matilda said.

"But she did come on this side, and she broke the door down."

"She's getting stronger and less fearful of coming here. Maybe she could do at any time and just chose not to. Perhaps she didn't have any intention of harming you, but just wanted you to go away, and is trying to scare you off."

"It's working," I said.

"But I believe this is the strong part of the house, where the family was most comfortable. Some people claim all dwellings have a center, a heart, a source of power, something that is inherent, and something borrowed from the living things around or in it, and this place must be it.

"American Indians believed all things had power, that they were alive. Rocks. Trees. They had spirits inside of them. Manitous, they called them. Nymph. Elemental. Manitou. Spirit. All the same thing...what I can't decide is if Elizabeth is angry because I left, or because someone else has moved into the house. Most likely a little of both."

We waited in the living room. The only light was a fire in the fireplace and a single lit candle I had placed in a jar lid on the end table by the couch. The night came, and as soon as the sky darkened, I knew it was coming, and I wished then I hadn't listened to Matilda, and that I had gone away as I had originally planned. There was a change in the air. It became heavy and oppressive, and within moments, on the back porch this time, I heard a heavy sound as if something were dragging itself.

"It's her," I said.

"Yes," she said. "It is."

I looked at Matilda. The fire in the hearth tossed shadows over one side of her face, and in those shadows she looked so much younger. I thought I could not only see the woman she was, but I could almost see the child she had once been.

There was a sudden wailing, like what I would think a banshee would sound like. Loud and raw and strange, it affected not only the ears, but the very bones inside of me. It was as if my skeleton moved and rattled and strained at my flesh.

"My God," I said.

"She is of older gods," Matilda said. "Calling to yours will do you no good."

The next sound was like thousands of whips being slapped against the house, as if an angry slave master were trying to tame it. I heard what was left of the glass in the kitchen and dining room windows tinkle out and to the floor.

And then everything went silent. But I knew it wasn't over, even though the silence reigned for quite some time. When it started up again, the sound was different. It was of the back door to the dog run being flung open, slammed back against the hall. Then there was a noise like something too large for the door pushing itself inside. I glanced toward the living room door to the dog run. It was swelling, and the cold from the dog run was seeping under it; the cold from outside, and the cold from Elizabeth.

The door warped in the middle and seemed sure to break, but it held. And then everything went silent.

I couldn't say where Elizabeth was at that moment, but it seemed to me that she was in the dog run, standing there, or lurking there. The door no longer swelled, but the cold had grown so that it now filled the room. Our candle guttered out. The fire in the fireplace lost its warmth, and the flames grew low.

And then there went up such a savage wail that I dropped to my knees with my hands over my ears. Matilda, she stood there, her arms spread. "Elizabeth," she called out. "It's me, Matilda."

The wail ended, but then the entire house shook, and the living room door to the dog run swelled again and vibrated.

"It's grown strong," Matilda said, and then the door blew apart in thousands of fragments, one of them striking me in the head as I perched on my knees. It didn't knock me out, but it hurt me badly, and it slammed me to the floor. The way pieces of the house were flying about, I stayed down, was so tight to the ground I felt as if I might become part of it.

Then the thrashing and the howling of the wind stopped. I looked up. Much of the house was in wreckage around me. The fireplace still stood, but the flames had been blown out.

I managed to get up. I called out for Matilda. No answer.

Where the walls had once stood, there was just the night, and beyond I could see something dark moving past the barn toward the woods. It looked like a knot of ropy coils and thrashing sticks, and in its midst, trapped in all those sticks and coils, I got a glimpse of Matilda.

I looked around and saw the axe lying by the fireplace, where I had split a few chunks of wood to start the fire. I picked it up and ran out into the night after Elizabeth. I was terrified, no doubt, but I thought of Matilda and felt I had no other alternative than to help her if I could.

The thing moved swiftly and without seeming to touch the ground. Trees leaned wide as it proceeded, not trees from the grove, but all manner of trees, pines and oaks, sweet-gums and hickory. They made plenty of room for it to pass.

What had felt like a long walk before only seemed to take moments this time, and soon I stood in the clearing, looking at the grove. The mass of limbs, the elemental, Elizabeth, was already closing in on the place, and there I stood with the axe in my hand, and absolutely no idea what to do with it; I felt small and useless.

I'm ashamed to say I was frozen. I watched as the thing laid Matilda's body on the ground, gently, and then the limbs whipped and sawed in all directions, and the coils of roots and boughs unknotted, and all those loose projections waved at the night sky.

And then, it was gone. In its place was a young girl in simple clothes, and even though I had not seen early photos of Matilda, I had seen that very child in her features. It was Elizabeth, looking as Matilda had looked those long years ago when she discovered the grove. I was seeing Elizabeth in the same way Matilda had seen her; she was an invisible child no longer.

Matilda was on the ground, but now she rose up on an elbow, struggled to sit. She looked directly at Elizabeth. As for me, I was frozen to my spot.

"Elizabeth," Matilda said. Her voice was sweet and clear and came to me where I stood at the end of the trail, looking at this fantastic occurrence; I think I was suffering from shock. "You don't want to hurt me any more than I want to hurt you."

The little girl stood there looking at Matilda, not moving. Matilda slowly stood up. She held out her hand, said, "We are friends. We have always been friends. Don't be angry. I didn't mean to leave. I had to leave."

The little girl reached out and touched Matilda's hand. When she did, I saw a sort of whipping movement at the back of her head and along her spine. It was like what she really was, was trying to escape.

"We are different, you and I, and both our times are ending," Matilda said. This seemed like a bad time to bring such things up, but then again, I was uncertain there was a perfect way for dealing with what Matilda had called an elemental.

The wind picked up and the trees in the grove waved at the night air. Matilda continued to talk, but I could no longer hear her. The howling wind was too loud. Limbs from trees, not only in the grove, but from the woods surrounding it, began to fly past me. The air filled with them. I crouched down, but one glanced against my head and knocked me out.

》《

There really isn't much to tell after that, and as I warned it's not all explained. But when I awoke, Matilda was leaning over me, cradling my head in her hands. I had been hit twice in one night, once hard enough to be knocked out, so I'll admit that my memory of the next few minutes is hazy.

I do remember that I looked in the direction of the grove and saw that it was gone, twisted out of the ground as if by a tornado. But I knew that storm had not been of this earth.

When I was able to get to my feet, Matilda and I walked back to the remains of the house. There was really nothing left of it but that chimney. My car was fine, however, and we sat in it to recover. I got some Kleenex out of the glove compartment and held a wad of it to my wounded head.

"What happened out there?" I asked.

"Elizabeth was lonely," Matilda said.

That wasn't exactly the answer I was looking for.

"I saw her," I said.

Matilda nodded. "Besides me, you are the first. I suppose she no longer cared if she was seen. I can't say, really."

"She was you?"

"She was a form of me. She still is."

"Still is?"

"I made her a deal. I would stay with her forever."

"But—"

"She is inside me. She and I are one. It was my trade-off. The grove must go. Her anger must go. And she could be with me until the end of my days."

I was stunned by this revelation, but I will tell you quite sincerely, I believed it; after what I had seen, I believed Matilda emphatically.

"What happens then?" I said. "At the end of your days?"

Matilda shook her head. "I don't know. But you know what? I feel really good having her back, and I know now that though I've been happy all my life, I have on some level still been missing something. That something was Elizabeth. The grove didn't make Elizabeth from its elemental powers, it pulled her out of me and gave her to me. She was another side of me, and she was a side I needed. A friend. I was happy because of her, not in spite of her, and now that the other part of me is back, my middle name, I feel refreshed. It's like having a missing arm sewn back on."

We sat there and talked for a long time, and some of what she said resonated with me, but most of it was merely confusing. Suffice to say, the house was gone, the grove was gone, and I never saw Elizabeth again. Matilda and I claimed the house had been taken down by a tornado, and who was to argue. Who was to guess an elemental force from time eternal had torn it down in a rage, and that what remained of it was now inside Matilda. Or so she claimed.

My head healed. You can still see a scar. I told Cliff the story, and he acted like he didn't believe me, but I think he did. I have a feeling he may have seen something strange there before I did, but didn't want to own up to it. Oddly enough, I never crossed William's path again. But I'm sure he had an experience in the house as well and that's why he left.

What else? Oh, the landlady got insurance money. Matilda and I stayed in touch until her death. I suppose she must have been ninety when she passed. They did discover one odd thing after her departure. Matilda had been confined to her bed, no longer able to walk, and in the last few months of her life, not capable of communicating. But during the night they heard a terrible noise, and when they rushed into her room they found her lying dead on her bed, but the room, well, it was torn apart. The window had been blown out and the bed clothes that had covered Matilda were missing, as if there had been some great suction that had taken them away, carried them out the window, along with fragments of a busted chair and all the paintings and easels in the room.

They were all gone, and never found. There were a number of theories, but no satisfactory explanations. My explanation is Elizabeth. I like to think maybe Matilda's soul went with her to some place nice and eternal. Again, I can't say for sure, and I can explain it no further than that.

I don't know what else there is to say. That's my story, and it's just what happened to me. I apologize for it not being a made-up tale, considering so many stories told tonight were good, and highly imaginative, but that's all I've got, and it's true, so I hope it'll do.

# OINK

Sometimes pigs come to visit me.
They are tall and stand on their hind legs.
They knock on the door,
carrying give-away bibles.
They're here to convert me.

Oink. Oink.

If I hide and don't answer.
They walk around the house,
trying to peek through windows.
They lean left, they lean right,
looking through gaps in the curtains.

Oink. Oink.

If they see me.
And they often do.
I smile and wave.
I feel obligated, and let them in.
They have wide nasty smiles.

Oink. Oink.

They show me the bible.
They ask for a drink of water and a cheese sandwich.
I hose down the backyard for them.
They roll in the mud.
When they leave, my couch stinks.

Oink. Oink.

When they're gone,
I tell myself, never again.
And the next time they come,
I'm ready.
I have props.

Oink. Oink.

On the table, in full color,
is a meat cutting chart,
with a pork cookbook nearby.
I offer them a ham sandwich.

Oink. Oink.

Back fires.
They know about the choice cuts of meat.
They eat the ham sandwich.
They burp, and fart,
and leave me,
with pamphlets.

Oink. Oink. And one spare Oink.

They'll be back.
They always are.
With their appetites and bibles.
So I bought a gun.
Real big bullets too.

Oink. Oink.

They came in the night.
While I slept.
Their hooves made marks in the carpet.
They took my gun.
They took my big bullets.

Oink. Oink. And double Oink.

I went to their homes.
One was made of straw.
The other I think was a canvas yurt.
Hard to tell.
I'm not into architecture.

Oink. Oink.

I burned Straw Pig's house up while he slept.
I detonated plastic explosives in the yurt.
In both cases, the meat was ruined.
There was lots of smoke.
Dogs ate the remains.

Ha. Ha. Oink that.

# STARLIGHT,
# EYES BRIGHT

E arlier she had been in the kitchen putting dishes in the washer, and she could hear the TV in the living room. The news.

After awhile Jim came into the kitchen and grabbed her from behind and put his arms around her waist, pushed aside her hair and kissed her on the back of the neck.

"That feels good," Connie said.

"It's supposed to," he said.

He let her go and went to the refrigerator and took out a pitcher of ice tea and poured a glass.

"Anything interesting on the news?" she asked.

He shook his head. "All bad," he said. "I think I'll take my walk."

》《

The curtains were drawn and the lights were out and it was night outside the window. But when the wind blew the curtains moved and showed not only a patch of night but a glitter of stars and the blush of a bright half moon. The wind came and went and when it came it was cool.

They lay in bed and Connie could hear Jim breathing, slow and even, and she thought he was nearly asleep, when he said, "I found something odd on my walk."

He always took a walk after dinner, and tonight when he came back from his walk she had been in the bath, and outside of a peck of a kiss, like a chicken bobbing for a corn kernel, and the words good night, they had discussed nothing and had pulled the slick sheets over them and turned out the light and stretched into position and curled around pillows. Some nights, after his walk, they made love, and others they said little because they liked to go to sleep and wake up early. And tonight she thought was that kind of night, but she had been wrong.

"I thought you were asleep, or close to it."

"No. I'm not really sleepy. I wanted to tell you what I found."

She rolled over in bed and faced him, but all she could see in the dark room was his outline, and then the wind blew and the curtains moved again, and she could see him clearly for a moment. He was lying on his side with his elbow on the bed and his hand holding up the side of his head. The moonlight made him look pale as a gravestone.

"I found the oddest piece of glass," he said.

"That's it? You're keeping me up about finding a piece of glass."

"It was broken."

"Now we're talking tragedy."

"I've never seen anything like it, and it got me to thinking."

"A piece of glass got you to thinking?"

"I don't think it's an ordinary piece of glass. When I first saw it I thought it was stained glass, but when I picked it up it was too thick for that, and the colors were far brighter and less even, and inside you could see the colors were like globs and the globs moved when you turned it."

"A piece of a child's toy. A lava lamp."

"No. It's not a lava lamp. It's nothing like a lava lamp. It's not a piece of a child's toy either. I think it's not really glass...not the way we think of it. I just don't know how else to describe it, but I had the sudden notion that it had fallen from space at one time, maybe long ago, and time and weather and years and men working, changing the landscape, earth being shifted and heaved, had caused it to work itself out of the ground."

"That's assuming a lot."

"I know. But I felt that way when I held it in my hand. I felt maybe it was waiting for me, for some reason."

"Waiting?"

"That's what comes to mind," he said. "More I think about it, the more thoughts about it fill my head."

"That's a little odd, Jim."

"I suppose so."

"You're more tired than you think. You can show it to me in the morning."

He ignored her invitation to sleep, said, "The moon is why I saw it. It was lying beside the road, and the moonlight, or the starlight, or both, seemed to be falling down right out of the heavens and into it. It was like there was some kind of connection between it and the rays of the moon and the stars, the vastness of space, and me. I suppose it could have been, or would have been, that way with someone else, but I think it was because everything was right. The night, the moon, and me."

"The vastness of space? The night. The moon and you. That's a funny way to talk."

"I know, but it's how I feel. It's what comes to me when I think about it. This thing lying on the ground, maybe thousands, maybe millions of years old, drinking in the moonlight."

"You can't know it's older than yesterday."

"True. But when I saw it... No, when I touched it, that was my first thought. That it's old, very old, and that it was here when dinosaurs roamed, and maybe even before that. That it was either heaved up out of the ground or fell here from the stars.

That's what I really think happened. That it fell, or that it was sent here, and that it doesn't belong here because we're all wrong. It's better than us. It fell long ago and was lost to time, and that maybe when it came, something came with it."

She had started to feel uncomfortable with all this talk, but she couldn't help but say, "What do you mean?"

"That it's not like you or me, and it doesn't exist like you or me, and that maybe it's imprisoned in the glass, or whatever that fragment is, glass, rock, something unknown. Maybe, somewhere out there, spread all over the ground for miles, and deep down too, is the rest of it. I think what I found was a piece of its eye."

She sat up in bed. "You're talking very strange."

"Am I?"

"You never talk like this. You're odd...your language... You... Kind of distant. It's... Well, it's strange. You've been working too hard."

"No. I'm hardly working, really. Work is going fine."

"All right, say you did find something unique. You couldn't know all the things about it you claim to know. Like it being a piece of something's eye. Do you know how that sounds?"

"I know. And I'm not saying I know all there is to know, but...I get sensations. I was walking, and then I saw it, and picked it up. When I looked at it, a golden glob of something moved inside it, and then there was a blip of something red inside the gold, and I felt...something. Something moved in the thing, and I felt it in my hand, and by the time I was home with it, I had begun to get sensations. I've been sorting them out ever since."

"Sensations? You got sensations? Well, I got one too. You need a really good night's rest. Tomorrow's Saturday. We can sleep in. We can skip the garage sale crawl and just sleep. Make love, go back to sleep. But now, just go to bed. It'll be okay."

"But nothing's wrong."

"You're tired."

"I'm not tired at all."

"But I am."

"I keep thinking about the poor thing."

"Poor thing?"

"Yes. I feel that it's trapped inside that glass, or some piece of it is, and it wants the other pieces of it found and brought together, and...I can feel something else... It's very close to me now."

"Close."

"The thing that it is," he said, "it's very close."

"The thing that it is... That's enough, hon. Lay down and go to sleep and you'll feel silly about this in the morning. Damn silly."

There was a pause.

"I feel as if I'm no longer of the human race," he said.

"That could be a good thing," she said.

"Yes. I think so."

"I was joking."

"It's no joke. I think we were meant to be like light. The way it feels when you're lost and lonely and way out there in the deep dark, and then suddenly, someone shows, first from a distance, with a light. And we perk up. Maybe a little afraid. Then comes a voice we know. A friendly voice, and the light bobs our way. It should always be that way, a moment of excitement that never becomes fear, because there's the light. A time and a place where we feel safe and wanted, and there's the light. And the closer it gets, the more we become a part of it."

Connie rolled over and looked at him.

"Are you sure you haven't been drinking?"

"I'm not drinking. But I'm drunk. The glass made me drunk. It showed me that once there were good forces in the universe, and they crashed. They crashed like we humans crashed. The good that was is down deep in the ground, and it's bright, and it's colorful, and it's ours for the asking, for the wanting, but not enough of us ask or want."

"The glass? The glass is there for us, and all we have to do is take it?"

"I can't explain it. Not really."

"Who could?"

"I can feel it, but I can't explain it. Talking about it is like talking about the other side of the sky. Like telling someone how love feels when it's fresh. Why a flight of ducks will cause you to lift your eyes."

"You know, Jim, maybe tomorrow, you feel this way... You really should see somebody."

"The glory of what IT was, what THEY were, before they crashed, it had no name. No language. No singular connection to anything to which something could be connected. They, if they is the correct word. It, this structure of color and life and everything precious, was a hive of joy because there was no reason to be otherwise because it's the only sensation they/it have. Humanity, as we know it, all the whats and ifs and buts did not apply. It just was, and what it was is part of what I feel. It was pure happiness, and then something went wrong. Some steering through space, or mechanism, powers outside of itself. Sun spots. A rocket blast from our tired old earth. A rift in time and space...I don't know. But down it went, and it's trying to come back. It wants to come back."

Jim lay back on his pillow and stared at the ceiling.

"We are our own destruction," he said. "They are the joy of the air and the sky and the earth and the beyond."

"Of course," Connie said.

"When I go," he said, "you should come with me. It's only done by choice. The glass is telling me. It wants me to be its rocket, its freedom. It wants me to bear it out and away. Come with me when I go, Connie. Link up with the pieces and let them ride you. Come with me."

"Ride me?"

"They need a host to hold their soul."

Connie was actually scared now.

"Sleep," she said.

"A third of life," he said, "lost in the bed and a dream. For them it's always life and it's always full of light, and happiness, things I can't explain with words."

"I've never heard you talk this way, ever, Jim."

"I've never been this way. I opened a door tonight. I found one piece, and it found me, and now all the others are easy to find. All the others will want me and I will become one of many that are one of the same."

He rose up again and put his hand under his head and rested on his elbow and looked at her in a way she thought was different than any way she had ever seen before.

Yes, she thought, drunk, or maybe some kind of drug. A trip. That's it. He got something from work and hid it, and when he took his walk, he took it. But a night's sleep and he's better. He's gone and done something he shouldn't do, and tomorrow he'll be all right, and we'll talk about it sensibly, and he'll never do it again. It's like that. It has to be like that.

Almost convinced, Connie lay down, shifted in bed, slid under the sheets, turned her back to him, and closed her eyes. She hadn't felt him move, and she visualized him in the same position, elbow on the bed, hand against his head, watching her.

"When they call," he said. "When I go. Don't make me leave without you. Don't let yourself be you. I'm no longer me. Let us be one."

She pretended not to hear him. She closed her eyes. She tried to think of pleasant things. Finally, she felt him lie down. She thought she wouldn't sleep after all that had been said, but perhaps, as a bit of respite from the strangeness of the night, the kicking in of an internal protection device, her body relaxed and in the silence that followed, she slept.

## 》《

In the middle of the night she awoke. She was uncertain why. She had been very tired, but now she was wide awake and she didn't know if a sound had awakened her or an impulse. She sat up in bed and saw that he was in a chair by the window. The wind whipped at the curtains and light sifted in and fell across his face. It made the eye on the right side of his face bright with shifting light, and then the wind ceased and the curtain fell back and he was in shadow again.

She sat up in bed, said, "What's the matter? Can't sleep?"

"I got up and looked at it again. I held it over my eye. It stayed there."

That was the light she had seen move across his face, moonlight on the piece of glass. She felt a chill move along her spine like a mountain climber wearing cold shoes.

"Take that off and come to bed," she said, like a mother asking her child to remove his play hat and call it a day.

"It won't come off my eye now," he said tapping at the glass across his right eye, "and honey, I have seen such amazing things inside of it and inside my head. My first sensations were right. It came from outer space, and it came in a ship made of night and light and all manner of matter from the creation of time. It fell here, millions and millions of years ago. Shattered on impact. Some malfunction. And the pieces went deep, lay there for a long time, then festered out of the earth like a splinter from a thumb. I saw it all inside my head, and now this piece of it lives deep inside my eye and inside my brain, and it is a dark place, a very dark place, and it moves in there, and it knows about all manner of horrors because of being here on our world. It knows horrors it never knew, and it seeks the light."

"You need rest. Come to bed."

"No. You keep saying that. I don't need rest. There are things I need, but rest is not one of them."

He moved his hands in the dark as if measuring something huge, and the hands appeared puffy, like oversized Mickey Mouse gloves. "Oh, the misery that we make. When really, all the world is waiting to be anew."

〉〈

Connie went to the bathroom and put the lid down on the toilet and sat there with the light on, thinking. She didn't know what to say to Jim, and she didn't know what to do. But one thing was certain. The desire for sleep was gone. Like a sailor too long at sea, it had mutinied, and now she was wide awake and nervous.

Jim had been working a lot, so maybe it was the stress of the new accounts at work. And then again, there was the glass, and it was over his eye, held in place by no visible means of support.

Of course it has support of some kind, she told herself. I just couldn't see it.

But why in hell would a grown man place a piece of colored glass over his eye and sit by the window and talk about space ships and aliens and poor sad creatures made of glass from another world?

After awhile, she got up and washed her face, went back to the bedroom. The chair by the window was empty, and he wasn't in bed.

She moved through the house in search of him, but he was nowhere to be seen. When she came to the kitchen, the back door that led to the porch was open, and there was a pleasant night breeze blowing in. She went out on the screened-in porch and looked for him, looked in the rocking chair where he liked to sit sometimes. He wasn't there. She glanced out toward the field that connected to the creek on their forty acres, and she could see him out there in the moonlight, just off the little rough path where he liked to walk. He was down on his hands and knees, digging in the grass with a trowel.

She started walking toward him, and then, perhaps through some motion of his body that gave her alert, or some hidden instinct wrapped up in her brain like a wet dog in a towel, she shivered and stepped behind a sweet gum tree, watched through a fork in the trunk.

He found something. He paused. He reached down, and a light jumped up, covered his face as if with a gel, and then the gel hardened and he shook his head, which looked like the globe of a kerosene lamp, well lit and the color of amber. More light came from the ground, and Connie saw it turn solid and pop against him and stick there like shards of glass, and then the glass writhed and rolled and stretched. More leaped up from the earth. More landed on Jim. The glass wrapped around him, and then he was off his knees and on his feet, spinning, stumbling. The glass spread and made scabs on his flesh the colors of cherries and lemons and oranges and apples.

Jim froze as the fragments flew up from the ground, came to roost on his flesh. He stood with his arms spread and his head drooping toward the ground.

The night crawled on. The insects ceased to buzz. The moon hazed with cloud cover. Somewhere a dog barked. Way, way out on the highway, far beyond, she heard a car hum like a bee in a jar.

Then Jim moved, and the way he moved, it was like the night had come undone and the morning had slipped out in a flash, and then Jim spread his arms high, flapped them rapidly up and down, and the movement radiated colors across the night. Jim's feet came unstuck. He skipped and flittered over the grass, stepping in such a way it was as if he were trying to avoid piles of dog do. He flapped his arms and skipped and hopped. He resembled a big butterfly made of stained glass, bright and eager, but earthbound. His arms kept flapping and the light from the flapping became solid, like wings, and the wings fluttered, and up he went, rising into the sky, covered in all the colors of the rainbow, and some that were not in the rainbow, and way up he rose, bright in the night, a palette of colors against the gold of the moon.

Connie felt something then. Things he had said suddenly made sense to her, and like he said, there were no words for it. She felt it because there was light from where he had leaped upward, and she could feel its warmth, taste what it was, and realize what she could have been with him.

She ran to the rainbow of color, screamed at the darting colors across the sky: "Come get me, Jim. Take me with you."

But the rainbow went away, and with it the light, and the streaks in the sky.

And so went, she realized in a hard, cold instant, her chance to be something other than what she was.

Her chance to be more than, and better than, human.

# DEAD SISTER

I had my office window open, and the October wind was making my hair ruffle. I was turned sideways and had my feet up, cooling my heels on the edge of my desk, noticing my socks. Once the pattern on the socks had been clocks, now the designs were so thin and colorless, I could damn near see my ankles through them.

I was looking out the window, watching the town square from where I sat, three floors up, which was as high as anything went in Mud Creek. It seemed pretty busy down there for a town of only eight thousand. Even a couple of dogs were looking industrious, as if they were in a hurry to get somewhere and do something important. Chase a cat, bite a mailman, or bury a bone.

Me, I wasn't working right then, and hadn't in a while. For me, 1958 had not been a banner year.

I was about to get a bottle of cheap whisky out of my desk drawer, when there was a knock on the door. I could see my name spelled backwards on the pebbled glass, and beyond that a shadow that had a nice overall shape.

I said, "Come on in, the water's fine."

A blond woman wearing a little blue pill hat came in. She was the kind of dame if she walked real fast she might set the walls on fire. She sat down in the client chair and crossed her legs and let her cool blue dress slide up so I could see her knees. She was wearing stockings so sheer, she might as well have not had any on. She lifted her head and stared at me with eyes that would make a monk set fire to his Bible.

She was carrying a cute little purse that might hold a compact, a couple of quarters and a pencil. She let it rest on her lap, laid her hand on it like it was a pet cat.

"Mr. Taylor? I was wondering if you could check on something for me?" she said.

"If it's on your person, no charge."

She smiled at me. "I heard you thought you were funny."

"Not really, but I try the stuff out anyway. See how this one works for you. I get fifty a day plus expenses."

"You might have to do some rough stuff."

"How rough?" I said.

"I don't know. I really don't know what's going on at all, but I think it may be someone who's not quite right."

"Did you talk to the police?" I asked.

She nodded. "They checked, watched for three nights. But nobody showed. Soon as they quit, it started over again."

"Where did they watch, and what did they watch?"

"The graveyard. They were watching a grave. I could swear someone was digging it up at night."

"You saw this?"

"If I saw it, I'd be sure, wouldn't I?"

"You got me there," I said.

"My sister, Susan. She died of something unexpected. Eighteen. Beautiful. One morning she's feeling ill, and then the night comes, and she's feeling worse, and the next day she's dead. Just like that. She was buried in the Sweet Pine Cemetery, and I go each morning on my way to work to bring flowers to her grave. The ground never settled. I got the impression it was being worked over at night. That someone was digging there. That they were digging up my sister, or trying to."

"That's an odd thing to think."

"The dirt was always disturbed," she said. "The flowers from the day before were buried under the dirt. It didn't seem right."

"So, you want me to check the place out, see if that's what's going on?"

"The police were so noisy and so obvious I doubt they got a true view of things. No one would try with them there. They thought I was crazy. What I need is someone who can be discreet. I would go myself, but I might need someone with some muscle."

"Yeah, you're too nice a piece of chicken to be wandering a graveyard. It would be asking for trouble. Your sister's name is Susan. What's yours?"

"Oh, I didn't tell you, did I? It's Cathy. Cathy Carter. Can you start right away?"

"Soon as the money hits my palm."

>><<

I probably didn't need a .38 revolver to handle a grave robber, but you never know. So, I brought it with me.

My plan was if there was someone actually there, to put the gun on him and make him lie down, tie him up, and haul him to the police. If he was digging up somebody's sister, the county cops downtown might not let him make it to trial. He might end up with a warning shot in the back of the head. That happened, I could probably get over it.

Course, it could be more than one. That's why the .38.

My take, though, was it was all hooey. Not that Cathy Carter didn't believe it. She did. But my guess was the whole business was nothing more than her grieving imagination, or a dog or an armadillo digging around at night.

I decided to go out there and look at the place during the day. See if I thought there was any kind of monkey business going on.

Sweet Pine isn't a pauper graveyard on the whole, but a lot of paupers are buried there, on the back, low end near Coats Creek. Actually on the other side of the graveyard fence. Even in death, they couldn't get inside with the regular people. Outsiders to the end.

There've been graves there since the Civil War. A recent flood had washed away a lot of headstones and broke the ground open and pushed some rotten bones and broken coffins around. It was all covered up in a heap with a dozer after that; sons and daughters, mothers and fathers, grandmas and grandpas, massed together in one big ditch for their final rest.

The fresher graves on the higher ground, inside the cemetery fence were fine. That's where Susan was buried.

I parked at the gate, which was a black ornamental thing with fence tops like spear heads. The fence was six feet high and went all around the cemetery. The front was a large open area with a horseshoe sign over it that read in metal curlicues: SWEET PINE CEMETERY.

That was just in case you thought the headstones were for show.

Inside, I went where Cathy told me Susan was buried, and found her grave easy enough. There was a stone marker with her name on it, and the dates of birth and death. The ground did look fresh dug. I bent down and looked close. There were scratches in the dirt, but they didn't look like shovel work. There were a bunch of cigarette butts heel-mashed into the ground near the grave.

I went over to a huge shade tree nearby and leaned on it, pulled out a stick of gum and chewed. It was comfortable under the tree, with the day being cool to begin with, and the shadow of the limbs lying on the ground like spilled night. I chewed the gum and looked at the grave for a long time. I looked around and decided if there was anything to what Cathy had said, then the cops wouldn't have seen it, or rather they would have discouraged any kind of grave-bothering soul from entering the cemetery in the first place. Those cigarette butts were the tipoff. My guess was they belonged to the cops, and they had stood not six feet from the grave, smoking, watching. Probably, like me, figuring it was all a pipe dream. Only thing was, I planned to give Cathy her whole dollar.

I drove back to the office and sat around there for a few hours, and then I went home and changed into some old duds, left my hat, grabbed a burger at Dairy Queen, and hustled my car back over to the cemetery. I drove by it and parked my heap about a half mile from the graveyard under a hickory nut tree well off the main road and hoped no one would bother it.

I walked back to the cemetery and stood under the tree near Susan's grave and looked up at it. There was a low limb and I got hold of that and pulled myself up, and then climbed higher. The oak had very few leaves, but the limbs were big, and I found a place where there was a naturally scooped-out spot in the wood and laid down on that. It wasn't comfortable, but I lay there anyway and chewed some gum, and waited for the sun to set. That wouldn't be long this time of year. By five-thirty or six the sun was gone and the night was up.

Night came and I lay on the limb until my chest hurt. I got up and climbed higher, found a place where I could stand on a limb and wedge my ass in a fork in the tree. From there I had a good look at the grave.

The dark was gathered around me like a blanket. To see me, you'd have to be looking for me. I took the gum out of my mouth and stuck it to the tree, and leaned back so that I was nestled firmly in the narrow fork. It was almost like an easy chair.

I could see the lights of the town from there, and I watched those for awhile, and watched the headlights of cars in the distance. It was kind of hypnotic. Then I watched lightning bugs. A few mosquitoes came to visit, but it was a little cool for them, so they weren't too bad.

I touched my coat pocket to make sure my .38 was in place, and it was. I had five shots. I didn't figure I would need to shoot anyone, and if I did, I doubted it would take more than five shots.

I added up the hours I had invested in the case, my expenses, which were lunch and a few packs of chewing gum. This wasn't the big score I was looking for, and I was beginning to feel silly, sitting in a tree waiting on someone to come along and dig around a grave. I wanted to check my watch, but I couldn't see the hands well enough, and though I had a little flashlight in my pocket, I didn't want any light to give me away.

I'll admit I wasn't much of a sentry. After awhile, I dozed.

What woke me was a scratching sound. When I came awake I nearly fell out of the tree, not knowing where I was. By the time I had it figured the sound was really loud. It was coming from the direction of the grave.

》《

When I looked down I saw an animal digging at the grave, and then I realized it wasn't a dog at all. I had only thought it was. It was a man in a long black jacket. He was bent over the grave and he was digging with his hands like a dog. He wasn't throwing the dirt far, just mounding it up. While I had napped like a squirrel in a nest, he had dug all the way down to the coffin.

I pulled the gun from my pocket and yelled: "Hey, you down there. Leave that grave alone."

The man wheeled then, looked up, and when he did, I got a glimpse of his face in the moonlight. It wasn't a good glimpse, but it was enough to nearly cause me to fall out of the tree. The face was as white as a nun's ass and the eyes were way too bright, even if he was looking up into the moonlight; those eyes looked the way coyote eyes look staring out of the woods.

He hissed at me, and went back to his work, which was now popping the lid off the coffin like it was a cardboard box. It snapped free, and he reached inside and pulled out the body of a girl. Her hair was undone and it was long and blond and fell over the dirty white slip she was wearing. He pulled her out of there before I could get down from the tree with the gun. The air was full of the stink of death. Susan's body, I guessed.

By the time I hit the ground, he had the body thrown over his shoulder, and he was running across the graveyard, between the stones, like a goddamn deer. I ran after him with my gun, yelling for him to stop. He was really moving. I saw him jump one of the tall upright gravestones like it was lying down and land so light he seemed like a crepe paper floating down.

Now that he was running, not crouching and digging like a dog, I could tell more about his body type. He was a long, skinny guy with stringy white hair and the long black coat that spread out around him like the wings of a roach. The girl bounced across his shoulder as though she was nothing more than a bag of dry laundry.

I chased him to the back fence, puffing all the way, and then he did something that couldn't be done. He sprang and leaped over that spear-tipped fence with Susan's body thrown over his shoulder, hit the ground running and darted down to the creek, jumped it, and ran off between the trees and into the shadows and out of my sight.

That fence was easily six feet high.

》《

I started to drive over to Cathy's place. I had her address. But I didn't know what to say. I didn't go there, and I didn't go home, which was a dingy apartment. I went to the office, which was slightly better and got the bottle out of the drawer, along with my glass, and poured myself a shot of my medicine. It wasn't a cure, but it was better than nothing. I liked it so much I poured another.

I went to the window with my fresh filled glass and looked out. The night looked like the night and the moon looked like the moon and the street looked like the street. I held my hand up in front of me. Nope. That was my hand and it had a glass of cheap whisky in it. I wasn't dreaming, and to the best of my knowledge I wasn't crazy.

I finished off the drink. I thought I should have taken a shot at him. But I didn't because of Susan's body. She wouldn't mind a bullet in the head, but I didn't want to have to explain that to her sister if I accidentally hit her.

I laid down on the couch for a little while, and the whisky helped me sleep, but when I came awake, and turned on the light and looked at my watch, it was just then midnight.

I got my hat and my gun and my car keys off the desk, went down to my car and drove back to the cemetery.

》《

I didn't park down from the place this time. I drove through the horseshoe opening and drove down as close as I could get to the grave. I got out and looked around, hoping I wouldn't see the man in the long coat, and hoping in another way I would.

I got my gun from my pocket and held it down by my side, and walked over to the grave. It was covered up, patted down. The air still held that stench as before. Less of it, but it still lingered, and I had this odd feeling it wasn't the stink of Susan's body after all. It was that man. It was his stink. I felt sure of it, but there was no reasoning as to why I thought that. Call it instinct. I looked down at the grave. It was closed up.

The hair on the back of my neck stood up like I had been shot with a quiver full of little arrows.

Looking every which way as I went, I made it back to the car and got inside and locked all the doors and started it up and drove back to town and over to Cathy's place.

》《

We were in her little front room sitting on the couch. There was coffee in cups on saucers sitting on the coffee table. I sipped mine and tried to do it so my hand didn't shake.

"So now you believe me," she said.

"But I don't know anyone else will. We tell the cops this, we'll both be in the booby hatch."

"He took her body?"

I nodded.

"Weren't you supposed to stop him?"

"I actually didn't think that was going to come up. But I couldn't stop him. He didn't look like much, but he was fast, and to leap like that, he had to be strong. He carried your sister's body like it was nothing."

"My heavens, what could he want with her?"

I had an idea, considering she only had on a slip. That meant he'd been there before, undressed her, and put her back without her burial clothes. But Cathy, she was on the same page.

"Now someone has her body," she said, "and they're doing who knows what to her... Oh, Jesus. This is like a nightmare. Listen, you've got to take me out there."

"You don't want to do that," I said.

"Yes I do, Mr. Taylor. That's exactly what I want to do. And if you won't do it, I'll go anyway."

She started to cry and leaned into me. I held her. I figured part of it was real and part of it was like the way she showed me her legs; she'd had practice getting her way with men.

## 》《

I drove her over there.

It was just about daybreak when we arrived. I drove through the gate and parked near the grave again. I saw that fellow, even if he was carrying two dead blondes on his shoulders, I was going to take a shot at him. Maybe two. That didn't work, I was going to try and run over him with my car.

Cathy stood over the grave. There was still a faint aroma of the stink from before.

Cathy said, "So he came back and filled it in while you were at your office, doing what did you say—having a drink?"

"Two actually."

"If you hadn't done that, he would have come back and you would have seen him."

"No reason for me to think he'd come back. I just came to look again to make sure I wasn't crazy."

As the sun came up, we walked across the cemetery, me tracing the path the man had taken as he ran. When I got to the fence, I looked to see if there was anything he could have jumped up on or used as a spring board to get over. There wasn't.

We went back to the car and I drove us around on the right side near the back of the cemetery. I had to park well before we got to the creek. It was muddy back there where the creek had rose, and there were boot prints in the mud from the flooding. The flood had made everything a bog.

I looked at the fence. Six feet tall, and he had landed some ten feet from the fence on this side. That wasn't possible, but I had seen him do it, and now I was looking at what had to be his boot tracks.

I followed the prints down to the creek, where he had jumped across. It was all I could do to stay on my feet, as it was such a slick path to follow, but he had gone over it as sure-footedly as a goat.

Cathy came with me. I told her to go back, but she wouldn't listen. We walked along the edge of the creek until we found a narrow spot, and I helped her cross over. The tracks played out when the mud played out. As we went up a little rise, the trees thickened even more and the land became drier. Finally we came to a nearly open clearing. There were a few trees growing there, and they were growing up close to an old saw mill. One side of it had fallen down, and there was an ancient pile of blackened sawdust mounded up on the other where it had been dumped from the mill and rotted by the weather.

We went inside. The floor boards creaked, and the whole place, large as it was, shifted as we walked.

"Come on," I said. "Before we fall all the way to hell."

On the way back, as we crossed the creek, I saw something snagged on a little limb. I bent over and looked at it. It stank of that smell I had smelled in the graveyard. I got out my handkerchief and folded the handkerchief around it and put it in my pocket.

Back in the car, driving to town, Cathy said, "It isn't just some kook, is it?"

"Some kook couldn't have jumped a fence like that, especially with a body thrown over its shoulder. It couldn't have gone across that mud and over that creek like it did. It has to be something else."

"What does something else mean?" Cathy said.

"I don't know," I said.

We parked out near the edge of town and I took the handkerchief out and unfolded it. The smell was intense.

"Throw it away," Cathy said.

"I will, but first, you tell me what it is."

She leaned over, wrinkled her pretty nose. "It's a piece of cloth with meat on it."

"Rotting flesh," I said. "The cloth goes with the man's jacket; the man I saw with Susan's body. Nobody has flesh like this if they're alive."

"Could it be from Susan?" she asked.

"Anything is possible, but this is stuck to the inside of the cloth. I think it came off him."

>> <<

In town I bought a shovel at the hardware store, and then we drove back to the cemetery. I parked so that I thought the car might block what I was doing a little, and I told Cathy to keep watch. It was broad daylight and I hoped I looked like a grave digger and not a grave robber.

She said, "You're going to dig up the grave?"

"Dang tootin'," I said, and I went at it.

Cathy didn't like it much, but she didn't stop me. She was as curious as I was. It didn't take long because the dirt was soft, the digging was easy. I got down to the coffin, scraped the dirt off, and opened it with the tip of the shovel. It was a heavy lid, and it was hard to do. It made me think of how easily the man in the coat had lifted it.

Susan was in there. She looked very fresh and she didn't smell. There was only that musty smell you get from slightly damp earth. She had on the slip, and the rest of her clothes were folded under her head. Her shoes were arranged at her feet.

"Jesus," Cathy said. "She looks so alive. So fair. But why would someone dig her up, and then bring her back?"

"I'm not sure, but I think the best thing to do is go see my mother."

>><<

My mother is the town librarian. She's one of those that believes in astrology, ESP, little green men from Mars, ghosts, a balanced budget, you name it. And she knows about that stuff. I grew up with it, and it never appealed to me. Like my dad, I was a hard-headed realist. And at some point, my mother had been too much for him. They separated. He lives in Hoboken with a show girl, far from East Texas. He's been there so long he might as well be a Yankee himself.

The library was nearly empty, and as always, quiet as God's own secrets. My mother ran a tight ship. Mom saw me when I came in and frowned. She's no bigger than a minute with over-dyed hair and an expression on her face like she's just eaten a sour persimmon.

I waved at her, and she waved me to follow her to the back, where her office was.

In the back, she made Cathy sit at a table near the religious literature, and took me into her office which was only a little larger than a janitor's closet, and closed the door. She sat behind her cluttered desk, and I sat in front of it.

"So, you must need money," she said.

"When have I asked you for any?"

"Never, but since I haven't seen you in a month of Sundays, and you live across town, I figured it had to be money. If it's for that floozy out there, to buy her something, forget it. She looks cheap."

"I don't even know her that well," I said.

She gave me a narrow-eyed look.

"No. It's not like that. She's a client."

"I bet she is."

"Listen, Mom, I'm going to jump right in. I have a situation. It has to do with the kind of things you know about."

"That would be a long list."

I nodded. "But this one is a very specialized thing." And then I told her the story.

She sat silent for a while, processing the information.

"Cauldwell Hogston," she said.

"Beg pardon?"

"The old graveyard, behind the fence. The one they don't use anymore. He was buried there. Fact is he was hanged in the graveyard from a tree limb. About where the old saw mill is now."

"There are graves there?" I asked.

"Well, there were. The flood washed up a bunch of them. Hogston was one of the ones buried there, in an unmarked grave. Here, it's in one of the books about the growth of the city, written in 1940."

She got up and pulled a dusty-looking book off one of her shelves. The walls were lined with them, and these were her personal collection. She put the book on her desk, sat back down and started thumbing through the volume, then paused.

"Oh, what the heck. I know it by heart." She closed the book and sat back down in her chair and said, "Cauldwell Hogston was a grave robber. He stole bodies."

"To sell to science?"

"No. To have...well, you know."

"No. I don't know."

"He had relations with the bodies."

"That's nasty," I said.

"I'll say. He would take them and put them in his house and pose them and sketch them. Young women. Old women. Just as long as they were women."

"Why?"

"Before daybreak, he would put them back. It was a kind of ritual. But he got caught and he got hung, right there in the graveyard. Preacher cursed him. Later they found his notebooks in his house, and his drawings of the dead women. Mostly nudes."

"But Mom, I think I saw him. Or someone like him."

"It could be him," she said.

"You really think so?"

"I do. You used to laugh at my knowledge, thought I was a fool. What do you think now?"

"I think I'm confused. How could he come out of the grave after all these many years and start doing the things he did before? Could it be someone else? Someone imitating him?"

"Unlikely."

"But he's dead."

"What we're talking about here, it's a different kind of dead. He's a ghoul. Not in the normal use of the term. He's a real ghoul. Back when he was caught, and that would be during the Great Depression, no one questioned that sort of thing. This town was settled by people from the old lands. They knew about ghouls. Ghouls are mentioned as far back as One Thousand and One Nights. And that's just their first known mention. They love the dead. They gain power from the dead."

"How can you gain power from something that's dead?"

"Some experts believe we die in stages, and that when we are dead to this world, the brain is still functioning on a plain somewhere between life and death. There's a gradual release of the soul."

"How do you know all this?"

"Books. Try them sometime. The brain dies slowly, and a ghoul takes that slow dying, that gradual release of soul, and feasts on it."

"He eats their flesh?"

"There are different kinds of ghouls. Some eat flesh. Some only attack men, and some are like Hogston. The corpses of women are his prey."

"But how did he become a ghoul?"

"Anyone who has an unholy interest in the dead, no matter what religion, no matter if they have no religion, if they are killed violently, they may well become a ghoul. Hogston was certainly a prime candidate. He stole women's bodies and sketched them, and he did other things. We're talking about, you know—"

"Sex?"

"If you can call it that with dead bodies. By this method he thought he could gain their souls and their youth. Being an old man, he wanted to live forever. Course, there were some spells involved, and some horrible stuff he had to drink, made from herbs and body parts. Sex with the bodies causes the remains of their souls to rise to the surface, and he absorbs them through his own body. That's why he keeps coming back to a body until it's drained. It all came out when he was caught replacing the body of Mary Lawrence in her grave. I went to school with her, so I remember all this very well. Anyway, when they caught him, he told them everything, and then there were his notebooks and sketches. He was quite proud of what he had done."

"But why put the bodies back? And, Susan, she looked like she was just sleeping. She looked fresh."

"He returned the bodies before morning because for the black magic to work, they must lie at night in the resting place made for them by their loved ones. Once a ghoul begins to take the soul from a body, it will stay fresh until he's finished, as long as he returns it to its grave before morning. When he drains the last of its soul, the body decays. What he gets out of all this, besides immortality, are powers he didn't have as a man."

"Like being strong and able to jump a six-foot fence flat-footed," I said.

"Things like that, yes."

"But they hung the old man," I said. "How in hell could he be around now?"

"They did more than hang him. They buried him in a deep grave filled with wet cement and allowed it to dry. That was a mistake. They should have completely destroyed the body. Still, that would have held him, except the flood opened the graves, and a bulldozer was sent in to push the old bones away. In the process, it must have broken open the cement and let him out."

"What's to be done?" I said.

"You have to stop it."

"Me?"

"I'm too old. The cops won't believe this. So it's up to you. You don't stop him, another woman dies, he'll take her body. It could be me. He doesn't care I'm old."

"How would I stop him?"

"That part might prove to be difficult. First, you'll need an axe, and you'll need some fire..."

>«

With Cathy riding with me, we went by the hardware store and bought an axe and a file to sharpen it up good. I got a can of paint thinner and a new lighter and a can of lighter fluid. I went home and got my twelve gauge, double barrel. I got a handful of shotgun shells. I explained to Cathy what I had to do.

"According to Mom, the ghoul doesn't feel pain much. But, they can be destroyed if you chop their head off, and then you got to burn the head. If you don't, it either grows a new head, or body out of the head, or some such thing. She was a little vague. All I know is she says it's a way to kill mummies, ghouls, vampires, and assorted monsters."

"My guess is she hasn't tried any of this," Cathy said.

"No, she hasn't. But she's well schooled in these matters. I always thought she was full of it, but turns out, she isn't. Who knew?"

"And if it doesn't work?"

"Look for my remains."

"I'm going with you," she said.

"No you're not."

"Do you really think you can stop me? It's my sister. I hired you."

"Then let me do my job."

"I just have your word for all this."

"There you are. I wouldn't tromp around in the dark based on my word."

"I'm going."

"It could get ugly."

"Once again. It's my sister. You don't get to choose for me."

》《

I parked my car across the road from the cemetery under a willow. As it grew dark, shadows would hide it reasonably well. This is where Cathy was to sit. I, on the other hand, would go around to the rear where the ghoul would most likely come en route to Susan's grave.

Sitting in my jalopy talking, the sun starting to drop, I said, "I'll try and stop him before he gets to the grave. But, if he comes from some other angle, another route, hit the horn and I'll come running."

"There's the problem of the six-foot fence," Cathy said.

"I may have to run around the graveyard fence, but I'll still come. You can keep honking the horn and turn on the lights and drive through the cemetery gate. But whatever you do, don't get out of the car."

I handed her my shotgun.

"Ever shot one of these?" I said.

"Daddy was a bird hunter. So, yes."

"Good. Just in case it comes to it."

"Will it kill him?"

"Mom says no, but it beats harsh language."

I grabbed my canvas shoulder bag and axe and got out of the car and started walking. I made it around the fence and to the rear of the graveyard, near the creek and the mud, about fifteen minutes before dark.

I got behind a wide pine and waited. I didn't know if I was in the right place, but if his grave had been near the sawmill this seemed like a likely spot. I got a piece of chewing gum and went to work on it.

The sun was setting.

I hoisted the axe in my hand, to test the weight. Heavy. I'd have to swing it pretty good to manage decapitation. I thought about that. Decapitation. What if it was just some nut, and not a ghoul?

Well, what the hell. He was still creepy.

I put the axe head on the ground and leaned on the axe handle.

I guess about an hour passed before I heard something crack. I looked out toward the creek where I had seen him jump with Susan's body. I didn't see anything but dark. I felt my skin prick, and I had a sick feeling my stomach.

I heard another cracking.

It wasn't near the creek.

It wasn't in front of me at all.

It was behind me.

**》《**

I wheeled, and then I saw the ghoul. He hadn't actually seen me, but he was moving behind me at a run, and boy could he run. He was heading straight for the cemetery fence.

I started after him, but I was too far behind and too slow. I slipped on the mud and fell. When I looked up, it was just in time to see the ghoul make a leap. For a moment, he seemed pinned against the moon, like a curious broach on a golden breast. His long white hair trailed behind him and his coat was flying wide. He had easily leaped ten feet high.

He came down in the cemetery as light as a feather. By the time I was off my ass and had my feet under me, he was running across the cemetery toward Susan's grave.

I ran around the edge of the fence, carrying the axe, the bag slung over my shoulder. As I ran, I saw him, moving fast. He was leaping gravestones again.

Before I reached the end of the fence, I heard my horn go off, and saw lights come on. Then car was moving. As I turned the corner of the fence, I could see the lights had pinned the ghoul for a moment, and the car was coming fast. The ghoul threw up its arm and the car hit him and knocked him back about twenty feet.

The ghoul got up as if nothing had happened. Its movements were puppet-like, as if he were being pulled by invisible strings.

Cathy, ignoring everything I told her, got out of the car. She had the shotgun.

The ghoul ignored her, and ran toward Susan's grave, started digging as if Cathy wasn't there. As I came through the cemetery opening, and past my car, Cathy cut down on the thing with the shotgun. Both barrels.

It was a hell of a roar and dust and cloth and flesh flew up from the thing. The blast knocked it down. It popped up like a Jack-in-the-Box and hissed like a cornered possum. It lunged at Cathy. She swung the shotgun by the barrel, hit the ghoul upside the head.

I was at Cathy's side now, and without thinking I dropped the axe and the bag fell off my shoulder. Before the ghoul could reach her, I tackled the thing.

It was easy. There was nothing to Cauldwell Hogston. It was like grabbing a hollow reed. But the reed was surprisingly strong. Next thing I knew I was being thrown into the windshield of my car, and then Cathy was thrown on top of me.

When I had enough of my senses back I tried to sit up. My back hurt. The back of my head ached, but otherwise, I seemed to be all in one piece.

The ghoul was digging furiously at the grave with its hands, throwing dirt like a dog searching for a bone. He was already deep into the earth.

Still stunned, I jumped off the car and grabbed the canvas bag and pulled the lighter fluid and the lighter out of it. I got as close as I dared, and sprayed a stream of lighter fluid at the creature. It soaked the back of its head. Hogston wheeled to look at me. I sprayed the stuff in his eyes and onto his chest, drenching him. He swatted at the fluid as I squeezed the can.

I dropped the can. I had the lighter, and I was going to pop the top and hit the thumb wheel, when the next thing I knew the ghoul leaped at me and grabbed me and threw me at the cemetery fence. I hit hard against it and lay there stunned.

When I looked up, the ghoul was dragging the coffin from the grave, and without bothering to open it this time, threw it over its shoulder and took off running.

I scrambled to my feet, found the lighter, stuffed it in the canvas bag, and swung the bag over my shoulder and picked up the axe. I yelled for Cathy to get in the car. She was still dazed, but managed to get in the car.

Sliding behind the wheel, I gave her the axe and the bag, turned the key, popped the clutch, and backed out of the cemetery. I whipped onto the road, jerked the gear into position, and tore down the road.

"He's over there!" Cathy said. "See!"

I glimpsed the ghoul running toward the creek with the coffin.

"I see," I said. "But I think I know where he's going."

》《

The saw mill road was good for a short distance, but then the trees grew in close and the road was grown up with small brush. I had to stop the car. We started rushing along on foot. Cathy carried the canvas bag. I carried the axe.

"What's in the bag?" she said.

"More lighter fluid."

Trees dipped their limbs around us, and when an owl hooted, then fluttered through the pines, I nearly crapped my pants.

Eventually, the road played out, and there were only trees. We pushed through some limbs, scratching ourselves in the process, and finally broke out into a partial clearing. The saw mill was in the center of it, with its sagging roof and missing wall and trees growing up through and alongside it. The moonlight fell over it and colored it like thin yellow paint.

"You're sure he's here," Cathy said.

"I'm not sure of much of anything anymore," I said. "But, his grave was near here. It's about the only thing he can call home now."

When we reached the saw mill, we took deep breaths, as if on cue, and went inside. The boards creaked under our feet. I looked toward a flight of open stairs and saw the ghoul moving up those as swift and silent as a rat. The coffin was on his shoulder, held there as if it were nothing more than a shoe box.

I darted toward the stairway, and the minute my foot hit them, they creaked and swayed.

"Stay back," I said, and Cathy actually listened to me. At least for a moment.

I climbed on up, and then there was a crack, and my foot went through. I felt a pain like an elephant had stepped on my leg. I nearly dropped the axe.

"Taylor," Cathy yelled. "Are you all right?"

"Good as it gets," I said.

Pulling my leg out, I limped up the rest of the steps with the axe, turned left at the top of the stairs—the direction I had seen it take. I guess I was probably thirty feet high by then.

I walked along the wooden walkway. To my right were walls and doorways without doors, and to my left was a sharp drop to the rotten floor below. I hobbled along for a few feet, glanced through one of the doorways. The floor on the other side was gone. Beyond that door was a long drop.

I looked down at Cathy.

She pointed at the door on the far end.

"He went in there," she said.

Girding my loins, I came to the doorway and looked in. The roof of the room was broken open, and the floor was filled with moonlight. On the floor was the coffin, and the slip Susan had worn was on the edge of the coffin, along with the ghoul's rotten black coat.

Cauldwell Hogston was in the coffin on top of her.

I rushed toward him, just as his naked ass rose up, a bony thing that made him look like some sad concentration camp survivor. As his butt came down, I brought the axe downward with all my might.

It caught him on the back of the neck, but the results were not as I expected. The axe cut a dry notch, but up he leaped, as if levitating, grabbed my axe handle, and would have had me, had his pants not been around his ankles. It caused him to fall. I staggered back through the doorway, and now he was out of his pants and on his feet, revealing that though he was emaciated, one part of him was not.

Backpedaling, I stumbled onto the landing. He sprang foward, grabbed my throat. His hands were like a combination of vise and ice tongs; they bit into my flesh and took my air. Up close, his breath was rancid as roadkill. His teeth were black and jagged and the flesh hung from the bones of his face like cheap curtains. The way he had me, I couldn't swing the axe and not hit myself.

In the next moment, the momentum of his rush carried us backwards, along the little walkway, and then, out into empty space.

〉〈

Falling didn't take anytime. When I hit the ground my air was knocked out of me, and the boards of the floor sagged.

The ghoul was straddling me, choking me.

And then I heard a click, a snap. I looked. Cathy had gotten the lighter from the bag. She tossed it.

The lighter hit the ghoul, and the fluid I had soaked him with flared. His head flamed and he jumped off of me, and headed straight for Cathy.

I got up as quickly as I could, which was sort of like asking a dead hippo to roll over. On my feet, lumbering forward, finding that I still held the axe in my hand, I saw that the thing's head was flaming like a match, and yet, it had gripped Cathy by the throat and was lifting her off the ground.

I swung the axe from behind, caught its left leg just above the knee. The blade I had sharpened so severely did its work. It literally cut the ghoul off at the knee, and he dropped, letting go of Cathy. She moved back quickly, holding her throat, gasping for air.

The burning thing lay on its side. I brought the axe down on its neck. It took me two more chops before its rotten, burning head came loose. I chopped at the head, sending the wreckage of flaming skull in all directions.

I faltered a few steps, looked at Cathy, said, "You know, when you lit him up, I was under him."

"Sorry."

And then I saw her eyes go wide.

I turned.

The headless, one-legged corpse was crawling toward us, swift as a lizard. It grabbed my ankle.

I slammed the axe down, took off the hand at the wrist, then kicked it loose of my leg. That put me in a chopping frenzy. I brought the axe down time after time, snapping that dry stick of a creature into thousands of pieces.

By the time I finished that, I could hardly stand. I had to lean on the axe. Cathy took my arm, said, "Taylor."

Looking up, I saw the fire from the ghoul had spread out in front of us and the rotten lumber and old sawdust had caught like paper. The canvas bag with the lighter fluid in it caught too, and within a second, it blew, causing us to fall back.

The only way out was up the stairs, and in the long run, that would only prolong the roasting. Considering the alternative, however, we were both for prolonging our fiery death instead of embracing it.

Cathy helped me up the stairs, because by now my ankle had swollen up until it was only slightly smaller than a Civil War cannon. I used the axe like a cane. The fire licked the steps behind us, climbed up after us, as if playing tag.

When we made the upper landing, we went through the door where Susan's body lay. I looked in the coffin. She was nude, looking a lot rougher than before. Perhaps the ghoul had gotten the last of her, or without him to keep her percolating with his magic she had gone for the last roundup; passed on over into true solid death. I hoped in the end, her soul had been hers, and not that monster's.

I let go of Cathy, and using the axe for support, made it to the window. The dark sawdust was piled deep below.

Stumbling back to the coffin, I dropped the axe, got hold of the edge, and said, "Push."

Cathy did just that. The coffin scraped across the floor. Smoke wafted up through cracks, and it was growing hot. Flame licked up now and then, as if searching for us.

We pushed the coffin and Susan out the window. She fell free of the box and hit the sawdust. We jumped after her.

When we were on the pile, spitting sawdust, trying to work our way down the side of it, the saw mill wall started to fall. We rolled down the side of the piled sawdust and hit the ground.

The burning wall hit the sawdust. The mound was high enough we were protected from it. We crawled out from under it and managed to get about fifty feet away before we looked back.

The sawmill, the sawdust pile, and poor Susan's body, and anything that was left of Cauldwell Hogston, was now nothing more than a raging mountain of sizzling, cracking flames.

# SHOOTING POOL

**M**y daddy told me it wasn't a place I ought to be because the owner, who had once been a good friend of his, and the owner's friends were troublesome, which was his way of saying they were no-accounts or hoods. My mother didn't want me there either, but after high school, about twice a week, sometimes three times a week, me and my friends Donald and Lee would go over to the pool hall to shoot a few runs of solids and stripes, which was the only pool game we knew.

I think what we liked about going there was that pool was thought of as a tough guy's game, a game played in bars with lots of cigarette and cigar smoke and some rough-looking characters hanging around. And that's just the way Rugger's Pool Hall was. I saw Jack Rugger and his friends at my father's garage from time to time where my daddy kept their cars running. My daddy was no shrinking violet either, but his strength and anger were generally of a positive sort and not directed at my person. Rugger and his pals were a mystery to me, because they talked about drinking and whoring and fighting and about how bad they were, and the thing was I knew they weren't just bragging.

I figured I was pretty bad myself, and so did Donald and Lee. They were my fan club. In school, with my six-three, two hundred-pound frame, and the bulk of it weight-lifting muscles, I was respected. I had even on occasion gotten into fights outside of school with older bigger college boys and whipped them. I had a few moves. I was always waiting for a chance to prove it.

So, this time I'm talking about, we walked over there from school to buy a couple of soda pops and shoot some pool, and slip a cigarette and talk about girls and tail, like we'd had any, and when we got there, Rugger's cousin, Ray Martin Winston, was there along with Rugger and a retarded kid who cleaned up and kept sodas in the soda machine. The kid always wore a red baseball cap and overalls, lived in the back, and Rugger usually referred to him as "the retard." The kid went along with this without any kickback and was as dedicated to Rugger as a seeing-eye dog, and was about as concerned with day-to-day activities as a pig was about the algebra.

Ray Martin was older than we were, but not by much. Maybe three years. He had dropped out of school as soon as he could, and I had no idea what he did for living, though it was rumored he stole and sold and ran a few whores, one of which was said to be his sister, though any of it could have been talk. He was a peculiar looking fella, one of those who seem as if their lives will be about trouble, and that was Ray Martin. He was lean but not too tall, had a shock of blond hair which he took great care to lightly oil and comb. It was his best feature. It was thick and fell down on his forehead in a beach boy kind of wave. His face always made me think of a hammerhead shark, it had to do with his beady black eyes and the way his nose dropped straight down from his thick forehead and along the length of his face until it stopped just above lips as thin as razor cuts. His chin looked like a block of stone. He had chunky white teeth, all them about the size of sugar cubes. He would have made a great Dick Tracy villain. He had a reptilian way of moving, or at least that's how it seemed to me, as if he undulated and squirmed. I guess, in the back of my head there was a piece of me itching to find out just how dangerous he really was.

We shot a game at our table, while Ray Martin shot alone at one of the other three, knocking the cue ball around, racking and breaking and taking shots. Free time had given him good aim and a good arm for the table.

I was feeling my oats that day, and I looked over, and said, "You're pretty good playin' yourself."

Ray Martin raised his head and twisted it, cracked his neck as he did, and gave me a look that I had never seen before. He studied me carefully, put his pool cue on the table, and stood up. Rugger came over quickly with a beer from the cooler and handed it to him, said, "Ought to be someone comin' in pretty soon. Maybe you can get a game up."

Ray Martin nodded, took the wet beer bottle and sipped it, examined me with the precision of a sniper about to pop off a shot. "Sure," he said. "That could happen."

He went over and sat in a chair by the wall and drank his beer and kept his eye on me, one hand in his baggy pants pocket. I turned back to the game, and Ronald leaned over close and said, "He didn't take that well. He thought it was some kind of crack."

"I meant it as a crack," I said.

"I know. And he took it as a crack."

"You think I'm worried?"

Ronald's face changed a little. He licked his lips. I thought his lower jaw shook. "No. I'm not worried about you. I know you can take care of yourself."

I didn't believe him altogether. I had seen that spark of doubt in his eyes, and it annoyed me. I didn't like him thinking I might not be as bad and tough as I thought I was. I saw the retarded kid glaring at me, his mouth hanging open, and it somehow hit me that the kid thought the same thing, though truth was if that kid had two thoughts they probably canceled each other out.

I gave Ray Martin a glance, just to show him my ball sack hadn't shrunk, and his stare was still locked on me. I won't lie to you, I was feeling brave, but there was something about the way he looked at me that clawed its way down inside of me. I had never seen anyone with that kind of look, and I wrote it off to the way his face was and that no matter what he was thinking and no matter where he was looking, he'd look like that. Hell, his old mother probably looked like that; she probably had to tie a pork chop around her neck to get fucked.

I peeked at Rugger. He was looking at me too, but with a different kind of look, like someone watching a dog darting across the highway in front of an eighteen-wheeler, wondering how it was going to turn out. I thought maybe he was hoping I'd make it. When he and my father were kids my daddy had been on his side in an oil field fight that had become a kind of Marvel Creek legend. Him and Dad against six others, and they had won, and in style, sending two of their foes to the hospital. I guess through my dad that gave me and the old man a kind of connection, though now that I look back on it, he wasn't that old. Probably in his forties then, balding, with a hard pot belly, arms that looked as if they had been pumped full of air, legs too short and thin for the bulk of his upper body; a barrel supported by reeds.

This concern and Ronald's doubt didn't set well with me, and it made me feel all the more feisty. I was about to say something smart to Ray Martin, when the front door opened and a man about thirty came in. He was wearing khaki pants and a plaid shirt and a blue jean jacket and tie up boots. He was as dark as Ray Martin was blond and pale. "How're y'all," he said. He sounded like someone that had just that day stepped off the farm for the first time and had left his turnips outside. I looked out through the front door, which was glass with a roll-down curtain curled above it, and parked next to the curb I could see a shiny new Impala. It wasn't a car that looked like it went with the fella, but it was his.

Rugger nodded at him, and the fella said, "I was wonderin' you could tell me how to get to Tyler?" Rugger told him, and then the hick asked, "You got any food to sell here?"

"Some potato chips, peanuts," Rugger said. "Got a Coke machine. We don't fry no hamburgers or nothin'."

"I guess I'll just have some peanuts then."

Rugger went over and pulled a package off the rack and the hick paid for them. He went to the Coke machine and lifted the lid and reached down in the cold water and threaded a cola through the little metal maze that led to where you pulled it out after putting in your money. You don't see those kind of machines anymore, but for a while, back in the sixties, they were pretty popular.

He pulled the cap off with the opener on the side of the box and turned around and said, "Ain't nothin' like a store-bought Co-Cola," as if there were any other kind. He swigged about half the drink in one gulp, pulled it down and wiped his mouth with his sleeve and tore open his bag of peanuts with his teeth and poured them into the Coke bottle and the salt made the soda foam a little. He swigged that and chewed on the wet peanuts and came over and watched us play for a moment.

"I've played this game," he said, showing me some crunched peanuts on his teeth.

"Yeah," I said. "Well, we got a full table."

"I see that. I do. I'm just sayin' I know how. My old pappy taught me how to play. I like it. I'm pretty good too."

"Well, good for you," I said. "Did your old pappy teach you not to bother folks when they're playin'?"

He smiled, looked a little wounded. "Yes, he did. I apologize."

"Hey, you," Ray Martin called.

We all looked.

"You want to play some pool?" he said to the hayseed. "I'll play you."

"Sure, I'll play," the hayseed said, shrugging his shoulders. "But I warn you, sometimes I like to play for nickels and such."

Ray Martin stretched his razor-thin lips and grinned those sugar-cube teeth. "That's all right, yokel. We'll play for such, as you call it."

"I reckon I am a bit of a yokel," said the fella, "but I prefer to be called Ross. That's what my old mama named me."

"Say she did?" Ray Martin said. "All right then, Ross, I'll ask you somethin'. You know how to play anything other than stripes and solids. You shoot straight pool?"

"I know how it's done," Ross said.

"Good. Let's you and me knock 'em around."

## 》《

It wasn't a very exciting game. Ross got to break on the flip of a coin, and he managed to knock the cue ball in the hole right off without so much as sending the ball's shadow in direction of any of his targets.

Ray Martin took his shoot, and he cleared about four balls before he missed. Ross shot one in with what looked like mostly a lucky shot, and then he missed, and then Ray Martin ran what was left. They had bet a dollar on the game, and Ross paid up.

"You're good," Ross said.

"I've heard that," Ray Martin said. "You want to go again?"

"I don't know."

"Sure you do. You want to get that dollar back, don't you?"

Ross scratched the side of his nose, then shifted his testicles with one hand, as if that would help him make a decision, said, "I reckon... Hell, all right. I'll bet you that dollar and two more."

"A high roller."

"I got paid, I can spare a little."

Ray Martin grinned at him as if he were a wolf that had just found an injured rabbit caught up in the briars.

By now we weren't shooting anymore, just leaning against the wall watching them, not really knowing how to play straight pool, but pretending we did, acting like we knew what was going on.

The game results were similar to the first. Ray Martin chalked his cue while Ross dug a few bucks out of his wallet and paid up. Ray Martin called out, "Hey, Retard, get over here and rack these balls. You keep them racked, I'll give you a quarter. You don't, I'll give you a kick in the ass."

The retard racked the balls. Ross said, "I don't know I want to play anymore."

"Scared?" Ray Martin asked.

"Well, I know a better pool player when I see them."

"How about one more," Ray Martin said. "Just one more game and we'll throw in the towel."

Ross pursed his lips and looked like he wished he were back on the farm, maybe fucking a calf.

"Hell, you can spare another two or three dollars, can't you?" Ray Martin said.

"I guess," Ross said, and did that lip pursing thing again. "But I tell you what. You want to go another game, let's go ahead and play it bigger. I ain't been winnin', but I'm gonna bet you can't do three in a row. My pappy always said bet on the third in a row cause that's your winner."

"He rich?" Ray Martin asked.

"Well, no," Ross said.

Ray Martin laughed a little, a sharp little laugh like a dog barking. "That's all right, even someone mostly wrong has got to be right now and again."

"Very well, then," Ross said, "I'm gonna trust my old pappy. I'll bet you...say ten dollars."

"That's bold."

"Yeah, and I'm about to change my mind, now that I think about it."

"Oh, no," Ray Martin said. "You made the offer."

"Now that I think about it, it was stupid of me," Ross said. "I guess I was feeling kind of full of piss and vinegar. How about we drop it? My old pappy ain't even right when he says it's gonna rain."

"No. You're on. Retard's got 'em racked. Come on, country boy, let's shoot."

Of course, when it got right down to it, we were all country boys, just some of us lived in town, as if in disguise, but this Ross, he was a regular turd knocker. He tried to get out of it, said, "Heck, I'll pay you a dollar to forget it. I shouldn't have bet anything. I ain't really no bettin' kind of man. I'm actin' bigger than my gol darn britches."

"You welchin' on a bet, Mister?" Ray Martin said, and when he said it he laid the pool cue on the table and stepped close to Ross. "You welchin'?"

"No. I'm not welchin'. I'm just tryin' to pay my way out so as I can get out cheaper."

Ray Martin shook his head. "Pick up your cue, farmer. You're in."

»«

Ross lost the coin toss on the break, and Ray Martin started out good, went for several shots before he missed. Ray Martin leaned on his pool cue then and looked smug. Ross picked up his cue, studied the table, shook his head, said, "I'll give it a try."

His first shot was a doozy. He busted two balls and both of them went into pockets. He said, "Now that's somethin'. Even a blind hog finds an acorn now and then." And then he started to shoot again. He didn't miss. Not one shot. When he finished, he looked up, surprised. "Maybe my old pappy was right."

Ray Martin paid Ross the money as if the bills he was peeling out of his wallet were strips of his own skin, and then he insisted on another game. Ross said he'd had enough, that he'd had a lucky run, but Ray Martin jumped the price up to fifty dollars, and after a bit of haggling, they went at it. Ross got the flip, and he started shooting. He didn't miss a shot, and once he even jumped the cue ball over another ball to make a shot. I'd never seen anything like it. The way he moved then was different. There was a fluid sort of way he had of going around the table, nothing like the gangly moves he'd shown before, and his face had changed as well; it was dark with concentration and there was a sparkle in his eye, as if he were actually powered by electricity.

When he was finished, he said, "I'm gettin' better."

"You sure are," Ray Martin said.

"I guess I could play another game, you want," Ross said.

Ray Martin shook his head, said, "You don't get that much better that quick, and seems to me you ain't talkin' slow as you were before. You sound a little uptown to me."

"Well, a Co-Cola and a good game perks me," Ross said. "I guess it's the sugar."

Ray Martin's eyes narrowed and his forehead wrinkled. "You're a hustler. You hustled me."

Ross looked as if he had just received a blow. "I can't believe you're talkin' like that. You wanted to play. I tried to quit. I tried to pay out on you."

"You were playin' me," Ray Martin said. "You and that car. That ain't no car like a cracker would have. I should have known. You ain't from around here. You're a pool hall hustler. You're makin' the towns, ain't you?"

"I'm just a man likes a good contest now and again," Ross said, "and I've had a lucky day."

"Tell you somethin'," Ray Martin said, "your goddamn luck just run out," and then Ray Martin's hand dipped into his pocket. We saw a flash of silver, and Ross made a face and Ray Martin's little cheap Saturday Night Special coughed and we all jumped, and then Ross, who was still holding the pool cue, dropped it, fanned his right knee out to the side, the collapsed as if someone had opened a trap door beneath him. The way he fell, the way he crumpled, there wasn't any doubt he was dead. A little hole in his forehead began to ooze blood. The air filled with the stench of what Ross had left in his pants.

Rugger said, "Oh, hell."

The retard said, "You hit him right 'tween the eyes, and he done shit on himself."

>> <<

**Ray Martin turned** and looked at me and my friends. We were as quiet as the walls around us. He pointed the gun in my direction. "You," he said, "you look in his pockets, see if you can find his keys."

I hesitated only a moment, and Rugger said, "I got it."

Rugger went over and pushed the guy around on the floor so that he could get to his pockets easy, found the keys, held them up, shook them.

"Now my money, and his too," Ray Martin said. "I'm claimin' some interest."

Rugger got the man's money and gave it to Ray Martin who folded it up and shoved it in the front pocket of his jeans. He tossed the keys on the pool table.

"All right," Ray Martin said, turning back to me. "I want you, tough guy, you and no one else to take those keys and go outside and unlock the trunk of his car, and then I want you back in here faster than a bunny fucks, you understand? Otherwise, you go in the trunk with him after I shoot your balls off. You got me, dry fuck?"

"Yeah," I said, and when I spoke my mouth was dust dry. The word came out more like a cough. This wasn't some scuffle in the halls at school, some after-school fist fight at the Dairy Queen. This was the real thing. This was the world where real tough guys lived, and I wasn't one of them.

I took the keys and went outside and unlocked the trunk of the Impala and lifted it up and went back inside. "Give me them keys," Ray Martin said. I gave them to him. He said, "I don't like nobody likes to cheat me. I got rules. Don't cheat me, don't hang with niggers, and don't let women tell you what to do. Keep your hands away from my wallet. And don't never back down. Them's my rules. He broke one of them."

"You didn't have to shoot him," Rugger said. "We could have just beat his ass and got your money back."

"You got him right 'tween the eyes," the retard said, suddenly overcome again with Ray Martin's marksmanship.

"Shut up, Retard," Rugger said. "Now we got a mess."

"Mess can get cleaned up," Ray Martin said. He looked at Donny. "You, nickel dick, go over there and lock the door and pull the blind down. Now."

Donald pulled the blind down over the glass and locked the door. Ray Martin waved the gun at Donald, said, "When I tell you, you look out there see ain't no one comin'. Someone's comin', you close the door and lock it. Ain't no one comin', you say so, and don't be wrong. Got me."

"Yes, sir," Donald said, as if he were speaking to a teacher.

"You, tough guy," he said to me, "you acted like you wanted some of my action. You still wantin' it?"

"No," I said.

"No, huh. That the way you talk to me? You heard how your friend spoke to me, let me hear some of that."

"No, sir," I said.

"Now you're talkin'. Stay sharp, I might need you to wipe my butt with your tongue. But right now, you get hold of this fucker's legs and you," he said to Lee, "you get his head, and you boys take him out and put him in the trunk of his car and close the lid and come back in, and don't screw around."

We picked up the body and a hair-covered fragment from the back of his skull fell against the tile with a sound like pottery being dropped. As we lifted him, I found myself drawn to his face. Ross's eyes were wide open, and I saw then that everything he had been or might have been, all of his plans and memories, dreams and schemes, they had fled, out through the hole in the back of his skull, across the floor in a puddle of blood and brain fragments, a piece of his skull. The body was empty. It was in that moment I knew something I had never really known before. Oh, I knew it on an intellectual basis. I knew we all died. But this wasn't like on TV. This guy didn't just look like a guy lying down. He was truly dead. Looking at him, in that moment, I knew there was nothing beyond the moment, nothing beyond our time on earth, that dead was dead, and I had never wanted to live more than I did in that moment with my eyes locked on Ross's face. Hell, he wasn't Ross anymore. He was just meat. Dead meat.

I got hold of Ross's feet. The mess in his pants smelled strong. Lee got his shoulders and we lifted him and carried him toward the door. When we were about there, Donald unlocked and opened the door and looked out, then pushed the door wide open. Me and Lee put Ross in the trunk of the Impala, curled him around his spare tire, and closed the lid. We went back inside. It was all like a dream.

"All right, now," Ray Martin said, "lock the door."

"What now," Rugger said, lighting a cigar. The smell wafted over the stink Ross had left.

"Get the retard to wipe the floor up... But not yet. The back-seat of that Impala, it's still got room." Ray Martin looked at us.

I said, "Wait a minute."

"We ain't gonna tell nobody," Donald said.

"Nobody," Lee said, just in case Donald hadn't stated our case firmly enough.

"Hell," Ray Martin said. "I know that. Dead men, they don't talk."

I didn't realize it, but I had backed up against the pool table. I remember it crossing my mind to grab a pool cue, a pool ball, anything. But I knew I wouldn't. I wouldn't do anything. I couldn't move. It was like I was glued to the floor. I thought maybe I was about to do in my pants what Ross had done in his.

"I know these boys," Rugger said softly. "They'd be missed. Their folks know they're here."

That was a lie, but it was a beautiful lie, and I clung to it, hoping.

"You can tell them they was here but they left," Ray Martin said. "I don't want to take chances. And this one," he said, point-ing the Saturday Night Special at me. "I don't like him. I didn't like him soon as I saw him."

"I know that," Rugger said, and I saw that when he pulled his cigar out of his mouth his hand was shaking. Even he, a man who had fought a mess of oil field guys with my daddy, he knew Ray Martin was beyond just trouble. Guys like him had invented trouble; they had given it its name. "This boy here," Rugger said, "his daddy and me once fought a bunch of oil field workers together."

"What's that mean to me?" Ray Martin said.

"It means me and him is kin," Rugger said, "and I'm asking a favor. It's not like you didn't get your money back."

Ray Martin went quiet. You could almost see his brain working behind his skull. "All right," he said. "I wasn't gonna do nothin'. Not really. Well, maybe with the tough guy here." He waved the gun at me. "But here's the thing, and you little turds listen tight as a nun's ass, cause you don't, you'll be seein' me and this here gun, maybe a knife or a tire tool...you didn't see a fuckin' thing."

"No. Nothin'," I said.

"What you gonna do with the hayseed?" Rugger asked.

"He wasn't no hayseed. He was a goddamn pool shark... I'm gonna drive him out to the river bottoms. I know a place you can drive that car off and it'll go deep. And you, Rugger, you're gonna follow me. Maybe we ought to pop the retard too, put him in the backseat."

Rugger shook his head. "He's all right. He won't remember nothin' come tomorrow mornin'. Hell, I got to tell him when to shit."

"You got him right 'tween the eyes," the retard said.

"Shut up," Rugger said. "You go on and sit down on that stool and shut up."

The retard hung his head and went and sat on the stool.

"You can get you a Co-Cola," Rugger said, and the retard got a soda and popped it and went and sat back on the stool and sipped it.

Ray Martin said, "I don't know, man. I'm thinking on it some more, and I don't know I should let these asswipes go."

"They ain't gonna say nothin'," Rugger said. "You boys... You ain't gonna say nothin', are you?"

"About what?" Donny said.

"There you go," Rugger said.

Ray Martin put the gun in his pocket, said, "Maybe."

"The retard finishes his Coke," Rugger said, "we'll have him wipe up that blood, spray some air freshener around. You drive the fella's car to the bottoms, Ray Martin, and I'll follow. We'll get rid of him... You boys, you go on out the back way. And don't you never say nothin'. Nothin'. Not a fuckin' word."

"No, sir," I said, "we won't," and then I looked at Ray Martin, said, "We won't say anything, sir. I promise."

Ray Martin grinned at me. His teeth reminded me of an animal trap. "Go on then, punks, before I bend you over this pool table and fuck you in the ass, one at a time."

We went quickly out the back door and didn't say a word, just split and went three different ways.

## 〉〈

Of course I saw Donny and Lee after that, in school, in the halls. We waved or smiled, but we didn't hang. I don't think they thought I was so tough anymore. We went our own ways after that. I never went back to the pool hall. I doubt they did. I thought about telling someone about what happened, but didn't, and to the best of my knowledge neither did Donny or Lee. I had nightmares. I still have nightmares.

I saw Rugger around town a few times, and nodded at him. He always looked at me like he'd never seen me before, and he never came back to the garage. Ray Martin, I never saw again, and I'm not bothered by that. I never even asked anyone about him, and I think I heard he was in prison somewhere for something or another. I think about Ross, a lot, that face, that empty face, all the life there was and ever would be gone from it, leaving the rest of us aware and alone, waiting.

# THE FOLDING MAN

(Based on the black car legend)

They had come from a Halloween party, having long shed the masks they'd worn. No one but Harold had been drinking, and he wasn't driving, and he wasn't so drunk he was blind. Just drunk enough he couldn't sit up straight and was lying on the backseat, trying, for some unknown reason, to recite The Pledge of Allegiance, which he didn't accurately recall. He was mixing in verses from the Star Spangled Banner and the Boy Scout oath, which he vaguely remembered from his time in the organization before they drove him out for setting fires.

Even though William, who was driving, and Jim, who was riding shotgun, were sober as Baptists claimed to be, they were fired up and happy and yelling and hooting, and Jim pulled down his pants and literally mooned a black bug of a car carrying a load of nuns.

The car wasn't something that looked as if it had come off the lot. Didn't have the look of any car maker Jim could identify. It had a cobbled look. It reminded him of something in old movies, the ones with gangsters who were always squealing their tires around corners. Only it seemed bigger, with broader windows through which he could see the nuns, or at least glimpse them in their habits; it was a regular penguin convention inside that car.

Way it happened, when they came up on the nuns, Jim said to William at the wheel, "Man, move over close, I'm gonna show them some butt."

"They're nuns, man."

"That's what makes it funny," Jim said.

William eased the wheel to the right, and Harold in the back said, "Grand Canyon. Grand Canyon. Show them the Grand Canyon... Oh, say can you see..."

Jim got his pants down, swiveled on his knees in the seat, twisted so that his ass was against the glass, and just as they passed the nuns, William hit the electric window switch and slid the glass down. Jim's ass jumped out at the night, like a vibrating moon.

"They lookin'?" Jim asked.

"Oh, yeah," William said, "and they are not amused."

Jim jerked his pants up, shifted in the seat, and turned for a look, and sure enough, they were not amused. Then a funny thing happened, one of the nuns shot him the finger, and then others followed. Jim said, "Man, those nuns are rowdy."

And now he got a good look at them, even though it was night, because there was enough light from the headlights as they passed for him to see faces hard as wardens and ugly as death warmed over. The driver was especially homely, face like that could stop a clock and run it backwards or make shit crawl up hill.

"Did you see that, they shot me the finger?" Jim said.

"I did see it," William said.

Harold had finally gotten the Star Spangled Banner straight, and he kept singing it over and over.

"For Christ sake," William said. "Shut up, Harold."

"You know what," Jim said, studying the rearview mirror, "I think they're speeding up. They're trying to catch us. Oh, hell. What if they get the license plate? Maybe they already have. They call the law, my dad will have my mooning ass."

"Well, if they haven't got the plate," William said, "they won't. This baby can get on up and get on out."

He put his foot on the gas. The car hummed as if it had just had an orgasm, and seemed to leap. Harold was flung off the backseat, onto the floorboard. "Hey, goddamnit," he said.

"Put on your seat belt, jackass," Jim said.

William's car was eating up the road. It jumped over a hill and dove down the other side like a porpoise negotiating a wave, and Jim thought: Goodbye, penguins, and then he looked back. At the top of the hill were the lights from the nuns' car, and the car was gaining speed and it moved in a jerky manner, as if it were stealing space between blinks of the eye.

"Damn," William said. "They got some juice in that thing, and the driver has her foot down."

"What kind of car is that?" Jim said.

"Black," William said.

"Ha! Mr. Detroit."

"Then you name it."

Jim couldn't. He turned to look back. The nuns' car had already caught up; the big automotive beast was cruising in tight as a coat of varnish, the headlights making the interior of William's machine bright as a Vegas act.

"What the hell they got under the hood?" William said. "Hyper-drive?"

"These nuns," Jim said, "they mean business."

"I can't believe it, they're riding my bumper."

"Slam on your brakes. That'll show them."

"Not this close," William said. "Do that, what it'll show them is the inside of our butts."

"Do nuns do this?"

"These do."

"Oh," Jim said. "I get it. Halloween. They aren't real nuns."

"Then we give them hell," Harold said, and just as the nuns were passing on the right, he crawled out of the floorboard and onto his seat and rolled the window down. The back window of the nuns' car went down and Jim turned to get a look, and the nun, well, she was ugly all right, but uglier than he had first imagined. She looked like something dead, and the nun's outfit she wore was not actually black and white, but purple and white, or so it appeared in the light from head beams and moonlight. The nun's lips pulled back from her teeth and the teeth were long and brown, as if tobacco stained. One of her eyes looked like a spoiled meatball, and her nostrils flared like a pig's.

Jim said, "That ain't no mask."

Harold leaned way out of the window and flailed his hands and said, "You are so goddamn ugly you have to creep up on your underwear."

Harold kept on with this kind of thing, some of it almost making sense, and then one of the nuns in the back, one closest to the window, bent over in the seat and came up and leaned out of the window, a two-by-four in her hands. Jim noted that her arms, where the nun outfit had fallen back to the elbows, were as thin as sticks and white as the underbelly of a fish and the elbows were knotty, and bent in the wrong direction.

"Get back in," Jim said to Harold.

Harold waved his arms and made another crack, and then the nun swung the two-by-four, the oddness of her elbows causing it to arrive at a weird angle, and the board made a crack of its own, or rather Harold's skull did, and he fell forward, the lower half of his body hanging from the window, bouncing against the door, his knuckles losing meat on the highway, his ass hanging inside, one foot on the floor board the other waggling in the air.

"The nun hit him," Jim said. "With a board."

"What?" William said.

"You deaf, she hit him."

Jim snapped loose his seat belt and leaned over and grabbed Harold by the back of the shirt and yanked him inside. Harold's head looked like it had been in a vise. There was blood everywhere. Jim said, "Oh, man, I think he's dead."

BLAM!

The noise made Jim jump. He slid back in his seat and looked toward the nuns. They were riding close enough to slam the two-by-four into William's car; the driver was pressing that black monster toward them.

Another swing of the board and the side mirror shattered.

William tried to gun forward, but the nuns' car was even with him, pushing him to the left. They went across the highway and into a ditch and the car did an acrobatic twist and tumbled down an embankment and rolled into the woods tossing up mud and leaves and pine straw.

## 》《

Jim found himself outside the car, and when he moved, everything seemed to whirl for a moment, then gathered up slowly and became solid. He had been thrown free, and so had William, who was lying nearby. The car was a wreck, lying on its roof, spinning still, steam easing out from under the hood in little cotton-white clouds. Gradually, the car quit spinning, like an old time watch that had wound down. The windshield was gone and three of the four doors lay scattered about.

The nuns were parked up on the road, and the car doors opened and the nuns got out. Four of them. They were unusually tall, and when they walked, like their elbows, their knees bent in the wrong direction. It was impossible to tell this for sure, because of the robes they wore, but it certainly looked that way, and considering the elbows, it fit. There in the moonlight, they were as white and pasty as potstickers, their jaws seeming to have grown longer than when Jim had last looked at them, their noses witchlike, except for those pig flare nostrils, their backs bent like long bows. One of them still held the two-by-four.

Jim slid over to William who was trying to sit up.

"You okay?" Jim asked.

"I think so," William said, patting his fingers at a blood spot on his forehead. "Just before they hit, I stupidly unsnapped my seat belt. I don't know why. I just wanted out I guess. Brain not working right."

"Look up there," Jim said.

They both looked up the hill. One of the nuns was moving down from the highway, toward the wrecked car.

"If you can move," Jim said, "I think we oughta."

William worked himself to his feet. Jim grabbed his arm and half pulled him into the woods where they leaned against a tree. William said, "Everything's spinning."

"It stops soon enough," Jim said.

"I got to chill, I'm about to faint."

"A moment," Jim said.

The nun who had gone down by herself, bent down out of sight behind William's car, then they saw her going back up the hill, dragging Harold by his ankle, his body flopping all over as if all the bones in his body had been broken.

"My God, see that?" William said. "We got to help."

"He's dead," Jim said. "They crushed his head with a board."

"Oh, hell, man. That can't be. They're nuns."

"I don't think they are," Jim said. "Least not the kind of nuns you're thinking."

The nun dragged Harold up the hill and dropped his leg when she reached the big black car. Another of the nuns opened the trunk and reached in and got hold of something. It looked like some kind of folded up lawn chair, only more awkward in shape. The nun jerked it out and dropped it on the ground and gave it a swift kick. The folded up thing began to unfold with a clatter and a squeak. A perfectly round head rose up from it, and the head spun on what appeared to be a silver hinge. When it quit whirling, it was upright and in place, though cocked slightly to the left. The eyes and mouth and nostrils were merely holes. Moonlight could be seen through them. The head rose as coatrack style shoulders pushed it up and a cage of a chest rose under that. The chest looked almost like an old frame on which dresses were placed to be sewn, or perhaps a cage designed to contain something you wouldn't want to get out. With more squeaks and clatters, skeletal hips appeared, and beneath that, long, bony legs with bent back knees and big metal-framed feet. Stick-like arms swung below its knees, clattering against its legs like tree limbs bumping against a windowpane. It stood at least seven feet tall. Like the nuns, its knees and elbows fit backwards.

The nun by the car trunk reached inside and pulled out something fairly large that beat its wings against the night air. She held it in one hand by its clawed feet, and its beak snapped wildly, looking for something to peck. Using her free hand, she opened up the folding man's chest by use of a hinge, and when the cage flung open, she put the black, winged thing inside. It fluttered about like a heart shot full of adrenaline. The holes that were the folding man's eyes filled with a red glow and the mouth hole grew wormy lips, and a tongue, long as a garden snake, dark as dirt, licked out at the night, and there was a loud sniff as its nostrils sucked air. One of the nuns reached down and grabbed up a handful of clay, and pressed it against the folding man's arms; the clay spread fast as a lie, went all over, filling the thing with flesh of the earth until the entire folding man's body was covered. The nun who had taken the folding man out of the car picked Harold up by the ankle, and as if he were nothing more than a blow-up doll, swung him over her head and slammed him into the darkness of the trunk, shut the lid, and looked out where Jim and William stood recovering by the tree.

The nun said something, a noise between a word and a cough, and the folding man began to move down the hill at a stumble. As he moved his joints made an un-oiled hinge sound, and the rest of him made a clatter like lug bolts being knocked together, accompanied by a noise akin to wire hangers being twisted by strong hands.

"Run," Jim said.

》《

**Jim began to** feel pain, knew he was more banged up than he thought. His neck hurt. His back hurt. One of his legs really hurt. He must have jammed his knee against something. William, who ran alongside him, dodging trees, said, "My ribs. I think they're cracked."

Jim looked back. In the distance, just entering the trees, framed in the moonlight behind him, was the folding man. He moved in strange leaps, as if there were springs inside him, and he was making good time.

Jim said, "We can't stop. It's coming."

**》《**

**It was low** down in the woods and water had gathered there and the leaves had mucked up with it, and as they ran, they sloshed and splashed, and behind them, they could hear it, the folding man, coming, cracking limbs, squeaking hinges, splashing his way after them. When they had the nerve to look back, they could see him darting between the trees like a bit of the forest itself, and he, or it, was coming quite briskly for a thing its size until it reached the lower down parts of the bottom land. There its big feet slowed it some as they buried deep in the mud and were pulled free again with a sound like the universe sucking wind. Within moments, however, the thing got its stride, its movements becoming more fluid and its pace faster.

Finally Jim and William came to a tree-thickened rise in the land, and were able to get out of the muck, scramble upwards and move more freely, even though there was something of a climb ahead, and they had to use trees growing out from the side of the rise to pull themselves upward. When they reached the top of the climb, they were surprised when they looked back to see they had actually gained some space on the thing. It was some distance away, speckled by the moonlight, negotiating its way through the ever-thickening trees and undergrowth.

But, still it came, ever onward, never tiring. Jim and William bent over and put their hands on their knees and took some deep breaths.

"There's an old graveyard on the far side of this stretch," Jim said. "Near the wrecking yard."

"Where you worked last summer."

"Yeah, that's the one. It gets clearer in the graveyard, and we can make good time. Get to the wrecking yard, Old Man Gordon lives there. He always has a gun and he has that dog, Chomps. It knows me. It will eat that thing up."

"What about me?"

"You'll be all right. You're with me. Come on. I kinda of know where we are now. Used to play in the graveyard, and in this end of the woods. Got to move."

»«

They moved along more swiftly as Jim became more and more familiar with the terrain. It was close to where he had lived when he was a kid, and he had spent a lot of time out here. They came to a place where there was a clearing in the woods, a place where lightning had made a fire. The ground was black, and there were no trees, and in that spot silver moonlight was falling down into it, like mercury filling a cup.

In the center of the clearing they stopped and got their breath again, and William said. "My head feels like it's going to explode... Hey, I don't hear it now."

"It's there. Whatever it is, I don't think it gives up."

"Oh, Jesus," William said, and gasped deep once. "I don't know how much I got left in me."

"You got plenty. We got to have plenty."

"What can it be, Jimbo? What in the hell can it be?"

Jim shook his head. "You know that old story about the black car?"

William shook his head.

"My grandmother used to tell me about a black car that roams the highways and the back roads of the South. It isn't in one area all the time, but it's out there somewhere all the time. Halloween is its peak night. It's always after somebody for whatever reason."

"Bullshit."

Jim, hands still on his knees, lifted his head. "You go down there and tell that clatter clap thing it's all bullshit. See where that gets you."

"It just doesn't make sense."

"Grandma said before it was a black car, it was a black buggy, and before that a figure dressed in black on a black horse, and that before that, it was just a shadow that clicked and clacked and squeaked. There's people go missing, she said, and it's the black car, the black buggy, the thing on the horse, or the walkin' shadow that gets them. But, it's all the same thing, just a different appearance."

"The nuns? What about them?"

Jim shook his head, stood up, tested his ability to breathe. "Those weren't nuns. They were like...I don't know...anti-nuns. This thing, if Grandma was right, can take a lot of different forms. Come on. We can't stay here anymore."

"Just another moment, I'm so tired. And I think we've lost it. I don't hear it anymore."

As if on cue, there came a clanking and a squeaking and cracking of limbs. William glanced at Jim, and without a word, they moved across the lightning-made clearing and into the trees. Jim looked back, and there it was, crossing the clearing, silver-flooded in the moonlight, still coming, not tiring.

They ran. White stones rose up in front of them. Most of the stones were heaved to the side, or completely pushed out of the ground by growing trees and expanding roots. It was the old graveyard, and Jim knew that meant the wrecking yard was nearby, and so was Gordon's shotgun, and so was one mean dog.

Again the land sloped upwards, and this time William fell forward on his hands and knees, throwing up a mess of blackness. "Oh, God. Don't leave me, Jim...I'm tuckered...can hardly... breathe."

Jim had moved slightly ahead of William. He turned back to help. As he grabbed William's arm to pull him up, the folding man squeaked and clattered forward and grabbed William's ankle, jerked him back, out of Jim's grasp.

The folding man swung William around easily, slammed his body against a tree, then the thing whirled, and as if William were a bullwhip, snapped him so hard his neck popped and an eyeball flew out of his skull. The folding man brought William whipping down across a standing gravestone. There was a cracking sound, like someone had dropped a glass coffee cup, then the folding man whirled and slung William from one tree to another, hitting the trees so hard bark flew off of them and clothes and meat flew off William.

Jim bolted. He ran faster than he had ever run, finally he broke free of the woods and came to a stretch of ground that was rough with gravel. Behind him, breaking free of the woods, was the folding man, making good time with great strides, dragging William's much-abused body behind it by the ankle.

》《

Jim could dimly see the wrecking yard from where he was, and he thought he could make it. Still, there was the aluminum fence all the way around the yard, seven feet high. No little barrier. Then he remembered the sycamore tree on the edge of the fence, on the right side. Old Man Gordon was always talking about cutting it because he thought someone could use it to climb over and into the yard, steal one of his precious car parts, though if they did, they had Gordon's shotgun waiting along with the sizeable teeth of his dog. It had been six months since he had seen the old man, and he hoped he hadn't gotten ambitious, that the tree was still there.

Running closer, Jim could see the sycamore tree remained, tight against the long run of shiny wrecking yard fence. Looking over his shoulder, Jim saw the folding man was springing forward, like some kind of electronic rabbit, William's body being pulled along by the ankle, bouncing on the ground as the thing came ever onward. At this rate, it would be only a few seconds before the thing caught up with him.

Jim felt a pain like a knife in his side, and it seemed as if his heart was going to explode. He reached down deep for everything he had, hoping like hell he didn't stumble.

He made the fence and the tree, went up it like a squirrel, dropped over on the roof of an old car, sprang off of that and ran toward a dim light shining in the small window of a wood and aluminum shack nestled in the midst of old cars and piles of junk.

As he neared the shack, Chomps, part pit bull, part just plain big ole dog, came loping out toward him, growling. It was a hard thing to do, but Jim forced himself to stop, bent down, stuck out his hand, and called the dog's name.

"Chomps. Hey, buddy. It's me."

The dog slowed and lowered its head and wagged its tail.

"That's right. Your pal, Jim."

The dog came close and Jim gave it a pat. "Good, boy."

Jim looked over his shoulder. Nothing.

"Come on, Chomps."

Jim moved quickly toward the shack and hammered on the door. A moment later the door flew open, and standing there in overalls, one strap dangling from a naked arm, was Mr. Gordon. He was old and near toothless, squat and greasy as the insides of the cars in the yard.

"Jim? What the hell you doing in here? You look like hell."

"Something's after me."

"Something?"

"It's outside the fence. It killed two of my friends..."

"What?"

"It killed two of my friends."

"It? Some kind of animal?"

"No... It."

"We'll call some law."

Jim shook his head. "No use calling the law now, time they arrive it'll be too late."

Gordon leaned inside the shack and pulled a twelve gauge into view, pumped it once. He stepped outside and looked around.

"You sure?"

"Oh, yeah. Yes, sir. I'm sure."

"Then I guess you and me and Pump Twelve will check it out." Gordon moved out into the yard, looking left and right. Jim stayed close to Gordon's left elbow. Chomps trotted nearby. They walked about a bit. They stopped between a row of wrecked cars, looked around. Other than the moon-shimmering fence at either end of the row where they stood, there was nothing to see.

"Maybe whatever, or whoever it is, is gone," Gordon said. "Otherwise, Chomps would be all over it."

"I don't think it smells like humans or animals."

"Are you joshin' an old man? Is this a Halloween prank?"

"No, sir. Two of my friends are dead. This thing killed them. It's real."

"What the hell is it then?"

As if in answer, there was the sound like a huge can opener going to work, and then the long, thin arm of the folding man poked through the fence and there was more ripping as the arm slid upwards, tearing at the metal. A big chunk of the fence was torn away, revealing the thing, bathed in moonlight, still holding what was left of William's ragged body by the ankle.

Jim and Gordon both stood locked in amazement.

"Sonofabitch," Gordon said.

Chomps growled, ran toward it.

"Chomps will fix him," Gordon said.

The folding man dropped William's ankle and bent forward, and just as the dog leaped, caught it and twisted it and ran its long arm down the snapping dog's throat, and began to pull its insides out. It flung the dog's parts in all directions, like someone pulling confetti from a sack. Then it turned the dog inside out.

When the sack was empty, the folding man bent down and fastened the dead, deflated dog to a hook on the back of what passed for its ankle.

"My God," Gordon said.

The thing picked up William by the ankle, stepped forward a step, and paused.

Gordon lifted the shotgun. "Come and get you some, asshole."

The thing cocked its head as if to consider the suggestion, and then it began to lope toward them, bringing along its clanks and squeaks, the dead dog flopping at the folding man's heel. For the first time, its mouth, which had been nothing but a hole with wormy lips, twisted into the shape of a smile.

Gordon said, "You run, boy. I got this."

Jim didn't hesitate. He turned and darted between a row of cars and found a gap between a couple of Fords with grass grown up around their flattened tires, ducked down behind one, and hid. He lay down on his belly to see if he could see anything. There was a little bit of space down there, and he could look under the car, and under several others, and he could see Gordon's feet. They had shifted into a firm stance, and Jim could imagine the old man pulling the shotgun to his shoulder.

And even as he imagined, the gun boomed, and then it boomed again. Silence, followed by a noise like someone ripping a piece of thick cardboard in half, and then there were screams and more rips. Jim felt light-headed, realized he hadn't been breathing. He gasped for air, feared that he had gasped too loudly.

Oh, my God, he thought. I ran and left it to Mr. Gordon, and now... He was uncertain. Maybe the screams had come from... It, the folding man? But so far it hadn't so much as made breathing sounds, let alone anything that might be thought of as a vocalization.

Crawling like a soldier under fire, Jim worked his way to the edge of the car, and took a look. Stalking down the row between the cars was the folding man, and he was dragging behind him by one ankle what was left of William's body. In his other hand, if you could call it a hand, he had Mr. Gordon, who looked thin now because so much had been pulled out of him. Chomps' body was still fastened to the wire hook at the back of the thing's foot. As the folding man came forward, Chomps dragged in the dirt.

Jim pushed back between the cars, and kept pushing, crawling backwards. When he was far enough back, he raised to a squat and started between narrower rows that he thought would be harder for the folding man to navigate; they were just spaces really, not rows, and if he could go where it couldn't go, then—

There was a large creaking sound, and Jim, still at a squat, turned to discover its source. The folding man was looking at him. It had grabbed an old car and lifted it up by the front and was holding it so that the back end rested on the ground. Being as close as he was now, Jim realized the folding man was bigger than he had thought, and he saw too that just below where the monster's thick torso ended there were springs, huge springs, silver in the moonlight, vibrating. He had stretched to accommodate the lifting of the car, and where his knees bent backwards, springs could be seen as well; he was a garage sale collection of parts and pieces.

For a moment, Jim froze. The folding man opened his mouth wide, wider than Jim had seen before, and inside he could glimpse a turning of gears and a smattering of sparks. Jim broke suddenly, running between cars, leaping on hoods, scrambling across roofs, and behind him came the folding man, picking up cars and flipping them aside as easily as if they had been toys.

Jim could see the fence at the back, and he made for that, and when he got close to it, he thought he had it figured. He could see a Chevy parked next to the fence, and he felt certain he could climb onto the roof, spring off of it, grab the top of the fence, and scramble over. That wouldn't stop the thing behind him, but it would perhaps give him a few moments to gain ground.

The squeaking and clanking behind him was growing louder.

There was a row of cars ahead, he had to leap onto the hood of the first, then spring from hood to hood, drop off, turn slightly right, and go for the Chevy by the fence.

He was knocked forward, hard, and his breath leaped out of him.

He was hit again, painfully in the chest.

It took a moment to process, but he was lying between two cars, and there, standing above him, was the folding man, snapping at him with the two dead bodies like they were wet towels. That's what had hit him, the bodies, used like whips.

Jim found strength he didn't know he had, made it to his feet as Mr. Gordon's body slammed the ground near him. Then, as William's body snapped by his ear, just missing him, he was once more at a run.

The Chevy loomed before him. He made its hood by scrambling up on hands and knees, and then he jumped to the roof. He felt something tug at him, but he jerked loose, didn't stop moving. He sprang off the car top, grabbed at the fence, latching his arms over it. The fence cut into the undersides of his arms, but he couldn't let that stop him, so he kept pulling himself forward, and the next thing he knew, he was over the fence, dropping to the ground.

It seemed as if a bullet had gone up through his right foot, which he now realized was bare, and that the tug he had felt was the folding man grabbing at his foot, only to come away with a shoe. But of more immediate concern was his foot, the pain. There hadn't been any bullet. He had landed crooked coming over the fence, and his foot had broken. It felt like hell, but he moved on it anyway, and within a few steps he had a limp, a bad limp.

He could see the highway ahead, and he could hear the fence coming down behind him, and he knew it was over, all over, because he was out of gas and had blown a tire and his engine was about to blow too. His breath came in chops and blood was pounding in his skull like a thug wanting out.

He saw lights. They were moving very quickly down the highway. A big truck, a Mack, was balling the jack in his direction. If he could get it to stop, maybe there would be help, maybe.

Jim stumbled to the middle of the highway, directly into the lights, waved his arms, glanced to his left—

—and there it was. The folding man. It was only six feet away.

The truck was only a little farther away, but moving faster, and then the folding man was reaching for him, and the truck was a sure hit, and Jim, pushing off his good foot, leaped sideways and there was a sound like a box of dishes falling downstairs.

### 》《

Jim felt the wind from the truck, but he had moved just in time. The folding man had not. As Jim had leaped aside, his body turned, through no plan of his own, and he saw the folding man take the hit.

Wood and springs and hinges went everywhere.

The truck bumped right over the folding man and started sliding as the driver tried to put on brakes that weren't designed for fast stops. Tires smoked, brakes squealed, the truck fishtailed.

Jim fell to the side of the highway, got up and limped into the brush there, and tripped on something and went down. He rolled on his back. His butt was in a ditch and his back was against one side of it, and he could see above it on the other side, and through some little bushes that grew there. The highway had a few lights on either side of it, so it was lit up good, and Jim could see the folding man lying in the highway, or rather he could see parts of it everywhere. It looked like a dirty hardware store had come to pieces. William, Gordon, and Chomps lay in the middle of the highway.

The folding man's big torso, which had somehow survived the impact of the truck, vibrated and burst open, and Jim saw the birdlike thing rise up with a squawk. It snatched up the body of Mr. Gordon and William, one in either claw, used its beak to nab the dog, and ignoring the fact that its size was not enough to lift all that weight, it did just that, took hold of them and went up into the night sky, abruptly became one with the dark.

Jim turned his head. He could see down the highway, could see the driver of the truck getting out, walking briskly toward the scene of the accident. He walked faster as he got closer, and when he arrived, he bent over the pieces of the folding man. He picked up a spring, examined it, tossed it aside. He looked out where Jim lay in the ditch, but Jim figured, lying as he was, brush in front of him, he couldn't be seen.

He was about to call out to the driver when the truck driver yelled, "You nearly got me killed. You nearly got you killed. Maybe you are killed. I catch you, might as well be, you stupid shit. I'll beat the hell out of you."

Jim didn't move.

"Come on out so I can finish you off."

Great, Jim thought, first the folding man, and now a truck driver wants to kill me. To hell with him, to hell with everything, and he laid his head back against the ditch and closed his eyes and went to sleep.

## 》《

The truck driver didn't come out and find him, and when he awoke the truck was gone and the sky was starting to lighten. His ankle hurt like hell. He bent over and looked at it. He couldn't tell much in the dark, but it looked as big as a sewer pipe. He thought when he got some strength back, he might be able to limp, or crawl out to the edge of the highway, flag down some help. Surely, someone would stop. But for the moment, he was too weak. He laid back again, and was about to close his eyes, when he heard a humming sound.

Looking out at the highway, he saw lights coming from the direction the trucker had come from. Fear crawled up his back like a spider. It was the black car.

The car pulled to the side of the road and stopped. The nuns got out. They sniffed and extended long tongues and licked at the fading night. With speed and agility that seemed impossible, they gathered up the parts of the folding man and put them in a sack they placed in the middle of the highway.

When the sack was full of parts, one nun stuck a long leg into the sack and stomped about, then jerked her leg out, pulled the sack together at the top and swung it over her head and slammed it on the road a few times, then she dropped the sack and moved back and one of the nuns kicked it. Another nun opened up and reached inside the sack and took out the folding man. Jim lost a breath. It appeared to be put back together. The nun didn't unfold the folding man. She opened the trunk of the car and flung it inside.

And then she turned and looked in his direction, held out one arm and waited. The bird-thing came flapping out of the last of the dark and landed on her arm. The bodies of William and Gordon were still in its talons, the dog in its beak, the three of them hanging as if they were nothing heavier than rags. The nun took hold of the bird's legs and tossed it and what it held into the trunk as well. She closed the lid of the trunk. She looked directly where Jim lay. She looked up at the sky, turned to face the rising sun. She turned quickly back in Jim's direction and stuck out her long arm, the robe folding back from it. She pointed a stick like finger right at him, leaned slightly forward. She held that pose until the others joined her and pointed in Jim's direction.

My God, Jim thought, they know I'm here. They see me. Or smell me. Or sense me. But they know I'm here.

The sky brightened and outlined them like that for a moment and they stopped pointing.

They got quickly in the car. The last of the darkness seemed to seep into the ground and give way to a rising pink; Halloween night had ended. The car gunned and went away fast. Jim watched it go a few feet, and then it wasn't there anymore. It faded like fog. All that was left now was the sunrise and the day turning bright.

# DREAD ISLAND

This here story is a good'n, and just about every word of it is true. It's tempting to just jump to the part about where we seen them horrible things, and heads was pulled off and we was in a flying machine and such. But I ain't gonna do it, cause Jim says that ain't the way to tell a proper yarn.

Anyhow, this here story is as true as that other story that was written down about me and Jim. But that fella wrote it down made all the money and didn't give me or Jim one plug nickel of it. So, I'm going to try and tell this one myself like it happened, and have someone other than that old fart write it down for me, take out most of the swear words and such, and give you a gussied up version that I can sell and get some money.

Jim says when you do a thing like that, trying to make more of something than it is, it's like you're taking a drunk in rags and putting a hat on him and giving him new shoes with ties in them, and telling everybody he's from uptown and has solid habits. But anyone looks at him, they're still gonna see the rags he's wearing and know he's a drunk cause of the stagger and the smell. Still, lots of drunks are more interesting than bankers, and they got good stories, even if you got to stand downwind to hear them in comfort.

If I get somebody to write it down for me, or I take a crack at it, is yet to be seen. All I know right now is it's me talking and you listening, and you can believe me or not, because it's a free country. Well, almost a free country, unless your skin ain't white. I've said it before: I know it ain't right in the eyes of God to be friends with a slave, or in Jim's case, an ex-slave that's got his free papers. But even if it ain't right, I don't care. Jim may be colored, but he has sure fire done more for me than God. I tried praying maybe a dozen times, and the only thing I ever got out of it was some sore knees. So, if I go to hell, I go to hell.

Truth is, I figure heaven is probably filled with dogs, cause if you get right down to it, they're the only ones deserve to be there. I don't figure a cat or a lawyer has any chance at all.

Anyway, I got a story to tell, and keep in mind—and this part is important—I'm trying to tell mostly the truth.

>> <<

Now, any old steamboater will tell you, that come the full moon, there's an island out there in the wide part of the Mississippi. You're standing on shore, it's so far out it ain't easy to see. But if the weather's just right, and you got some kind of eye on you, you can see it. It don't last but a night—the first night of the full moon—and then it's gone until next time.

Steamboats try not to go by it, cause when it's there, it has a current that'll drag a boat in just like a fella with a good stout line pulling in a fish. I got word about it from half a dozen fellas that knew a fella that knew a fella that had boated past it and been tugged by them currents. They said it was all they could do to get away. And there's plenty they say didn't get away, and ain't never been heard of again.

Another time, me and Tom Sawyer heard a story about how sometimes you could see fires on the island. Another fella, who might have been borrowing the story from someone else, said he was out fishing with a buddy, and come close to the island,

and seen a post go up near the shore, and a thing that wasn't no kind of man was fastened to it. He said it could scream real loud, and that it made the hairs on the back of his neck stand up. He said there was other things dancing all around the post, carrying torches and making a noise like yelling or some such. Then the currents started pulling him in, and he had to not pay it any more mind, because he and his buddy had to row for all they was worth to keep from being sucked onto the island.

When we got through hearing the story, first thing Tom said was, "Someday, when the moon is right, and that island is there, I'm gonna take a gun and a big Bowie knife, and I'm going to go out there. I'll probably also have to pack a lunch."

That danged old island is called Dread Island, and it's always been called that. I don't know where it got that name, but it was a right good one. I found that out because of Tom and Joe.

Way this all come about, was me and Jim was down on the bank of the river, night fishing for catfish. Jim said there was some folks fished them holes by sticking their arms down in them so a catfish would bite. It wasn't a big bite, he said, but they clamped on good and you could pull them out that way, with them hanging on your arm. Then you could bust them in the head, and you had you something good to eat. He also said he wouldn't do that for nothing. The idea of sticking his hand down in them holes bothered him to no end, and just me thinking on it didn't do me no good either. I figured a gator or a moccasin snake was just as likely to bite me, and a fishing line with a hook on it would do me just as good. Thinking back on that, considering I wouldn't put my hand in a hole for fear something might bite it, and then me going out to Dread Island, just goes to show you can talk common sense a lot more than you can act on it.

But anyway, that ain't how this story starts. It starts like this.

So, there we was, with stinky bait, trying to catch us a catfish, when I seen Becky Thatcher coming along the shoreline in the moonlight.

Now Becky is quite a nice looker, and not a bad sort for a girl; a breed I figure is just a step up from cats. Jim says my thinking that way is because I'm still young and don't understand women's ways. He also explained to me their ways ain't actually understandable, but they sure do get a whole lot more interesting as time goes on.

I will say this. As I seen her coming, her hair hanging, and her legs working under that dress, the moonlight on her face, I thought maybe if she wasn't Tom's girl, I could like her a lot. I'm a little ashamed to admit that, but there you have it.

Anyway, she come along, and when she saw us, she said, "Huck. Jim. Is that you?"

I said, "Well, if it ain't, someone looks a whole lot like us is talking to you."

She come over real swift like then. She said, "I been looking all over for you. I figured you'd be here."

"Well," I said, "we're pretty near always around somewhere or another on the river."

"I was afraid you'd be out on your raft," she said.

"We don't like to go out on the water the night Dread Island is out there," I said.

She looked out over the water, said, "I can't see a thing."

"It looks just like a brown line on top of the water, but it's sharp enough there in the moonlight," I said. "If you give a good look."

"Can you see it too, Jim?" she asked.

"No, Miss Becky, I ain't got the eyes Huck's got."

"The island is why I'm looking for you," she said. "Tom has gone out there with Joe. He's been building his courage for a long time, and tonight, he got worked up about it. I think maybe they had some liquid courage. I went to see Tom, and he and Joe were loading a pail full of dinner into the boat. Some cornbread and the like, and they were just about to push off. When I asked what they were doing, Tom told me they were finally going to see Dread Island and learn what was on it. I didn't know if he was serious. I'm not even sure there is an island, but you tell me you can see it, and well... I'm scared he wasn't just talking, and really did go."

"Did Tom have a big knife with him?" I asked.

"He had a big one in a scabbard stuck in his belt," she said. "And a pistol."

"What do you think, Jim?" I asked.

"I think he's done gone out there, Huck," Jim said. "He said he was gonna, and now he's got that knife and gun and dinner. I think he's done it."

She reached out and touched my arm and a shock run through me like I'd been struck by lightning. It hurt and felt good at the same time, and for a moment there, I thought I'd go to my knees.

"Oh, my God," she said. "Will they be all right?"

"I reckon Tom and Joe will come back all right," I said, but I wasn't really that sure.

She shook her head. "I'm not so certain. Could you and Jim go take a look?"

"Go to Dread Island?" Jim said. "Now, Miss Becky, that ain't smart."

"Tom and Joe went," she said.

"Yes, ma'am," Jim said, like she was a grown woman, "and that proves what I'm saying. It ain't smart."

"When did they go?" I said.

"It was just at dark," she said. "I saw them then, and they were getting in the boat. I tried to talk Tom out of it, because I thought he was a little drunk and shouldn't be on the water, but they went out anyway, and they haven't come back."

I figured a moment. Nightfall was about three or four hours ago.

I said, "Jim, how long you reckon it takes to reach that island?"

"Couple of hours," Jim said, "or something mighty close to that."

"And a couple back," I said. "So what say we walk over to where Tom launched his boat and take a look. See if they done come in. They ain't, me and Jim will go take a gander for him."

"We will?" Jim said.

I ignored him.

## »«

**Me and Jim** put our lines in the water before we left, and figured on checking them later. We went with Becky to where Tom
and Joe had pushed off in their boat. It was a pretty far piece.
They hadn't come back, and when we looked out over the water,
we didn't see them coming neither.

Becky said, "Huck, I think I see it. The island, I mean."

"Yeah," I said, "there's a better look from here."

"It's just that line almost even with the water, isn't it?" she said.

"Yep, that's it."

"I don't see nothing," Jim said. "And I don't want to."

"You will go look for him?" Becky said.

"We'll go," I said.

"We will?" Jim said again.

"Or I can go by myself," I said. "Either way."

"Huck," Jim said, "you ought not go out there. You ain't got
no idea what's on that island. I do. I heard more stories than
you have, and most of it's way worse than an entire afternoon in
church and having to talk to the preacher personal like."

"Then it's bad," I said, and I think it was pretty obvious to
Becky that I was reconsidering.

Becky took my arm. She pulled herself close. "Please, Huck.
There's no one else to ask. He's your friend. And then there's
Joe."

"Yeah, well, Joe, he's sort of got his own lookout far as I'm
concerned," I said. I admit I said this cause I don't care for Joe
Harvey much. I ain't got no closer friend than Jim, but me and
Tom was friends too, and I didn't like that he'd asked Joe to
go with him out there to Dread Island and not me. I probably
wouldn't have gone, but a fella likes to be asked.

"Please, Huck," she said, and now she was so close to me I
could smell her, and it was a good smell. Not a stink, mind you,
but sweet like strawberries. Even there in the moonlight, her

plump, wet lips made me want to kiss them, and I had an urge to reach out and stroke her hair. That was something I wasn't altogether understanding, and it made me feel like I was coming down sick.

Jim looked at me, said, "Ah, hell."

## »《

Our raft was back where we had been fishing, so I told Becky to go on home and I'd go look for Tom and Joe, and if I found them, I'd come back and let her know or send Tom to tell her, if he hadn't been ate up by alligators or carried off by mermaids. Not that I believed in mermaids, but there was them said they was out there in the river. But you can't believe every tall tale you hear.

All the while we're walking back to the raft, Jim is trying to talk me out of it.

"Huck, that island is all covered in badness."

"How would you know? You ain't never been. I mean, I've heard stories, but far as I know, they're just stories."

I was talking like that to build up my courage; tell the truth, I wasn't so sure they was just tall tales.

Jim shook his head. "I ain't got to have been. I know someone that's been there for sure. I know more than one."

I stopped walking. It was like I had been stunned with an ox hammer. Sure, me and Tom had heard a fella say he had been there, but when something come from Jim, it wasn't usually a lie, which isn't something I can say for most folks.

"You ain't never said nothing before about that, so why now?" I said. "I ain't saying you're making it up cause you don't want to go. I ain't saying that. But I'm saying why tell me now? We could have conversated on it before, but now you tell me."

Jim grabbed my elbow, shook me a little, said, "Listen here, Huck. I ain't never mentioned it before because if someone tells you that you ought not to do something, then you'll do it. It's a weakness, son. It is."

I was startled. Jim hadn't never called me son before, and he hadn't never mentioned my weakness. It was a weakness me and Tom shared, and it wasn't something I thought about, and most of the time I just figured I did stuff cause I wanted to. But with Jim saying that, and grabbing my arm, calling me son, it just come all over me of a sudden that he was right. Down deep, I knew I had been thinking about going to that island for a long time, and tonight just set me a purpose. It was what them preachers call a revelation.

"Ain't nobody goes over there in they right mind, Huck," Jim said. "That ole island is all full of haints, they say. And then there's the Brer People."

"Brer People," I says. "What in hell is that?"

"You ain't heard nothing about the Brer People? Why I know I ain't told you all I know, but it surprises me deep as the river that you ain't at least heard of the Brer People. They done come on this land from time to time and do things, and then go back. Them fellas I know been over there and come back, both of them colored, they ain't been right in they heads since. One of them lost a whole arm, and the other one, he lost his mind, which I figure is some worse than an arm."

"You sure it's because they went out to Dread Island?"

"Well, they didn't go to Nantucket," Jim said, like he had some idea where that was, but I knew he didn't. It was just a name he heard and locked onto.

"I don't know neither them to be liars," Jim said, "and the one didn't lose his senses said the Brer People was out there, and they was lucky to get away. Said the island was fading when they got back to their boat. When it went away, it darn near pulled them after it. Said it was like a big ole twister on the water, and then it went up in the sky and was gone."

"A twister?"

"What they said."

I considered a moment. "I guess Brer People or not, I got to go."

"You worried about that Miss Becky," Jim said, "and what she thinks?"

"I don't want her upset."

"I believe that. But you thinking you and her might be together. I know that's what you thinking, cause that's what any young, red-blooded, white boy be thinking about Miss Becky. I hope you understand now, I ain't crossing no color lines in my talk here, I'm just talking to a friend."

"Hell, I know that," I said. "And I don't care about color lines. I done decided if I go to hell for not caring about that, at least you and me will be there to talk. I figure too that danged ole writer cheated us out of some money will be there too."

"Yeah, he done us bad, didn't he?"

"Yeah, but what are these Brer People?"

We had started walking again, and as we did, Jim talked.

"Uncle Remus used to tell about them. He's gone now. Buried for some twenty years, I s'pect. He was a slave. A good man. He knew things ain't nobody had an inkling about. He come from Africa, Huck. He was a kind of preacher man, but the gods he knew, they wasn't no god of the Bible. It wasn't no Jesus he talked about, until later when he had to talk about Jesus, cause the massas would beat his ass if he didn't. But he knew about them hoodoo things. Them animals that walked like men. He told about them even to the whites, but he made like they was little stories. I heard them tales when I was a boy, and he told them to me and all the colored folks in a different way."

"You ain't makin' a damn bit of sense, Jim."

"There's places where they show up. Holes in the sky, Uncle Remus used to say. They come out of them, and they got them some places where they got to stay when they come out of them holes. They can wander some, but they got to get back to their spot a'fore their time runs out. They got 'strictions. That island, it's got the same 'strictions."

"What's 'strictions'?"

"Ain't exactly sure, but I've heard it said. I think it means there's rules of a sort."

By this time we had come to the raft and our fishing lines, which we checked right away. Jim's had a big ole catfish on it.

Jim said, "Well, if we gonna go to that dadburn island, we might as well go with full bellies. Let's get out our gear and fry these fish up."

"You're going then?" I said.

Jim sighed. "I can't let you go out there by yourself. Not to Dread Island. I did something like that I couldn't sleep at night. Course, I didn't go, I would at least be around to be without some sleep."

"Go or don't go, Jim, but I got to. Tom is my friend, and Becky asked me. If it was you, I'd go."

"Now, Huck, don't be trying to make me feel bad. I done said I'd go."

"Good then."

Jim paused and looked out over the river.

"I still don't see it," Jim said, "and I'm hoping you just think you do."

## 》《

We cooked up those catfish and ate them. When we was done eating, Jim got his magic hairball out of the ditty bag he carried on a rope around his waist. He took a gander at it, trying to divine things. That hairball come from the inside of a cow's stomach, and Jim said it had more mystery in it than women, but was a lot less good to look at. He figured he could see the future in it, and held stock by it.

Jim stuck his big thumbs in it and moved the hair around and eyeballed it some, said, "It don't look good, Huck."

"What's that hairball telling you?" I was looking at it, but I didn't see nothing but a big ole wad of hair that the cow had licked off its self and left in its stomach before it got killed and eat up; it smelled like an armpit after a hard day of field work.

Jim pawed around some more, then I seen his face change.

He said, "We go out there, Huck, someone's gonna die."

"You ain't just saying that about dying cause you don't want to go, are you?" I said.

He shook his head. "I'm saying it, cause that's what the hairball says."

I thought on that a moment, then said, "But that don't mean it's me or you dying, does it?"

Jim shook his head again. "No. But there ain't no solid way of telling."

"It's a chance we have to take," I said.

Jim stood for a moment just looking at me, shoving that hairball back into his pants pocket.

"All right," he said. "If that's how it is, then put this in your left shoe."

He had whittled a little cross, and it was small enough I could slide it down the side of my shoe and let it press up against the edge of my foot. Jim put a cross in his shoe too. We didn't normally have no shoes, but some Good Samaritans gave them to us, and we had taken to wearing them now and again. Jim said it was a sure sign we was getting civilized, and the idea of it scared me to death. Civilizing someone meant they had to go to jobs; and there was a time to show up and a time to leave; and you had to do work in between the coming and leaving. It was a horrible thing to think about, yet there I was with shoes on. The first step toward civilization and not having no fun anymore.

I said, "Is that cross so Jesus will watch over us?"

"A cross has got them four ends to it that show the four things make up this world. Fire, wind, earth, and water. It don't do nothing against a regular man, but against raw evil, it's supposed to have a mighty big power."

"But you don't know for sure?" I said.

"No, Huck, I don't. There ain't much I know for sure. But I got these too."

Jim held up two strings, and each of them had a big nail tied to it.

"These supposed to be full of power against evil," he said.

"Ain't the nails on account of Jesus?" I said. "Them being stuck in his hands and feet and such. I think I was told that in Sunday school. It's something like a cymbal."

"A cymbal? Like you hit in a band?"

"You know, I ain't sure, but I think that's what I was told."

"I don't see it being about no cymbals," Jim said. "Iron's got magic in it, that's all I know. It had magic in it before anyone ever heard of any Jesus. It's just iron to us, but to them haints, well, it's a whole nuther matter. Here. Loop this here string over your neck and tie the other end back to the nail. Make you a necklace of it. That ought to give you some protection. And I got some salt here in little bags for us. You never know when you might have the devil on your left, which is where he likes to stay, and if you feel him there, you can toss salt over your left shoulder, right into his eye. And we can use some of it on something to eat, if we got it."

"Finally," I said, "something that sounds reasonable."

When I had the nail around my neck, the cross in my shoe, and the bag of salt in my pocket, and my pocketknife shoved down tight in my back pocket, we pushed off the raft. Moment later we was sailing out across the black night water toward Dread Island.

The water was smooth at first, and the long pushing poles helped us get out in the deep part. When we got out there, we switched to Jim using the tiller, and me handling the sails, which is something we had added as of recent. They worked mighty good, if you didn't shift wrong; and, of course, there had to be wind.

It had been pretty still when we started out, and that had worried me, but before long, a light wind come up. It was just right, filling that canvas and pushing us along.

### 》《

It didn't seem long before that line of dark in the water was a rise of dark, and then it was sure enough an island. Long and low and covered in fog, thick as the wool on a sheep's ass.

The raft started moving swift on account of it was caught up in a current, and before we knowed it, we was going through the fog and slamming up on the bank of Dread Island. We got out and used the docking rope to drag the raft on shore. It was a heavy rascal out of the water, and I thought I was gonna bust a gut. But we finally got it pulled up on solid ground.

Right then, there wasn't much to see that was worth seeing. The fog was heavy, but it was mostly around the island. On the island itself it was thin. Off to my right, I could see briars rising up about ten feet high, with dark thorns on them bigger than that nail I had tied around my neck. The tips of them were shiny in the moonlight, and the bit of fog that was off the water, twisted in between them like stripped wads of cotton. To the left, and in front of us, was some woods; it was as dark in there as the inside of a dog's gut.

"Well, here we is all ready for a rescue," Jim said. "And we don't even know they here anywhere. They may have done come and gone home. They could have come back while we was frying catfish and I was looking at my hairball."

I pointed to the mud gleaming in the moonlight, showed Jim there was a drag line in it.

"That looks like the bottom of a boat," I said.

Jim squatted down and touched the ground with his fingers. "It sure do, Huck."

We followed the drag line until we come to a patch of limbs. I moved them back, and seen they had been cut and was thrown over the boat to hide it.

"I figure this is their boat," I said. "They're exploring, Jim. They done hid the boat, and gone out there."

"Well, they didn't hide it so good," he said, "cause it took us about the time it takes a duck to eat a June bug to find it."

We got a big cane knife off the raft, and Jim took that and cut down some limbs, and we covered the raft up with them. It wasn't a better hiding place than Tom and Joe's boat, but it made me feel better to do it.

With Jim carrying the cane knife, and me with a lit lantern, we looked for sign of Tom and Joe. Finally, we seen some footprints on the ground. One was barefoot, and the other had on shoes. I figured Tom, who had been getting civilized too, would be the shoe wearer, and Joe would be the bare footer.

Their sign led off in the woods. We followed in there after them. There was hardly any moon now, and even with me holding the lantern close to the ground, it wasn't no time at all until we lost track of them.

We kept going, and after a while we seen a big old clock on the ground. I held the lantern closer, seen it was inside a skeleton. The skeleton looked like it belonged to an alligator. Inside them alligator bones was human bones, all broke up, along with what was left of a hat with a feather in it, a boot, and a hook of the sort fits on a fella with his hand chopped off.

It didn't make no sense, but I quit thinking about, because I seen something move up ahead of us.

I wasn't sure what I had seen, but I can tell you this, it didn't take but that little bit of a glance for me to know I didn't like the looks of it.

》《

Jim said, "Holy dog turd, was that a man with a rabbit's head?"

I was glad he said that. I had seen the same darn shadowy thing, but was thinking my mind was making it up.

Then we saw movement again, and that thing poked its head out from behind a tree. You could see the ears standing up in the shadows. I could see some big white buckteeth too.

Jim called out, "You better come out from behind that tree, and show yourself good, or I'm gonna chop your big-eared head off with this cane knife."

That didn't bring the thing out, but it did make it run. It tore off through them woods and underbrush like its tail was on fire.

And it actually had a tail. A big cotton puff that I got a good look at, sticking out of the back of a pair of pants.

I didn't figure we ought to go after it. Our reason for being here was to find Tom and Joe and get ourselves back before the light come up. Besides, even if that thing was running, that didn't give me an idea about chasing it down. I might not like it if I caught it.

So, we was standing there, trying to figure if we was gonna shit or go blind, and that's when we heard a whipping sound in the brush. Then we seen torches. It didn't take no Daniel Boone to figure that it was someone beating the bushes, driving game in front of it. I reckoned the game would be none other than that thing we saw, so I grabbed Jim's arm and tugged him back behind some trees, and I blowed out the light. We laid down on our bellies and watched as the torches got closer, and they was bright enough we could see what was carrying them.

Their shadows come first, flickering in the torchlight. They was shaped something odd, and the way they fell on the ground, and bent around trees, made my skin crawl. But the shadows wasn't nothing compared to what made them.

Up front, carrying a torch, was a short fella wearing blue pants with rivets up the side, and he didn't have on no shirt. His chest was covered in a red fur and he had some kind of pack strapped to his back. His head, well, it wasn't no human head at all. It was the head of a fox. He was wearing a little folded hat with a feather in it. Not that he really needed that feather to get our attention. The fact that he was walking on his hind paws, with shoes on his feet, was plenty enough.

With him was a huge bear, also on hind legs, and wearing red pants that come to the knees. He didn't have no shoes on, but like the fox, he wasn't without a hat. Had a big straw one like Tom Sawyer liked to wear. In his teeth was a long piece of some kind of weed or another. He was working it from one side of his mouth to the other. He was carrying a torch.

The other four was clearly weasels, only bigger than any weasels I had ever seen. They didn't have no pants on at all, nor shoes neither, but they was wearing some wool caps. Two of the weasels had torches, but the other two had long switch limbs they was using to beat the brush.

But the thing that made me want to jump up and grab Jim and run back toward the raft was this big nasty shape of a thing that was with them. It was black as sin. The torch it was carrying flickered over its body and made it shine like fresh licked licorice. It looked like a big baby, if a baby could be six foot tall and four foot wide. It was fat in the belly and legs. It waddled from side to side on flat, sticky feet that was picking up leaves and pine needles and dirt. It didn't have no real face or body; all of it was made out of that sticky black mess. After awhile, it spit a stream that hit in the bushes heavy as a cow pissing on a flat rock. That stream of spit didn't miss me and Jim by more than ten feet. Worse, that thing turned its head in our direction to do the spitting, and when it did, I could see it had teeth that looked like sugar cubes. Its eyes was as blood-red as two bullet wounds.

I thought at first it saw us, but after it spit, it turned its head back the way it had been going, and just kept on keeping on; it and that fox and that bear and them weasels. The smell of its spit lingered behind, and it was like the stink of turpentine.

After they was passed, me and Jim got up and started going back through the woods the way we had come, toward the raft. Seeing what we seen had made up our minds for us, and discussion about it wasn't necessary, and I knowed better than to light the lantern again. We just went along and made the best of it in the darkness of the woods.

As we was about to come out of the trees onto the beach, we seen something that froze us in our tracks. Coming along the beach was more of them weasels. Some of them had torches, some of them had clubs, and they all had hats. I guess a weasel don't care for pants, but dearly loves a hat. One of them was carrying a big, wet-looking bag.

We slipped back behind some trees and watched them move along for a bit, but was disappointed to see them stop by the water. They was strung out in a long line, and the weasel with the bag moved in front of the line and the line sort of gathered around him in a horseshoe shape. The weasel put the bag on the ground, opened it, and took out something I couldn't recognize at first. I squatted down so I could see better between their legs, and when I did, I caught my breath. They was passing a man's battered head among them, and they was each sitting down and taking a bite of it, passing it to the next weasel, like they was sharing a big apple.

Jim, who had squatted down beside me, said, "Oh, Huck, chile, look what they doing."

Not knowing what to do, we just stayed there, and then we heard that beating sound we had heard before. Off to our left was a whole batch of torches moving in our direction.

"More of them," Jim said.

Silent, but as quick as we could, we started going away from them. They didn't even know we was there, but they was driving us along like we was wild game cause they was looking for that rabbit, I figured.

After a bit, we picked up our pace, because they was closing. As we went more quickly through the woods, two things happened. The woods got thicker and harder to move through, and whatever was behind us started coming faster. I reckoned that was because now they could hear us. It may not have been us they was looking for, but it was darn sure us they was chasing.

It turned into a full-blowed run. I tossed the lantern aside, and we tore through them woods and vines and undergrowth as hard as we could go. Since we wasn't trying to be sneaky about it, Jim was using that cane knife to cut through the hard parts; mostly we just pushed through it.

Then an odd thing happened. We broke out of the woods and was standing on a cliff. Below us, pretty far down, was a big pool of water that the moon's face seemed to be floating on. Across from the pool was more land, and way beyond that was some mountains that rose up so high the peaks looked close to the moon.

I know. It don't make no sense. That island ought not to have been that big. It didn't fit the facts. Course, I reckon in a place where weasels and foxes and bears wear hats, and there's a big ole thing made of a sticky, black mess that spits turpentine, you can expect the facts to have their problems.

Behind us, them weasels was closing, waving torches, and yipping and barking like dogs.

Jim looked at me, said, "We gonna have to jump, Huck. It's all there is for it."

It was a good drop and wasn't no way of knowing what was under that water, but I nodded, aimed for the floating moon and jumped.

»«

It was a quick drop, as it usually is when you step off nothing and fall. Me and Jim hit the water side by side and went under. The water was as cold as a dead man's ass in winter. When we come up swimming and spitting, I lifted my head to look at where we had jumped from. At the edge of the cliff was now the pack of weasels, and they was pressed up together tighter than a cluster of chiggers, leaning over and looking down.

One of them was dedicated, cause he jumped with his torch in his hand. He come down right in front of us in the water, went under, and when he come up he still had the torch, but of course it wasn't lit. He swung it and hit Jim upside the head.

Jim had lost the cane knife in the jump, so he didn't have nothing to hit back with. He and the weasel just sort of floated there eyeing one another.

There was a chittering sound from above, as all them weasels rallied their man on. The weasel cocked back the torch again, and swung at me. I couldn't backpedal fast enough, and it caught me a glancing blow on the side of my head. It was a hard enough lick that for a moment, I not only couldn't swim, I wouldn't have been able to tell you the difference between a cow and a horse and a goat and a cotton sack. Right then, everything seemed pretty much the same to me.

I slipped under, but the water, and me choking on it, brought me back. I clawed my way to the surface, and when I was sort of back to myself, I seen that Jim had the weasel by the neck with one hand, and had its torch arm in his other. The weasel was pretty good sized, but he wasn't as big as Jim, and his neck wasn't on his shoulders as good neither. The weasel had reached its free hand and got Jim's throat and was trying to strangle him; he might as well have been trying to squeeze a tree to death. Jim's fingers dug into the weasel's throat, and there was a sound like someone trying to spit a pea through a tight-rolled cigar, and then the next thing I knowed, the weasel was floating like a turd in a night jar.

Above, the pack was still there, and a couple of them threw torches at us, but missed; they hissed out in the water. We swam to the other side, and crawled out. There was thick brush and woods there, and we staggered into it, with me stopping at the edge of the trees just long enough to yell something nasty to them weasels.

》《

The woods come up along a wall of dirt, and thinned, and there was a small cave in the dirt, and in the cave, sleeping on the floor, was that rabbit we had seen. I doubted it was really a rabbit back then, when we first seen it in the shadows, but after the fox and bear and weasels, and Mr. Sticky, it was hard to doubt anything.

The moonlight was strong enough where the trees had thinned, that we could see the rabbit had white fur and wore a red vest and blue pants and no shoes. He had a pink nose and pink in his big ears, and he was sleeping. He heard us, and in a move so quick it was hard to see, he come awake and sprang to his feet. But we was in front of the cave, blocking the way out.

"Oh, my," he said.

A rabbit speaking right good American was enough to startle both me and Jim. But as I said, this place was the sort of place where you come to expect anything other than a free boat ride home.

Jim said slowly, "Why, I think I know who you are. Uncle Remus talked about you and your red vest. You Brer Rabbit."

The rabbit hung his head and sort of collapsed to the floor of the cave.

"Brer Rabbit," the rabbit said, "that would be me. Well, Fred actually, but when Uncle Remus was here, he knowed me by that name. I had a family once, but they was all eat up. There was Floppsy and Mopsy and Fred, and Alice and Fred Two and Fred Three, and then there was... Oh, I don't even remember now, it's been so long ago they was eaten up, or given to Cut Through You."

There was a roll of thunder, and rain started darting down on us. We went inside the cave with Brer Rabbit and watched lightning cut across the sky and slam into what looked like a sycamore tree.

"Lightning," Jim said, to no one in particular. "It don't leave no shadow. You got a torch, it leaves a shadow. The sun makes a shadow on the ground of things it shines on. But lightning, it don't leave no shadow."

"No," Brer Rabbit said, looking up and out of the cave. "It don't, and it never has. And here, on this island, when it starts to rain and the lightning flashes and hits the ground like that, it's a warning. It means time is closing out. But what makes it bad is there's something new now. Something really awful."

"The weasels, you mean," Jim said.

"No," Brer Rabbit said. "Something much worse."

"Well," Jim said, "them weasels is bad enough. We seen them eating a man's head."

"Riverboat captain probably," Brer Rabbit said. "Big ole steamboat got too close and got sucked in. And then there was the lady in the big, silver mosquito."

"Beg your pardon," I said.

"Well, it reminded me of a mosquito. I ain't got no other way to explain it, so I won't. But that head, it was probably all that remains of that captain. It could have been some of the others, but I reckon it was him. He had a fat head."

"How do you know all this?" I said.

Brer Rabbit looked at me, pulled his paw from behind his back, where he had been keeping it, and we saw he didn't have a hand on the end of it. Course, he didn't have a hand on the one showing neither. He had a kind of paw with fingers, which is the best I can describe it, but that other arm ended in a nubbin.

The rabbit dropped his head then, let his arm fall to his side, like everything inside of him had turned to water and run out on the ground. "I know what happened cause I was there, and was gonna be one of the sacrifices. Would have been part of the whole thing had I not gnawed my paw off. It was the only way out. While I was doing it, it hurt like hell, but I kept thinking, rabbit meat, it ain't so bad. Ain't that a thing to think? It still hurts. I been running all night. But it ain't no use. I am a shadow of my former self. Was a time when I was clever and smart, but these days I ain't neither one. They gonna catch up with me now. I been outsmarting them for years, but everything done got its time, and I reckon mine has finally come. Brer Fox, he's working up to the Big One, and tonight could be the night it all comes down in a bad way. If ole Cut Through You gets enough souls."

"I'm so confused I feel turned around and pulled inside out," I said.

"I'm a might confused myself," Jim said.

The rain was really hammering now. The lightning was tearing at the sky and poking down hot yellow forks, hitting trees, catching them on fire. It got so there were so many burning, that the inside of our cave was lit up for a time like it was daylight.

"This here rain," Brer Rabbit said. "They don't like it. Ain't nobody likes it, cause that lightning can come down on your ass sure as it can on a tree. The Warning Rain we call it. Means that there ain't much time before the next rain comes. The Soft Rain, and when it does, it's that time. Time to go."

"I just thought I was confused before," I said.

"All right," Brer Rabbit said. "It ain't like we're going anywhere now, and it ain't like they'll be coming. They'll be sheltering up somewhere nearby to get out of the Warning Rain. So, I'll tell you what you want to know. Just ask."

"I'll make it easy," I said. "Tell us all of it."

And he did. Now, no disrespect to Brer Rabbit, but once he got going, he was a dad burn blabbermouth. He told us all we wanted to know, and all manner of business we didn't want to know. I think it's best I just summarize what he was saying, keeping in mind it's possible I've left out some of the important parts, but mostly, I can assure you, I've left out stuff you don't want to hear anyway. We even got a few pointers on how to decorate a burrow, which seemed to be a tip we didn't need.

## 》《

The rain got so thick it put those burning trees out, and with the moon behind clouds, it was dark in that cave. We couldn't even see each other. All we could do was hear Brer Rabbit's voice, which was a little squeaky.

What he was telling us was, there was gonna be some kind of ceremony. That whoever the weasels could catch was gonna be a part of it. It wasn't no ceremony where there was cake and prizes and games, least not any that was fun. It was gonna be a ceremony in honor of this fella he called Cut Through You.

According to Brer Rabbit, the island wasn't always a bad place. He and his family had lived here, along with all the other brother and sister animals, or whatever the hell they were, until Brer Fox found the stones and the book wrapped in skin. That's how Brer Rabbit put it. The book wrapped in skin.

Brer Fox, he wasn't never loveable, and Brer Rabbit said right up front, he used to pull tricks on him and Brer Bear all the time. They was harmless, he said, and they was mostly just to keep from getting eaten by them two. Cause as nice a place as it was then as measured up against now, it was still a place where meat eaters lived alongside them that wasn't meat eaters, which meant them that ate vegetables was the meat eater's lunch, if they got caught. Brer Rabbit said he figured that was just fair play. That was how the world worked, even if their island wasn't exactly like the rest of the world.

It dropped out of the sky come the full moon and ended up in the big wide middle of the Mississippi. It stayed that way for a few hours, and then come the Warning Rain, as he called it, the one we was having now; the one full of lightning and thunder and hard falling water. It meant they was more than halfway through their time to be on the Mississippi, then there was gonna come the Soft Rain. It didn't have no lightning in it. It was pleasant. At least until the sky opened up and the wind came down and carried them away.

"Where does it take you?" I asked.

Brer Rabbit shook his head. "I don't know I can say. We don't seem to know nothing till we come back. And when we do, well, we just pick up right where we was before. Doing whatever it was we was doing. So if Brer Fox has me by the neck, and the time comes, and we all get sucked away, when it blows back, we gonna be right where we was; it's always night and always like things was when we left them."

He said when that funnel of wind dropped them back on the island, sometimes it brought things with it that wasn't there before. Like people from other places. Other worlds, he said. That didn't make no sense at all to me. But that's what he said. He said sometimes it brought live people, and sometimes it brought dead people, and sometimes it brought Brer People with it, and sometimes what it brought wasn't people at all. He told us about some big old crawdads come through once, and how they chased everyone around, but ended up being boiled in water and eaten by Brer Bear, Brer Fox, and all the weasels, who was kind of butt kissers to Brer Fox.

Anyway, not knowing what was gonna show up on the island, either by way of that Sticky Storm—as he named it cause everything clung to it—or by way of the Mississippi, made things interesting; right before it got too interesting. The part that was too interesting had to do with Brer Fox and that Book of Skin.

Way Brer Rabbit figured, it come through that hole in the sky like everything else. It was clutched in a man's hand, and the man was deader than a rock, and he had what Brer Rabbit said was a towel or a rag or some such thing wrapped around his head.

Brer Rabbit said he seen that dead man from a hiding place in the woods, and Uncle Remus was with him when he did. Uncle Remus had escaped slavery and come to the island. He fit in good. Stayed in the burrow with Brer Rabbit and his family, and he listened to all their stories.

But when the change come, when that book showed up, and stuff started happening because of it, he decided he'd had enough and tried to swim back to shore. Things he saw made him think taking his chance on drowning, or getting caught and being a slave again, was worth it. I don't know how he felt later, but he sure got caught, since Jim knew him and had heard stories about Dread Island from him.

"He left before things really got bad," Brer Rabbit said. "And did they get bad. He was lucky."

"That depends on how you look at it," Jim said. "I done been a slave, and I can't say it compares good to much of anything."

"Maybe," Brer Rabbit said. "Maybe."

And then he went on with his story.

Seems that when the storm brought that dead man clutching that book, Brer Fox pried it out of his hands and opened it up and found it was written in some foreign language, but he could read it. Brer Rabbit said one of the peculiars about the island is that everyone—except the weasels, who pretty much got the short end of the stick when it come to smarts—could read or speak any language there was.

Now, wasn't just the book and the dead man come through, there was the stones. They had fallen out of the sky at the same time. There was also a mass of black goo with dying and dead fish in it that come through, and it splattered all over the ground. The stones was carved up. The main marking was a big eye, then there was all manner of other scratchings and drawings. And though the Brer Folk could read or speak any language possible, even the language in that book, they couldn't speak or read what was on them stones. It had been put together by folk spoke a tongue none of their mouths would fit around. Least at first.

Brer Fox went to holding that book dear. Everyone on the island knew about it, and he always carried it in a pack on his back. Brer Bear, who was kind of a kiss ass like the weasels, but smarter than they was—and, according to Brer Rabbit, that was a sad thing to think about, since Brer Bear didn't hardly have the sense to get in out of the Warning Rain—helped Brer Fox set them stones up in that black muck. Every time the storm brought them back, that's what they did, and pretty soon they had the weasels helping them.

Fact was, Brer Fox all but quit chasing Brer Rabbit. He instead sat and read by firelight and moonlight, and started chanting, cause he was learning how to say that language that he couldn't read before, the language on the stones, and he was teaching Brer Bear how to do the same. And one time, well, the island stayed overnight.

"It didn't happen but that once," Brer Rabbit said. "But come daylight, here we still was. And it stayed that way until the next night come, and finally before next morning, things got back to the way they was supposed to be. Brer Fox had some power from that book and those stones, and he liked it mighty good."

Now and again he'd chant something from the book, and the air would fill with an odor like rotting fish, and then that odor got heavy and went to whirling about them stones; it was an odor that made the stomach crawl and the head fill with all manner of sickness and worry and grief.

Once, while Brer Rabbit was watching Brer Fox chant, while he was smelling that rotten fish stink, he saw the sky crack open, right up close by the moon. Not the way it did when the Sticky Storm come, which was when everything turned gray and the sky opened up and a twister of sorts dropped down and sucked them all up. It was more like the night sky was just a big black sheet, and this thing with one, large, nasty, rolling eye and more legs than a spider—and ropey legs at that—poked through and pulled at the night.

For a moment, Brer Rabbit thought that thing—which from Brer Fox's chanting he learned was called Cut Through You— was gonna take hold of the moon and eat it like a flapjack. It had a odd mouth with a beak, and it was snapping all the while.

Then, sudden like, it was sucked back, like something got hold of one of its legs and yanked it plumb out of sight. The sky closed up and the air got clean for a moment, and it was over with.

After that, Brer Fox and ole One Eye had them a connection. Every time the island was brought back, Brer Fox would go out there and stand in that muck, or sit on a rock in the middle of them carved stones, and call out to Cut Through You. It was a noise, Brer Rabbit said, sounded like something straining at toilet while trying to cough and yodel all at the same time.

Brer Fox and Brer Bear was catching folk and tying them to the stones. People from the Mississippi come along by accident; they got nabbed too, mostly by the weasels. It was all so Brer Fox could have Cut Through You meetings.

Way it was described to me, it was kind of like church. Except when it come time to pass the offering, the sky would crack open, and ole Cut Through You would lean out and reach down and pull folk tied to the stones up there with him.

Brer Rabbit said he watched it eat a bunch a folk quicker than a mule skinner could pop goober peas; chawed them up and spat them out, splattered what was left in that black mud that was all around the stones.

That was what Brer Fox and Brer Bear, and all them weasels, took to eating. It changed them. They went from sneaky and hungry and animal like, to being more like men. Meaning, said Brer Rabbit, they come to enjoy cruelty. And then Brer Fox built the Tar Baby, used that book to give it life. It could do more work than all of them put together, and it set up the final stones by itself. Something dirty needed to be done, it was Tar Baby done it. You couldn't stop the thing, Brer Rabbit said. It just kept on a coming, and a coming.

But the final thing Brer Rabbit said worried him, was that each time Cut Through You came back, there's more and more of him to be seen, and it turned out there's a lot more of Cut Through You than you'd think; and it was like he was hungrier each time he showed.

Bottom line, as figured by Brer Rabbit, was this: if Brer Fox and his bunch didn't supply the sacrifices, pretty soon they'd be sacrifices themselves.

Brer Rabbit finished up his story, and it was about that time the rain quit. The clouds melted away and the moonlight was back. It was clear out, and you could see a right smart distance.

I said, "You ain't seen a couple of fellas named Tom and Joe, have you? One of them might be wearing a straw hat. They're about my age and size, but not quite as good looking."

Brer Rabbit shook his head. "I ain't," he said. "But they could be with all the others Brer Fox has nabbed of late. Was they on the riverboat run aground?"

I shook my head.

Jim said, "Huck, you and me, we got to get back to the raft and get on out of this place, Tom and Joe or not."

"That's right," Brer Rabbit said. "You got to. Oh, I wish I could go with you."

"You're invited," I said.

"Ah, but there is the thorn in the paw. I can't go, cause I do, come daylight, if I ain't on this island, I disappear, and I don't come back. Though to tell you true, that might be better than getting ate up by Cut Through You. I'll give it some considering."

"Consider quick," Jim said, "we got to start back to the raft."

"What we got to do," Brer Rabbit said, "is we got to go that way." He pointed.

"Then," he said, "we work down to the shore, and you can get your raft. And I'm thinking I might just go with you and turn to nothing. I ain't got no family now. I ain't got nothing but me, and part of me is missing, so the rest of me might as well go missing too."

Jim said, "I got my medicine bag with me. I can't give you your paw back, but I can take some of the hurt away with a salve I got."

Jim dressed Brer Rabbit's paw, and when that was done, he got some wool string out of that little bag he had on his belt and tied up his hair—which had grown long—in little sheaves, like dark wheat. He said it was a thing to do to keep back witches.

I pointed out witches seemed to me the least of our worries, but he done it anyway, with me taking my pocketknife out of my back pocket to cut the string for him.

When he had knotted his hair up in about twenty gatherings, we lit out for the raft without fear of witches.

》《

Way we went made it so we had to swim across a creek that was deep in places. It was cold water, like that blue hole we had jumped in, and there was fish in it. They was curious and would bob to the top and look at us; their eyes was shiny as wet stones in the moonlight.

On the other side of the creek, we stumbled through a patch of woods, and down a hill, and then up one that led us level with where we had been before. In front of us was more dark woods.

Brer Rabbit said beyond the trees was the shoreline, and we might be able to get to our raft if the weasels hadn't found it. Me and Jim decided if they had, we'd try for Tom's and Joe's boat and wish them our best. If their boat was gone, then, there was nothing left but to hit that Mississippi and swim for it. We had about as much chance of making that swim as passing through the eye of a needle, but it was a might more inviting than Cut Through You. Least, that way we had a chance. Me and Jim was both good swimmers, and maybe we could even find a log to push off into the water with us. As for Brer Rabbit, well, he was thinking on going with us and just disappearing when daylight come; that was a thing made me really want to get off that island. If he was willing to go out that way, then that Cut Through You must be some nasty sort of fella. Worse yet, our salt had got all wet and wasn't worth nothing, and we had both lost the cross in our shoes. All we had was those rusty nails on strings, and I didn't have a whole lot of trust in that. I was more comfortable that I still had my little knife in my back pocket.

We was coming down through the woods, and it got so the · trees were thinning, and we could see the bank down there, the river churning along furious like. My heart was starting to beat in an excited way, and about then, things turned to dog doo.

The weasels come down out of the trees on ropes, and a big net come down with them and landed over us. It was weighed down with rocks, and there wasn't no time to get out from under it before they was tugging it firm around us, and we was bagged up tighter than a strand of gut packed with sausage makings.

As we was laying there, out of the woods come Brer Fox and Brer Bear. They come right over to us. The fox bent down, and he looked Brer Rabbit in the eye. He grinned and showed his teeth. His breath was so sour we could smell it from four feet away; it smelled like death warmed over and gone cold again.

Up close, I could see things I couldn't see before in the night. He had fish scales running along the side of his face, and when he breathed there were flaps that flared out on his cheeks; they was gills, like a fish.

I looked up at Brer Bear. There were sores all over his body, and bits of fish heads and fish tails poking out of him like moles. He was breathing in and out, like bellows being worked to start up a fresh fire.

"You ain't looking so good," Brer Rabbit said.

"Yeah," Brer Fox said, "but looks ain't everything. I ain't looking so good, but you ain't doing so good."

Brer Fox slung his pack off his back and opened it. I could see there was a book in there, the one bound up in human skin. You could see there was a face on the cover, eyes, nose, mouth, and some warts. But that wasn't what Brer Fox was reaching for. What he was reaching for was Brer Rabbit's paw, which was stuffed in there.

"Here's a little something you left back at the ceremony spot." He held up the paw and waved it around. "That wasn't nice. I had plans for you. But, you know what? I got a lucky rabbit's foot now. Though, to tell the truth, it ain't all that lucky for you, is it?"

He put the paw in his mouth and clamped down on it and bit right through it and chewed on it some. He gave what was left of it to Brer Bear, who ate it up in one big bite.

"I figured you wouldn't be needing it," Brer Fox said.

"Why, I'm quite happy with this nubbing," Brer Rabbit said. "I don't spend so much time cleaning my nails now."

Brer Fox's face turned sour, like he had bitten into an unripe persimmon. "There ain't gonna be nothing of you to clean after tonight. And in fact, we got to go quick like. I wouldn't want you to miss the meeting, Brer Rabbit. You see, tonight, he comes all the way through, and then, me and my folk, we're gonna serve him. He's gonna go all over the Mississippi, and then all over the world. He's gonna rule, and I'm gonna rule beside him. He told me. He told me in my head."

With those last words, Brer Fox tapped the side of his head with a finger.

"You gonna get ate up like everyone else," Brer Rabbit said. "You just a big ole idiot."

Brer Fox rose up, waved his hand over his head, yelled out, "Bring them. And don't be easy about it. Let's blood them."

What that meant was they dragged us in that net. We was pressed up tight together, and there was all manner of stuff on the ground to stick us, and we banged into trees and such, and it seemed like forever before we broke out of the woods and I got a glimpse at the place we was going.

Right then I knew why it was Brer Rabbit would rather just disappear.

》《

We was scratched and bumped up and full of ticks and chiggers and poison ivy by the time we got to where we was going, and where we was going didn't have no trees and there wasn't nothing pretty about it.

There was this big stretch of black mud. You could see dead fish in it, and some of them was mostly bones, but there were still some flopping about. They were fish I didn't recognize. Some had a lot of eyes and big teeth and were shaped funny.

Standing up in the mud were these big dark slabs of rock that wasn't quite black and wasn't quite brown, but was somewhere between any color you can mention. The moonlight laid on them like a slick of bacon grease, and you could see markings all over them. Each and every one of them had a big ole eye at the top of the slab, and below it were all manner of marks. Some of the marks looked like fish or things with lots of legs, and beaks, and then there was marks that didn't look like nothing but chicken scratch. But, I can tell you this, looking at those slabs and those marks made my stomach feel kind of funny, like I had swallowed a big chaw of tobacco right after eating too many hot peppers and boiled pig's feet, something, by the way, that really happened to me once.

Standing out there in that black muck was the weasels. On posts all around the muck right where it was still solid ground, there was men and women with their hands tied behind their backs and then tied to rings on the posts. I reckoned a number of them was from the steamboat wreck. There was also a woman wearing a kind of leather cap, and she had on pants just like a man. She was kind of pretty, and where everyone else was hanging their heads, she looked mad as a hornet. As we was pulled up closer to the muck, I saw that Tom and Joe was there, tied to posts, drooping like flowers too long in the hot sun, missing Bowie knife, gun, and packed lunch.

When they seen me and Jim, they brightened for a second, then realized wasn't nothing we could do, and that we was in the same situation as them. It hurt me to see Tom like that, all sagging. It was the first time I'd ever seen him about given up. Like us, they was all scratched up and even in the moonlight, you could see they was spotted like speckled pups from bruises.

Out behind them I could see parts of that big briar patch we had seen when we first sailed our raft onto the island. The briars twisted up high, and the way the moonlight fell into them, that whole section looked like a field of coiled ropes and nails. I hadn't never seen a briar patch like that before.

There were some other things out there in the muck that I can't explain, and there was stuff on the sides of where the muck ended. I figured, from what Brer Rabbit had told us, they was stuff from them other worlds or places that sometimes come through on the Sticky Storm. One of them things was a long boat of sorts, but it had wings on it, and it was shiny silver and had a tail on it like a fish. There was some kind of big crosses on the wings, and it was just sitting on wheels over on some high grass, but the wheels wasn't like any I'd ever seen on a wagon or buggy.

There was also this big thing looked like a gourd, if a gourd could be about a thousand times bigger; it was stuck up in the mud with the fat part down, and the thinner part in the air, and it had little fins on it. Written on it in big writing was something that didn't make no sense to me. It said: HOWDY ALL YOU JAPS.

Wasn't a moment or two passed between me seeing all this, then we was being pulled out of the net and carried over to three empty posts. A moment later, they wasn't empty no more. We was tied to the wooden rings on them tight as a fishing knot.

I turned my head and looked at Jim.

He said, "You're right, they ain't no witch problems around here."

"Maybe," I said, "it's because of the string. Who knows how many witches would be around otherwise."

Jim grinned at me. "That's right. That's right, ain't it?"

I nodded and smiled at him. I figured if we was gonna be killed, and wasn't nothing we could do about it, we might as well try and be cheerful.

Right then, coming across that black mud, its feet splattering and sucking in the muck as it pulled them free for each step, was the Tar Baby.

Now that he was out under the moonlight, I could see he was stuck all over with what at first looked like long needles, but as he come closer, I saw was straw. He was shot through with it. I figured it was a thing Brer Fox used to help put him together, mixing it with tar he got from somewhere, and turpentine, and maybe some things I didn't want to know about; you could smell that turpentine as he waddled closer, spitting all the while.

He sauntered around the circle of folks that was tied to the posts, and as he did, his plump belly would flare open, and you could see fire in there and bits of ash and bones being burned up along with fish heads and a human skull. Tar Baby went by each of them on the posts and pushed his face close to their faces so he could enjoy how they curled back from him. I knew a bully when I seen one, cause I had fought a few, and when I was younger, I was kind of a bully myself, till a girl named Hortense Miller beat the snot out of me, twisted my arm behind my back and made me say cotton sack, and even then, after I said it, she made me eat a mouthful of dirt and tell her I liked it. She wasn't one to settle an argument easy like. It cured my bully days.

When the Tar Baby come to me and pushed his face close, I didn't flinch. I just looked him in his red eyes like they was nothing, even though it was all I could do to keep my knees from chattering together. He stayed looking at me for a long time, then grunted, left the air around me full of the fog and stink of turpentine. Jim was next, and Jim didn't flinch none either. That didn't set well with Tar Baby, two rascals in a row, so he reached out with a finger and poked Jim's chest. There was a hissing sound and smoke come off Jim. That made me figure he was being burned by the Tar Baby somehow, but when the Tar Baby pulled his chubby, tar finger back, it was him that was smoking.

I leaned out and took a good look and seen the cause of it—the nail on the string around Jim's neck. The Tar Baby had poked it and that iron nail had actually worked its magic on him. Course, problem was, he had to put his finger right on it, but in that moment, I gathered me up a more favorable view of the hoodoo methods.

Tar Baby looked at the end of his smoking finger, like he might find something special there, then he looked at Jim, and his mouth twisted. I think he was gonna do something nasty, but there come a rain all of a sudden. The Soft Rain Brer Rabbit told us about. It come down sweet smelling and light and warm. No thunder. No lightning. And no clouds. Just water falling out of a clear sky stuffed with stars and a big fat moon; it was the rain that was supposed to let everyone know it wouldn't be long before daylight and the Sticky Storm.

The weasels and Brer Fox and Brer Bear, and that nasty Tar Baby, all made their way quick like to the tallest stone in the muck. They stood in front of it, and you could tell they was nervous, even the Tar Baby, and they went about chanting. The words were like someone spitting and sucking and coughing and clearing their throat all at once, if they was words at all. This went on for a while, and wasn't nothing happening but that rain, which was kind of pleasant.

"Huck," Jim said, "you done been as good a friend as man could have, and I ain't happy you gonna die, or me neither, but we got to, it makes me happy knowing you gonna go out with me."

"I'd feel better if you was by yourself," I said, and Jim let out a cackle when I said it.

There was a change in things, a feeling that the air had gone heavy. I looked up and the rain fell on my face and ran in my mouth and tasted good. The night sky was vibrating a little, like someone shaking weak pudding in a bowl. Then the sky cracked open like Brer Rabbit had told us about, and I seen there was light up there in the crack. It was light like you'd see from a lantern behind a wax paper curtain. After a moment, something moved behind the light, and then something moved in front of it. A dark shape about the size of the moon; the moon itself was starting to drift low and thin off to the right of the island.

Brer Rabbit had tried to describe it to us, ole Cut Through You, but all I can say is there ain't no real way to tell you how it looked, cause there wasn't nothing to measure it against. It was big and it had one eye that was dark and unblinking, and it had a beak of sorts, and there were all these ropey arms; but the way it looked shifted and changed so much you couldn't get a real handle on it.

I won't lie to you. It wasn't like standing up to the Tar Baby. My knees started knocking together, and my heart was beating like a drum and my insides felt as if they were being worked about like they was in a milk churn. Them snaky arms on that thing was clawing at the sky, and I even seen the sky give on the sides, like it was about to rip all over and fall down.

I pressed my back against the post, and when I did, I felt that pocketknife in my back pocket. It come to me then that if I stuck out my butt a little and pulled the rope loose as possible on the ring I was tied to, I might be able to thumb that knife out of my pocket, so I give it a try.

It wasn't easy, but that thing up there gave me a lot of will power. I worked the knife with my thumb and long finger, and got it out, and flicked it open, and turned it in my hand, almost dropping it. When that happened, it felt like my heart had leaped down a long tunnel somewhere. But when I knew I still had it, I turned it and went to cutting. Way I was holding it, twisted so that it come back against the rope on the ring, I was doing a bit of work on my wrists as well as the tie. It was a worrying job, but I stayed at it, feeling blood running down my hands.

While I was at it, that chanting got louder and louder, and I seen off to the side of Cut Through You, another hole opening up in the sky; inside that hole it looked like a whirlpool, like you find in the river; it was bright as day in that hole, and the day was churning around and around and the sky was widening.

I figured then the ceremony was in a kind of hurry, cause Cut Through You was peeking through, and that whirling hole was in competition to him. He wouldn't have nothing to eat and no chanting to hear, if the Sticky Storm took everyone away first.

You see, it was the chanting that was helping Cut Through You get loose. It gave him strength, hearing that crazy language.

From where we was, I could see the pink of the morning starting to lay across the far end of the river, pushing itself up like the bloom of a rose, and that ole moon dipping down low, like a wheel of rat cheese being slowly lowered into a sack.

So, there we were, Cut Through You thrashing around in the sky, the Sticky Storm whirling about, and the sun coming up. The only thing that would have made it worse was if I had had to pee.

Everything started to shake, and I guess that was because Cut Through You and that storm was banging together in some way behind night's curtain, and maybe the sun starting to rise had something to do with it. The Sticky Storm dipped out of that hole and it come down lower. I could see all manner of stuff up there in it, but I couldn't make out none of it. It looked like someone had taken some different mixes of paint and thrown them all together; a few light things on the ground started to float up toward the storm, and when they did, I really understood why Brer Rabbit called it a Sticky Storm; it was like it was flypaper and all that was sucked up got stuck to it like flies.

About then, I cut that rope in two, and pulled my bleeding hands loose. I ran over to Jim and cut him loose.

Brer Fox and the others didn't even notice. They was so busy looking up at Cut Through You. I didn't have the time, but I couldn't help but look up too. It had its head poking all the way through, and that head was so big you can't imagine, and it was lumpy and such, like a bunch of melons had been put in a tow sack and banged on with a boat paddle; it was leaking green goo that was falling down on the ground, and onto the worshipers, and they was grabbing it off the muck, or off themselves, and sticking their fingers in their mouths and licking them clean.

It didn't look like what the Widow Douglas would have called sanitary, and I could see that them that was eating it, was starting to change. Sores, big and bloody, was popping up on them like a rash.

I ran on around the circle to Tom and Joe and cut them loose, and then we all ran back the other way, cause as much as I'd like to have helped them on that farther part of the circle, it was too late. On that side the ground was starting to fold up, and their posts was coming loose. It was like someone had taken a sheet of paper and curled one end of it. They was being sucked up in the sky toward that Sticky Storm, and even the black mud was coming loose and shooting up in the sky.

On the other end of the circle, things was still reasonably calm, so I rushed to Brer Rabbit and cut him loose, then that lady with the pants on. Right about then, Cut Through You let out with a bellow so loud it made the freckles on my butt crawl up my back and hide in my hair, or so it felt. Wasn't no need to guess that Cut Through You was mad that he was running out of time, and he was ready to take it out on most anybody. He stuck long ropey legs out of the sky and went to thrashing at Brer Fox and the others. I had the pleasure of seeing Brer Fox getting his head snapped off, and then Brer Bear was next.

The weasels, not being of strong stuff to begin with, started running like rats from a sinking ship. But it didn't do them no good. That Cut Through You's legs was all over them, grabbing their heads and jerking them off, and them that wasn't beheaded, was being pulled up in the sky by the Sticky Storm.

I was still on that side of the circle, cutting people loose, and soon as I did, a bunch of them just ran wildly, some right into the storm. They was yanked up, and went out of sight. All of the island seemed like it was wadding up.

Brer Rabbit grabbed my shoulder said, "It's every man for his self," and then he darted along the edge of the Sticky Storm, dashed between two whipping Cut Through You legs, and leaped right into that briar patch, which seemed crazy to me. All the while he's running and jumping in the briars, I'm yelling, "Brer Rabbit, come back."

But he didn't. I heard him say, "Born and raised in the briar patch, born and raised," and then he was in the big middle of it, even as it was starting to fold up and get pulled toward the sky.

Now that we was free, I didn't know what to do. There didn't seem no place to go. Even the shoreline was starting to curl up.

Jim was standing by me. He said, "I reckon this is it, Huck. I say we let that storm take us, and not Cut Through You."

We was about to go right into the storm, cause the side of it wasn't but a few steps away, when I got my elbow yanked. I turned and it was Tom Sawyer, and Joe with him.

"The lady," Tom said. "This way."

I turned and seen the short-haired lady was at that silver boat, and she was waving us to her. Any port in a storm, so to speak, so we run toward her with Tom and Joe. A big shadow fell over us as we run, and then a leg come popping out of the sky like a whip, and caught Joe around the neck, and yanked his head plumb off. His headless body must have run three or four steps before it went down.

I heard Tom yell out, and stop, as if to help the body up. "You got to run for it, Tom," I said. "Ain't no other way. Joe's deader than last Christmas."

So we come up on the silver boat with the wings, and there was an open door in the side of it, and we rushed in there and closed it. The lady was up front in a seat, behind this kind of partial wheel, looking out through a glass that run in front of her. The silver bug was humming, and those crosses on the wings was spinning. She touched something and let loose of something else, and we started to bounce, and then we was running along on the grass. I moved to the seat beside her, and she glanced over at me. She was white faced, but determined looking.

"That was Noonan's seat," she said.

I didn't know what to say to that. I didn't know if I should get out of it or not, but I'll tell you, I didn't. I couldn't move. And then we was bouncing harder, and the island was closing in on us, and Cut Through You's rope legs was waving around us. One of them got hit by the crosses, which was spinning so fast you could hardly make them out. They hit it, and the winged boat was knocked a bit. The leg come off in a spray of green that splattered on the glass, and then the boat started to lift up. I can't explain it, and I know it ain't believable, but we was flying.

The sun was really starting to brighten things now, and as we climbed up, I seen the woods was still in front of us. The lady was trying to make the boat go higher, but I figured we was gonna clip the top of them trees and end up punched to death by them, but then the boat rose up some, and I could feel and hear the trees brush against the bottom of it, like someone with a whisk broom snapping dust off a coat collar.

With the island curling up all around us and starting to come apart in a spray of color, being sucked up by the Sticky Storm, and that flying boat wobbling and a rattling, I figured we had done all this for nothing.

The boat turned slightly, like the lady was tacking a sail. I could glance up and out of the glass and see Cut Through You.

He was sticking his head out of a pink morning sky, and his legs was thrashing, but he didn't look so big now; it was like the light had shrunk him up. I seen Tar Baby too, or what was left of him, and he was splattering against that big gourd thing with the writing on it, splattering like someone was flicking ink out of a writing pen. He and that big gourd was whipping around us like angry bugs.

Then there was a feeling like we was an arrow shot from a bow, and the boat jumped forward, and then it went up high, turned slightly, and below I seen the island was turning into a ball, and the ball was starting to look wet. Then it, the rain, every dang thing, including ole Cut Through You, who was sucked out of his hole, shot up into that Sticky Storm.

Way we was now, I could still see Tar Baby splashed on that gourd, and the gourd started to shake, then it twisted and went as flat as a tapeworm, and for some reason, it blowed; it was way worse than dynamite. When it blew up, it threw some Tar Baby on the flying boat's glass. The boat started to shake and the air inside and out had blue ripples in it.

And then—

—the island was gone and there was just the Mississippi below us. Things was looking good for a minute, and then the boat started coughing, and black smoke come up from that whirly thing that had cut off one of Cut Through You's legs.

The boat dropped, the lady pulling at that wheel, yanking at doo-dads and such, but having about as much luck taking us back up as I'd have had trying to lift a dead cow off the ground by the tail.

"We are going down," she said, as if this might not be something we hadn't noticed. "And there is nothing else to do but hope for the best."

Well, to make a long story short. She was right.

Course, hope only goes so far.

She fought that boat all the way down, and then it hit the water and skipped like it was a flat rock. We skipped and skipped, then the whirly gigs flew off, and one of them smashed the glass. I was thrown out of the seat, and around the inside of the boat like a ball.

Then everything knotted up, and there was a bang on my head, and the next thing I know there's water all over. The boat was about half full inside. I suppose that's what brought me around, that cold Mississippi water.

The glass up front was broke open, and water was squirting in around the edges, so I helped it by giving it a kick. It come loose at the edges, and I was able to push it out with my feet. Behind me was Tom Sawyer, and he come from the back like a farm mule in sight of the barn. Fact was, he damn near run over me going through the hole I'd made.

By the time he got through, there wasn't nothing but water, and I was holding my breath. Jim grabbed me from below, and pushed me by the seat of my pants through the hole. Then it was like the boat was towed out from under me. Next thing I knew I was on top of the water floating by Tom, spitting and coughing.

"Jim," I said, "where's Jim?"

"Didn't see him come up," Tom said.

"I guess not," I said. "You was too busy stepping on my head on your way out of that flying boat."

Tom started swimming toward shore, and I just stayed where I was, dog paddling, looking for Jim. I didn't see him, but on that sunlit water there come a big bubble and a burst of something black as the tar baby had been. It spread over the water. It was oil. I could smell it.

Next thing, I felt a tug at my leg. I thought it was one of them big catfish grabbing me, but it wasn't. It was Jim. He bobbed up beside me, and I grabbed him and hugged him and he hugged me back.

"I tried to save her, Huck. I did. But she was done dead. I could tell when I touched her, she was done dead."

"You done what you could."

"What about Tom?" Jim said.

I nodded in the direction Tom had gone swimming. We could see his arms going up and down in the water, swimming like he thought he could make the far shore in about two minutes.

Wasn't nothing to do but for us to start swimming after him. We done that for a long time, floating some, swimming some. And I'm ashamed to say Jim had to pull me along a few times, cause I got tuckered out.

When we was both about gone under, a big tree come floating by, and we climbed up on it. We seen Tom wasn't too far away, having gotten slower as he got tired. We yelled for him, and he come swimming back. The water flow was slow right then, and he caught up with us pretty quick, which is a good thing, cause if he hadn't, he'd have sure enough drowned. We clung and floated, and it was late that afternoon when we finally was seen by some fishermen and pulled off the log and into their boat.

## 》《

There isn't much left to tell. All I can say is we was tired for three days, and when we tried to tell our story, folks just laughed at us. Didn't believe us at all. Course, can't blame them, as I'm prone toward being a liar.

It finally got so we had to tell a lie for it to be believed for the truth, and that included Tom who was in on it with us. We had to say Joe drowned, because they wouldn't believe Cut Through You jerked his head off. They didn't believe there was a Cut Through You. Even the folks believed there was a Dread Island didn't believe our story.

Tom and Becky got together, and they been together ever since. Five years have passed, and dang if Tom didn't become respectable and marry Becky. They got a kid now. But maybe they ain't all that respectable. I count eight months from the time they married until the time their bundle of joy come along.

Last thing I reckon I ought to say, is every year I go out to the edge of the Mississippi with Jim and toss some flowers on the water in memory of the lady who flew us off the island in that winged boat.

As for Dread Island. Well, here's something odd. I can't see it no more, not even when it's supposed to be there.

Jim says it might be my eyes, cause when you get older you lose sight of some things you used to could see.

I don't know. But I think it ain't out there no time anymore, and it might not be coming back. I figure it, Brer Rabbit and Cut Through You is somewhere else that ain't like nothing else we know. If that's true, all I got to say, is I hope Brer Rabbit is hid up good, far away from Cut Through You, out there in the thorns, out there where he was raised, in the deep parts of that big old briar patch.

# STORY NOTES FOR
# *BLEEDING SHADOWS*

**D**ear readers, these are the story notes in order
of appearance in the book, but I am lumping all the
poems together under one piece at the end of the notes.
I'll explain why when you get there. But for now, these
are the notes for this collection. If you are someone who enjoys
this sort of thing, as I do, then this may be right down your alley.
If not, well partner, you have wrapped up this collection of stories
and are ready to move onto something new and you can ignore
this section altogether.

## TORN AWAY

In the 1960s this great television series came along. It was
called *The Twilight Zone*. I was already in love with weird and
unusual stories, but this was something else. It was O'Henry for
fantasy lovers. It was one of the things that changed my life and
drove me not only toward writing, which I had already decided I
wanted to do, but ultimately toward fantastic fiction. I have written
a lot of non-fantastic fiction as well, but this imprinted me deeply.

I am often asked which is my favorite kind of story. It depends, I say. But you know, it may well be this sort of fiction when it comes to shorter tales. In fact, I think fantastic, science fiction, and horror tales work better at the shorter length most of the time. Exceptions to everything, but for my tastes most novels in these fields fall apart, especially fantasy and horror and whimsy. *The Twilight Zone* touched on all these forms, but it was contemporary fantasy and whimsy that it excelled at, often with a coating of social and political satire or allegory.

But what it did best was simply this: it gave its viewers fantastic stories that were unlike anything on television at the time. This led to me reading many of the writers who wrote for *The Twilight Zone*, or writers who influenced it, like Ray Bradbury. Among these writers were Richard Matheson and Charles Beaumont. They were the kind of writers that helped change my course as a writer from one who wanted to write Edgar Rice Burroughs pastiches to something more ambitious.

Some years later, in the eighties, I discovered this very cool-looking magazine titled *The Twilight Zone*, owned by Carol Serling, the wife of Rod Serling, who created the television show *The Twilight Zone*. He was also its onscreen narrator. He appeared at the first of all the programs, and at the end, the way Hitchcock did with his series, *Alfred Hitchcock Presents*, another favorite of mine. I ended up writing several stories for the magazine, as well as conducting interviews and writing a nonfiction piece, and I believe it may well have been the most important place where I was published early on. It gave my stock more value.

Some years later I was asked if I would like to contribute a *Twilight Zone*-style story to an anthology honoring the television show and Rod Serling. Although I had written for the magazine, I had never truly written what I thought was a true *Twilight Zone*-style story, so I jumped at the chance. I wanted to do it up right; something for then, as well as for now. This is what I wrote. I think I nailed it, but that is for you to decide.

# THE BLEEDING SHADOW

Lovecraft has crossed my path many times. I must be honest and say I am not a Lovecraft fanatic, but I am very fond of his mythos, the idea that there are some pretty nasty and evil entities waiting beyond the dimensional veil, and that they are easily perceived by man as gods, or demons, or devils. I always like the writers he influenced more than Lovecraft himself. Robert Bloch comes immediately to mind.

I have also for some time loved blues music and been attracted to the legendary story of Robert Johnson, who according to some sold his soul to the devil. Now, I don't believe in the devil, but I believe in a good story, and I always wanted to write something based on this legend, if not purely about Robert Johnson. I had touched on it before in comics and prose, but this was my first attempt to really get at the source of the story.

Lovecraft's evil entities, Robert Bloch's forward driving storytelling style, blues music, private eye fiction, deals with the devil (or his ilk), and Robert Johnson all boiled together in this one. I didn't even know how much I had been thinking about it until Gardner Dozois and George R.R. Martin asked me to write a story for their anthology *Down These Strange Streets*, which was a combination of noir and the supernatural. Having written so much "realistic" stuff, I jumped at the chance. All of the odds and ends I had been thinking about lined up like soldiers, and this popped out.

I might also add that this was written under tremendous pressure. We suffered a broken water pipe that destroyed part of our house and about 2,000 books in my library, as well as magazines, movie posters, some of my own work, and important papers. I was really down about it for about two days, but I managed to write this story with my computer on a board, with the bottom floor torn out beneath me, with deadlines looming, and my wonderful daughter and son-in-law downstairs doing all they could to organize things and help me deal with the water damage. They did this so I could work and meet my deadlines and to prepare for the construction that was to follow. That's the kind of family I have, and I am grateful.

# A VISIT WITH FRIENDS

Frankly, I'm sick of zombies. Oh, there are exceptions. I like a good zombie story or movie now and then, am a fan of *The Walking Dead*, and was even executive producer on an oddball, independent zombie film titled *Christmas with the Dead*, based on a short story by me of the same title, the screenplay written by my son, Keith, directed by my friend Terrill Lee Lankford. I read a very fine young adult novel not too long ago titled *Rotters*, and liked that. So there's good stuff out there, but it's hard to find due to the mass of zombies that are now rampaging the countryside. They are everywhere, including television commercials.

Many years ago, before the current stampede of zombie tales, I wrote a weird western novel titled *Dead in the West*, and a little later, a story titled "On the Far Side of the Cadillac Desert with Dead Folks". Both were about zombies, but at the time they weren't all the rage. They were almost a cult interest. Now, they are everywhere.

It's like vampires. I once liked the genre, until films, books and comics became so thick with vampires I lost interest. Especially romantic vampires. They are as common as sin these days, but less interesting.

But, that said, in the last few years I have written a handful of stories that take place in this zombified universe, and my emphasis has been on something other than the zombies. I have said enough. I leave the story with you.

# CHRISTMAS WITH THE DEAD

Christmas with the Dead was a simple idea. What if the world is full of zombies, and there are only a few survivors, and one of the survivors misses Christmas, and decided one year to put up Christmas lights. Only problem, he has to go get them and bring them home and put them up, and the zombies are in the way. But putting up those damn Christmas lights becomes his obsession. It was a simple story, but it sort of rang a Christmas bell. It was published first by PS Publishing in England, picked up for a Best of the Year, and was later adapted to film by my son, Keith Lansdale. Keith's script is based on my story, and the beginning and the end are very similar, a few elements from the middle. But as Keith said, "Had I followed Dad's story our movie would have been twenty minutes long."

He was right. When he was doing the script for the film, which my wife and I helped produce, I gave him two bits of advice. Get rid of the dog, as they are notorious actors, and get rid of the kid as soon as possible because they are notorious actors as well. He did that, and added in a lot of new elements, and the thing got filmed. It starred Damian Maffei, who did a terrific job, Brad Maule, who used to play Doctor Tony on *General Hospital*, as well as my daughter, Kasey, and Chet Williamson, a very fine writer, and actor. My son-in-law, Adam Coats has a part, and there are a number of others. Part of the music was co-written and co-produced by my daughter. She sang two songs. Judy Pancoast, a Grammy nominee did three songs, a friend who is an amazing musician wrote "Dead Beat" for our film, and we had the luck of having the great Tasmanian Orchestra to do the rest of the soundtrack, not to mention the Southern Gospel Choir. Nice make-up and special effects by Cat Bernier and Marcus Koch, and so many people I haven't the room to list. It was directed by Terrill Lee Lankford, and we had the assistance of Stephen F. Austin University.

It came out well, has been featured at the Torino Film Festival, played at the British Fantasy Convention, several other conventions, and has moved on to others, and with a little luck, we will soon have distribution.

Anyway, all that came from a simple short story.

# QUARRY

I mentioned how much I loved *The Twilight Zone*, and Richard Matheson, one of the writers for that show, became one of my favorite writers. He wrote short stories, novels, screenplays and so on. Three of his stories were made into a made-for-television movie titled *Trilogy of Terror*.

The one everyone remembers, and the only one Matheson scripted of the three—William F. Nolan, a fine writer in his own right, scripted the other two—was one called "Prey." It starred Karen Black. It was a creepy little story about a Zuni doll that was more than a little dangerous. There was a later television adaptation of the story as well, but it was too pyrotechnic for me. The charm of the original story was lost, and I hardly remember it at all.

Not long ago a book celebrating Matheson's career was designed. It's called *He Is Legend*, a variation on his famous novel *I Am Legend*, which has been filmed three times with mixed results, and would, I believe, be best filmed as a mini-series.

Anyway, for *He Is Legend* the trick was for writers to write sequels, or associative stories based on one of Matheson's works. I was asked and honored to be one of those writers. There were many of his stories I might have enjoyed writing sequels to, but "Prey" was always one of my favorites.

The story wrote itself, and it was fun. It's my tribute to one of the best and most influential writers to ever write in the horror and modern fantasy field, as well as other fields. I see his influence everywhere, from stories to books to movies to TV shows, to cartoons and commercials. His ideas and his wonderful ability to make paranoia entertaining have permeated the culture. You can't do better than that.

Anyway, this is my tribute. It can't match the original, but maybe it will entertain and my respect for the writer who created the little monster in this story will come through.

# SIX-FINGER JACK

*Lone Star Noir* was a book of, obviously, Texas crime stories. I was asked to be in it, but at the time couldn't make the deadline. I joked to the editors via email that it wouldn't be a true Texas Noir without a story from me. They took me seriously, said I was right, and could I please write one after all, as they would very much like to have me in the book.

I wanted to be in the book, but I just didn't have the time. Still, I debated on it, decided I couldn't do it, as I was up to my neck in alligators, which is my common situation these days, and was about to pass when this hit. I jumped up in the middle of the night, darted down to my study and started the story, went to bed, got up the next morning and wrote the rest of it quickly. I decided to just go for it, both in the style of language as well as the events in the story. I had great fun, and feel like the short deadline accounts for one of the more positive things about the story—momentum.

# MR. BEAR

I love stories that are absurd, yet somehow believable. I'm not sure what inspired the story, but I'm sure being asked to write a story for a humorous anthology was the main impetus. It alerted my storytelling machine and it went shopping for ideas, without me even knowing it. Anyway, like a lot of my stories it hit me fast and hard, and I went at it, hammer and tongs.

The story came out in a book titled *Blood Lite*. This humorous anthology was primarily promoting the works of best-selling horror writers, primarily those that wrote about vampires. I think it attracted those fans and put off readers who wanted a broader approach to horror. Actually, the book was broader than that, but the way it was marketed you wouldn't think so. Most of the comments I saw on the book were that they read one story by their favorite author and didn't care about the others, or didn't care about short stories, which wasn't exactly a perfect situation for those of us who love short stories and were buried in a book with a somewhat deceptive marketing campaign. The title and cover led most readers to think it was strictly a vampire story collection, which I think was their plan. A story about an angry bear sort of got lost here, which I thought was too bad. I think it's one of my best, and a personal favorite.

There were comments I saw here and there on internet reviews that tickled me. One complaint about my story was that bears couldn't fly on airplanes.

"No shit, Sherlock. And there aren't any vampires either."

# OLD MAN IN THE MOTORIZED CHAIR

My friend Bill Crider was editing an anthology about old guy detectives, and since he and I are the best of friends, going back over thirty years now, I had no choice. I didn't want to see him cry.

Anyway, I wrote this one for an anthology titled *Damn Near Dead, Volume 2.* I wanted to write something simple, but fun, and of an older school of crime writing I used to read but had hardly touched on as a writer. When I was learning to write, teaching myself, I used all manner of sources. *Ellery Queen* and *Alfred Hitchcock* magazines were among them. I tried a few stories for them early on, and missed, and once I started selling I was writing other types of stories, so I never really came back to that kind much, and when I did, it was usually pre-sold somewhere. Meaning I had been asked to write a story for a magazine or anthology, and it went there without going out into the broader market. Also, as a short story writer I had mostly moved out of the crime arena. My short stories were primarily of the hardcore realism or absurd fantasy, or marginal fantasy and horror and science fiction school, or to be more precise, a bit of all those things, and often at the same time, which was an unintentional by-product.

I will say among the influences for this were the character of Mycroft, from the Sherlock Holmes stories, "The Old Man in the

Corner" stories, which are mostly forgotten today, as well as Rex Stout's Nero Wolfe stories, though I confess I was never a big fan of Nero Wolfe.

Anyway, here it is. I even thought I might write more about the character, but I haven't, and this may be the only appearance for this old, cantankerous man who likes to watch television, especially dark nature programs, and solve crimes off the cuff, without leaving his chair or room.

As a side note, Busted Flush Press, the press that published this story, was owned and operated by David Thompson, a very fine person who was a co-owner of Murder by the Book in Houston, Texas, one of the best bookstores around. Its specialty, as you might have gleaned from the name, is crime and mystery. David died suddenly of an unknown heart problem, and I forever have his memory and this story tied together. He was a fine young man and died well before his time. I miss him. I remember when he was just a kid that worked in the store, and then he was the co-owner with his wife McKenna. In my mind he's still just a kid. He was like a big puppy, rushing here, rushing there, laughing in place of barking. He was someone who truly loved his work and loved the field of crime and mystery writing. I miss you David.

# SOLDIER'N and HIDE AND HORNS

This will serve as the introduction for two stories because they are related.

For many years I have wanted to write a western-historical novel I call *The True Life Adventures of Deadwood Dick*. It would be a big sprawling novel about a black cowboy and buffalo soldier. I have been trying to write it since the early eighties, and probably had the seed for it before that.

I have researched and thought about it and started it a few times without success, mostly due to the fact that there are other things I want to write as well, things more likely to get done sooner and find a market. This book would be a labor of love, and I'm at the point where I'm just about to break down and do it.

On my way to writing it, I wrote two stories about the character. They lack some of the backstory I plan to provide, and only hint at all the character will go through in the course of the novel, but I am very fond of them.

Once I was asked my favorite novels and films and realized a large number of them are Westerns, or are Western-like, and it has been pointed out more than once that the Hap and Leonard series, as well as other novels of mine, owe a lot to the Western. I agree.

Anyway, here's a taste of the character and his times. I hope to write the novel soon.

# THE STARS ARE FALLING

This has some of the Western flavor I talked about earlier, but it takes place a little later, after the First World War. It's not a mystery, in that it's not trying to fool anyone, though some have thought it was a mystery. Some have thought it a kind of horror story. It was in a Best of the Year crime and mystery anthology as well as a horror anthology. It's not really a mystery, and there's nothing supernatural about it. It's a dark story of inevitability. It was at one time to be the opening section of a novel that would use these characters as a jumping off point. I don't know if that will happen or not. I may have satisfied myself with this one. I feel it to be one of my best novellas, and one of my best works, period.

# THE METAL MEN OF MARS

I have often said that Edgar Rice Burroughs is my sentimental favorite author. I can't read him with the same wide-eyed enthusiasm I did when I was a boy, but the way he made me feel as a young reader is forever in my heart.

His imagination was second to none. Along with Jack London, it's one of the things Philip José Farmer and I talked about once in Dallas, Texas when he invited my wife and me, along with our infant son, up to his and his wife's hotel room to have a cold drink. I was a pretty new writer then, and he didn't know us from fried rice, but he saw we were hot and tired and the child was wearing us down. We were living on pennies, eating outside the hotel, and rooming in a flea bag motel farther away. I think he and his wife deduced this immediately.

I'll never forget that kindness, and the passion that we both had for Edgar Rice Burroughs and Jack London. Nor will I forget that one of my favorite writers, someone I admired deeply, did such a kind thing for us.

Anyway, when I got the opportunity to write a John Carter of Mars story I jumped at the chance. I had already finished a Tarzan novel that ERB had left unfinished and in his safe. It had remained there fifty years after his death. The novel I finished was called *Tarzan's Lost Adventure*. I actually got to collaborate with one of my childhood heroes. That was way cool.

This time out, asked to write a John Carter of Mars story, I was even more excited. Like so many young readers of Edgar Rice Burroughs, mostly boys, I had stood out under the night sky and stretched my arms out to Mars, hoping I would be pulled across the vastness of space to the Red Planet like John Carter. Shot straight to a Mars with thin, but breathable air, four-armed, giant, green warriors called Tharks, four-armed white apes, and a lovely, naked red-skinned princess named Deja Thoris. What we didn't consider as young boys was that had we been pulled across that dark emptiness of space to arrive on a thin-aired Mars with living creatures, within less than fifteen minutes we would have been pulled apart by those white apes, or chopped up by the Tharks. And if we survived long enough to view that fine princess without her drawers she would have made us blush and kick dirt and probably run away.

Still, it was a wonderful dream. That's what Burroughs was. He tapped into the primal part of my brain, and frankly, he and his worlds have never left. They camp there comfortably and with my permission.

The magic of Burroughs' Mars often comes to me before sleep. I dream I am lying sleepily in one of the fliers that John Carter rode in, skimming just above the Martian sands. I am a warrior wrapped in sleeping silks, my sword by my side. Deja Thoris is at the controls, watching over me, and as I drift into the darkness of sleep, all is right with the red world of Mars, and with me.

It would be wonderful to think that when it comes time for me to die, that would be the way I would go. Drifting down into the sleepy world of Edgar Rice Burroughs, racing in a flyer above the deserts of Mars.

## MORNING, NOON, AND NIGHT

This was the other story written for the reloaded version of *By Bizarre Hands*. It's a story about some well-known creatures of mythology, though it offers a different version, and a different kind of explanation for their existence. It, like much of my fiction, has a science fiction heart, even if it may in fact be horror. I really don't care. Labels actually bore, and even annoy, me at times. It's a story that contains the elements that I love: mystery, horror, science fiction, and just plain odd and creepy.

## SANTA AT THE CAFÉ

This is another one of those crime stories I wrote later in life, but is very much like a number I tried to write, unsuccessfully, early in life. It would probably have fit a magazine that was gone by the time I started to write, *Manhunt*. But I read many of those magazines. I collected them when I could and a friend of mine had quite a few of them that he loaned out for me to read.

*The Strand Magazine* requested a story by me, and though I didn't have the time, the idea of writing for such a prestigious name as that, a modern version of the magazine that Arthur Conan Doyle had written his Sherlock Holmes stories for, was just too much of a temptation. I thought I'd like to write a *Manhunt* kind of story.

It was fun.

# WHAT HAPPENED TO ME

I love ghost stories with a passion, especially those of an earlier age. I don't believe in the supernatural or an afterlife, but I have always found ghost stories fun. A good one will make me believe, at least during the time it takes to read it. That's the challenge for all writers of the fantastic, to make their audience believe what they otherwise know to be untrue.

This is loosely based on real events, and though some were unexplained, I didn't actually believe them to be the result of ghosts. Still, at twenty years old, living in the depths of the country, in an old house with an outhouse for a bathroom and no running water inside the house, it was prime real estate for someone like me. Little clanks and creaks, and a number of very odd moments were enough to make my skin crawl and set my imagination free. I wasn't writing stories at the time I lived in that house, but I knew I wanted to, and I had these events in my mind for years and knew there was a story there, but I could never quite put it together.

Then, not quite forty years later, I had a period where for some reason or another I was all about nostalgia. I re-read old science fiction and horror stories, and certainly a large number of ghost stories. I own a lot of collections and anthologies of this kind of stuff, and I was reading two or three volumes a week. Some of those stories were about psychic investigators. I came up with my own investigator and wrote four stories about that character, two of which still await publication. When I thought I was through with this period of writing, I was asked to write a haunted house story. Those events of long ago found shape and form, and I wrote this. It doesn't have my psychic investigator in it, and technically I guess it isn't actually a pure ghost story, but the tone is certainly the same, and finally I feel satisfied, having written a story that was with me for so long, though I didn't exactly know what that story was.

Now I do.

For the record, my favorite short ghost story is "The Upper Berth" by Marion Crawford.

## STARLIGHT, EYES BRIGHT

I can't explain this one, other than I was asked to write some new stories for a new edition of my first short story collection, *By Bizarre Hands*. That collection has gained considerable fame over the years, and I really appreciate that. It is often cited as one of the best horror short story collections out there, and I'll take that, true or not. I believe I've written stories just as good since, but that collection, when it came out, was unique to the field. I want to believe those who have told me or written about it, that it was, as they say, a game changer for the field of horror and the fantastic. All writers who love to write and care about their work want to believe that something they have written matters. It's great to think you gave someone a few hours of entertainment, but it's even better if that entertainment has echo.

Both of the new stories I wrote for the revamped edition are included here. This one is about... Well, I won't say. It's a little odd and a little obtuse, and I offer no apologies for that. The opening came to me and lay around inside the workings of my word processor until this reboot of *By Bizarre Hands* came along, and then it clicked for me and was finished quickly.

## DEAD SISTER

About the time I was asked to write the story that became *The Bleeding Shadow* for a horror-noir anthology, another one, this one edited by Ellen Datlow was being shaped. It was called *Supernatural Noir.* I wanted to write an old style private eye story with something of a *Night Stalker* feel. For those who might not know, *The Night Stalker* was a character created by Jeff Rice, and then adapted to a couple of made-for-TV movies by Richard Matheson, and then there was a series. It starred Darren McGavin as Kolchak, an intrepid newspaper reporter who kept running across strange and unexplained occurrences. He always investigated, figured out the truth, and then no one would believe him.

It's a show that's a little dated now, but still fun to watch, and McGavin is great. It was revived not long ago with another actor and put into modern form, and it wasn't too good. The charisma that McGavin had was lost, and the modern reporting just didn't have the charm of the original hard-nosed newspaper reporter in his straw hat and worn-out suit.

Anyway, I was looking for that kind of feel, and this is what came out, a light but entertaining read, I hope.

# SHOOTING POOL

When I was in high school one of my schoolmates told me elements of this story and claimed it was true. I have made up a lot of it, but the basic story was supposed to have happened, and he swore he was there and saw it. I didn't know what to think of it at the time, and frankly, it never occurred to me to tell the police about it. I assume that's because I didn't really believe it.

As the years have passed, I've wondered. Maybe it was just a story, or more likely a story this fellow I knew had heard and repeated and put himself into as an observer. I don't know. I actually doubt the veracity of it, because I never heard about anything that might fit this episode, and on the other hand, maybe the people who did it got away with it. So many years removed, I wonder.

# THE FOLDING MAN

This is one of my oddest stories, and as many of my stories do, it came out of dream. It, like a couple of others here, was written during the time of house repairs that were necessary due to a broken water pipe that destroyed a lot of my books and magazines and personal items. Fear not, it was a small portion of what I owned and might well have been a good thing, causing me to decide to get rid of a lot of unnecessary baggage, sell some things, and do long needed repairs on our house.

I wrote this with my chair and computer desk and computer on a few planks over the rafters of our middle floor. The flooring itself had been torn out due to the flood, and I could look down to what had once been our storeroom and see piles of damaged books. I focused on the writing, and I think because I was sleeping so badly, remembering which books I had lost, which ones were signed by writers I had met, or who were dear friends, that this oddball idea took root and seemed perhaps more real to me than what the flood waters had done. I certainly needed a distraction.

# DREAD ISLAND

I love novellas, and as time has gone on it's become my favorite thing to write. It's long enough to manage characterization and texture, short enough to get on with the story and get it over with. One reason I prefer shorter works, short stories or novellas, is that you can cover so much more ground than with novels. You can write about so many different subjects, ideas, and then move on.

I have a passion for Mark Twain. He is one of my favorite writers. I love his novel *Huckleberry Finn*, and it is my favorite after Harper Lee's *To Kill a Mockingbird*, but unlike Lee, Twain wrote a lot, and he wrote well. He was a humorist, a satirist, and he could be deadly serious while making you laugh.

I am also, as should seem obvious, a fan of horror. I am not a fanatic of Lovecraft, but I admire his creations, his ideas.

When I was a child, the first thing I remember having read to me, before I could read myself, were Uncle Remus stories. I remember especially the story of Brer Rabbit and Brer Fox and the tar baby, and when I got older I found a volume of these stories and read them. They were considered racist by many because of the dialect. I don't know about that. I think the author of the stories, a white man named Joel Chandler Harris, was trying to capture the black dialect as he heard it. In many ways, he preserved much that would have been lost, and that primarily being the stories that he claimed were told by an old black man, a slave, named Uncle Remus. The stories had connections to African folk tales, and had been "Americanized," but they bear a lot of resemblance to trickster stories from many cultures.

Lovecraft, Twain, and Uncle Remus all came together to result in this. It was for an anthology of mash-up tales, utilizing real characters and fictional characters colliding in alternate universes. Mine was liked well enough to get its own book before being collected in the main collection. Still, it seemed to me that the marketing of the book was off, and not enough people saw either my independent story, or the anthology it appeared in. I hope for my story this will help correct that oversight and introduce it to a wider audience.

# THE POETRY

First thing I remember writing was a poem about my dog. Fortune has been kind in that it has not survived. It was the one and only time until recently that I wrote, or wanted to write, a poem.

I have never been someone who read a lot of poetry. When I was a kid I read the Iliad and the Odyssey, and they are considered poems of a sort. I read poetry in school, and when I was very young, I even took a kind of independent course, not associated with the schools, called Expression. My mother wisely insisted that I do it. The lady that taught it may have been named Ms. Sessions, but it's been so long ago I can't be sure. I remember that she had me memorize poems and plays and all manner of things. I took Expression for some time. It changed me for the better. It gave me confidence as someone who could read and speak aloud. It led to my being in a play that was performed at the school using this lady's students. I guess it was first or second grade and I played a character called Santa Claus, Jr., and the way I remember it I was awesome and am surprised that someone didn't snatch me right off the stage and haul me off to Broadway to perform on the Great White Way.

But they didn't.

I already loved stories, but Expression taught me how to love words. The sound of them, their meaning, imagery; a lot of that was taught through poetry. That said, I never really thought of myself as someone who loved poetry. I read Edgar Alan Poe, and I really did like his poetry. I read Robert Frost and loved "Stopping by the Woods" and I read and liked Shakespeare's sonnets. I read all manner of poetry taught in school, and later at universities. I never got a degree, but I did read a lot of poetry as part of the classes I took, and I did a bit of independent reading as well. But poetry, frankly, I respected it, but it never held me hostage the way prose does. I loved poetic prose, however, and it's one of the main reasons I loved Bradbury's stories, but oddly, didn't care for his poetry at all.

I did love song lyrics. The ones I thought were good, like Dylan and Lennon and McCartney, and so on. But other poetry, well, I seldom bought it, and usually when I did it was because a friend wrote it. I sometimes read it and liked it, but, again, not a poetry fanatic.

Then one day Al Sarrantonio contacted me and said he was editing an anthology of Halloween poetry, and would I give it a try. I wrote one, and then two, and then five or six. He accepted them all and put some of them in the book under another name.

They weren't very good, but they were amusing, and I guess that was the point.

But this sort of opened a gate. It got me to thinking about poetry. Now, I said I rarely bought poetry, but I had some in old school books I kept, and after writing the Halloween poems, I pulled them down and reread a few of the older poems. Okay. Good stuff, but I wasn't excited. And then I went to my Charles Bukowski collection. I had his prose, and I really enjoyed his novels and short stories. I think Bukowski was a bit of a bullshitter and the kind of guy I wouldn't have liked much in person, but I did enjoy his work. He wrote simply and clearly and about things a lot of writers would be afraid to touch. I had a book that had his poetry mixed in with some prose, and I started reading. Something clicked. I liked his poetry. A lot.

All of a sudden I was on fire to write some. And I did. Mine was nothing like his, and certainly nowhere as good. I don't claim to be a true poet. But I wrote some for fun, and it came out pretty well, and about the time I was doing this, I was asked to write something for *The Horror Zine*. I had the poetry and sent it, and it was accepted. It fired me up even more. I found I was writing poetry in bursts, mostly at night. I would go to bed, and then would be moved to leap up and bound downstairs and turn on my machine, and then I would write. It was sometimes a line that drove me downstairs, sometimes an entire poem. I did this and wrote a lot, and... It went away.

I moved on, wrote stories and novels and screenplays and comic scripts and articles, and what have you, and then... It came back. I wrote a bunch more. I tended to write anywhere from three or four to twenty at a sitting. I have even gotten to the point where I may soon have enough for a book of poetry. Provided anyone wanted a book of poetry.

I don't claim to be a great poet. I think I'm a good writer of prose, but poetry, I don't know the form, and frankly, I don't want to learn it. If I do I'll never write another. I'll know what's expected. I put it on the page the way I want the reader to see it, with the location of the words providing the emphasis for how I want it read. Knowing what is proper would just mess me up. The poems here speak enough for themselves and intros to them individually would be ridiculous. Let me just say they are a kind of flash fiction disguised as poems. I think that's what Bukowski did. He wrote short stories as poems, but if they weren't written as poems they would never have existed as short stories. Same for these.

I don't know how many poems I'll write in my lifetime. Maybe I'm through, and I must be honest, I still much prefer prose and find it more magical and satisfying than poetry.

Enough of that. Let me end with this: WARNING. This book contains something that passes for poetry.